ARIS & PHILLIPS HISPANIC CLASSICS

PERO LÓPEZ DE AYALA

CHRONICLE OF KING PEDRO

Crónica del rey don Pedro

Volume III

1363–1369

*(1363–1365: years 14–16 of the reign of King Pedro
1366–1369: years 1–4 of the reign of King Enrique
and years 17–20 of the reign of King Pedro)*

Translated with an introduction and notes by

Peter Such

Spanish text taken from Pero López de Ayala, *Crónica del rey don Pedro
y del rey don Enrique, su hermano, hijos del rey don Alfonso Onceno*.
Volume 1, edited and with notes by Germán Orduna, and preliminary
study by Germán Orduna and José Luis Moure.
Volume 2 edited and with notes by Germán Orduna.
SECRIT, Buenos Aires, 1994 and 1997.

LIVERPOOL UNIVERSITY PRESS

First published 2020 by
Liverpool University Press
4 Cambridge Street
Liverpool
L69 7ZU

www.liverpooluniversitypress.co.uk

Copyright © 2020 Peter Such

The right of Peter Such to be identified as the author of this book has been asserted by him in accordance with the Copyright, Designs and Patents Act 1988.

All rights reserved. No part of this book may be reproduced, stored in a retrieval system, or transmitted, in any form or by any means, electronic, mechanical, photocopying, recording, or otherwise, without the prior written permission of the publisher.

British Library Cataloguing-in-Publication data
A British Library CIP record is available

ISBN 978-1-78962-134-1 hardback

Typeset by Tara Montane

Printed and bound by CPI Group (UK) Ltd, Croydon CR0 4YY

Cover image: King Pedro kneeling in prayer (Museo Arqueológico Nacional)

CONTENTS

Volume III

THE *CHRONICLE OF KING PEDRO*
Text, Translation and Notes
Years XIV–XVI of the reign of King Pedro: 1363–1365
   Year XIV   (1363)   2
   Year XV   (1364)   30
   Year XVI (1365)   50

Years I–IV of the reign of King Enrique
(Years XVII–XX of the reign of King Pedro): 1366–1369
   Year I / Year XVII   (1366)   60
   Year II / Year XVIII (1367)   124
   Year III / Year XIX   (1368)   274
   Year IV / Year XX   (1369)   300
Notes   344

CHRONICLE OF KING PEDRO

(CRÓNICA DEL REY DON PEDRO)

AÑO QUATORZENO

del rrey don Pedro, que fue año del Señor mill e trezientos e sesenta e tres, e de la era de Çesar mill e quatroçientos e uno.

Capitulo primero. Commo el rrey don Pedro fizo sus ligas con el rrey de Inglaterra e con el prinçipe de Gales su fijo.

En el quatorzeno año sobredicho que el rrey don Pedro rregno, que fue en el año del Señor mill e trezientos e sesenta e tres años, e de la era de Çesar mill e quatroçientos e uno, e del Criamiento del mundo, segund la cuenta de los ebreos, en çinco mill e çiento e veynte e [tres] años, e del año de los alarabes en sieteçientos e sesenta e çinco, el rrey don Pedro enbio vn su cauallero que dizian Dia Sanchez de Terrazas e vn su alcalde que dizian Aluar Sanchez de Cuellar al rrey Eduarte de Inglaterra e al prinçipe de Gales, su fijo, por los quales les enbio dezir que el queria seer su amigo e aliado con ellos contra todos los onbres del mundo. E esto fazia el rrey don Pedro por quanto se rreçelaua del rrey de Françia e de los sus amigos por la muerte de la rreyna doña Blanca. E al rrey de Inglaterra e al prinçipe de Gales, su fijo, plogo mucho con esta mensageria que el rrey de Castilla les enbio dezir, e enbiaron con los dichos mensageros otros sus caualleros, e llegaron al rrey don Pedro a la villa de Calatayud, ca el rrey era ý llegado, que venia de Seuilla para entrar a fazer guerra a Aragon, e alli fizieron sus ligas e rrecabdos. E fincaron el rrey don Pedro e el rrey de Inglaterra e el prinçipe de Gales, su fijo, amigos e aliados en vno contra todos los omnes del mundo.

Otrosi al comienço deste año el rrey ayunto muchas conpañas e entro en Aragon e gano estos lugares que eran del dicho rregno de Aragon en la comarca de Calatayut: Fuentes e Chodes e Arandiga e Maluenda e otros muchos logares. E çerco la çibdat de Taraçona e

YEAR FOURTEEN (1363)

of the reign of King Pedro, which was the year of the Lord 1363 and, counting from the era of Caesar, 1401.

1363: CHAPTER I

How King Pedro formed an alliance with the king of England and with his son, the prince of Wales.

These events occurred in the fourteenth year of the reign of King Pedro, which was the year of the Lord 1363; in 1401, counting from the era of Caesar; 5,123 years from the creation of the world by the reckoning of the Hebrews; and, according to that of the Arabs, it was in the year 765. King Pedro sent one of his knights, called Día Sánchez de Terrazas, and a judge by the name of Álvar Sánchez de Cuéllar to King Edward of England and his son the prince of Wales. The message they carried was that King Pedro wished to be their friend and ally against any men in the world, and that he was taking this step as he feared the reaction of the king of France and his allies to the death of Queen Blanche. The king of England and his son the prince were much in favour of this proposal brought to them from the king of Castile and they sent back some of their own knights with his emissaries. They came to King Pedro in the town of Calatayud in which he had now arrived – having left Seville in order to embark on a campaign against Aragon – and it was there that the alliance was concluded and the details drawn up. King Pedro and the king of England, together with his son the prince of Wales, were now confirmed in their bond of friendship and in their alliance against any men in the world.

Moreover, at the beginning of this year the king assembled large numbers of troops and invaded Aragon, capturing Fuentes, Chodes, Arándiga, Maluenda and numerous other Aragonese possessions in the area of Calatayud. He laid siege to the city of Tarazona and

cobrola e tomo alli preso a frey Alberte, vn cauallero de la horden de Sand Iohan, e enbiolo preso a la taraçana de Seuilla e alli morio. E gano la villa de Borja e tomo ý presos dos caualleros que dizian don Iohan Ximenez de Sand Peyre e don Carro[z], e gano a Magallon e tomo ý presos al vizconde de Ylla e otros caualleros e escuderos de Cataluña e de Rosellon. E todos estos presos enbio a Seuilla, e entro por fuerça a Cariñana e fizo matar a quantos ý fallo.

Capitulo segundo. Commo el rrey don Pedro fizo jurar sus fijas por herederas del rregno e commo paso contra algunos caualleros de Castilla.

Este año desque el rrey ouo ganado Borja e Magallon, fizo su ayuntamiento de los señores e caualleros que ý eran, otrossi de los procuradores de çibdades e villas del rregno que ý mandara venir con sus poderes bastantes, en vn lugar de aquella comarca de Borja e de Magallon que dizian Burueta. E alli dixo el rrey a los suyos que pues el infante don Alfonso, su fijo, era muerto, que era heredero del rregno e lo auian jurado en Seuilla todos los del rregno, segund dicho auemos, que el queria que las infantas, sus fijas, que eran tres, doña Beatriz e doña Costança e doña Ysabel, fuessen juradas para heredar los rregnos de Castilla e de Leon, cada vna en subçession de la otra, en guisa que doña Beatriz fuesse la primera, e si desta non fincasse heredero, que heredasse el rregno doña Costança e sus herederos legitimos, e si della non fuesen legitimos herederos, que heredase despues doña Ysabel. E esto se entiende non auiendo el rrey fijo varon legitimo para heredar el rregno, e fizieronlo assy estando presentes las dichas infantas fijas del rrey, e juraronlo todos los del rregno que alli eran. E fizosse desto vn libro de todos los que esta jura fizieron e pusieron sus nonbres.

captured it, and there he took prisoner Fray Albert, a knight of the Order of Saint John, whom he sent to the shipyards prison in Seville where he died. King Pedro also captured the town of Borja, taking prisoner two knights called Don Joan Ximéneç de Sent Pere and Don Carroç. He seized Magallón, where he captured the viscount of Illa and other knights and squires of Catalonia and Roussillon. He sent all of these prisoners to Seville. He then took Cariñena by force, ordering everyone that he found there to be put to death.

1363: CHAPTER II

How King Pedro had an oath of allegiance sworn to his daughters as heiresses to the kingdom, and how he issued a formal condemnation of some Castilian knights.

During this year, having taken Borja and Magallón, the king held an assembly of the lords and knights who were present and also of the authorized procurators that he had summoned from the cities and towns of the kingdom. They met in a village called Bureta situated in the area of Borja and Magallón, where the king informed his people that, since his son Don Alfonso was dead – and he had been heir to the kingdom and all its citizens had pledged their allegiance to him in Seville, as we have already related – he now desired that an oath of allegiance be sworn to his three daughters, Doña Beatriz, Doña Constanza and Doña Isabel. Their right to inherit the kingdoms of Castile and León was to be recognized and this was to be in the following order: Doña Beatriz was to be first in line, and if she left no heir then the throne was to pass to Doña Constanza and her legitimate heirs; if Doña Constanza left no legitimate heirs, next in line to the throne would be Doña Isabel. This was on the understanding that there was no legitimate male heir to inherit the kingdom, and it was agreed in the presence of the princesses, the daughters of the king. All the representatives of the kingdom who were gathered there swore an oath of assent and a book was produced containing a list of those who did so, in which they signed their names.

Otrossi estando el rrey en esta comarca de Aragon estonçe, segund que dicho auemos, dio sentençia contra algunos caualleros que eran naturales de Castilla e estauan en Aragon con el conde don Enrrique, su hermano, en lo qual fizo lo que era su merçed, que estonçes los perdio para siempre, e algunos caualleros gelo dixeron, los que amauan su seruiçio, que non era bien que el pasasse contra aquellos caualleros; pero el non los quiso creer, e despues fallo que lo non fiziera bien e le touo grand daño, e por quanto la obra fue assi fecha voluntaria mente, non los nonbramos aqui aquellos caualleros contra los quales paso.

Capitulo IIIº. Quales conpañas vinieron en ayuda del rrey don Pedro a esta guerra que auia con Aragon este año.

En este año llego al rrey don Pedro de Castilla con acorro del rrey don Pedro de Portogal, que le enbio en su ayuda a esta guerra que auia con el rrey de Aragon a don Gil Ferrandes de Caruallo, maestre de Santiago de Portogal, e traxo consigo trezientos caualleros e escuderos muy buenos del rregno de Portogal. E llego quando el rrey tenia çercada la villa de Taraçona.

Otrossi vino en este año a esta guerra en ayuda del rrey, don Luys infante de Nauarra, hermano del rrey de Nauarra, e el cabtal de Buche, que era vn grand señor de Gujana e muy buen cauallero, e mucha buena conpaña con ellos, de cauallo e de pie. Otrossi llego estonçe vn cauallero del rrey de Granada que dizian don Farax Rodoan, con seysçientos ginetes, que el rrey Mahomad enbiaua en ayuda del rrey de Castilla.

During the time that he spent – as we have already said – in that area of Aragon, the king published a condemnation of a number of knights who were natives of Castile but were in Aragon with his brother Count Enrique. In doing so he was acting wilfully and thereby he lost these men for good. Some loyal knights told him this, pointing out that he had not been right to condemn the men, but he was not willing to believe them. He later discovered that he had committed an error, and this did him great harm; and since this act was committed arbitrarily in this way we shall not at this point name those knights on whom he passed sentence.

1363: CHAPTER III

Concerning the forces which arrived during this year in support of King Pedro in his war with Aragon.

During this year King Pedro of Castile was joined by Don Gil Fernandes de Carvalho, master of the Order of Santiago in Portugal. Don Gil was bringing him support sent by King Pedro of Portugal to aid the Castilian monarch in his war with the king of Aragon: 300 very fine knights and squires from the kingdom of Portugal. Don Gil Fernandes arrived while King Pedro had the town of Tarazona under siege.

Also during this year the king received support in the war from Prince Luis of Navarre, the king of Navarre's brother, and the captal de Buch, who was a great lord in Guyenne and a very fine knight. With them they brought a large number of troops of high quality, both mounted and on foot. In addition, a knight of the king of Granada called Don Faraj ibn Ridwān, sent by King Muhammad in support of the king of Castile, arrived with 600 light cavalry.

Capitulo IIII°. Que lugares gano de Aragon el rrey don Pedro en esta guerra e en este año, e commo llego a Valençia del Çid e commo el rrey de Aragon vino a la fuente de Almenara por pelear.

El rrey don Pedro despues que fizo jurar sus fijas por herederas del rregno e ouo dado sentençia contra algunos caualleros naturales de Castilla que estauan en Aragon, segund dicho auemos, partio luego de aquella comarca donde estaua con todas aquellas conpañas que dicho auemos, asi las que el tenia commo las que le venieron a ayudar de Portogal e de Nauarra e de Granada, e fue para Tiruel, que es vna villa de Aragon muy fuerte e muy fermosa, e cobrola por pleytesia e dierongela luego otro dia que alli llego. E cobro algunos castillos de enderredor, que son Castil Habibo e Adamuz e Villel e otros castillos que luego se le dieron. E dende fuesse para la çibdat de Segorbe e cobrola e tomo ý preso a don Pero Maça, vn rrico omne que estaua en el castillo de la dicha çibdat. E cobro a Xerica, que es vna villa que tiene muy fuerte e muy fermoso castillo, e tomo ý preso vn cauallero que dizian Ximen de Oriz. E dende fue a la villa de Monuiedro e touola çercada algunos dias e cobrola por pleytesia.

E estando en Monuiedro cobro estos lugares: Almenara e [Chiva], Buñol e Macasta e Benaguazil e Liria e El Puche e otros castillos. E en todas estas villas e castillos que el rrey cobraua de Aragon, en todas ponia gentes suyas para las defender e las mandaua labrar e rreparar e fuele muy dañoso, ca derramaua sus gentes e fazia grandes costas, segund adelante paresçio.

E dende fue el rrey a la çibdat de Valençia e llego ý domingo dia de Çinquesma veynte e vn dias de mayo, e estando ý por capitan el conde

1363: CHAPTER IV

Concerning which places King Pedro won from Aragon during this year of the war; how he reached the Cid's city of Valencia; and how the king of Aragon came to do battle at the spring of Almenara.

After having an oath of allegiance sworn to his daughters as his successors to the throne and having proclaimed a condemnation of some knights who were natives of Castile but were in Aragon – as we said above –, King Pedro lost no time in moving on from that area, where he had assembled all the forces of which we have spoken: both his own army and the troops that had come to assist him from Portugal, Navarre and Granada. He then headed for Teruel, an Aragonese town which was both well fortified and highly attractive, and he took it through negotiation so that it was handed over to him on the very first day after his arrival. He also captured some castles in the surrounding area: Castielfabib, Ademuz and Villel and some others which were quickly surrendered to him. From there he went on to the city of Segorbe, which he captured, taking prisoner Don Pero Maça, a magnate who was present in the city castle. He also seized Jérica, a town with a very fine and heavily fortified castle, where he captured a knight by the name of Ximèn d'Oris. From Jérica he advanced to Murviedro and, after besieging it for a few days, he negotiated the town's surrender.[1]

Moreover, while he was in Murviedro, he captured Almenara, Chiva, Buñol, Macasta, Benaguacil, Liria and Alpuche, as well as a number of other castles. In all of these towns and castles which the king seized from Aragon he placed troops of his own for their defence and instructed them to undertake building work and repairs. This turned out to be greatly to his disadvantage, for he was spreading his troops thinly, and this proved very costly, as became apparent in due course.

From there the king moved on to the city of Valencia, where he arrived on the Sunday of Pentecost, the 21st of May. Serving as

de Denia que dizian don Alfonso, fijo del infante don Pedro e nieto del rrey don Jaymes de Aragon, que fue despues marques de Villena en Castilla. E estudo alli el rrey ocho dias, e peleauan cada dia los suyos con los de la çibdat. E posaua el rrey en vn monesterio fuera de la çibdat que dizian la Çaydia, que era de dueñas, e ellas estauan en la çibdat e dexaron el monesterio.

E estando el rrey don Pedro sobre Valençia, sopo commo el rrey de Aragon e el infante don Ferrando, su hermano del rrey de Aragon, que era marques de Tortosa, e el conde don Enrrique e don Tello e don Sancho, sus hermanos, eran ya venidos de Françia, donde estauan, para Aragon, e que todos estos que con el rrey de Aragon venian por pelear, eran tres mill de cauallo. E el rrey don Pedro desque esto sopo, partio de sobre Valençia e vinosse para la villa de Monuiedro, que auia ganado.

E el rrey de Aragon e los que con el eran llegaron fasta la fuente que dizen de Almenara, que es a dos leguas de Monuiedro, e pusieron alli su batalla; pero el rrey estaua en Monuiedro e non quiso pelear con ellos. E el rrey de Aragon desque non fallo pelea, tornosse con toda su hueste para Burriana. E el rrey enbio a Martin Lopez de Cordoua, su priuado e su rrepostero mayor, con dos mill de la gineta, e corrian muchos dias delante el rreal del rrey de Aragon. E el rrey de Aragon quando aquellos ginetes llegauan, ponia sus gentes en buena hordenança e non le pudian los ginetes fazer enojo.

Otrossi estando el rrey don Pedro en Monuiedro, pasaron vn dia por la mar seys galeas de Aragon, que leuauan consigo quatro galeas de Castilla, que auian tomado çerca la villa de Almeria. E peso al rrey mucho dello, que estaua esse dia en la rribera de la mar.

governor of the city was Don Alfons, count of Denia, son of Prince Pere and grandson of King Jaume of Aragon, and who later became marquis of Villena in Castile. King Pedro remained there for a week and each day his army fought against the troops from the city. The king lodged in a convent called La Zaidia which stood outside Valencia: the nuns abandoned the convent and stayed within the city.

While King Pedro was outside Valencia he learned of the approach of the king of Aragon and his brother Prince Ferran, marquis of Tortosa, together with Count Enrique, Don Tello and Don Sancho, King Pedro's brothers, who had now returned from France and arrived back in Aragon.[2] In all there were 3,000 horsemen who had come to fight alongside the king of Aragon, and once King Pedro received reports of this he abandoned his attack on Valencia and returned to the town of Murviedro which he had taken previously.

The king of Aragon and the men in his company reached what is known as the spring of Almenara, situated two leagues from Murviedro, and there they drew up their lines of battle; but King Pedro remained in Murviedro and chose to avoid a clash with them.[3] Then the king of Aragon, once he saw that there would be no battle, returned with his whole army to Burriana. King Pedro sent Martín López de Córdoba, his confidant and lord high butler, with 2,000 light cavalry and they raided close to the king of Aragon's encampment for several days. When these horsemen appeared, King Pere drew up his troops in good order in such a way that the light cavalry could not trouble him.

Also during the time that King Pedro was in Murviedro, one day six Aragonese galleys went by out at sea, taking with them four Castilian galleys which they had seized off Almería. The king, who that day was watching from the shore, was greatly annoyed.

Capitulo V°. De las pleytesias que se tratauan entre el rrey don Pedro de Castilla e el rrey de Aragon.

Estando el rrey don Pedro en Monuiedro, el abad de Fiscan andaua por mandado del cardenal de Boloña, que viniera en Castilla e Aragon por legado, e trayendo tratos entre los rreyes de Castilla e de Aragon, e sobre algunas cosas secretas, las quales adelante contaremos, e sobre otros secretos, que se diran en su lugar. E fuera tratado que el infante don Luys, hermano del rrey de Nauarra, que era alli con el rrey don Pedro, fuesse al rrey de Aragon sobre las pleytesias que el abad de Fiscan traya, e assi lo fizo.

E despues torno del rrey de Aragon e vinieron a Monuiedro para el rrey don Pedro, a fablar con el de partes del rrey de Aragon, el conde de Denia don Alfonso, fijo del infante don Pedro e nieto del rrey don Jaymes de Aragon, que deximos que estaua en Valençia por capitan, que fue despues marques de Villena, e don Bernal de Cabrera. E desque llegaron el conde de Denia e don Bernal de Cabrera al rrey don Pedro, estudieron con el en Monuiedro e luego otro dia se tornaron para el rrey de Aragon; pero en la venida que fizieron a Monuiedro non dexaron cosa asossegada, saluo lo que trataua el abad de Fiscan secreta mente, e dezian que don Bernal de Cabrera trataua en esta guisa: que el rrey don Pedro de Castilla, que estaua biudo, ca era muerta la rreyna doña Blanca su muger, otrosi que era muerta doña Maria de Padilla, que el dixo en las cortes que fizo en Seuilla que era su muger legitima, que casase con vna su fija del rrey de Aragon que dizian doña Iohana, que ouiera de vna rreyna con quien fuera casado, que era hermana del rrey de Nauarra, e que el rrey de Aragon le diesse con ella en dote la villa de Calatayud con sus castillos, que auia muy buenos en la comarca, con çinco partidas de rrios; los quales

1363: CHAPTER V

Concerning the negotiations which took place between King Pedro of Castile and the king of Aragon.

While the king of Castile was in Murviedro, the abbot of Fécamp was involved in negotiations on the instructions of the cardinal of Boulogne, who had come as legate to Castile and Aragon. He was conveying proposals between the kings of Castile and Aragon with regard to some confidential matters of which we shall tell in due course and other secrets which will be revealed at the appropriate point. It had been arranged that Prince Luis, brother of the king of Navarre, who was accompanying the king of Castile, should go and see the king of Aragon about the proposals brought by the abbot of Fécamp, and he went ahead and did this.

After Prince Luis returned from seeing the king of Aragon, King Pedro was approached in Murviedro on behalf of King Pere by Don Alfons, count of Denia, son of Prince Pere and grandson of King Jaume of Aragon. Don Alfons, as we have already said, was serving as governor in Valencia and was later to become marquis of Villena. Don Bernat de Cabrera was also involved and, once the count of Denia and Don Bernat had joined King Pedro, they stayed with him in Murviedro before going back to the king of Aragon on the following day. However, during their visit to Muviedro they settled nothing, except the secret business of the abbot of Fécamp. It was said that Don Bernat de Cabrera put forward the following proposals: Don Pedro was a widower, for his wife Queen Blanche was dead as well as Doña María de Padilla, whom at his *cortes* in Seville he claimed to have been his legitimate wife; and so the proposal was made that he marry a daughter of the king of Aragon called Doña Joana, born to King Pere and the sister of the king of Navarre who had been his wife and queen. It was also proposed that the king of Aragon, as Doña Joana's dowry, should make a gift to King Pedro of the town of Calatayud, together with its castles – for there were some fine castles in the surrounding area – and stretches of five rivers: the Jalón,

dizian el rrio de Xalon e rrio de Maluenda e el rrio de Verdejo e el rrio de Xiloca e el rrio de Miedes. E que le diesse mas el rrey de Aragon a la dicha su fija, la villa de Hariza e la çibdat de Taraçona e las villas de Borja e Magallon, lo qual todo esto tenia el rrey don Pedro en su poder e lo auia ganado del rrey de Aragon. Otrossi que le diesse e desenbargasse el rrey de Aragon al rrey don Pedro de Castilla libre mente, sin condiçion, las villas e castillos de Orihuela e Elche e Creuillen e Alicante e Guardamar e la Val de Elda. E que si el rrey don Pedro de Castilla ouiesse dos fijos de la dicha fija del rrey de Aragon, que el segundo fijo fuesse duque de Calatayud e de Hariza e de los otros lugares, e vasallo del rrey de Castilla e rrespondiesse a el con el señorio de los dichos lugares. E si non ouiesse segundo fijo, que fuessen los logares del que heredase el rregno de Castilla; enpero que las villas de Elche e Alicante e Creuillen e Guardamar e la Val de Elda fuessen libres e esentas e fincassen sienpre de la corona de Castilla. Otrossi que el infante don Iohan, fijo primo genito del rrey de Aragon, que era estonçe duque de Girona, casasse con la infanta doña Beatriz, fija del rrey don Pedro e de doña Maria de Padilla, e que el rrey don Pedro diesse con ella en dote las villas de Monuiedro e Chiva e Xerica e Segorbe e Tiruel e otros lugares que el rey don Pedro auia ganado de Aragon en el rregno de Valençia con esta condiçion: que si el duque de Girona, fijo del rrey de Aragon ouiesse dos fijos de la dicha doña Beatriz, fija del rrey de Castilla, que el segundo fijo del dicho fijo del rrey de Aragon fuesse duque e señor de los dichos lugares de Monuiedro e Xerica e Segorve e Chiva e Tiruel e los otros logares, e que se llamasse duque de Xerica. Pero si non ouiesse fijo de la dicha doña Beatriz, que los dichos logares tornassen a la corona de Castilla o diesse el rrey de Aragon por ellos çierta contia de moneda, que estaua avn por concordar entre ellos. E esta pleytesia fecha e firmada, pusieron que el rrey don Pedro de Castilla se fuesse para tierra de Çaragoça a vn lugar que dizen Mallen, que es vn castillo de la horden de Sand Iohan e auialo ganado el rrey don Pedro, e que alli se firmasen todas estas cosas.

 E el rrey don Pedro partio de Monuiedro e fue para Mallen, e el rrey de Aragon fuesse para Çaragoça. Pero despues que alli llegaron, el abad de Fiscan, que era tratador en estos fechos rrequirio al rrey

the Maluenda, the Berdejo, the Jiloca and the Miedes. The king of Aragon should also make over to his daughter the town of Ariza, the city of Tarazona and the towns of Borja and Magallón – all of which King Pedro already had under his control, having won them from the Aragonese monarch. In addition, the king of Aragon was to hand over unconditionally and free of all encumbrance the towns and castles of Orihuela, Elche, Crevillente, Alicante, Guardamar and the Elda valley. However, if the said daughter of the king of Aragon bore King Pedro of Castile two sons, the second should be duke of Calatayud and Ariza and of the other specified places and a vassal of the king of Castile, answering to him in his capacity as their lord. And, if she did not bear him a second son, the places in question should belong to the person who inherited the kingdom of Castile, although the towns of Elche, Alicante, Crevillente, Guardamar and the Elda valley were to be free and exempt and always remain the property of the Crown of Castile. It was also proposed that Prince Joan, the first-born son of the king of Aragon who at that time was duke of Girona, should marry Princess Beatriz, daughter of King Pedro and Doña María de Padilla. King Pedro was to give his daughter as her dowry the towns of Murviedro, Chiva, Jérica, Segorbe, Teruel and some other places in the kingdom of Valencia which he had won from Aragon. This was on the condition that, if the king of Aragon's son, the duke of Girona, fathered two sons by the king of Castile's daughter, Doña Beatriz, the second of them would become duke and lord of Murviedro, Jérica, Segorbe, Chiva, Teruel and the other places, and that he would take the title of duke of Jérica. However, if Doña Beatriz did not bear him a child, those places were to revert to the Crown of Castile or, otherwise, in return for them the king of Aragon was to pay a sum of money, the amount of which they still had to agree between themselves. When these terms had been set out and signed, it was decided that King Pedro of Castile was to go to a place called Mallén in the area of Saragossa. Mallén is a castle of the Order of Saint John which King Pedro had captured, and it was there that all the terms of this agreement were to be ratified.

 King Pedro set off from Murviedro for Mallén and the king of Aragon travelled to Saragossa. However, once they had arrived at their destinations, the abbot of Fécamp, who was the arbiter in this

de Castilla que pues el ouiera firmados estos tratos, que le pluguiesse de lo conplir. E el rrey don Pedro dixo que non se fallaua en aquella pleytesia e que en ninguna manera non le rrequiriesse mas sobre ello. E segund dizia despues el rrey don Pedro, la rrazon por que non quiso estar por esta pleytesia era esta: dizia el rrey don Pedro que quando el conde de Denia e don Bernal de Cabrera venieran a el a Monuiedro a tratar estas pleytesias, que el fablara con don Bernal de Cabrera secreta mente que le dixiesse e tratasse con el rrey de Aragon que pues el casaua con su fija e tomaua tan grande debdo con el, que el sabia bien que el infante don Ferrando e el conde don Enrrique, que estauan en Aragon, eran sus enemigos, e que el dicho rrey de Aragon los fiziesse prender o matar. E dizia el rrey don Pedro que don Bernal de Cabrera le fiziera fiuza que el rrey de Aragon lo faria. E asi agora desque le acometian que fiziesse el dicho su casamiento con la fija del rrey de Aragon, e pidia el que el rrey de Aragon matasse primero a los dichos infante e conde. E assi non se fizo mas en la dicha pleytesia.

Otrossi en este tienpo que el rrey don Pedro vino a Mallen por conplir la pleytesia que fiziera en Monuiedro, por la qual auia de casar con la fija del rrey de Aragon, en este mesmo tiempo que era en el mes de setienbre, estando el rrey en Ma[llen] le nasçiera vn fijo de vna dueña que tenia, que dezian doña Ysabel. E el rrey queria grand bien a la dicha doña Ysabel e ouo nonbre el fijo don Sancho e nasçio en Almaçan. E queria el rrey que el don Sancho fuesse su heredero e que casaria con su madre doña Ysabel. E assy por todas estas rrazones se desbarato la pleytesia que en Monuiedro era tratada e acordada.

affair, formally requested of the king of Castile – as he had put his signature to these terms – that he now agree to fulfil his obligations. King Pedro informed him that he was not in agreement with what had been negotiated and that in no way should the matter be put to him again. As King Pedro later explained, his reason for not wishing to be bound by these terms was as follows: when the count of Denia and Don Bernat de Cabrera had come to him at Murviedro to negotiate this agreement, he had spoken in secret with Don Bernat de Cabrera asking him to discuss a certain subject with the king of Aragon. This concerned the fact that that, since he was marrying the daughter of the king of Aragon and entering into a close family bond with him, and as he was well aware that Prince Ferran and Count Enrique – who were in Aragon – were his enemies, he was now requesting that the king of Aragon have these men either arrested or put to death. King Pedro claimed that Don Bernat de Cabrera had given him an assurance that the king of Aragon would do this. And therefore, now that he was being urged to go ahead with his marriage to the king of Aragon's daughter, he asked that first King Pere put the prince and the count to death. For this reason no more progress was made with the negotiations.

Another event occurred during this time when King Pedro came to Mallén to fulfil the terms that he had agreed in Murviedro – by which he was to marry the daughter of the king of Aragon. During the same month of September when the king was in Mallén, a son had been born to him and to a lady called Doña Isabel that he had taken as his mistress and of whom he was very fond. The son, who was given the name Don Sancho, was born in Almazán.[4] King Pedro wanted Don Sancho to be his heir and said that he intended to marry the child's mother, Doña Isabel. And so, for all these reasons, the treaty which had been negotiated and agreed in Murviedro came to nothing.

Capitulo VI°. Commo el infante don Ferrando fue muerto e lo fiziera matar el rrey de Aragon su hermano.

El rrey de Castilla estudo en Mallen algunos dias e dende vinose para Calatayud e despues de alli partio para Seuilla. E en estos dias el rrey de Aragon estando en Castellon de Burriana entendio que el infante don Ferrando, su hermano, marques de Tortosa, non se tenia por contento de las maneras de la su corte, ca dixo al rrey de Aragon, su hermano, que el queria yr a Françia. E estonçes dizian que la guerra de Françia e de Ynglaterra, que se bolvia, e auia cobrado estonçe el dicho infante don Ferrando todos los mas caualleros e escuderos de Castilla que estauan con el conde don Enrrique, e don Tello e don Sancho, sus hermanos, eran con el dicho infante don Ferrando. E tenia el infante todas las conpañas en vn lugar çerca de Burriana que dizian Almançora.

E el infante don Ferrando e el conde don Enrrique estonçe estauan sobre estas cosas mal abenidos, e fue dicho al rrey de Aragon commo el infante su hermano auia llegado a si todos los castellanos que eran en Aragon, los quales pudian seer fasta mill de cauallo muy buenos e que si el infante fuesse con aquellas gentes para Françia e se partiesse del rregno de Aragon, que el rrey de Castilla faria mas dura la guerra contra Aragon e que se veria el rrey de Aragon en gran menester. E acordo el rrey de Aragon con consejo del conde don Enrrique e de don Bernal de Cabrera de lo fazer prender al dicho infante su hermano. E mando el rrey de Aragon al conde de Vrgel e al conde de Cardona, que querian bien al infante don Ferrando, que le enbiassen dezir que se viniese alli a Castellon de Burriana e que el rrey de Aragon queria fazer todo lo que el infante quisiesse en tal que se non partiesse del rregno de Aragon. E el conde de Cardona e el conde de Vrgel fueron dello muy alegres e fuesse luego el conde de Cardona a Almançora, do estaua el infante don Ferrando, e dixole lo que el rrey de Aragon le enbiaua dezir. Otrossi le dixeron de partes del rrey de Aragon que otro dia comiesse con el rrey, el al infante plogo dello.

1363: CHAPTER VI

How Prince Ferran was killed on the orders of his brother the king of Aragon.

The king of Castile remained in Mallén for some days and from there he travelled to Calatayud before setting off again for Seville. During this time, while he was in Castellón de Burriana, the king of Aragon understood that his brother Prince Ferran, marquis of Tortosa, was not satisfied with the way things were in his court: the prince had informed him that it was his wish to go to France.[5] It was then being reported that war was in the course of breaking out again between France and England. Moreover, by now Prince Ferran had drawn to him most of the Castilian knights and squires who had been with Count Enrique; and the count's brothers Don Tello and Don Sancho were now accompanying Prince Ferran, who had assembled all his troops in a place near Burriana called Almazora.

Prince Ferran and Count Enrique were now in dispute over these matters and it was reported to the king of Aragon that his brother, the prince, had gathered around him all the Castilians in Aragon, who may have numbered as many as 1,000 horsemen of quality; and it was put to him that, if the prince were to go to France taking all those troops with him and leaving the kingdom of Aragon, then the king of Castle would intensify his campaigning against Aragon and King Pere would find himself in great difficulty. Therefore the king of Aragon, on the advice of Count Enrique and Don Bernat de Cabrera, resolved to order the arrest of his brother the prince. He instructed the counts of Urgel and Cardona, who were on very good terms with Prince Ferran, to send word to him that he should come to Castellón de Burriana; they were to tell him that the king of Aragon was prepared to do all that the prince wished provided that he did not leave the kingdom of Aragon. The counts of Cardona and Urgel were delighted at this and the count of Cardona went at once to Prince Ferran in Almazora and passed on to him what the king of Aragon had sent him to say. They also gave him an invitation from the king to eat with him on the next day, which the prince accepted.

E otro dia, que era domingo, fue el infante para Castellon de Burriana e vino al rrey e comio con el. E desque ouieron comido fuesse el infante para vna camara que ý estaua en la posada del rrey. E estauan con el infante Diego Perez Sarmiento e Luys Manuel, fijo de Sancho Manuel e nieto de don Iohan Manuel, e dos caualleros de Aragon, vno que dezian don Iohan Ximenez de Vrrea e otro, don Gunbal de Tr[amaçet]. E todo lo que era sobre este fecho hordenado sabialo el conde don Enrrique e don Bernal de Cabrera. E despues que el infante don Ferrando ouo comido e estaua ya en su camara en los palaçios del rrey, enbio el rrey de Aragon vn su alguazil que le dezian don Bernal de Escala que le dixiesse commo era su merçed que el fuesse alli preso. E el alguazil fuesse para el infante do estaua en la camara e dixogelo. E el infante era de muy grand coraçon e de grand esfuerço e touo que aquello le venia a el por consejo del conde don Enrrique e de don Bernal de Cabrera, que el queria mal; mas que la voluntad del rrey de Aragon, su hermano, non pudia seer que lo a el mandasse prender, e dixo al alguazil que non era el omne para seer preso. E el alguazil torno al rrey e dixogelo asi, e torno el alguazil al infante e por mandado del rrey dixole que el rrey le enbiaua dezir que se non touiese por desonrrado en ser su preso. E estonçe dixole Diego Perez Sarmiento, que estaua ý con el infante: 'Señor, mas vos vale morir que seer preso'. E luego el infante puso mano a vna espada que tenia. E el rrey de Aragon quando sopo que el infante se ponia en armas, mando destablar la camara do el infante estaua de partes del techo. E quando aquello vio, el infante sallio de la camara do estaua, la espada en la mano, e mato luego vn escudero del conde don Enrrique que fallo delante si, que dizian Rodrigo de Montoya, que se pusiera delante el conde don Enrrique, con quien bivia. E morio el infante don Ferrando aquel dia e mataron con el a Luys Manuel e a Diego Perez Sarmiento.

E fue muy mal rrazonado al rrey de Aragon la muerte del infante por que era su hermano e muy noble señor, de lo qual todo el rregno de Aragon fue muy quexado. E por esta rrazon morio despues don

On the following day, which was a Sunday, the prince went to the king in Castellón de Burriana and ate with him. Then, once they had eaten, the prince went into a chamber in the royal apartments, accompanied by Diego Pérez Sarmiento and Luis Manuel, son of Sancho Manuel and grandson of Don Juan Manuel, and two Aragonese knights, called Don Joan Ximéneç d'Urrea and Don Gombau de Tramacet. Every detail of what had been arranged was known to Count Enrique and Don Bernat de Cabrera. After Prince Ferran had eaten and now that he was in his chamber in the royal apartments, the king of Aragon sent one of his constables, by the name of Don Bernat d'Escala, to inform him that it was the king's will that he should be held there under arrest. The constable went to where the prince was in the chamber and said this to him. The prince was a man of great spirit and valour and he considered that he was being treated in such a way on the advice of Count Enrique and Don Bernat de Cabrera, with whom he was on bad terms. On the other hand, he believed, it could not be the wish of his brother the king of Aragon to order him to be detained: he told the constable that he was not the man to be placed under arrest. So the constable went back to the king and put this to him. He then returned to the prince and, following the king's command, he explained that King Pere had instructed him to say that the prince should see no dishonour in being his prisoner. And then Diego Pérez Sarmiento, who was present there with the prince, said to him, 'My lord, it would be better for you to die than to be made a captive.' At once the prince grasped a sword that he carried with him. The king of Aragon, when he learned that Prince Ferran was having recourse to arms, gave instructions for the chamber in which the prince was standing to be dismantled from the ceiling down; and, when he saw what was being done, Prince Ferran rushed out sword in hand and promptly killed one of Count Enrique's squires whom he found in his path. This man's name was Rodrigo de Montoya and he had positioned himself in front of Count Enrique, of whose household he was a member. Prince Ferran met his death that day and with him Luis Manuel and Diego Pérez Sarmiento were also killed.

The king of Aragon was very ill advised in ordering the death of the prince, for he was his brother and a lord of great nobility, and the whole of the kingdom of Aragon was greatly aggrieved at what

Bernal de Cabrera, por que dizian que fiziera el rrey de Aragon esta muerte del infante por su consejo. E los dos caualleros que dezian don Iohan Ximenez de Vrrea e don Gunbal de Tr[amaçet], que estauan con el, sallieron por vnas finiestras de la camara, e escaparon.

Capitulo VII°. Commo fizieron don Tello e otros caualleros que eran de la parte del infante don Ferrando desque sopieron que el era muerto, e commo en este año entro el rrey don Pedro en Aragon e gano muchos castillos.

Don Tello e don Sancho, ermanos del conde don Enrrique, e los otros caualleros que eran de la parte del infante don Ferrando, que posauan en Almançora, quando supieron que el infante don Ferrando era muerto, pensaron que el rrey de Aragon e los suyos venian contra ellos para matarlos, ca se temian del conde don Enrrique por quanto los mas se auian partido del e eran venidos para el infante, e sabian que quando el infante moriera, que el conde llegara ý armado, e avn se dezia que Pero Carrillo, vn cauallero que era con el conde, feriera al infante de la primera ferida, e por esto se temian mucho del conde don Enrrique. E armaronsse don Tello e todos los caualleros que estauan en el dicho logar de Almançora, e tomaron el pendon del infante don Ferrando, que ellos tenian consigo, e sallieron fuera del lugar de Almançora, diziendo que mas querian morir en aquel canpo, pues su señor el infante era muerto, que seer presos o morir de otra manera.

  E el rrey de Aragon ouo su consejo luego que el infante morio, e enbio sus mensageros a don Tello e a los caualleros e conpañas del infante que posauan en Almançora, a les dezir e rrogar que estudiessen quedos e que ninguno dellos non se temiesse. E eso mesmo el conde

happened. Moreover, as a result of this in due course Don Bernat de Cabrera was also to die, for it was said that the king of Aragon had brought about the prince's death on his advice. The two knights called Don Joan Ximèneç d'Urrea and Don Gombau de Tramacet, who had been accompanying Prince Ferran, escaped by making their exit through some of the chamber's windows.

1363: CHAPTER VII

Concerning the reaction of Don Tello and other knights who were supporters of Prince Ferran once they learned of his death; and how during this year King Pedro invaded Aragon and captured several castles.

Count Enrique's brothers Don Tello and Don Sancho and the other knights who were supporters of Prince Ferran and were staying in Almazora, on learning of Prince Ferran's death, thought that the king of Aragon and his troops were coming for them to kill them. For they were in fear of Count Enrique, as most of them had broken away from him and transferred their allegiance to the prince. They knew that at the time that the prince had died the count had arrived armed for combat and it was even said that Pero Carrillo, a knight who was in the count's service, had struck the first blow against the prince. It was on account of this, then, that they were greatly in fear of Count Enrique, and so Don Tello and all the knights who were in Almazora took Prince Ferran's standard, which they carried with them, and rode out from Almazora, saying that – since their lord the prince was dead – they preferred to die there on the field of battle rather than to be taken prisoner or meet their death in some other way.

Immediately after the prince's death, the king of Aragon consulted his advisers and sent envoys to Don Tello and all the prince's knights and troops staying in Almazora to inform and to beseech them that they should remain calm and that none of them should be in fear. Likewise, Count Enrique sent envoys to hold discussions with many

don Enrrique enbio fablar e falagar muchos dellos por los cobrar, e assi lo fizo e asossegaronse todos.

E el rrey don Pedro de Castilla desque sopo que el infante don Ferrando era muerto ouo muy grand plazer, e partiera poco tienpo auia de la comarca de Calatayud donde estaua e era ydo a Seuilla.

E luego en el invierno deste año, entro el rey don Pedro por el rregno de Murçia en Aragon e gano estos castillos: Alicante e Elche e Creuillen e la Muela e Callosa e Monforte e [Aspe e Elda] e algunos otros castillos. E gano Denia e Gallinera e Rebollet e otros lugares en el rregno de Valençia.

Capitulo VIIIº. Commo los rreyes de Aragon e de Nauarra e el conde don Enrrique se vieron en el castillo de Soz e por que rrazon.

Agora tornaremos a contar de vna fabla que fue fecha entre los rreyes de Aragon e de Nauarra despues desta muerte del infante don Ferrando. Assi fue que quando don Bernal de Cabrera se vio con el rrey don Pedro en Monuiedro, segund avemos contado, dizen que fue tratado que el rrey de Aragon matasse al infante don Ferrando de Aragon e al conde don Enrrique, e que el rrey de Castilla tornaria al rrey de Aragon toda la tierra que le tenia ganada e faria con el paz por çient años. E don Bernal de Cabrera lo dixo eso mesmo al rrey de Aragon. Otrossi trataua con el rrey de Nauarra que fuesse en esto e que el rrey de Castilla le daria la villa de Logroño. E los rreyes de Aragon e de Nauarra consintieron en este fecho.

E assi fue que vn dia, despues que el infante don Ferrando moriera, torno el rrey de Aragon por fazer esto e dixo al conde don Enrrique que el rrey de Nauarra queria seer con ellos en esta guerra e ayudarlos, e que era bien que se viessen en vno. E el conde don Enrrique dixo que le plazia de las vistas; enpero que acordasen en qual castillo se

of them, paying court to them in order to win them over. By doing this he managed to placate them all.

When he learned of the death of Prince Ferran, King Pedro of Castile was delighted; he had only recently left the area of Calatayud and travelled to Seville.

Not long afterwards, in the winter of this year, King Pedro invaded Aragon from the kingdom of Murcia, capturing the following castles: Alicante, Elche, Crevillente, la Muela, Callosa, Monforte, Aspe, Elda and a number of others; and he also took Denia, Gallinera, Rebollet and other places in the kingdom of Valencia.[6]

1363: CHAPTER VIII

How the kings of Aragon and Navarre and Count Enrique held a meeting in the castle of Sos and for what reason.

Now we shall turn to an account of negotiations which took place between the kings of Aragon and Navarre after the death of Prince Ferran. In fact it is said that an agreement had been reached when Don Bernat de Cabrera met with King Pedro in Murviedro – as we have related –: the king of Aragon was to put to death both Prince Ferran of Aragon and Count Enrique and then the king of Castile would return to the king of Aragon all the land that he had won from him and make peace with him, to last 100 years. Don Bernat de Cabrera said exactly this to the king of Aragon and was also negotiating with the king of Navarre for him to lend his support to the agreement, in return for which the king of Castile would give him the town of Logroño. The kings of Aragon and Navarre agreed to this proposal.

So it was that one day, after the death of Prince Ferran, the king of Aragon again turned his attention to this matter. He informed Count Enrique that the king of Navarre wished to collaborate with them in their campaign and give them his support, and that therefore it was advisable for them all to meet. Count Enrique said that he agreed to the meeting, but that they should decide in which castle it would

verian e quien los ternia seguros. E fallaron que el rrey de Aragon tenia vn castillo frontero de Aragon e de Nauarra, que dizian Soz, e era bueno que se viessen alli. E el conde dixo que el non entraria en aquel castillo saluo teniendolo caualleros de quien el fuesse seguro, e por ende acordaron que lo touiesse vn cauallero que dizian don Iohan Ramirez de Arellano, que era nauarro e camarero del rrey de Aragon; pero era omne de quien el conde don Enrrique se fiaua e fue fecho assi.

E el castillo de Soz fue entregado al dicho don Iohan Ramirez e el puso ý vn su hermano que dizian Ramiro de Arellano con treynta omnes de armas e veynte ballesteros e treynta lançeros. E desque fue entregado el dicho castillo a don Iohan Ramirez, llegaron ý el rrey de Aragon e el rrey de Nauarra e acogieron los cada vno con dos seruidores e vinieron ý don Bernal de Cabrera e el abad de Fiscan, que era frances, que viniera con el cardenal de Boloña legado del papa. E despues vino el conde don Enrrique e traxo ochoçientos omnes de cauallo, e pusieron todos los suyos su rreal çerca del castillo. E el conde don Enrrique entro en el castillo con dos seruidores, segund era hordenado, e desque fueron todos en el castillo fablaron de muchas cosas. E los rreyes de Aragon e de Nauarra non fallaron en el alcayde esfuerço para conplir lo que querian fazer, ca les dixo que en ninguna manera el non seria en fazer tal muerte. E desque esto vieron encubrieronsse lo mejor que pudieron e partieron dende.

Capitulo IXº. De lo que en este año acaesçio en tierra de Gascueña.

En este año pelearon el conde de Fox e el conde de Armiñac en la plaça de Leonat en Gascueña e fue vençido el conde de Armiñaque e fueron presos el conde de Armiñaque e el señor de Lebret, su sobrino, e otros

take place and who would ensure their safety. They concluded that the king of Aragon possessed a castle called Sos which stood on the frontier between Aragon and Navarre and that it was appropriate for them to gather there. The count said that he would not set foot in that castle unless it was in the hands of knights on whom he could rely, and for this reason they agreed that the castle should be placed under the control of a knight by the name of Don Juan Ramírez de Arellano: he was from Navarre and was the chamberlain of the king of Aragon, but he was also a man that Count Enrique trusted, and so the decision was taken.

The castle of Sos was placed in the hands of Don Juan Ramírez and he installed in it his brother Ramiro de Arellano with 30 men-at-arms, 20 crossbowmen and 30 men armed with javelins. Then, once the castle had been handed over to Don Juan Ramírez, the kings of Aragon and Navarre arrived and each of them was admitted with two men in his service; the next to come were Don Bernat de Cabrera and the abbot of Fécamp, a Frenchman who had come to Spain with the cardinal of Boulogne, the papal legate. Then finally Count Enrique arrived, bringing 800 horsemen, and all of his followers set up their encampment near to the castle. Count Enrique entered the castle with two retainers, as had been arranged, and, once they were all inside, they discussed a wide range of subjects. The kings of Aragon and Navarre did not find in the castellan the spirit necessary to carry out what they had planned to do: he told them that in no way would he be party to committing such a murder. And so, once they had seen this to be the case, they covered up their intentions as well as they could and left the castle.

1363: CHAPTER IX

Concerning what happened during this year in Gascony.

During this year the count of Foix and the count of Armagnac did battle near the fortified town of Launac in Gascony.[7] The count of Armagnac was defeated and was taken prisoner, along with his nephew

del linaje de Lebret e el conde de Comenga e el conde de Fresinsac e el conde de Monlusu e otros muchos de la partida del conde de Armiñac. E vençiolos el conde de Fox e pagaron muy grandes rrendiçiones. E ayudauan ese dia al conde de Fox çinco capitanes de las conpañias, los quales eran: Espiota e Senesorgas d'Alemaña e Bretuquin e Petit Mençin e mosen Iohan Almerique, que eran muy buenos onbres de armas, e tenian muy buenas conpañas. E ouo esse dia grand honrra el conde de Fox e grandes rrendiçiones, de los quales presos, segund dizian, montauan treynta cuentos desta moneda de Castilla.

the lord of Albret, other members of the Albret family, the counts of Comminges, Fezensac and Motlezun and many other supporters of the count of Armagnac. They were defeated by the count of Foix and paid extremely large ransoms. On that day the count of Foix had the support of five captains of the Companies: Espiote, Johan Hazenorgue from Germany, Bertuchin, Petit-Meschin and Sir John Amory, who were fine soldiers and had troops of very high quality.[8] It was a day on which the count of Foix won great honour and gained a large sum of money in ransoms for those prisoners, which is said to have amounted to 30 million in our Castilian currency.

AÑO QUINZENO

del rrey don Pedro, que fue año del Señor mill e trezientos e sesenta e quatro, e de la era de Çesar mill e quatroçientos e dos.

Capitulo primero. Commo el rrey don Pedro puso su rreal en El Grao çerca la çibdat de Valençia.

En el año quinzeno que el sobredicho rrey don Pedro rregno, que fue año del Señor mill e trezientos e sesenta e quatro, quando andaua la era de Çesar en mill e quatroçientos e dos, e del Criamiento del mundo segund la cuenta de los ebreos, en çinco mill e çiento e veynte e [quatro] años, e del año de los alarabes en sieteçientos e sesenta e seys, en el comienço deste año el rrey don Pedro vino para el rregno de Murçia e entro en Aragon por el rregno de Valençia ganando algunos lugares e faziendo mucho daño. E primero ganara a Alicante, que es vna villa e vn castillo rribera de la mar muy fermoso, e gano a Xixona e Gandia e Oliua e otros lugares, e llego a Monuiedro.

E luego partio dende para Burriana, entendiendo yr por aquella comarca faziendo mal e daño en el rregno de Valençia. E quando llego çerca de Burriana vio galeas del rrey de Aragon, que venian por la mar, e otros nauios que trayan viandas a la çibdat de Valençia, ca estaua muy menguada dellas, e tornose del camino por destoruar aquellas viandas por que non se pusiesen en Valençia. E puso su rreal en El Grao que es rribera de la mar a media legua de la çibdat de Valençia. E esperaua cada dia la su flota que mandara armar en Seuilla, que eran veynte galeas e quarenta naos; otrossy atendia diez galeas del rrey don Pedro de Portogal su tio, que le enbiaua en su ayuda contra el rrey de Aragon, que avn non eran llegadas. E toda esta flota era ya en Cartajena ayuntada, pero non auia tienpo para venir, de lo qual el rrey estaua muy quexado.

# YEAR FIFTEEN (1364)

of the reign of King Pedro, which was the year of the Lord 1364 and, counting from the era of Caesar, 1402.

1364: CHAPTER I

How King Pedro established his encampment at El Grao near to the city of Valencia.

These events occurred in the fifteenth year of the reign of King Pedro, which was the year of the Lord 1364; in 1402, counting from the era of Caesar; 5,124 years from the creation of the world by the reckoning of the Hebrews; and, according to that of the Arabs, it was in the year 766. At the beginning of this year, King Pedro moved into the kingdom of Murcia and entered Aragon through the kingdom of Valencia, making some conquests and causing great devastation. Having first taken Alicante, a very handsome city and castle on the coast, he also seized Jijona, Gandía and Oliva and a number of other places, advancing as far as Murviedro.

From there he set off without delay for Burriana with the intention of raiding throughout that region and causing harm and destruction in the kingdom of Valencia. When he arrived near Burriana he saw galleys of the king of Aragon approaching from out at sea and other ships bringing provisions to the city of Valencia, where they were in very short supply, and he made a detour in order to prevent those supplies from being taken into the city. He established his camp at El Grao, which is on the coast half a league from the city, and each day he waited for the fleet of 20 galleys and 40 sailing ships which he had ordered to be fitted out for battle in Seville. He was also awaiting 10 galleys which his uncle King Pedro of Portugal was sending to assist him against the king of Aragon but which had not yet arrived. All of this fleet was already assembled in Cartagena but the weather did not allow it to sail, which was causing the king great annoyance.

E estando el rrey alli, çerco la çibdat de Valençia, e de cada dia se fazian muchas peleas de los suyos con los de la dicha çibdat. E los de Valençia auian mucha gente e mucha vallesteria, e era estonçe en aquella çerca capitan de la çibdat de Valençia vn cauallero natural dende que dizian don Pero Buyl. Pero en la çibdat de Valençia auia pocas viandas e estaua ya la çibdat de Valençia muy afincada e entendia el rrey que se non podria defender, e pan ya non lo tenian si non poco, e los mas se mantenian de arroz e de aquello non auian mucho. E vn dia ouo ý grand pelea don Ferrando de Castro con caualleros suyos e otros vasallos del rrey e Ferrand Aluarez de Toledo con escuderos del cuerpo del rrey, de los quales el era cabdillo, que eran dozientos escuderos muy buenos. Llegaron todos estos a la puerta que dizian de Sand Viçente e ouieron grand pelea, e morio ý vn grand cauallero de Gallizia vasallo del rrey, que dizian Ferrand Perez de Grades, e perdio el vn ojo Ferrand Aluarez de Toledo.

Otrossi en este tienpo ouo el rrey don Pedro nueuas commo matara en Aragon el conde don Enrrique a Pero Carrillo, vn cauallero de Castilla que sienpre andudiera en sus guerras con el, por su mano con vna lança, andando vn dia a monte, por que le dizian que auia fama con doña Iohana, su hermana del conde, muger que fuera de don Ferrando de Castro, la qual estaua con el conde su hermano en Aragon. E plogo mucho dello al rrey por quanto Pero Carrillo era uno de los buenos caualleros que andauan con el conde. E despues caso esta doña Iohana con vn rrico onbre de Aragon que dizian don Felipe de Castro, del qual diremos adelante.

Chronicle of King Pedro

Encamped at El Grao, King Pedro laid siege to the city of Valencia and each day several encounters took place between his army and the forces of the city. The defenders of Valencia could count on numerous troops and a large force of crossbowmen, and Don Pere Boïl, a knight who was a native of the city, was governor of Valencia during the period of the siege. However, as Valencia was short of supplies and by now the city was hard pressed, the king realized that it could not hold out. They had a very limited supply of bread and most of the people survived on rice – and of that too they had only a small amount. One day Don Fernando de Castro was involved in a major confrontation there along with some of his knights, some other vassals of the king and Fernán Álvarez de Toledo accompanied by squires from the king's corps, of which he was the head: this was a body of 200 fine squires. All of these men advanced as far as what was known as the Gate of Sant Vicenç, where they took part in a violent clash, in which the death occurred of a great lord from Galicia and vassal of the king called Fernán Pérez de Grades and Fernán Álvarez de Toledo lost an eye.

Also at this time King Pedro received a report of how in Aragon Count Enrique had killed Pero Carrillo, a Castilian knight who had always accompanied him on his campaigns. The count had killed him one day with his own hand, with a lance while out riding, because he had heard that there were rumours about him and his sister Doña Juana, who had been the wife of Don Fernando de Castro and was with her brother the count in Aragon. This news gave King Pedro great pleasure as Pero Carrillo was one of the finest knights accompanying the count. Doña Juana later married an Aragonese magnate called Don Felipe de Castro, about whom we shall speak in due course.[1]

Capitulo IIº. Commo vn escudero de Castilla que andaua con don Tello, aperçibio al rrey don Pedro que el rrey de Aragon venia a pelear con el.

Estando el rrey don Pedro sobre la çibdat de Valençia en aquel lugar que dicho auemos, que dizen El Grao, que es a media legua de Valençia, e non sabiendo nueuas ningunas del rrey de Aragon, llego a el vn escudero natural de Castilla, de la villa de Castro d'Urdiales, que auia nonbre Marcos Garçia e andaua en Aragon con don Tello, e algunos dizian que don Tello lo enbiara, ca sienpre don Tello fiziera asaz cosas tales e non era pagado de andar con el conde don Enrrique su hermano.

E dixo aquel escudero al rrey que por quanto era su natural que le venia aperçibir e que sopiesse que el rrey de Aragon e todos los mayores de su rregno; otrossy el conde don Enrrique e don Tello e don Sancho, sus hermanos, que eran en Burriana, que pudian seer fasta tres mill de cauallo e pieça de gentes de pie, e que venian por la mar e en par dellos, doze galeas e pieça de nauios cargados de viandas. E que su ardid era venir encubierta mente por pelear con el ante que de alli partiesse en guisa que auia ya tres noches que non fazian fuego por non seer descubiertos, e que fuesse çierto que otro dia, al alua del dia, serian con el en aquel lugar do estaua.

E el rrey touogelo en seruiçio lo que el escudero dixiera e le aperçibiera por quanto el rrey estaua muy sin cuydado deste fecho e non sabia ningunas nueuas del rrey de Aragon. E mando luego armar todos los suyos e partio del Grao, la noche cayda, para Monuiedro que era a quatro leguas de alli.

1364: CHAPTER II

How a Castilian squire in Don Tello's company warned King Pedro that the king of Aragon was coming to do battle with him.

While King Pedro was outside Valencia half a league from the city – in the place which, as we said, is called El Grao – and having heard no reports of the king of Aragon, he was approached by a squire called Marcos García, who was Castilian by birth, from the town of Castro Urdiales. This man was accompanying Don Tello in Aragon, and it was said by some people that Don Tello had sent him, for he had always been in the way of doing such things since he took little pleasure in the company of his brother Count Enrique.

This squire informed the king that he had come to give him warning as he was his vassal by birth and that he should be aware that the king of Aragon and all the greatest and finest men of his kingdom – together with Count Enrique and his brothers Don Tello and Don Sancho – were in Burriana. He explained that their forces might well include as many as 3,000 horsemen together with a substantial body of men on foot, and that at the same time 12 galleys and several ships laden with provisions were approaching by sea. The strategy of the Aragonese forces was to approach unobserved in order to do battle with King Pedro before he could withdraw, and so for three nights they had lit no fires in order not to be detected. King Pedro should be in no doubt that the next day at dawn they would come upon him where he was encamped.

The king was very grateful for the squire's action in informing and warning him as he had not suspected these developments and had received no reports of the king of Aragon's movements. He rapidly ordered his men to arm themselves for battle and departed from El Grao after nightfall, heading for Murviedro, four leagues away.

Capitulo III°. Commo el rrey de Aragon vino a la çibdat de Valençia.

Otro dia en la grand mañana, el rrey de Aragon e todos los que venian con el suyos, e el conde don Enrrique e don Tello e don Sancho, sus hermanos, e los castellanos que pudian seer todos –entre castellanos e aragoneses– tres mill de cauallo. E fueron rribera de la mar, paso e en buena hordenança las sus batallas, entre Monuiedro e la mar, quanto a vna legua de Monuiedro, e las sus galeas e naos en par dellos con muchas viandas. E la flota del rrey avn non era llegada.

E el rrey don Pedro estaua çerca la villa de Monuiedro e los ginetes suyos otrossi seysçientos de cauallo moros, que ý eran con don Farax Rodoan, cabdillo del rrey de Granada, yuan lançar lanças en la hueste del rrey de Aragon e fazer sus espolonadas en guisa que los ginetes suelen e acostunbran de fazer. Pero el rrey de Aragon e los que con el yuan non se partian de la hordenança de la su batalla que leuauan, e tenian todos su camino derecho para la çibdat de Valençia, e assy lo fizieron fasta que llegaron en Valençia.

E los de la çibdat de Valençia quando vieron que eran acorridos assi por mar commo por tierra e auian viandas assaz, fizieron muy grandes alegrias, ca en tal priesa auian estado. Otrossi el rrey de Aragon les agradesçio a los de la çibdat de Valençia e les touo en grado e señalado el seruiçio e el trauajo que auian sofrido.

E en este tienpo, estando el rrey en Monuiedro, cada dia yuan los ginetes e los moros que eran con el rrey don Pedro en su seruiçio, a la çibdat de Valençia. E pudian seer los ginetes e los moros fasta dos mill e quinientos de cauallo, e los de la çibdat sallian a ellos e peleauan alli e faziansse grandes peleas entre los vnos e los otros.

E despues desto, a cabo de doze dias, llego la flota del rrey don Pedro de Castilla, que eran veynte galeas suyas e diez galeas del rrey don Pedro de Portogal e quarenta naos de Castilla.

1364: CHAPTER III

How the king of Aragon made his way to the city of Valencia.

Early the following morning, the king of Aragon approached with his whole army, together with Count Enrique and his brothers Don Tello and Don Sancho and the Castilians. Including both Castilians and Aragonese there may have been 3,000 horsemen altogether. They advanced along the coast, at a measured pace and in close formation, between Murviedro and the sea just a league away; and their galleys and sailing ships, bringing a large supply of provisions, approached along with them. King Pedro's fleet had not yet arrived.

King Pedro was near to the town of Murviedro: his light cavalry, and also 600 Moorish horsemen who were there under Don Faraj ibn Ridwān, a commander for the king of Granada, rode out to hurl javelins at the king of Aragon's army, launching their rapid attacks as is the way and custom of such horsemen. However the king of Aragon and his troops did not break away from their battle formation and they rode straight on towards Valencia, continuing in this fashion until they reached the city.

The people of the city of Valencia, having found themselves in such a difficult position, rejoiced greatly when they saw that they were receiving assistance by both sea and land and that they now had an ample supply of provisions. Moreover, the king of Aragon was very grateful to them and gave them thanks and praise for their loyalty and for enduring so much hardship.

During this time that the king was in Murviedro, every day the light cavalry and the Moors who were in King Pedro's service rode up to the city of Valencia – including light cavalry and Moors the horsemen probably numbered as many as 2,500 – and the troops from the city came out to do battle with them, with violent encounters taking place between the two armies.

It was after this, twelve days later, that the fleet of King Pedro of Castile arrived, consisting of 20 of his own galleys, 10 galleys belonging to King Pedro of Portugal and 40 Castilian sailing ships.

Capitulo IIIIº. Commo el rrey de Castilla se ouiera a perder en la tormenta de la mar en Cullera.

Los que estauan en las galeas del rrey de Aragon, quando vieron la flota del rrey de Castilla, ouieron grand miedo e pusieronsse en vn rrio que dizen de Cullera. E el rrey don Pedro entro luego en la flota suya que entonçes llegara, dexando en Monuiedro toda su cauallería. E fuesse para la boca del rrio de Cullera do estauan las galeas e la flota del rrey de Aragon, cuydandolas alli tomar, pero non pudieron entrar en el rrio, que es estrecho. E assi fue que vna de las galeas del rrey de Aragon que alli se pusiera con los otros, desque vio que eran çercados e que estauan en grand peligro para seer tomados, auenturosse e sallio del rrio e nunca la pudieron tomar.

E estando alli el rrey don Pedro, ouo vn viento leuante que dizian 'solano', que es trauesia en aquella mar, tan grande que todos pensaron que la flota del rrey de Castilla yria a tierra. E el rrey de Aragon e el conde don Enrrique e los que con ellos eran llegados ý, todos e muchos de pie, teniendo, con esfuerço de aquel viento, que aquella flota del rrey de Castilla se perderia e vernia a tierra, e non ponian dubda en ello. E las galeas del rrey de Castilla estauan muy allegadas a la tierra, e el viento se esforçaua toda via mas. E aquel dia la galea del rrey de Castilla era la primera que estaua en la boca del rrio de Cullera e auia ya quebrado tres cables e perdido tres ancoras, e estaua ya sobre el quarto cable e vna ancora; pero Dios quisole ayudar e a la ora del sol puesto, amanso el viento e çeso aquella tormenta. E fue aquel dia el rrey don Pedro en muy grand peligro de su persona e fizo muchos botos de rromeria e de soltar presos, e tornosse para Monuiedro.

1364: CHAPTER IV

How the king of Castile came close to being shipwrecked in the sea storm at Cullera.

On seeing the fleet of the king of Castile, the men in the king of Aragon's galleys were filled with fear and sailed up a river known as the Cullera.[2] The king lost no time in embarking on the fleet which had just arrived, leaving all his cavalry at Murviedro. He then made for the estuary of the River Cullera where the galleys and the fleet of the king of Aragon were anchored, intending to seize them, but his ships could not sail up the river, which is too narrow. What then happened was that one of the king of Aragon's galleys which had anchored there with the rest, seeing that they were hemmed in and in serious danger of capture, made a break and sailed out from the river, eluding all attempts to seize it.

While King Pedro was there, an easterly wind blew up. This wind is known as a 'solano' and blows onshore from the sea, across the ships, and it was so strong that everyone thought the king of Castile's fleet would be forced onto the coast.[3] The king of Aragon, Count Enrique and the men accompanying them, including many footsoldiers, had massed there believing that, with the force of the wind, the king of Castile's fleet would be wrecked and carried onto the coast; of this they were in no doubt. The king of Castile's galleys were very close to land and the wind continued to strengthen. That day the king of Castile's galley was the first one anchored in the estuary of the river Cullera. It had already broken three cables and lost three anchors and was by now on the fourth cable and a single anchor. However, it was God's will to come to King Pedro's assistance and at the hour of sunset the wind dropped and the storm eased. That day the king's person was in grave danger and so he vowed repeatedly to take part in a pilgrimage and to release prisoners. He made his way back to Murviedro.

Capitulo V°. Commo el rrey don Pedro partio de Monuiedro e se torno para su rregno de Castilla.

El rrey don Pedro partio de alli por el camino de Segorbe e sallio a vna villa suya que dizian Cañete, que es en el rregno de Castilla, e dexo en Monuiedro por fronteros de Valençia e para defender la dicha villa por mayor a don Gomez Perez de Porres prior de Sand Iohan, e otrossi dexo ý con el muy grandes caualleros, ca dexo ay a Pero Manrrique adelantado mayor de Castilla e a don Aluar Perez de Castro e a don Alfonso Ferrandez de Monte Mayor, e don Egas de Cordoua e Garçi Gutierrez Tello el moço, e Iohan Duque e Pero Gomez de Porres e Ruy Gonçalez de Boz Mediano e a Gomez Perez de Valderrauano e Lope Gutierrez de Cordoua e otros muchos caualleros e escuderos muy buenos de Castilla e de Leon e de la frontera. E dexoles ý muchos buenos vallesteros de la flota e de los que con el andauan, e muchas viandas. E podian seer los que fincauan en Monuiedro ochoçientos de cauallo e mucha gente de pie. E el rrey fuesse para Seuilla e enbio los otros caualleros a sus fronteras, segund solian estar.

E el rrey de Aragon desque sopo que el rrey de Castilla era ydo para su rregno, partio de Valençia con todas sus conpañas e con mucha ballesteria, e llego a Monuiedro cuydandola tomar con la grand ballesteria que tenia. E los de la villa pelearon muy bien, e morio ý estonçe Ruy Gonçalez de Boz Mediano, que el rrey auia dexado en Monuiedro, e peleara aquel dia muy bien.

E el rrey de Aragon desque llegara a Monuiedro e non pudo mas fazer, partiosse de alli e fuesse para el rregno de Aragon, toda via con entençion de tornar a çercar a Monuiedro.

1364: CHAPTER V

How King Pedro departed from Murviedro and made his way back to his kingdom of Castile.

King Pedro set off from Murviedro along the Segorbe road and reached a town called Cañete which belonged to him and is situated in the kingdom of Castile. In Murviedro he left field commanders against Valencia and for the defence of the town itself: he left the prior of Saint John, Don Gómez Pérez de Porres, as overall commander, and along with him a number of very distinguished knights: Pero Manrique, governor general of Castile, Don Álvar Pérez de Castro, Don Alfonso Fernández de Montemayor, Don Egas de Córdoba, Garci Gutiérrez Tello the Younger, Juan Duque, Pero Gómez de Porres, Ruy González de Vozmediano, Gómez Pérez de Valderrábano, Lope Gutiérrez de Córdoba and many other very fine knights and squires from Castile, León and the Frontier region. With them he left many skilled crossbowmen from the fleet and from his own company and he also furnished them with a good supply of provisions. Those who remained behind in Murviedro probably numbered 800 horsemen and there was also a substantial force of footsoldiers. The king then travelled to Seville, dispatching the remainder of the knights to the frontier posts that they had usually occupied.

Once the king of Aragon learned that the king of Castile had left for his own kingdom, he set off from Valencia with all his troops and a large force of crossbowmen. He reached Murviedro expecting to capture it with his numerous crossbowmen, but the men holding the town put up firm resistance. On that occasion Ruy González de Vozmediano, whom the king had left in Murviedro, met his death there, having fought very bravely on the day.

Having come to Murviedro and not having been able to achieve any more than this, the king of Aragon withdrew and headed for his own kingdom, still with the intention of returning to besiege Murviedro.

Capitulo VI°. Commo el rrey don Pedro tomo a Castil Habibi e otros castillos e lo que fizo este año.

Este año en el mes de agosto, despues que el rrey don Pedro de Castilla sopo commo el rrey de Aragon viniera sobre Monuiedro, partio de Seuilla donde estaua e vinosse para Calatayud. E luego partio dende e fue çercar vna villa e castillo çerca Tiruel, que dizian Castil Habibi, por quanto el lo auia ganado e dexara ý vn cauallero suyo natural de Toledo que lo touiesse. E los de la villa mataron al cauallero e alçaronse con la dicha villa e castillo, e touolo çercado vn mes tirandole con muchos engeños, e cobrolo. E dende partio e fuesse entrar en el rregno de Valençia e gano la villa e castillo de Ayora e otros castillos enderredor.

E quando el rrey partio de Castil Habibi desque lo ouo ganado, enbio dende al maestre de Alcantara, que dizian don Gutier Gomez de Toledo, que pusiesse algunas rrecuas de viandas en Monuiedro por que los que ý dexara el rrey le enuiaron dezir que auian menester viandas. E el maestre de Alcantara con otros caualleros vasallos del rrey fuesse para Segorbe, que es en la frontera de aquella comarca, por poner las viandas en Monuiedro e alli allegaua las rrecuas para las leuar.

E el rrey don Pedro de Castilla fuesse para Alicante, que estaua por el, e dende entro e gano algunos castillos en esa comarca, que dizian Guadaleste, e Castil de Castiel e otros, e dende tornosse para Elche, que es çerca del rregno de Murçia, que lo auia ganado antes.

E los que estauan en Orihuela, que es a quatro leguas de Elche, rreçelaron que los querria el rrey çercar, e non tenian viandas e auian enbiado por acorro al rrey de Aragon.

1364: CHAPTER VI

How King Pedro captured Castielfabib and some other castles, and what he did during this year.

This year, during the month of August, after learning that the king of Aragon had tried to take Murviedro, King Pedro of Castile set off from Seville where he had been staying and advanced as far as Calatayud. From there he moved on to besiege a town and castle near Teruel by the name of Castielfabib. He took this step because, although he had taken the town and appointed one of his knights, a native of Toledo, to be its governor, its citizens had killed the knight and seized control of the town and castle. So now he besieged Castielfabib for a month, using a large number of siege engines, and he captured it. He promptly left and entered the kingdom of Valencia, taking the town and castle of Ayora and a number of other castles in the surrounding area.

When the king departed from Castielfabib after its capture, he dispatched the master of Alcántara, Don Gutier Gómez de Toledo, to escort into Murviedro some mule trains carrying provisions, as the men that he had left there had sent word to him that they were in need of supplies. The master of Alcántara, with other knights who were vassals of the king, went to Segorbe, situated on the edge of that area, to assemble the mule trains with which to take the provisions to Murviedro.

King Pedro of Castile went to Alicante, which was in the hands of his supporters, and from Alicante he moved out into the surrounding region, capturing the castles of Guadalest and Castell de Castells, along with some other fortresses, and returning from there to Elche, situated close to the kingdom of Murcia and which he had already captured on a previous occasion.

The people in Orihuela, which was four leagues from Elche, were afraid that the king intended to lay siege to them: they were short of supplies and had appealed to the king of Aragon for help.

Capitulo VIIº. Commo el rrey de Aragon vino por su cuerpo e basteçio la villa de Orihuela.

El rrey don Pedro de Aragon estaua en tierra de Valençia e por esa comarca e desque ouo cartas e mensageros de la villa de Orihuela, en que le enbiauan pedir que los acorriesse con viandas, que las non tenian e auian rresçelo que el rrey de Castilla los çercasse e los tomaria por fanbre, partio luego de alli e con el fasta dos mill de cauallo de su rregno, e con el conde don Enrrique e don Tello e don Sancho, sus hermanos, e caualleros de Castilla que pudian seer todos fasta tres mill de cauallo e mucha gente vallesteros e lançeros.

E el rrey de Aragon fizo cargar muchos nauios de pan e que se viniessen en derecho de Orihuela, que es ý la mar assaz cerca. E el e las conpañas que con el venian, segund dicho auemos, venian acorrer a la villa de Orihuela e la basteçer de aquellas viandas que auia enbiado por la mar, e paso dos leguas de Elche, donde el rrey de Castilla estaua. E el rrey don Pedro de Castilla non quiso pelear con el e estudo en Elche e alli enderredor tenia toda su hueste.

E el rrey de Aragon puso su rreal çerca de Orihuela e estudo alli çinco dias faziendo traer las viandas que estauan en los nauios. E basteçio la villa de Orihuela lo mejor que pudo, e dende tornosse por el camino do veniera. E el rrey don Pedro de Castilla enbio a Martin Lopez de Cordoua, su camarero mayor e su priuado, con dos mill ginetes e algunos caualleros de Castilla. E fueron veer la hueste del rrey de Aragon, e aquel dia que primera mente los alcançaron pusieron los en grand rrebate e ouieron el rrey de Aragon e los que con el yuan a tomar vn grand rreues. E esse dia puso el rrey de Aragon su rreal muy çerca del pinar de Villena. E Martin Lopez de Cordoua e los ginetes

1364: CHAPTER VII

How the king of Aragon came in person, bringing provisions to the town of Orihuela.

King Pere of Aragon was on Valencian territory and in that same area, and once he received letters and envoys sent by the town of Orihuela appealing to him to come to their aid with provisions – for they were very short of supplies and were afraid that the king of Castile would besiege them and starve them into submission – he set off at once. He took with him some 2,000 horsemen from his kingdom and was also accompanied by Count Enrique and his brothers Don Tello and Don Sancho, together with Castilian knights: altogether there may well have been as many as 3,000 horsemen and a large force of crossbowmen and men armed with javelins.

The king of Aragon had several ships loaded with bread and ordered them to head straight for Orihuela, which stands quite near to the sea. He and the troops with him – as we have explained – had come to assist the town of Orihuela and to provide it with supplies from the provisions that he had sent by sea. He passed two leagues from Elche where the king of Castile was encamped, but King Pedro of Castile was unwilling to do battle with him, remaining in Elche, where – as well as in the surrounding area – he had his whole army.

The king of Aragon established his encampment close to Orihuela and he remained there for five days while he had the provisions which were on the ships taken to the town. He equipped the town of Orihuela with supplies as far as he could and from there he returned retracing the route by which he had come. King Pedro then dispatched Martín López de Córdoba, his master chamberlain and his confidant, with 2,000 light cavalry and some Castilian knights. They went to confront the king of Aragon's army, and on the first day that they caught up with them they threw them into considerable confusion and King Pere and his troops suffered a serious reverse. That day the king of Aragon established his camp very near to the pine woods of Villena. Then Martín López de Córdoba and the light cavalry advanced right up to

llegaron a ellos, pero non los fallaron mal rreglados commo el primero dia, ca los fallaron en mejor ordenança e non los pudieron enpesçer. E dende tornosse Martin Lopez para el rrey, e el rrey de Aragon tornosse a Valençia e dende por el rregno de Aragon, ca ya yua en acuerdo de tornar a çercar la villa de Monuiedro.

Capitulo VIIIº. Commo el rrey don Pedro de Castilla entro fazer guerra en Aragon e commo sopo que el maestre de Alcantara era muerto en pelea, e commo fue maestre de Alcantara Martin Lopez de Cordoua.

El rrey don Pedro de Castilla partio estonçe de Elche e entro por el rregno de Valençia e gano algunos castillos e llego a Denia que estaua por el, e basteçiola e basteçio otros castillos que eran en esa comarca, que estauan por el. E estando sobre vn lugar que dizen Calpe, que es rribera de la mar e lo tenia çercado, llegaronle nueuas commo don Gutier Gomez de Toledo maestre de Alcantara, al qual el rrey mandara poner rrecuas de viandas en Monuiedro, que entrara por poner la rrecua e que sallieran a el el conde de Denia, que fue despues marques de Villena, e don Pero Moñiz, que estonçes andaua en Aragon e se llamaua maestre de Calatrava, e el conçejo de Valençia, e pelearon con el dicho maestre de Alcantara en vn lugar que dizen Las Alcobillas e que lo desbarataron e lo mataron e le tiraron la rrecua. E peso mucho dello al rrey.

E fue muerto vn cauallero de Toledo que dizian Pero Alfonso Çeruatos e preso Iohan Martinez de Rojas e muertos otros e presos. E hordeno el rrey que fuesse maestre de Alcantara Martin Lopez de Cordoua, su rrepostero mayor, e enbio por los freyres e mando gelo fazer assi. E el rrey desque ouo estado algunos dias en aquella tierra

the Aragonese troops. However, they did not find them as disorganized as on the first day but rather in better order, and they were unable to inflict any damage on them. From there Martín López returned to King Pedro, whilst the king of Aragon made his way back to Valencia and then through the kingdom of Aragon, having already resolved to return to besiege the town of Murviedro.

1364: CHAPTER VIII

How King Pedro of Castile invaded Aragon, how he learned that the master of Alcántara had been killed in battle, and how Martín López de Córdoba was created master.

Then King Pedro of Castile set out from Elche and entered the kingdom of Valencia, capturing a number of castles. He came to Denia, which was in the hands of his supporters, and he supplied it with provisions, as he did for other castles in that area which were held by his forces. Then, while he was camped outside a settlement on the coast called Calpe which he was besieging, he received reports of the master of Alcántara, Don Gutier Gómez de Toledo, whom he had instructed to escort a mule train carrying provisions into Murviedro: Don Gutier had made his way in to escort the pack train and had been intercepted by the count of Denia, later to become marquis of Villena, and Don Pero Muñiz, currently campaigning in Aragon and terming himself master of Calatrava, together with the militias of Valencia. They did battle with the master of Alcántara at a place called Alcublas, defeating and killing him and seizing the mule train. The king was deeply saddened.

In addition to this, a knight from Toledo called Pero Alfonso Cervatos was killed, Juan Martínez de Rojas was captured and a number of other men died or were taken prisoner. The king instructed that his lord high butler, Martín López de Córdoba, be made master of Alcántara, and he sent for the brothers and commanded that this be put into effect. Then, once he had spent some days in those territories belonging to the kingdom of Valencia, he returned to Murcia and from

del rregno de Valençia, tornosse para Murçia e dende tornosse para Seuilla, e enbio los caualleros a sus fronteras.

Capitulo IX°. Commo el rrey don Pedro fizo matar todas las gentes de çinco galeas de Aragon e commo sopo que Monuiedro estaua çercada.

Luego que llego el rrey don Pedro de Castilla en Seuilla, sopo commo galeas suyas que andauan en la mar, de las quales era capitan Martin Yañes de Seuilla, auian tomado çinco galeas de catalanes e las auian traydas a Cartajena. E luego el rrey partio de Seuilla e fuesse para Cartajena e fallo ý las galeas de los catalanes, e fizo matar todas las conpañas que fallo de las dichas galeas, que non escapo ninguno, saluo los que eran rremollares, que eran omnes que sabian adobar rremos, por quanto non los auia en Seuilla deste ofiçio estonçe quantos auia menester.

E despues que ouo esto fecho, partio de Cartajena e fuesse para Murçia, e sopo alli commo el rrey de Aragon e sus gentes e el conde don Enrrique e don Tello e don Sancho, sus hermanos, eran todos sobre Monuiedro e la tenian çercada.

Capitulo X°. De lo que en este año acaesçio en Françia.

En este año que fue año del Señor mill e trezientos e sesenta e quatro, e de la era de Çesar mill e quatroçientos e tres años, fino el rrey don Iohan de Françia, primero que assi ouo nonbre, e rregno en su lugar su fijo Carlos quinto, que era primero dolfin de Viana. E rregno el rrey don Iohan de Françia, treze años.

there made his way back to Seville, sending his knights back to their posts on the frontiers.

1364: CHAPTER IX

How King Pedro ordered the execution of all those on board five Catalan galleys and how he learned that Murviedro had been placed under siege.[4]

As soon as King Pedro of Castile reached Seville, he learned how some of his galleys roaming the sea under the command of Martín Yáñez de Sevilla had captured five Catalan galleys and brought them to Cartagena. At once the king left Seville for Cartagena, where he found the Catalan galleys. He ordered the deaths of all the men that he found on them. Not one of those on board escaped with his life, except for men who were oar-makers by trade, as at that time there was a shortage in Seville of individuals who possessed this skill.

Once he had dealt with this, King Pedro left Cartagena and went on to Murcia, where he learned how the king of Aragon and his forces, together with Count Enrique and his brothers Don Tello and Don Sancho, were all outside Murviedro, laying siege to the town.

1364: CHAPTER X

Concerning what happened during this year in France.

During this year, which was the year of the Lord 1364, 1403 counting from the era of Caesar, the death occurred of King Jean of France, the first ruler to bear that name.[5] In his place Charles V, who had previously been Dauphin de Vienne, succeeded to the throne. King Jean of France had reigned for 13 years.

AÑO DIEZ E SEYS

que el rrey don Pedro de Castilla rregno, que fue año del Señor mill e trezientos e sesenta e çinco, e de la era de Çesar mill e quatroçientos e tres años.

Capitulo primero. Commo el rrey don Pedro çerco a Orihuela e la tomo.

En el año diez e seys que el rrey don Pedro rregno, que fue año del Señor mill e trezientos e sesenta e çinco, e de la era de Çesar mill e quatroçientos e tres, e del Criamiento del mundo segund la cuenta de los ebreos, en çinco mill e çiento e veynte e [çinco], e de los alarabes en sieteçientos e sesenta e siete, por quanto el rrey don Pedro non queria pelear con el rrey de Aragon, cataua todas las maneras de guerra que podia fallar. E desque sopo commo el rrey de Aragon tenia çercada a Monuiedro, fue luego el çercar la villa de Orihuela, que era del rrey de Aragon e era en frontera de Murçia, e fizola vn dia conbatir. E mataron alli a don Alfonso Perez de Guzman, fijo de don Iohan Alfonso de Guzman, e fue el conbate jueues treynta dias de mayo, e luego dende a ocho dias fue entregada la villa de Orihuela, a siete dias de junio.

E estudo el rrey alli fasta que gano el castillo, que es uno de los mas fuertes e fermosos del mundo. E morio ý estonçe vn cauallero del rrey de Aragon muy bueno, que tenia el dicho castillo de Orihuela, que llamauan don Iohan Martinez d'Eslaua e era rrico omne. E morio el dicho don Iohan Martinez llamandolo a fabla algunos de los del rrey e el segurandose en ellos, e estaua el rrey don Pedro en la bastida que tenia fecha e dos ballesteros con el, e fizole tirar de dos saetas al dicho don Iohan Martinez e dieronle por el rrostro, e ouo de fazer su pleytesia con el rrey e diole el castillo. E despues dizen que los

YEAR SIXTEEN (1365)

of the reign of King Pedro, which was the year of the Lord 1365 and, counting from the era of Caesar, 1403.

1365: CHAPTER I

How King Pedro besieged and captured Orihuela.

These events occurred in the sixteenth year of the reign of King Pedro, which was the year of the Lord 1365; in 1403, counting from the era of Caesar; 5,125 years from the creation of the world by the reckoning of the Hebrews; and, according to that of the Arabs, it was in the year 767. Since King Pedro did not wish to do battle with the king of Aragon, he looked for every form of waging war that he could find. Once he learned that the king of Aragon had placed Murviedro under siege, he quickly moved to besiege the town of Orihuela which belonged to the king of Aragon and stood on the frontier with Murcia. One day he ordered an attack to be made on the town and in this attack the death occurred of Don Alfonso Pérez de Guzmán, son of Don Juan Alfonso de Guzmán. The encounter took place on Thursday the 30th of May and just a week later, on the 7th of June, the town of Orihuela was surrendered.

The king remained there until he had taken the castle, which is one of the finest and most heavily fortified in the world. During that time a distinguished knight serving the king of Aragon met his death there. He was the man in charge of the castle of Orihuela, a member of the upper nobility by the name of Don Joan Martínez d'Eslava. Don Joan Martínez died when he was called to parley by some of the king's men and placed his trust in them. King Pedro was on the assault tower which he had had set up, together with two crossbowmen, and he instructed them to fire two bolts at Don Joan Martínez which hit him in the face, forcing him to negotiate with the king and hand the castle

çurujanos que lo catauan por mandado del rrey pusieron yeruas en el unguento en guisa que morio el dicho don Iohan Martinez. E desque el rrey ouo ganado a Orihuela dexo ý gente para la defender e partio e fuesse para Seuilla.

Capitulo segundo. Commo el rrey de Aragon çerco a Monuiedro e la gano por pleytesia que los de la villa fizieron con el rrey.

Commo quier que el rrey de Aragon tenia çercada a Monuiedro e los de la villa non tenian viandas e enbiauan rrequerir de cada dia al rrey que los acorriesse e el rrey non lo fazia, ca el non pudia acorrer saluo por batalla. E el rrey de Castilla por algunas cosas assi de muerte que auia fecho de algunos caualleros commo por todos los de su rregno que non eran contentos del, non se atreuia a dar batalla. E el rrey de Aragon estudo sobre Monuiedro e ouo muchas peleas con los de la villa, ca se defendian muy bien e peleauan sienpre fuera de la villa. E fue la mengua de las viandas mucha, ca comian los cauallos e las mulas que ya non tenian pan, e con el grand afincamiento de fanbre que tenian, ouieron de fazer su pleytesia en esta manera: que le diessen al rrey de Aragon la villa e ellos que salliessen todos seguros de vidas e mienbros e de prision e con todo lo suyo e los pusiessen en saluo en Castilla a do ellos quisiessen e fizieronlo assi.

E el prior de Sand Iohan, que era capitan, e los caualleros que ý eran salieron de la villa vn dia todos armados e de pie e pudian estonçe seer fasta seysçientos omnes de armas e partida de omnes de pie e vallesteros, e dieron la villa al rrey de Aragon. E el conde don Enrrique que ý era comenzo a tratar con los caualleros que sallieron de Monuiedro diziendoles que ellos sabian que el rrey de Castilla

over to him. They say that afterwards the surgeons caring for Don Joan Martínez at the king's command put poison in the ointment used on him in order to cause his death. Then, having taken Orihuela, the king left a garrison to defend it and set off for Seville.

1365: CHAPTER II

How the king of Aragon besieged Murviedro and took it by negotiation with the town's defenders.

The king of Aragon was besieging Murviedro and the people inside the town, whose supplies had run out, were sending daily appeals to King Pedro for help. However, he did not come to their aid, for he could not do so except by giving battle: and this, as a result of some of his actions such as the killing of some knights, and on account of all those people in his kingdom who were unhappy with him, King Pedro did not dare to do. The king of Aragon, meanwhile, continued to besiege Murviedro and had many encounters with the town's defenders, for they put up stout resistance and constantly fought outside the walls. The shortage of supplies was very serious, for they were eating the horses and mules now that they had run out of bread, and so they were forced by the great hunger that they were enduring to negotiate the following terms: they were to surrender the town to the king of Aragon and in return they were all to leave safe in life and limb, without fear of captivity and with all their possessions; and they were to be given safe conduct to wherever they wished in Castile. This agreement was honoured.

The prior of Saint John, who was in charge of the defence of Murviedro, together with the knights who were there, left the town one day, all of them armed and on foot – there could well have been as many as 600 men-at-arms and a good number of footsoldiers and crossbowmen – and they handed the town over to the king of Aragon. Count Enrique, who was present, began to negotiate with the knights who had left Murviedro, telling them that they were well

nunca los querria bien –teniendo que ellos serian querellosos por que los non acorriera– e que era omne muy peligroso, e que por auentura los mataria, e si a ellos pluguiesse que el e ellos fuessen vna conpañia e que el nunca les fallesçeria. E otrossi que los faria çiertos que el rrey de Aragon traya sus pleytesias con algunas conpañias de gentes de armas que andauan en Françia e en Gascueña, e que era çierto que le venian ayudar: lo uno por grand suma de dineros que el rrey de Aragon les enbiara prometer, otrossi por quanto el dicho conde don Enrrique auia estado en seruiçio del rrey don Iohan de Françia e ouiera vn dia de pelear con las dichas conpañias çerca vna çibdat de Françia que es en Aluernia, que dizen Claramonte, do eran muchos capitanes de las conpañias e todos estos fazian daño en la tierra de Françia. Enpero que se abinieron con el conde don Enrrique en esta manera: que el rrey de Françia les diesse çierta suma de dineros e que ellos salliessen del rregno de Françia e non fiziessen en el mas guerra, e por quanto ellos veyan que el conde don Enrrique era omne estrangero, que andaua fuera del rregno de Castilla donde era nasçido por miedo del rrey de Castilla, su hermano, que cada vez que el pudiesse auer manera para entrar en el rregno de Castilla e los ouiesse menester, que le farian compañia. E desto le fizieron juras e firmezas muy fuertes, seyendo rrequeridos por el que le viniessen ayudar. E el rrey de Aragon tenia su fecho concertado con los dichos capitanes e sus tratos; otrossy el conde don Enrrique les enbiara ya rrequerir del juramento e omenaje que le fizieran, segund dicho avemos, por le ayudar, e tenia çierto que todas aquellas conpañas serian en Aragon al comienço del año primero que viene, e luego el rrey de Aragon les libraria por tal manera que el dicho conde con ellos pudiesse entrar en Castilla e muy poderosa mente, ca la gente era mucha que tenian que las conpañas solas serian diez o doze mill conbatientes de gentes buenas de cauallo e omnes de armas husados de guerra, e que el rrey de Aragon le daua de los suyos mill de cauallo e que el tenia mill

aware that the king of Castile would never be on good terms with them, as he would believe them to be resentful towards him for not having gone to their assistance. He told them that King Pedro was a very dangerous man and that it was possible that he would kill them; and Count Enrique suggested to them that they might be prepared to join with him and, if so, he would never fail them. Moreover he added that he would give them firm evidence that the king of Aragon was in negotiation with some companies of men-at-arms who were campaigning in France and Gascony and that it was certain that they were coming to his assistance. This was partly because of the large sum of money that the king of Aragon had undertaken to pay them but also because Count Enrique had been in the service of King Jean of France and at one point had fought against those forces near to a French city by the name of Clermont situated in the region of Auvergne.[1] Several captains of the Companies were in that area, all laying waste to the lands of France, but they came to the following agreement with Count Enrique: the king of France was to pay them a certain sum of money and in return they were to leave the kingdom of France and no longer wage war there. Moreover, they could see that Count Enrique was a foreigner in exile from the kingdom of Castile where he had been born – out of fear for his brother the king of Castile –, and therefore they agreed that, at any time when he might have an opportunity to invade the kingdom of Castile and be in need of their assistance, they would fight at his side. They had sworn and given a firm assurance that on being called on by him they would come to his aid. The king of Aragon had made a pact and negotiated terms with those captains and Count Enrique now also sent word to them calling on them to comply with the terms of their oath and of the formal bond into which they had entered with him; for by this they had undertaken – as we have explained – to come to his aid. Thus the count was in no doubt that those companies would be in Aragon by the beginning of the following year and that the king of Aragon would free them from their commitment to him so that he could enter Castile in great strength. Indeed, the army was so large that the Companies alone were reckoned to number 10,000 to 12,000 fine cavalry and battle hardened men-at-arms, whilst the king of Aragon was providing Count Enrique

omnes de armas o mas, e que tenia que todas estas gentes entrando en Castilla que podrian fazer grand obra, e que si Dios le ayudasse a cobrar aquel rregno que el non lo queria si non para lo partir con ellos, e que les rrogaua que pensasen en todo esto.

E los que sallieron de Monuiedro oyeron e supieron todas estas cosas que el dicho conde les dixo, e lo mas era que se rresçelauan del rrey de Castilla e auian temor que los mataria e que non cataria commo lo fizieran con grand desanparo. E los mas caualleros e escuderos que en Monuiedro estudieron aseguraron sus fechos con el conde don Enrrique e fincaron por suyos, e otros algunos ouo que non quisieron fincar ally e fueronsse para el rrey de Castilla.

E vna de las cosas que mayor daño touo al rrey don Pedro en perder estos caualleros fue que vn año antes acaesçio que don Iohan Alfonso de Benauides justiçia mayor de la casa del rrey, vn cauallero muy grande en el rregno de Leon e muy enparentado e muy heredado e de mucha buena fama, e quien auia seruido al rrey don Alfonso su padre entrando en la villa de Tarifa quando la çercaron los rreyes de Benamarin e de Granada, e la defendio fasta que el rrey don Alfonso los acorrio. E tenia este don Iohan Alfonso de Benauides por el rrey don Pedro a Segorbe, que es a quatro leguas de Monuiedro, la qual ganara el rrey don Pedro, e menguaron las viandas e non se pudo defender. E antes que se perdiesse el dicho logar de Segorbe, el dicho don Iohan Alfonso fue al rrey don Pedro, a Seuilla, a le dezir en que estado estaua el lugar. E dexo ý parientes suyos e gentes assaz. E el rrey non le quiso oyr mas mandole prender e lleuar al castillo de Almodouar del Rio e ý morio. E los que esto oyeron auian grant rreçelo del rrey, señalada mente los caualleros que dieran a Monuiedro.

with 1,000 of his own horsemen and the count himself also had at least 1,000 men-at-arms. Count Enrique said he believed that an army of such a size entering Castile could achieve a great deal and that if God helped him to take control of that kingdom he wanted it not for himself but rather in order to share it with them. He now asked them to give consideration to all of this.

The men who had abandoned Murviedro heard and took in all of these things that the count put to them, but their strongest concern was their distrust of the king of Castile and their fear that he would put them to death without taking into consideration how their action had been the result of being in a hopeless situation. Most of the knights and squires who had been in Murviedro struck their deals with Count Enrique and pledged him their allegiance, although there were some others who did not wish to remain there and so went off to join the king of Castile.

One of most harmful factors for King Pedro which contributed to the loss of these knights was what had occurred a year previously in the case of Don Juan Alfonso de Benavides, chief justice for the king's household. Don Juan Alfonso was a very prominent knight in the kingdom of León, a member of an eminent family, well endowed with lands and of distinguished reputation, who had lent important service to King Pedro's father, King Alfonso, by entering the town of Tarifa when it was being besieged by the kings of the Marinids and of Granada and defending it until King Alfonso came to their assistance. Don Juan Alfonso had charge of Segorbe – situated four leagues from Murviedro – on behalf of King Pedro, who had captured the town. Supplies ran very low and resistance became impossible, but before the town of Segorbe was finally lost Don Juan Alfonso went to King Pedro in Seville to explain to him about the state that the place was in. In Segorbe he left members of his family and a good number of troops. However the king would not listen to him but instead ordered him to be arrested and taken to the castle of Almodóvar del Río, where he died. There was great fear of the king among the people who heard about this and particularly among the knights who had surrendered Murviedro.

Capitulo IIIº. Commo el conde don Enrrique se aparejaua para entrar en Castilla.

El rrey de Aragon despues que ouo cobrado la villa de Monuiedro, fue para Barçelona e dende enbio sus mensageros a las conpañias para que le viniessen luego a ayudar, e enbioles sus pagas. E venieron a el alli a Barçelona algunos capitanes e firmaron sus fechos con el rrey de Aragon e con el conde don Enrrique para seer en Aragon por todo el mes de febrero del año primero que venia, con todas las gentes de armas que tenian.

E en este año el rrey don Pedro de Castilla era en Seuilla e sabia desto e enbiaua sus cartas por todo su rregno a les aperçebir que se ayuntassen todos con el.

E en este año morio en Seuilla don Martin Gil señor de Alburquerque, fijo de don Iohan Alfonso e de doña Ysabel su muger, e dezian que morio con yeruas que le dieron.

1365: CHAPTER III

How Count Enrique made ready to invade Castile.

After taking the town of Murviedro, the king of Aragon headed for Barcelona, from where he sent his envoys to the Companies, requesting them to come at once to give him their support and sending them their payment. Some of their captains then came to him there in Barcelona, where they put their names to agreements with the king of Aragon and with Count Enrique, undertaking to be in Aragon for the month of February of the coming year, together with all the men-at-arms at their disposal.

Over the course of this year King Pedro was in Seville. He was aware of these developments and he sent letters to people throughout his kingdom giving them notice that they were all to go and rally to him.

Also during this year the death occurred of the lord of Alburquerque, Don Martín Gil, the son of Don Juan Alfonso and his wife Doña Isabel. His death was said to have been caused by poison that he was given.

AÑO DIEZ E SIETE

del rrey don Pedro, que fue año del Señor mill e trezientos e sesenta e seys, e de la era de Çesar mill e quatroçientos e quatro años.

Capitulo primero. Commo el rrey don Pedro sopo que el conde don Enrrique e las conpañias entrauan en Castilla.

En el año diez e siete que el rrey don Pedro rregnara, que fue año del Señor mill e trezientos e sesenta e seys, e de la era de Çesar segund costunbre de España, en mill e quatroçientos e quatro, e del Criamiento del mundo segund la cuenta de los ebreos, en çinco mill e çiento e veynte e [seys], e de los alarabes en sieteçientos e sesenta e ocho, el rrey don Pedro, estando en Seuilla en el comienço deste año, sopo por çierto commo los capitanes de las gentes de las conpañias, de quien auemos ya dicho, con quien el rrey de Aragon trataua para los fazer venir, que entrasen en Castilla con el conde don Enrrique, que auia estado con el rrey en Barçelona, e eran ya en todo abenidos con el e auian ydo para traer las conpañas darmas. E eso mesmo sopo commo algunos rricos omnes e caualleros de Aragon, los quales eran: el conde de Denia, que fue despues marques de Villena, e don Felipe de Castro e don Iohan Martinez de Luna e don Pero Ferrandez d'Yxar e don Pero Buyl e otros caualleros de Aragon eran prestos para venir con el conde don Enrrique para entrar en Castilla.

E partio el rrey don Pedro de Seuilla e vino su camino derecho para la çibdat de Burgos a do auia enbiado mandar que se llegassen todos los suyos. E desque llego el rrey en Burgos, venieron a el el señor de Lebret, que es vn grand señor en Gujana e era omne que sienpre amaua seruiçio del rrey de Castilla, e vinieron con el otros caualleros que amauan su seruicio. E dixeron en commo algunos señores e caualleros de aquellos que venian en aquellas conpañias que auian de

YEAR SEVENTEEN (1366)

of the reign of King Pedro, which was the year of the Lord 1366 and, counting from the era of Caesar, 1404.

1366: CHAPTER I

How King Pedro learned that Count Enrique and the Companies were invading Castile.

These events occurred in the seventeenth year of the reign of King Pedro, which was the year of the Lord 1366; in 1404, counting from the era of Caesar, according to Spanish custom; 5,126 years from the creation of the world by the reckoning of the Hebrews; and, according to that of the Arabs, it was in the year 768. While King Pedro was in Seville at the beginning of this year, he received reliable reports about the captains of the Companies. We have already said that the king of Aragon was negotiating to bring them to take part in the invasion of Castile with Count Enrique, who had been with King Pere in Barcelona. Now their agreement with him was complete and they had gone to bring their companies of men-at-arms. King Pedro, moreover, also learned how some Aragonese magnates and knights were ready to accompany Count Enrique into Castile. These were the count of Denia, who later became marquis of Villena, Don Felipe de Castro, Don Juan Martínez de Luna, Don Pedro Ferrándiz d'Ixar, Don Pere Boïl and other Aragonese knights.

King Pedro left Seville and made his way directly to the city of Burgos, where he had sent instructions for all his forces to gather. Following his arrival in Burgos, he was joined by the lord of Albret, who is a great lord in Guyenne and had always been a loyal ally of the king of Castile, and by other knights who served him faithfully. They spoke of how some of the lords and knights who were part of the force about to enter Castile had a family bond with them and with

entrar en Castilla, eran omnes que auian debdo con ellos e con la casa de Armiñac, cuyos parientes ellos eran, e que la casa de Armiñac e de Lebret querian e amauan seruiçio del rrey de Castilla, e si su merçed fuesse del rrey de Castilla que el señor de Lebret fablaria e trataria con ellos commo se partiessen de aquella conpañia e que farian de dos cosas la vna: o que se vernian para el rrey a le seruir e ayudar si el les quisiesse dar sueldo e mantenimiento o que se tornarian para sus tierras partiendo el rrey con ellos de lo suyo, e que si esto le pluguiese al rrey, que fuesse su merçed de les mandar enbiar alguna quantia para la despensa que auian fecho para se aparejar con los otros a fazer esta caualgada en Castilla. E esto dezia el señor de Lebret con buena entençion e con buen amor que el auia de seruir al rrey e al rregno de Castilla. E el rrey commo non era vsado de partir sus thesoros, dixoles luego que non les daria ninguna cosa, ca el entendia que todos los que en aquella coñpania venian que non le pudian enpeesçer en la entrada que agora querian fazer. E el señor de Lebret dixo que le non consejauan bien algunos sus priuados, ca çiertos fuessen que le seria mejor por algunas maneras catar commo pusiessen desuario entre aquellas conpañas que llegar con ellas a la prueua, ca alli venian grandes e nobles caualleros e buenos omnes de armas. E desque vio que el rrey non le tornaua rrespuesta a lo que el por su seruiçio le venia a dezir, tornosse para su tierra.

the House of Armagnac, to which they were related, and they affirmed that the Houses of Armagnac and Albret sought and desired to be loyal servants of the king of Castile. They suggested that, if it was the will of the king of Castile, the lord of Albret would put to those men a proposal that they break away from the company of which they formed part and then do one of two things: either come over to the king to give him their service and support – if he was willing to pay them a salary and the cost of their maintenance – or return to their own lands with the king sharing with them some of his wealth. They also requested that, if King Pedro was in agreement, he be prepared to arrange for a sum of money to be sent to cover the expenses that those lords and knights had incurred in preparing, along with the others, to make this foray into Castile. This proposal was made by the lord of Albret with a good intention and in his desire to be of service to the king and the kingdom of Castile. However, since King Pedro was not in the way of sharing his treasures, he was quick to tell them that he would give them nothing at all, for he could see that all those men who were part of that company could not harm him by means of the invasion that they were now planning. The lord of Albret told him that he was being badly advised by some of his confidants: they should be aware that he would be better served by finding some means of sowing discord among the Companies than by bringing the affair to a battle, for the the invading force included great and noble knights and fine men-at-arms. So, once he saw that the king was giving him no response to what he had come out of loyalty to say to him, he returned to his own land.

Capitulo segundo. Quales caualleros entraron con el conde don Enrrique en Castilla assi de Françia commo de otras partidas.

Estando el rrey don Pedro en la çibdat de Burgos, sopo commo el conde don Enrrique era ya pasado de Çaragoça para venir a Castilla e que todos los capitanes que venian para entrar en Castilla eran ya con el. E eran estos los capitanes de Françia mosen Beltran de Claquin, que era vn cauallero muy bueno natural de Bretaña, que fue despues conde estable de Françia e, por que era omne vsado de guerras e auia buenas venturas en las armas, todos le tomaron por capitan en esta caualgada maguer que venian otros señores de mayor linaje, ca venia ý el conde de las Marchas, que es de la flor de lis del linage del rrey de Françia, e el señor de Beaju, que es vn grant señor de Françia, e el mariscal d'Aude[nan] que era buen cauallero de armas, mariscal de Françia, natural de Picardia, e muchos otros caualleros e escuderos e omnes de armas de Françia. Otrossi venia ý de Yngla terra mossen Hugo de Carualoy e mossen Eustaçio e mossen Mayeu de Gornay e mossen Guillen Alemant e mossen Iohan de Ebreus e otros muchos grandes caualleros e escuderos e omnes de armas de Ingla terra. Otrossi venian de Gujana e Gascueña muchos buenos caualleros e escuderos e omnes de armas. E toda esta coñpana llego en la villa de Alfaro do estaua Yñigo Lopez de Horozco por frontero, que el rrey lo mandara ý estar, e non curaron de conbatir la villa.

E llegaron otro dia a Calahorra, que es vna çibdat que non era fuerte, e los que en ella estauan non se atreuieron a la defender e fizieron su pleytesia con el conde don Enrrique e acogieronlo alli. E estaua en Calahorra por el rrey, don Ferrand Sanchez de Touar e don Ferrando obispo de Calahorra e otros vasallos del rrey.

1366: CHAPTER II

Concerning which knights entered Castile along with Count Enrique, both from France and from elsewhere.

While he was in the city of Burgos, King Pedro learned how Count Enrique had already moved beyond Saragossa on his way towards Castile and that by now all the captains who had come to invade Castile were with him. These included the French captains, among them Monsieur Bertrand du Guesclin, a very fine knight who was a native of Brittany and who later became Constable of France. As he had considerable experience of warfare and he had enjoyed great success in battle, he was universally accepted as the commander on this campaign even though other lords of nobler birth were also involved. For also present were the count of La Marche, who bore the *fleur-de-lis* of the line of the king of France, the lord of Beaujeu, a great French lord, and the marshal d'Audrehem – a distinguished knight-at-arms, a marshal of France and native of Picardy – and many other French knights, squires and men-at-arms. Also, coming from England, there were Sir Hugh Calveley, Sir Eustace, Sir Matthew Gournay, Sir William Allamant, Sir John Devereux and a large number of other renowned English knights, squires and men-at-arms.[1] In addition, many fine knights, squires and men-at-arms had come from Guyenne and Gascony. The whole of this force arrived before the town of Alfaro, where Íñigo López de Orozco had been posted by the king as field commander, but they did not go to the trouble of attacking the town.

The following day they came to Calahorra. This city was not heavily fortified and those holding it dared not attempt to defend it. Instead, they negotiated its surrender with Count Enrique and allowed him to enter. In the city on King Pedro's behalf were Don Fernán Sánchez de Tovar, Bishop Fernando of Calahorra and other vassals of the king.

Capitulo IIIº. Commo el conde don Enrrique se fizo llamar rrey en Calahorra.

Desque la çibdat de Calahorra fue assi cobrada, ouieron nueuas el conde don Enrrique e los que con el venian commo el rrey don Pedro estaua en Burgos e tenia ý sus gentes ayuntadas, e sopieron de çierto que non auia voluntad de pelear con ellos, e ouieron ally en Calahorra todos su acuerdo e su consejo. E de todas las gentes de estrangeros que alli venian, eran los que hordenauan todo el fecho dos, por quanto auian visto muchos fechos de armas e de guerra, los quales eran el uno mossen Beltran de Claquin, que era breton del señorio del rrey de Françia, e el otro mossen Hugo de Carualoy, que era ingles de Ingla terra. E estos e todos los otros estrangeros dixeron al conde don Enrrique que, pues tan nobles gentes commo aquellos que venian con el eran acordados de lo guardar e tener por mayor en esta caualgada e el auia cobrado vna çibdat de Castilla, que le rrogauan que se fiziesse llamar rrey de Castilla e tomasse titulo de rrey, ca ellos tenian segund las nueuas que el sauia de la tierra, que el rrey don Pedro non podria defender la tierra. E en este acuerdo mesmo fueron el conde de Denia, que fue despues marques de Villena, e los otros rricos omnes e caualleros de Aragon que alli venian. E commo quier que al conde don Enrrique luego non le pudian tener a esto, pero segund paresçio, plogole mucho dello.

E luego que llego alli en la dicha çibdat de Calahorra le nonbraron rrey, e andudieron por la çibdat llamando: 'Real por el rrey don Enrrique'. E luego los que alli venian con el le demandaron muchos donadios e merçedes en los rregnos de Castilla e de Leon, e otorgogelos de muy buen talante, ca assi le cunplia e avn estauan por cobrar. E luego que esto assi fue fecho, el dicho conde de aqui adelante se fizo llamar rrey. E fue este año el primero que el rregno, que fue en el año del Señor mill e trezientos e sesenta e seys, e de la era de Çesar mill e quatrozientos e quatro. E era estonçe papa e apostoligo en Roma Vrbano Quinto, que fue abad de Sand Vitor de Marsella, e era

1366: CHAPTER III

How Count Enrique had himself proclaimed king in Calahorra.

Once Count Enrique had taken possession of the city of Calahorra in this way, he and those accompanying him received reports of how King Pedro was in Burgos, where he had assembled his forces, and they acquired certain knowledge that he had no desire to do battle with them. There in Calahorra they were all involved in giving counsel and advice; and of all the foreign soldiers who had come there, two were most influential in the whole matter as they had great experience of deeds of arms and of warfare: Monsieur Bertrand du Guesclin, a Breton lord in the service of the king of France, and Sir Hugh Calveley, of English birth and nationality. These and all the other foreigners said to Count Enrique that, since such distinguished soldiers as those that he had in his company were resolved to support him and take him as their commander in this campaign, and as he had captured a Castilian city, they beseeched him to have himself proclaimed king of Castile and to take the title of King; for they considered, to judge by the reports that he had received from the territory, that King Pedro would not be able to defend the kingdom. This opinion was also expressed by the count of Denia, later to become marquis of Villena, and the other Aragonese magnates and knights who were present. Although in the first instance they could not persuade Count Enrique to take this step, he appears to have been greatly attracted by the proposal.

Then, as soon as he arrived there in the city of Calahorra, they proclaimed him king and went through the city crying 'Long live King Enrique!'. The men in his company were quick to request many grants of possessions and favours in the kingdoms of Castile and León. He conceded these willingly, for it was fitting that he should do so and they had not yet received payment. From the moment that this had all taken place, the count took the title of King. This was the first year of his reign, which was the year of the Lord 1366, and 1404 counting from the era of Caesar. At that time the Pope and Pontiff in Rome was Urban V, who had been abbot of Saint-Victor in

enperador d'Alemaña Carlos rrey que fue de Bohemia. En Françia era rrey Carlos Quinto, fijo del rrey don Iohan, e rregnaua el rrey don Pedro en Aragon, e en Portogal el rrey don Pedro, e en Navarra el rrey don Carlos, e en Napol la rreyna doña Iohana, e en Inglaterra el rrey Eduarte, e en Granada el rrey Mahomad. E partio luego el dicho rrey don Enrrique de Calahorra e tomo su camino derecho para Burgos do estaua el rrey don Pedro, e llego a vna villa que llaman Nauarrete e quisierala conbatir; pero la villa non era fuerte, e diosele. E teniala vn cauallero que era adelantado por el rrey de Castilla, que dezian Aluar Rodriguez de Cueto. E dende fue para otra villa que dizen Briuiesca e fizola conbatir e tomaronla por la fuerça. E fue ý preso vn cauallero de Galizia que dizian Men Rodriguez de Senabria, que le mandara el rrey ý estar para defender la dicha villa con otras conpañas que el rrey le diera. E fue preso el dicho Men Rodriguez en la barrera peleando, e prisolo vn cauallero gascon que dezian mossen Bernal de la Sala.

Capitulo IIIIº. Commo el rrey don Pedro partio de Burgos e desanparo la çibdat, e las conpañas que alli eran con el.

El rrey don Pedro estando en Burgos sopo commo el conde don Enrrique e los capitanes que con el venian llegaron a Calahorra e la cobraran, e commo el conde don Enrrique se llamaua rrey de Castilla e de Leon e commo auia partido todos los ofiçios del rregno e auia fecho e prometido muchos donadios, e commo tomara a Navarrete e Briuiesca, e ouo grand rreçelo de todo esto.

E vn dia sabado biespera de Ramos, en la mañana sin dezir ninguna cosa a los señores e caualleros que con el estauan, caualgo para se partir e desanparar la çibdat de Burgos. E los de la çibdat quando lo supieron, venieron a el a su palaçio los mayores e mejores de la

Marseille, and the emperor of Germany was Karel, who was also king of Bohemia.[2] In France the king was Charles V, son of King Jean; in Aragon King Pere was on the throne, in Portugal King Pedro, in Navarre King Carlos, in Naples Queen Giovanna, in England King Edward and in Granada King Muhammad. King Enrique then set out from Calahorra without delay and headed straight for Burgos, where King Pedro was to be found. King Enrique came to a town called Navarrete, which he had intended to attack, but it was not heavily fortified and so it surrendered to him. It had been held by a knight by the name of Álvar Rodríguez de Cueto, who was governor on behalf of the king of Castile. From there King Enrique went on to another town called Briviesca; he ordered an attack to be made on it and it was taken by force. At Briviesca a Galician knight by the name of Men Rodríguez de Sanabria was taken prisoner: he had been posted there by King Pedro to be in charge of the defence of the town with the aid of other companies of troops given to him by the king. Men Rodríguez was captured fighting at the outworks by a Gascon knight called Monsieur Bernardon de la Salle.

1366: CHAPTER IV

How King Pedro set out from Burgos leaving the city without protection; and concerning the companies of troops that were there with him.

While King Pedro was in Burgos he learned how Count Enrique and the captains accompanying him had reached Calahorra and captured the city, how Count Enrique had taken the title of King of Castile and León, distributed all the offices of the kingdom and promised many grants of land, and how he had taken Navarrete and Briviesca. All of this filled King Pedro with fear.

One Saturday morning – it was the eve of Palm Sunday –, without giving any warning to the lords and knights accompanying him, he mounted ready to depart and abandon the city of Burgos. When the

çibdat e dixeronle e rrequirieronle e pidieronle por merçed que los non quisiesse asi dexar e desenparar, ca el tenia alli muchas buenas conpañas e tenia algo assaz para las poder mantener e sy mas algo auia menester que ellos le darian quanto en el mundo auian, e que deste rrequirimiento que le fazian pedian a los escriuanos que ý estauan que les diesse instrumentos. E el rrey estaua a la puerta del palaçio do posaua e queria ya caualgar para se partir de ally, e rrespondioles que el les agradesçia mucho todas las buenas rrazones que le dizian e que era bien çierto que ellos assi lo farian commo dizian e conosçia bien la lealtad suya dellos que era grande e buena segund la guardaron sienpre a los rreyes onde el venia; pero el non podia escusar de partir de alli, ca el sabia por nueuas çiertas, que el conde don Enrrique e las conpañas que con el venian querian tomar el camino de Seuilla, do el tenia sus fijos e sus tesoros, e que por esta rrazon partia de alli para poner rrecabdo en ello.

E los de la çibdat de Burgos tornaron otra vez a le rrequerir que se non partiesse de alli de la çibdat e que non creyesse por ninguna manera tales nueuas commo le dizian, antes fuesse çierto que el conde e todas aquellas conpañas que eran en Briuiesca a ocho leguas dende, que su entençion era venir a Burgos. E sobre esto porfiaron los de la çibdat de Burgos mucho con el. E quando vieron que el non los queria oyr preguntaronle asy: 'Sennor, pues vuestra merçed sabe de vuestros enemigos que estan a ocho leguas de aqui e vos non los queredes aqui atender en esta vuestra muy noble çibdat de Burgos con tantas buenas conpañas commo aqui tenedes, que nos mandades a nos otros fazer commo nos podamos defender'. E el rrey les dixo estonçe: 'Yo vos mando que fagades lo mejor que vos pudieredes'. E ellos le dixeron: 'Señor, nos querriamos auer tanta buena ventura que pudiessemos defender a esta vuestra çibdat de todos vuestros enemigos, mas do vos, con tantas gentes e con tantas buenas conpañas, non vos atreuedes a la defender, ¿que queredes que nos fagamos? E por ende, señor, lo que Dios non quiera, si tal caso fuere que nos non podamos defender,

citizens learned of this, the great and good of the city came to his royal apartments and addressed him, formally requesting and begging him that it should not be his will to leave and abandon them in this way: for he had there with him many fine companies of troops and he had ample resources to keep them in supplies, and, if more was needed, they would give him anything in the world that they possessed. The people of Burgos also asked the notaries who were present to draw up for them a formal record of this request. Meanwhile the king was at the gateway to the royal apartments where he had been lodging and was anxious to ride off and be away from Burgos; and he replied to them that he was grateful to them for all the fine words that they had spoken to him, and that he was certain that they would do as they said: he was well acquainted with their immense and genuine loyalty to him, the same loyalty that they had invariably displayed towards the line of kings from which he came. Nevertheless, he had no choice but to leave the city, for he had received unequivocal reports that Count Enrique and the troops accompanying him intended to take the road to Seville, where he had his children and his treasures; and for this reason he was leaving Burgos in order to ensure that all was safe.

The citizens of Burgos once again requested him not to leave the city and not to give any credence to the kind of reports that he was receiving. Rather, they said, he could be certain that the count and all of those troops that were in Briviesca, eight leagues away, were intending to come to Burgos. On this point the citizens of Burgos argued insistently with King Pedro, and, when they realized that he was not willing to listen to them, they put to him the following question: 'Lord king, since your Grace is aware that your enemies are eight leagues from here and you are not willing to await them here in this your most noble city of Burgos, with so many troops of such quality as you have with you, we ask you to instruct us as to what we must do in order to defend ourselves.' 'My command', the king then said to them, 'is that you do the best you can.' And they said to him, 'Lord king, our wish would be to have the good fortune to be able to defend this your city against all your enemies, but where you, with so many troops and with such fine companies of men, do not dare to defend it, what do you expect us to do? And so, lord king – and may

quitades nos el pleyto e omenaje que por esta çibdat vos tenemos fecho vna e dos e tres vezes'. E el rrey les dixo: 'Si.' E ellos pidieron a los escriuanos que alli estauan que les diessen instrumentos.

E luego antes que el rrey dende partiesse, llego a el vn rrecabdador mayor del dicho obispado de Burgos, que dizian Ruy Perez de Mena, e tenia el castillo de la dicha çibdat de Burgos por quanto solia tener en el dicho castillo los marauedis que cobraua de las rrentas del rrei e rrequirio al rrey que le mandaua fazer del dicho castillo pues el se partia de la çibdat de Burgos, ca el non lo pudia defender. E el rrey le dixo que lo defendiesse. E el Ruy Perez le dixo: 'Señor, non he yo poder para lo defender pues vos dexades vuestra çibdat de Burgos.' E el rrey non le rrespondio. E esse dia que el rrey partio de Burgos en la mañana, fiziera matar en el castillo de la dicha çibdat a Iohan Ferrandez de Touar, hermano de Ferrand Sanchez de Touar, el qual tenia preso, e esto fue por saña que auia de don Ferrand Sanchez su hermano por que acogiera en la çibdat de Calahorra al conde don Enrrique.

E partio el rrey de la çibdat de Burgos sabado biespera de Ramos, que fue veynte e ocho dias de março deste dicho año e fue comer a Lerma, que es a siete leguas de Burgos, e fue dormir a Gomiel, otras çinco leguas, asi que andudo aquel dia doze leguas. E de los escuderos e caualleros de Castilla fueron muy pocos con el, ca todos los mas fincaron en la çibdat de Burgos, ca non le querien bien, antes les plogo de todo esto, ca auia algunos dellos a quien matara los parientes e estauan sienpre a muy grand miedo. E fueron con el rrey don Pedro estonçes Martin Lopez de Cordoua maestre de Alcantara e Yñigo Lopez de Horozco e Pero Gonçalez de Mendoça e Pero Lopez de Ayala e Iohan Gonçalez de Auellaneda e Lope Ochoa, su hermano, e Iohan Rodriguez de Torquemada e Pero Ferrandez Cabeça de Vaca e don Alfonso Ferrandez de Monte Mayor e Lope Gutierrez, su hermano, e don Gonçalo Ferrandez de Cordoua e Diego Ferrandez alcayde de los donzeles, su hermano. Otrossi yuan con el rrey seysçientos de cauallo moros que el rrey de Granada le auia enbiado con vn cauallero suyo

God not be willing for this to happen! – in case it turns out that we cannot defend it, we ask you to free us from the oath of homage for this city which we have sworn to you one, two and three times.' And the king replied to them, 'Yes, I will do this.' They then requested the notaries there present to draw up for them legally binding documents.

Just before the king departed from Burgos, he was approached by a head collector of taxes for the diocese of Burgos by the name of Ruy Pérez de Mena. This man held the city castle as this was where he used to store the coins of gold and silver which he collected as royal revenue, and he sought an answer from the king with regard to what he commanded him to do about the castle: for, as the king was leaving Burgos, Ruy Pérez could not defend it. The king told him to defend the castle, and Ruy Pérez said to him, 'Lord king, since you are leaving your city of Burgos, I do not have the resources to defend the castle.' And the king did not give him a reply. Moreover, on that morning when the king set off from Burgos, he had ordered the death in the city castle of the brother of Fernán Sánchez de Tovar, Juan Fernández de Tovar, whom he had been holding prisoner; and this was out of spite towards the man's brother, Don Fernán Sánchez, for having allowed Count Enrique to enter the city of Calahorra.

The king departed from the city of Burgos on Saturday the eve of Palm Sunday, which was the 28th of March of the year in question, and he went to eat in Lerma, seven leagues from Burgos, and to sleep in Gumiel, a further five leagues away; and so that day he travelled 12 leagues. Very few of the Castilian squires and knights accompanied him, for most of them remained behind in the city of Burgos: they did not support him but rather were pleased at all these developments; for there were some of them whose relatives he had killed and who were constantly in great fear. Those who went with the king at that time were the master of Alcántara Martín López de Córdoba, Íñigo López de Orozco, Pero González de Mendoza, Pero López de Ayala, Juan González de Avellaneda and his brother Lope Ochoa, Juan Rodríguez de Torquemada, Pero Fernández Cabeza de Vaca, Don Alfonso Fernández de Montemayor and his brother Lope Gutiérrez, Don Gonzalo Fernández de Córdoba and his brother Diego Fernández, master of the pages. The king was also accompanied by

que dizian don Mahonad el Cabesçani. E aquel dia que el rrey partio de Burgos enbio el rrey sus cartas a todos los caualleros e otros que tenian por el las fortalezas que auia ganado en el rregno de Aragon, que se veniessen para el e desenbargasen las fortalezas e las quemasen si pudiessen e las destruyessen, e anssi lo fizieron. Enpero algunos destos que tenian las fortalezas e castillos en Aragon se vinieron para el rrey don Pedro e otros fueron para el rrey don Enrrique que nueua mente estonçes venia.

E despues que el rrei don Pedro partio de la çibdat de Burgos, llego a el don Garçia Aluarez maestre de Santiago, que estaua por su mandado en Logroño, e vinieron con el Ruy Diaz de Rojas e Rodrigo Rodriguez de Torquemada e Iohan Rodriguez de Biedma. Otrossi vino a el don Diego Garçia de Padilla maestre de Calatraua, que estaua por mandado del rrey en Agreda. Otrossi vino a el Ferrand Aluarez de Toledo, hermano del maestre de Santiago, el qual estaua por su mandado en la villa de Calatayud. E vino a el don Ferrand Perez de Ayala, el qual estaua por su mandado en Castil Habibi, que ganara el rrey en Aragon. E vino al rrey Diego Gomez de Toledo, el qual estaua por su mandado en la villa de Tiruel, e Diego Gomez de Castañeda. E vino al rrey miçer Gil Boca Negra, su almirante, el qual estaua por su mandado en Chiua. E vino al rrey Men Rodriguez de Biedma, el qual estaua por su mandado en Xerica. E de cada dia le llegauan assaz conpañas, pero el rrey non cataua por al saluo por tener su camino para Seuilla. E commo quier que Yñigo Lopez de Horozco le dizia que algunos capitanes ingleses de los que venian con el rrey don Enrrique trayan sus pleytesias con el para se venir a el, non lo queria oyr nin curaua dello. E mando a Yñigo Lopez e a Pero Gonçalez de Mendoça que se tornassen a Guadalfajara e estudiessen alli. E de tal manera yuan los negoçios e los fechos que todos los mas que del se partian auian su acuerdo de non boluer mas a el.

600 Moorish horsemen whom the king of Granada had sent him under the command of one of his knights called Muhammad el Cabezani.[3] On that day when the king set out from Burgos he wrote to all the knights and other men who held on his behalf the fortresses that he had captured in the kingdom of Aragon, instructing them to report to him, abandoning the fortresses and, if they could, burning and destroying them. They obeyed his command, although, while some of the men who held the fortresses in Aragon came to support King Pedro, others went over to King Enrique, who at that time had just arrived in Castile.

Then, after King Pedro set off from the city of Burgos, he was joined by the master of Santiago Don Garci Álvarez, who had been in Logroño at his command, together with Ruy Díaz de Rojas, Rodrigo Rodríguez de Torquemada and Juan Rodríguez de Biedma. He was also joined by the master of Calatrava Don Diego García de Padilla, who at the king's command had been in Ágreda; by Fernán Álvarez de Toledo, brother of the master of Santiago, whom King Pedro had posted to the town of Calatayud; by Don Fernán Pérez de Ayala, stationed in Castielfabib, a town won by the king in Aragon; by Diego Gómez de Toledo, who at his command was in the town of Teruel; by Diego Gómez de Castañeda; and also by his admiral Miçer Gil Boccanegra, whom he had assigned to Chiva, and by Men Rodríguez de Biedma, who at his command had been in Jérica. Each day the king was being joined by a substantial number of troops, but he thought of nothing other than making his way to Seville. Moreover, although Íñigo López de Orozco told him that some of the English captains accompanying King Enrique were bringing proposals for King Pedro with regard to coming over to him, he did not wish to hear about the matter and cared nothing for it. He commanded Íñigo López and Pero González de Mendoza to return to Guadalajara and remain there. Indeed the nature of his dealings and the state of events were such that most of those who took their leave of him were determined never more to return to his side.

Capitulo V°. Commo el rrey don Pedro llego a la çibdat de Toledo e el rrecabdo que alli dexo.

Despues que el rrey don Pedro partio de la çibdat de Burgos, segund que auemos contado, llego a la çibdat de Toledo e estudo ý algunos dias hordenando los que alli auian de quedar por quanto el yua para Seuilla.

E dexo en Toledo por capitan mayor e guarda de la çibdat a don Garçi Aluarez de Toledo maestre de Santiago e con el a Ferrand Aluarez, su hermano, e a Ruy Diaz de Rojas e a Rodrigo Rodriguez de Torquemada e otros caualleros fijos dalgo, assi de Castilla commo de la çibdat de Toledo, que eran por todos seysçientos de cauallo. E dende fue el rrey para Seuilla, e tornaremos a contar commo fizieron los de la çibdat de Burgos despues que el rrey don Pedro dende partio.

Capitulo VI°. Commo fizieron los de la çibdat de Burgos despues que el rrey don Pedro dende partio.

Agora tornaremos a contar commo fizieron los de la çibdat de Burgos despues que el rrey don Pedro partiera dende. E asi fue que los de la çibdat de Burgos desque vieron los fechos en tal estado e que el rrey don Pedro se yua para Seuilla sin les poner cobro alguno, entendieron que se non podrian anparar, ca todas las conpañas que eran ý llegadas por mandado del rrey don Pedro se partian dende e se yuan al conde don Enrrique, e otros se partian para sus tierras. E por tanto los de la çibdat de Burgos ouieron su consejo commo farian, ca vieron que en ninguna manera del mundo se podrian defender e que sy tardassen en

1366: CHAPTER V

How King Pedro arrived in the city of Toledo, and concerning the garrison that he left there.

After King Pedro made his departure from the city of Burgos – as we have already related – he came to the city of Toledo, where he remained for some days organizing the men who were going to be left there, as he was on his way to Seville.

In Toledo he left as overall commander and governor of the city the master of Santiago Don Garci Álvarez de Toledo. With the master were his brother Fernán Álvarez, Ruy Díaz de Rojas, Rodrigo Rodríguez de Torquemada and other knights of noble birth, drawn both from Castile and from the city of Toledo, altogether 600 horsemen. From there the king went on to Seville; and we shall return to the account of the action that the citizens of Burgos took once King Pedro had left.

1366: CHAPTER VI

The action that the citizens of Burgos took after King Pedro's departure.

We shall now return to the account of the steps taken by the citizens of Burgos following King Pedro's departure. The fact is that, once they saw that events had reached such a state and that King Pedro was leaving for Seville without providing them with any protection, the citizens of Burgos realized that they could not defend themselves, for all the companies of troops that had come there at the king's command were leaving: some were going over to Count Enrique whilst others were going off to their own lands. So the citizens of Burgos discussed together what action they were to take, for they could see that there was no way in the world that they could defend themselves and that if they took a long time over further lengthy negotiations they

otras luengas pleytesias, que podrian auer grand peligro, que la çibdat de Burgos non era estonçe bien çercada, ca el muro era muy baxo.

E todas las conpañas de armas assi de estrangeros commo de castellanos que venian con el rrey don Enrrique contra el rrey don Pedro estauan ya muy çerca dende, ca estauan el rrey don Enrrique e todas sus conpañas en Briuiesca a ocho leguas de Burgos, la qual auia tomado por fuerça segund dicho auemos. E por esto enbiaron los de Burgos sus mensajeros a Briuiesca llamandole 'conde' e desque fuesse en Burgos e les jurasse de guardar sus libertades, que le llamarian 'rrey', e pidiendole por merçed que se viniesse para Burgos, ca ellos lo acogerian commo su rrey e su señor, e lo podrian muy bien fazer sin caer en yerro e en verguença, ca tenian quito el pleyto e omenaje que fizieran al rrey don Pedro e ge lo quitara quando dende partio.

E el rrey don Enrrique ouo muy grand plazer con los dichos mensageros de Burgos e con las cartas que la çibdat de Burgos le enbio. E partio luego de Briuiesca e vinosse para la çibdat de Burgos e fue en ella acogido muy honrrada mente con grandes proçessiones e alegrias. E el alcayde que tenia el castillo de la çibdat, de quien auemos dicho, vino a el e entrego gelo.

Capitulo VIIº. Commo el rrey don Enrrique rregno e se corono en Burgos.

Despues que el rrey don Pedro partio de la çibdat de Burgos, segund auemos contado, e llego el rrey don Enrrique e fue tomado por rrey, e fue este el segundo rrey que assy ouo nonbre de los rreyes que rregnaron en Castilla e en Leon.

E fizo luego el rrey don Enrrique fazer en Las Huelgas, que es vn monesterio rreal de dueñas çerca la çibdat de Burgos, que ouieron

might be in serious danger: at that time Burgos did not have proper fortifications, as its city wall was far from being of sufficient height.

Moreover, all the companies of men-at-arms – both those consisting of foreigners and those made up of Castilians – who were supporting King Enrique against King Pedro were now very close by, for King Enrique and all his forces were eight leagues from Burgos in Briviesca, which, as we have already related, he had taken by force.[4] And therefore the people of Burgos sent their emissaries to Briviesca, addressing him as 'Count' but saying that, once he was in Burgos and had sworn to preserve their freedoms, they would call him 'King'. They begged him that it be his will to come to Burgos, for they would welcome him as their king and their lord. Indeed, they would be able to do so without falling into error or dishonour as they had been released from the oath of homage that they had sworn to King Pedro, who had freed them from its bond on leaving the city.

King Enrique was delighted by the emissaries from Burgos and by the letter that the city had sent him. He left Briviesca without delay and made his way to the city of Burgos, where he was welcomed with great honour and with great processions and celebrations. The castellan responsible for the city castle, whom we have already mentioned, came to King Enrique and formally surrendered the castle to him.

1366: CHAPTER VII

How King Enrique ascended to the throne and had himself crowned in Burgos.

After King Pedro had left Burgos – as we have related –, King Enrique arrived at the city and was welcomed as king, the second to bear that name among the monarchs who reigned over Castile and León.

King Enrique lost no time in having elaborate preparations made in las Huelgas, a royal convent of nuns situated near to the city and which had been founded by the kings of Castile, and there he had

fundado los rreyes de Castilla, muy grandes aparejos e coronosse alli por rrey, e de aqui adelante en esta coronica se llama 'rrey'. E desque el rrey don Enrrique fue coronado, besaronle la mano por su rrey e su señor los de la çibdat de Burgos e muchos caualleros fijos dalgo que alli eran e muchos otros que a el vinieron. E llegaron a el muchos procuradores de las çibdades e villas del rregno a lo tomar por su rrey e por su señor, asi que a cabo de veynte e çinco dias que el se corono en la çibdat de Burgos todo el rregno fue en su obediençia e señorio, saluo don Ferrando de Castro, que estaua en Galizia, e la villa de Agreda e el castillo de Soria e el castillo de Arnedo e Logroño e Sand Sebastian e Guetaria. E el rrey don Enrrique rresçibiolos muy bien a todos los que a el vinieron e otorgoles todas las libertades e merçedes que le demandauan, en manera que ningund omne del rregno que a el vinia non le era negado cosa que pidiesse.

 E alli en Burgos ouo el rrey mucho thesoro de lo del rrey don Pedro, que le dio Ruy Perez de Mena alcayde del castillo de Burgos, e fuera su rrecabdador del rrey don Pedro en aquella tierra. Otrossi ouo el rrey don Enrrique muchos dineros de la juderia de Burgos, que le dieron en seruiçio vn cuento, e partio con todos los que vinieron con el, assi estrangeros commo castellanos e aragoneses. E dio a don Alfonso conde de Denia, del rregno de Aragon, que venia con el, la tierra que fuera de don Iohan fijo del infante don Manuel, maguer pertenesçia a la rreyna doña Iohana su muger del dicho rrey don Enrrique, que era fija legitima del dicho don Iohan Manuel, e mando que le llamassen 'marques de Villena'. E dio a mosen Beltran de Claquin, que era breton, a Molina, e diole mas el condado de Trastamara e que se llamasse conde de Trastamara. E dio a mossen Hugo de Carualoy, que era ingles, a Carrion, e mando que se llamasse conde de Carrion. E mando a don Tello su hermano que se llamasse conde de Vizcaya e de Lara e de Aguilar e señor de Castañeda. E commo quier que primera mente que don Tello salliesse del rregno el tenia el señorio de Vizcaya e de Lara por rrazon de doña Iohana su muger, fija de don Iohan Nuñez, e tenia el señorio de Aguilar, que gelo diera el rrey don

himself crowned king.[5] And so from this point on in our chronicle he is called a 'king'. Once King Enrique had been crowned, the citizens of Burgos, numerous knights of noble birth there present and many others who came to join him all kissed his hand in homage as their king and lord. Many procurators from the cities and towns of the kingdom also came to take him as their king and lord, and so within 25 days of his coronation in Burgos the whole kingdom had pledged obedience and accepted his lordship, with the exception of Don Fernando de Castro in Galicia, the town of Ágreda, the castle of Soria, the castle of Arnedo, and Logroño, San Sebastián and Guetaria. King Enrique gave all those who came over to him a very warm welcome and granted them all the freedoms and favours that they sought of him, to such an extent that no man in the kingdom who came to him was denied anything that he asked.

There in Burgos the king took possession of a large amount of King Pedro's treasure, which was handed over to him by Ruy Pérez de Mena, the castellan of the castle of Burgos who had been King Pedro's collector of taxes for that area. King Enrique also obtained a large amount of money from the Jewish community of Burgos, who paid a levy of a million *maravedís*. He used this wealth to pay all those who had come with him, both Castilians and men of Aragon. In addition, to Count Alfons of Denia, from the kingdom of Aragon, who had come with him, he granted the lands which had belonged to Don Juan, son of Prince Manuel. This was in spite of the fact that these lands belonged to Queen Juana, King Enrique's wife and legitimate daughter of Don Juan Manuel. King Enrique also commanded that Count Alfons now be known as the 'Marquis of Villena'. In addition, he granted Molina to the Breton Monsieur Bertrand du Guesclin and also gave him the county of Trastámara so that he would be known as the 'Count of Trastámara'.[6] And to the Englishman Sir Hugh Calveley he granted Carrión, instructing that he take the title 'Count of Carrión'. He commanded that his brother Tello be known as 'Count of Vizcaya, Lara and Aguilar' and 'Lord of Castañeda'. Before Don Tello had left the kingdom he had held the lordship of Vizcaya and Lara through his wife Doña Juana, daughter of Don Juan Núñez, and he had also held the lordship of Aguilar, granted to him by his father King Alfonso.

Alfonso su padre; enpero agora quando el rrey don Enrrique entro en el rregno, la dicha doña Iohana, muger de don Tello, era finada, ca la fiziera matar el rrey don Pedro, segund suso auemos contado. Otrossi fiziera matar a doña Ysabel, su hermana de la dicha doña Iohana, e non fincaua heredero que fuesse fijo del dicho don Iohan Nuñez e de doña Maria, que heredasse a Lara e a Vizcaya. E por tanto diolas el rrey don Enrrique, que agora rreynara, al dicho don Tello, e diole mas a Castañeda, la qual tierra auia dado primero el rrey don Pedro a Diego Perez Sarmiento, e despues que Diego Perez se fuera para Aragon, tenia la dicha tierra el rrey don Pedro. E a don Sancho, su hermano, diole todos los bienes que fueron de don Iohan Alfonso de Alburquerque e de doña Ysabel su muger, fija de don Tello de Meneses, que non dexara fijos herederos algunos, e mando que se llamasse conde de Alburquerque. E diole mas al dicho don Sancho el señorio de Ledesma con las Çinco Villas e diole mas las villas de Haro e de Briones e Bilhorado e Çerezo. E a los otros rricos omnes e caualleros que con el venian dioles villas e logares e castillos por heredat. E a todos los otros fizo muchas e muy grandes merçedes.

E de alli de Burgos enbio el rrey don Enrrique por la rreyna doña Iohana a Aragon, su muger, que era fija de don Iohan fijo del infante don Manuel, e por sus fijos, el infante don Iohan e la infanta doña Leonor, fija del rrey de Aragon, que era puesto su casamiento de la dicha infanta doña Leonor con el infante don Iohan su fijo. E venieron a Burgos despues que el rrey don Enrrique dende partio [e] fuesse para Toledo, e vino con ellos el arçobispo de Çaragoça que dizian don Lope Ferrandez de Luna.

Capitulo VIII°. Commo el rrey don Enrrique llego a Toledo e la cobro.

El rrey don Enrrique desque todo esto ouo assossegado, partio de Burgos e fue su camino derecho para la çibdat de Toledo, e antes que alla llegasse se vinieron muchos caballeros a su merçed e se le dieron

Nevertheless now, when King Enrique invaded the kingdom, Don Tello's wife Doña Juana was dead, killed at King Pedro's command, as we related above. King Pedro had also ordered the death of Doña Juana's sister Doña Isabel, and so no offspring of Don Juan Núñez and Doña María remained to inherit Lara and Vizcaya. And therefore King Enrique, now that he had ascended to the throne, granted them to Don Tello. He also gave him Castañeda, a territory which King Pedro had given initially to Diego Pérez Sarmiento and which later, once Diego Pérez had left for Aragon, had been held by King Pedro himself. To his brother Don Sancho, King Enrique gave everything that had belonged to Don Juan Alfonso de Alburquerque and his wife Doña Isabel, daughter of Don Tello de Meneses, for no heirs at all had remained; and he commanded that Don Sancho be known as 'Count of Alburquerque'. As well as this, he granted to Don Sancho the lordship of Ledesma with the Five Towns and also the towns of Haro, Briones, Beldorado and Cerezo.[7] To the other magnates and knights in his company King Enrique granted in perpetuity towns, villages and castles, and on all the others he bestowed many and substantial favours.

From Burgos King Enrique sent to Aragon for his wife Queen Juana, daughter of Prince Manuel's son Don Juan, and for his son Prince Juan and his future daughter-in-law Princess Elionor, daughter of the king of Aragon: for arrangements had been made for them to marry. They arrived in Burgos after King Enrique's departure for Toledo, accompanied by Don Lope Fernández de Luna, archbishop of Saragossa.

1366: CHAPTER VIII

How King Enrique arrived before Toledo and how he took possession of the city.

Once he had settled all of this, King Enrique set out from Burgos and headed straight for Toledo, and before he arrived many knights came to him offering homage, and many cities and towns pledged him

muchas çibdades e villas. E vino a el don Diego Garçia de Padilla maestre de Calatrava e Yñigo Lopez de Horozco e Pero Gonçalez de Mendoza e Garçi Laso de la Vega e Ruy Gonçalez de Çisneros e Pero Ruyz Sarmiento e Gonçalo Gomez de Çisneros e Iohan Alfonso de Haro e muchos otros caualleros de Castilla e de Leon saluo muy pocos que yuan con el rrey don Pedro. E quando el rrey don Enrrique llego çerca la çibdat de Toledo ouo en la çibdat grand buelta, ca el rrey don Pedro dexaua ý por capitan a don Garçi Aluarez de Toledo maestre de Santiago e a Ferrand Aluarez su hermano e algunos caualleros de Castilla con el segund dicho auemos. Pero en la çibdat querian algunos que el rrey don Enrrique entrasse en la çibdat e otros non, e Diego Gomez de Toledo alcalde mayor de la dicha çibdat tenia el alcaçar, e otros caualleros sus parientes touieron que el rrey don Enrrique entrasse en la çibdat, e sobre esto ouieron grand porfia; pero final mente todos acordaron que lo acogiessen. E don Garçia Aluarez maestre de Santiago, que el rrey don Pedro dexara en Toledo por capitan, non ouo poder de fazer al, ca muchos caualleros de la çibdat querian que el rrey don Enrrique entrasse. E estos tenian en Toledo el alcaçar e la puente de Alcantara e muchos parientes e gentes en la çibdat segund dicho es, e asi se fizo. E por quanto venia con el rrey Enrrique Gonçalo Mexia, que se llamaua maestre de Santiago e estudiera con el sienpre en Aragon e en todas la partidas do el rrey don Pedro andudiera, fue tratado que don Garçi Aluarez de Toledo, que eso mesmo se llamaua maestre de Santiago, dexasse el maestradgo al dicho don Gonçalo Mexia e que el rrey don Enrrique le diesse a don Garçi Aluarez por juro de heredat a Val de Corneja e Oropesa e çincuenta mill marauedis en tierra. E todo esto assi acordado, el rrey don Enrrique entro en la çibdat de Toledo, e todos lo rresçibieron con grand plazer e con grandes alegrias, e estudo alli quinze dias pagando sus gentes. E estonçe el aljama de los judios de la dicha çibdat de Toledo le seruieron para pagar las conpañas que venian con el de vn cuento, e fue pagado en quinze dias. E el rrey don Enrrique, desque ouo cobrada la çibdat de Toledo, venieron a el los procuradores de

their support. The master of Calatrava Don Diego García de Padilla came over to him, with Íñigo López de Orozco, Pero González de Mendoza, Garci Laso de la Vega, Ruy González de Cisneros, Pero Ruiz Sarmiento, Gonzalo Gómez de Cisneros, Juan Alfonso de Haro, and many other knights of Castile and León – with the exception of just a few who were accompanying King Pedro. When King Enrique arrived near to Toledo there was great unrest in the city: King Pedro had left in charge of it the master of Santiago Don Garci Álvarez de Toledo, together with his brother Fernán Álvarez and some Castilian knights, as we have already stated. However, some people in the city wanted King Enrique to make his entry whilst others did not. The chief judge of the city Diego Gómez de Toledo, who held the *alcázar*, and other knights related to him, were in favour of King Enrique entering the city. There was a heated argument about this, but finally they all agreed on granting King Enrique entry. The master of Santiago Don Garci Álvarez de Toledo, whom King Pedro had left as his commander in the city, had no power to do otherwise, for many knights there wanted King Enrique to make his entry, and these people held the *alcázar* and the Bridge of Alcántara in Toledo, and they had many relatives and supporters in the city, as has already been pointed out. And so it was done. Moreover, since King Enrique was being accompanied by Don Gonzalo Mejía, who held the title of master of Santiago and had consistently remained with him in Aragon and wherever he went on campaign, it was arranged that Don Garci Álvarez de Toledo, who also held the title of master of Santiago, should renounce the mastership in favour of Don Gonzalo Mejía and that King Enrique should give to Don Garci Álvarez, with right of inheritance, the lordship of Valdecorneja and Oropesa, together with land to the value of 50,000 *maravedís*. Once all of this had been agreed, King Enrique made his entry into Toledo, where everyone welcomed him with great joy and celebration. He remained there for two weeks while he made payment to his followers. Then the Jewish community of the city of Toledo raised within two weeks the sum of a million *maravedís*, a levy which the king imposed upon them in order to pay the troops accompanying him. And, once King Enrique had taken possession of the city of Toledo, the procurators of Ávila,

Auila e Segouia e Talauera e Madrid e Cuenca e Villa Real e muchas otras villas e lugares, e fizieronle omenaje e tomaronle por su rrey e por su señor. E el rrey don Enrrique dexo en guarda para apoderar e rregir la dicha çibdat a don Gomez Manrrique arçobispo que era de la dicha çibdat e omne de grand linaje e muy amado de todos. E dexo con el un su sobrino que dizian don Iohan Garçia Manrrique arçidiano de Calatraua, e era fijo de don Garçi Ferrandez Manrrique, hermano del dicho arçobispo don Gomez Manrrique, e fue despues este arçidiano arçobispo de Santiago. E el rrey fue para el Andalozia.

Capitulo IXº. Commo fizo el rrey don Pedro en Seuilla quando sopo que el rrey don Enrrique cobrara la çibdat de Toledo.

Quando el rrey don Pedro sopo en Seuilla commo el rrey don Enrrique era entrado en Toledo, ouo su acuerdo con Martin Lopez de Cordoua, que era estonçes maestre de Alcantara, e con Matheos Ferrandez su chançeller del sello de la poridad e con Martin Yañes de Seuilla su thesorero, que estos eran sus priuados, que enbiasse pedir ayuda al rrey don Pedro de Portogal su tio, que era hermano de la rreyna doña Maria su madre.

E para encargar mas al dicho rrey de Portogal por que ayuda le feziesse, enbiaua le dezir que, por quanto era puesto casamiento de la infante doña Beatriz, fija del rrey don Pedro e de doña Maria de Padilla, con el infante don Ferrando, fijo del rrey don Pedro de Portogal, que enbiaua luego toda aquella quantia de auer que era puesto de le dar al tiempo que casasen e que la dicha doña Beatriz fincasse heredera de los rregnos de Castilla e de Leon. E enbiola luego de Seuilla, e enbio con ella a Marti Martinez de Trugillo, vn omne de quien fiaua, e enbio con ella çierta quantia de doblas que fincaron de doña Maria de Padilla, que dexara a la infanta doña Beatriz su fija, con otras joyas e aljofar.

Segovia, Talavera, Madrid, Cuenca, Villa Real and many other towns and communities came to him and did homage to him, accepting him as their king and their lord. King Enrique left Archbishop Gómez Manrique in charge to take responsibility for and govern the city: he was a native of Toledo, a member of a distinguished family and much loved by all. The king also appointed to accompany the archbishop his nephew the archdeacon of Calatrava, son of Don Garci Fernández Manrique, the archbishop's brother. This archdeacon was later to become archbishop of Santiago. And the king then headed for Andalusia.

1366: CHAPTER IX

Concerning what King Pedro did in Seville when he learned that King Enrique had taken control of the city of Toledo.

When King Pedro learned in Seville of how King Enrique had made his entry into Toledo, he agreed together with Martín López de Córdoba, who was then the master of Alcántara, with his chancellor of the confidential seal, Matheos Fernández, and with his treasurer Martín Yáñez de Sevilla – for these men were his confidants – that he should send a request for assistance to his uncle King Pedro of Portugal, the brother of his mother Queen María.

Moreover, in order to add further weight to the request for help that he was making to the king of Portugal, he wrote to inform him that, since a marriage had been arranged between Princess Beatriz, the daughter of King Pedro and Doña María de Padilla, and King Pedro of Portugal's son Fernando, he was sending without delay the full sum of money that it had been agreed that he would pay at the time of their marriage; and in addition Doña Beatriz was to be heiress to the kingdoms of Castile and León. He lost no time in sending her from Seville, and with her he sent Martín Martínez de Trujillo – a man in whom he trusted – and also a sum in *doblas* which remained from Doña María de Padilla's legacy to her daughter Doña Beatriz, together with jewels and pearls.

E desque fue la infanta doña Beatriz partida de Seuilla, ouo el rrey nueuas commo era partido el rrey don Enrrique de Toledo e se venia para Seuilla, estonçes ouo el rrey don Pedro su consejo con los dichos sus priuados e con otros priuados que eran estonçe con el, que enbiasse por todo el thesoro que tenia en el castillo de Almodouar, que era thesoro monedado en oro e en plata que tenia por el Martin Lopez.

E mando armar vna galea en Seuilla e puso en ella a Martin Yañes de Seuilla su thesorero con todo este auer e con todo el otro auer que tenia en Seuilla, e mandole que fuesse para Tauira, vna villa de Portogal, e mando que la galea en que yua Martin Yañes que le esperasse ý fasta que el ý fuesse.

E el rrey estando en Seuilla para partir dende dixeron le commo todas las gentes de la çibdat estauan alboroçadas contra el e que querian venir sobre el alcaçar do el estaua por le rrobar, e ouo muy grand themor. E estonçe ouo su acuerdo de partir dende e yrsse a Portogal e leuo conssigo sus fijas doña Costança e doña Ysabel, ca doña Beatriz la mayor ya la auia enbiado segund dicho auemos. E fue con el rrey Martin Lopez de Cordoua maestre de Alcantara e Mateos Ferrandez su chançeller, e estos eran sus priuados. Otrossi fueron con el rrey Diego Gomez de Castañeda e Pero Ferrandez Cabeça de Vaca e otros.

E antes que llegase a Portogal, el rrey don Pedro de Portogal le enbio dezir que el infante don Ferrando su fijo non queria casar con la infanta doña Beatriz su fija e que el que lo non pudia ver. E el rrey don Pedro ouo estonçe su acuerdo de yr a Alburquerque a dexar ý sus fijas e todas sus cargas por quanto le llegaron nueuas que miçer Gil Boca Negra su almirante armara en Seuilla vna galea e otros nauios e fuera tomar la galea en que yua Martin Yañes, e queria saber el rrey en que estado eran estos fechos, ca non sabia que faria de sy.

E llego el rrey don Pedro al castillo de Alburquerque e non lo acogieron en el, antes entraron en el dicho castillo e se partieron del rrey algunos de los que yuan con el.

Then, after Princess Beatriz had set out from Seville, the king received reports of how King Enrique had left Toledo and was on his way to Seville. King Pedro determined, in consultation with the advisers that we mentioned above and others who were with him at the time, that he should send for all the treasure that he possessed in the castle of Almodóvar, in the form of gold and silver coin being held for him by Martín Yáñez.[8]

In Seville King Pedro had a galley armed and he had his treasurer Martín Yáñez de Sevilla embark with all this wealth as well as all of that which the king possessed in that city, commanding him to make for Tavira, a Portuguese town, and giving instructions for the galley carrying Martín Yáñez to await him there until he arrived.

While the king was in Seville about to depart, he was told how there was unrest directed against him throughout the city and that the people intended to attack the *alcázar* where he was residing in order to rob him. This filled him with fear. So at that point he resolved to set off for Portugal, and with him he took his daughters Doña Constanza and Doña Isabel, having already sent his eldest daughter, Doña Beatriz, as we have explained. The king was accompanied by his confidants the master of Alcántara Martín López de Córdoba and his chancellor Matheos Fernández, and also by Diego Gómez de Castañeda, Pero Fernández Cabeza de Vaca and others.

However, before King Pedro reached Portugal, the Portuguese king sent word to him that his son Prince Fernando did not wish to marry the Castilian monarch's daughter Princess Beatriz, and that he was unable to see him. King Pedro then determined to go to Alburquerque and leave his daughters there together with everything that he was carrying with him, for he had received reports that in Seville his admiral Miçer Gil Boccanegra had armed a galley and other ships and set out to capture the galley carrying Martín Yáñez: the king was keen to know the state of these affairs, for he just did not know which way to turn.

King Pedro reached the castle of Alburquerque but he was not granted entry. Instead, some of those who had been accompanying him went into the castle and severed their ties with him.

Capitulo X°. Commo el rrey don Pedro paso por Portogal e fue para Galizia.

Despues que el rrey don Pedro partio de Alburquerque enbio al rrey de Portogal su tio a dezir que le enbiase segurar que pudiesse pasar por su rregno de Portogal, por quanto auia rresçelo del infante don Ferrando su fijo. E esto fazia el rrey e se temia del dicho infante de Portogal por quanto era sobrino de la rreyna doña Iohana, muger del rrey don Enrrique, que agora nueua mente entrara en el rregno de Castilla, ca era fijo de doña Costança, fija de don Iohan Manuel, hermana de la rreyna doña Iohana.

E el rrey de Portogal enbio a don Aluar Perez de Castro e a don Iohan Alfonso Tello conde de Barçelos que se fuessen con el rrey don Pedro e lo pusiessen en saluo en Galizia.

E los dichos don Aluar Perez e el conde de Barçelos vinieron al rrey don Pedro e yuan con el, e quando llegaron con el a la Guardia dixeronle que se querian tornar por quanto auian miedo del infante don Ferrando que los enbiara amenazar por que yuan con el. E el rrey dioles seys mill doblas e dos estoques e dos çintas de plata muy rricas que fuessen con el fasta Galizia, e ellos llegaron con el fasta Lamego e dende se tornaron. E tomaronle estonçe a doña Leonor, fija del rrey don Enrrique, la qual leuaua presa el rrey don Pedro, que auia tienpo que ella era presa en su poder, e traxieronla al rrey de Portogal.

E el rrey don Pedro fuesse camino de Chaues e de Monterrey assaz desanparado.

1366: CHAPTER X

How King Pedro passed through Portugal and headed for Galicia.

After King Pedro left Alburquerque, he sent a request to his uncle the king of Portugal for a guarantee of safe conduct through his kingdom, as he distrusted the king's son Prince Fernando. He took this measure on account of his fear of the prince of Portugal, given that the prince was a nephew of Queen Juana, wife of King Enrique, who had recently invaded the kingdom of Castile: the prince was the son of Doña Constanza, Don Juan Manuel's daughter and sister of Queen Juana.

The king of Portugal sent Don Álvar Pérez de Castro and João Afonso Telo, count of Barcelos, to accompany King Pedro and ensure him safe conduct as far as Galicia.

Don Álvar Pérez and the count of Barcelos came to meet King Pedro and travelled with him, but when they had gone with him as far as Guarda they informed him that they wished to turn back as they were afraid of Prince Fernando, who had sent messages threatening them because they were accompanying him. The king gave them 6,000 *doblas*, two estocs and two very elaborate silver belts in return for accompanying them as far as Galicia; and so they went with them as far as Lamego, at which point they turned back.[9] They removed from King Pedro's custody Doña Leonor, King Enrique's daughter, whom he was taking with him as a prisoner having held her captive for some time, and they delivered her to the king of Portugal.

King Pedro travelled on, with little protection, to Chaves and Monterrey.

Capitulo XI°. Del consejo que el rrey don Pedro ouo en Monterrey.

Despues que el rrey don Pedro llego en Monterrey, vna villa de Galizia, ouo nueuas commo en Çamora estaua en el alcaçar Iohan Ganso, vn comendador de la horden de Sand Iohan que estaua por el e tenia su boz. E enbio luego a mas andar cartas a el e cartas a Soria e a Logroño, que estauan por el, a los esforçar e fazer sauer commo era en la dicha tierra de Gallizia e que los queria acorrer. E otrosy enbio sus cartas al rrey de Nauarra e al prinçipe de Gales a les fazer sauer commo era en la dicha tierra de Galizia e queria sauer que esfuerço tenia en ellos.

E el espero alli en Monterrey al arçobispo de Santiago e a don Ferrando de Castro. E el arçobispo non vino e vino ý don Ferrando e ouieron su consejo. E estonçes el rrey traya conssigo dozientos de cauallo, e dezian que en Galizia que avria otros quinientos de cauallo e dos mill omnes de pie e que era bien que se fuesse para Çamora e dende, camino derecho fasta Logroño por quanto el rrey don Enrrique e todas sus conpañas estauan en Seuilla, e que non auria el rrey don Pedro quien gelo pudiesse estoruar este camino.

E en este consejo eran Martin Lopez de Cordoua maestre de Alcantara e Diego Gomez Castañeda e Iohan Alfonso de Mayorga e Pero Ferrandez Cabeça de Vaca. Enpero Matheos Ferrandez su chançeller del sello de la poridad e Iohan Diente, vn comendador de Santiago que era su priuado, touieron el contrario diziendo que non era rrazon que el rrey se pusiesse en poder de los que le assi auian echado del rregno, ca tan poco deuia fiar en los de Galizia commo en los de las çibdades que agora estauan por el. E don Ferrando de Castro fue en este consejo que era bien de yr a Çamora e dende por el camino fasta Logroño, e que algunas villas que estauan alçadas tomarian su boz desque viesen que el rrey andaua por el rreyno. Otrosi que la

1366: CHAPTER XI

Concerning the counsel that King Pedro was given in Monterrey.

After he arrived in Monterrey, a town in Galicia, King Pedro received reports of how Juan Ganso, a commander of the Order of Saint John who had taken his side and declared his support for him, was holding the *alcázar* in Zamora. He lost no time in writing to him and also to Soria and Logroño, which likewise were supporting him, to give them encouragement and to let them know that he was in Galicia and wanted to come to their assistance. In addition he wrote to the king of Navarre and to the prince of Wales to inform them that he was in Galicia and that he wished to know what support he could rely on from them.

There in Monterrey he awaited the archbishop of Santiago and Don Fernando de Castro. The archbishop did not come but Don Fernando did, and they consulted together. At that time the king had with him 200 horsemen and it was said that in Galicia he would have another 500 mounted troops and 2,000 footsoldiers; they considered that it was right for him to head for Zamora and from there carry straight on to Logroño, for King Enrique and all his troops were in Seville and, if he followed this route, King Pedro would have nobody to obstruct his path.

In favour of this were the master of Alcántara Martín López de Córdoba, Diego Gómez de Castañeda, Juan Alfonso de Mayorga and Pero Fernández Cabeza de Vaca. On the other hand, the king's chancellor of the confidential seal Matheos Fernández and Juan Diente, a commander of the Order of Santiago who was his confidant, held the opposing point of view, arguing that it was not right that the king should place himself at the mercy of the people who had driven him from his kingdom, for he should place little trust in either the people of Galicia or those from the cities who were now giving him their support.[10] Don Fernando de Castro was of the opinion that it was right to make for Zamora and from there to follow the road to Logroño, and he argued that some towns which had risen up would declare their support for King Pedro once they saw that he was moving across the

çibdat de Çamora tomaria su boz, de mas pues que auia entrada por el alcaçar, ca lo tenia Iohan Ganso, cauallero de la horden de Sand Iohan, por el rrey don Pedro. Otrossi Astorga eso mesmo estaua por el, ca auia auido nueuas que estaua ý Diego Felipes vn cauallero dende, que tenia la boz del rrey don Pedro.

E en estos conssejos estiedieron tres semanas que nunca declararon cosa fasta que ouo el rrey nueuas de Soria e de Logroño commo estauan por el. Otrossi ouo rrespuesta de mensageros que enbiara al rrey de Nauarra. E don Ferrando e todos tomaron aquel acuerdo: que era bien de yr a Çamora e dende a Logroño. Enpero touosse el rrey al conssejo de Mateos Ferrandez e de Iohan Diente, que era mejor yrsse a la Curuña e meterse en la mar e yrsse a Uayona de Ingla terra e catar sus acorros con el prinçipe de Gales.

Capitulo XIIº. Commo el rrey don Pedro fue para Santiago e commo mataron al arçobispo de Santiago e al dean de la dicha iglesia.

El rrey partio luego de Monterrey e fue tener el Sand Iohan a la çibdat de Santiago. E el arçobispo de Santiago don Suero, natural de Toledo, nieto de don Diego Garçia de Toledo e de don Ferrand Gomez de Toledo, vino ý a el e traxo dozientos de cauallo, e desque vio al rrey e fablo con el, tornosse para la Rocha, que es vn castillo llano suyo çerca de la çibdat de Santiago.

E fablo el rrey esse dia con don Ferrando de Castro que queria prender al arçobispo e tomarle las fortalezas. E Mateos Ferrandez e Iohan Diente fueron en la fabla, e Suer Yañez de Parada, vn cauallero

kingdom. In addition he said that the city of Zamora would declare for the king, especially as it was possible to enter it through the castle, which was being held on King Pedro's behalf by Juan Ganso, a knight of the Order of Saint John. He also said that Astorga was likewise giving the king its backing, for he had received reports that a knight from Astorga called Diego Felípez was present in the town and had declared his support for him.

They took three weeks over these discussions before they made any declaration, waiting until the king received news from Soria and Logroño of how these cities were giving him their support. King Pedro also received a reply from the emissaries that he had sent to the king of Navarre. Don Fernando and the others all agreed that it was right to go to Zamora and from there on to Logroño. Nevertheless, the king opted to follow the advice of Matheos Fernández and Juan Diente who argued that it would be preferable for him to go to La Coruña and from there set sail for the English city of Bayonne, where he would seek the assistance of the prince of Wales.

1366: CHAPTER XII

How King Pedro went to Santiago and how they killed the archbishop of Santiago and the dean of the cathedral.

Without delay the king set out from Monterrey and went to spend the Feast Day of Saint John in the city of Santiago.[11] Archbishop Suero of Santiago, a native of Toledo and grandson of Don Diego García de Toledo and of Don Fernán Gómez de Toledo, came to meet him there bringing with him a force of 200 horsemen; and, once he had seen the king and spoken with him, he returned to La Rocha, a castle in his possession which was situated in a valley near to the city of Santiago.

That day the king spoke with Don Fernando de Castro, who was in favour of arresting the archbishop and seizing his fortresses. Matheos Fernández and Juan Diente took part in the discussion and also party to it was Suer Yáñez de Parada, a Galician knight who was no friend

de Galizia que queria mal al arçobispo, fue en este consejo. E todos estos consejaron al rrey que lo matasse.

E el dia de Sand Pedro despues de Sand Iohan vino el arçobispo de la Rocha, en la tarde, a veer al rrey a Santiago, ca enbiaua el rrey por el que viniesse a consejo, que queria auer con don Ferrando e con el e con los otros que ý eran. E mando el rrey a Ferrand Perez Corruchao e a Gonçalo Gomez Gallinato, dos caualleros de Galizia que querian mal al arçobispo, que le estudiessen esperando con veynte de cauallo a la puerta de la villa e que lo matassen, e ellos fizieronlo assi. E pusieronsse a vnas puertas de vnas posadas que eran çerca por do el arçobispo avia de venir e en veniendo el arçobispo entrando por la çibdat, fue luego muerto esse dia a la puerta de la iglesia de Santiago. E mataronlo Ferrand Perez Corruchao e los otros que eran con el.

Otrossi mataron esse dia luego ý el dean de Santiago que dezian Pero Aluarez, omne muy letrado e natural de Toledo, e alli fino delante el altar de Santiago. E el rrey estaua esse dia ençima de la iglesia donde veya todo esto. E el rrey tomole quanto tenia en la Rocha el arçobispo, e tomo todas las fortalezas e mandolas entrar a don Fernando de Castro e a los que mataron al arçobispo.

E fueronsse para la puente de Aulla, que es a tres leguas de Santiago, do estaua don Aluar Perez de Castro, hermano de don Ferrando, que venia veer al rrey. E commo sopo don Aluar Perez que mataron al arçobispo tornosse para su tierra con rresçelo que ouo del rrey. E Andres Sanchez de Grez, otro cauallero de Gallizia que estaua en la villa con el rrey, fuxo dende e tomaron boz del rrey don Enrrique luego que fueron en sus comarcas el don Aluar Perez e Andres Sanchez.

of the archbishop. All of these men advised the king to kill Archbishop Suero.

On the afternoon of the Feast Day of Saint Peter following that of Saint John, the archbishop came from La Rocha to see the king in Santiago, for King Pedro had sent for him to attend a discussion which he wished to hold with him, with Don Fernando and with the others who were present. The king instructed Fernán Pérez Churruchao and Gonzalo Gómez Gallinato – two Galician knights who were hostile to the archbishop – to await him with 20 horsemen at the city gate and kill him. This they did: they positioned themselves in the doorways of some dwellings which stood close to the route that the archbishop was to follow and, as soon as he made his way into the city, he was killed there and then at the door of Santiago cathedral. He died at the hands of Fernán Pérez Churruchao and his companions.

That same day they likewise killed the dean of Santiago, a very learned man from Toledo called Pero Álvarez, who died there before the altar of Santiago. On that day King Pedro had taken up a position high up on the cathedral from which he watched all of these events. He took all of the possessions that the archbishop had in La Rocha and seized all his fortresses, ordering them to be given to Don Fernando de Castro and the men who had killed the archbishop.[12]

They left for the bridge over the River Ulla, situated three leagues from Santiago, to meet up with Don Fernando's brother, Don Álvar Pérez de Castro, who had come to see the king. On learning of how the archbishop had been killed, Don Álvar returned to his own lands out of the fear that he felt for the king. Likewise, Andrés Sánchez de Gres, another Galician knight who had been in the town with the king, fled from there, and he and Don Álvar Pérez declared their support for King Enrique as soon as they had reached their own territory.

Capitulo XIII°. Commo el rrey don Pedro fue para Bayona de Inglaterra.

El rrey don Pedro desque todas estas cosas asi pasaron, ouo su consejo de yr para Bayona de Inglaterra e partio de Santiago e fuesse luego para la Curuña, e mando armar vna galea que estaua ý, e tomo todas las naos que estauan en la costa para se yr a Bayona.

E llegaron ý al rrey el señor de Poyana e otro cauallero de Burdeu, que enbio a el el prinçipe de Gales, e enbiole dezir que se fuesse para el señorio del rrey de Inglaterra, su padre, e que el que le ayudaria a cobrar su rregno, e asi ge lo enbio prometer.

E el rrey partio de la Curuña e levo consigo veynte e dos naos e vna carraca e la galea en que fuera e vn panfil que tomo a vnos genoueses. E el rrey yua en la carraca e leuaua consigo sus fijas las infantas, que eran tres: doña Beatriz e doña Costança e doña Ysabel. E dexo a don Ferrando de Castro en Gallizia con poder bastante, e en Gallizia e en tierra de Leon commo adelantado, e todos los ofiçios de la tierra acomendo a el.

E el rrey don Pedro partio de Galizia e pusose en la mar en la Curuña e fuesse para vna su villa de Guipuzcoa que dizen Sand Sebastian, e levo consigo sus fijas e el thesoro que traya alli consigo, que eran treynta e seys mill doblas e non mas en moneda de oro, ca todo lo al dexara en la galea que auia de traer Martin Yanes su tesorero. Pero leuaua muchas joyas de oro e aljofar e piedras presçiosas.

1366: CHAPTER XIII

How King Pedro went to the English city of Bayonne.

Once all these events had taken place, King Pedro resolved to go to the English city of Bayonne and he set out from Santiago, heading directly for La Coruña. He gave instructions for the arming of a galley that was waiting there and took possession of all the sailing ships on the coast in order to make his way to Bayonne.

While he was there, King Pedro was approached by the lord of Poyanne and another knight from Bordeaux, sent to him by the prince of Wales to inform him that he should go to the territories of the prince's father, the king of England, for he would help him to win back his kingdom. This was the promise that he sent to King Pedro.

King Pedro left La Coruña, taking with him 22 sailing ships, a carrack and the galley on board which he had been travelling, and also a small Genoese galley of which he had taken possession. The king now travelled in the carrack, taking with him the three princesses: Doña Beatriz, Doña Constanza and Doña Isabel. He left Don Fernando de Castro in Galicia with full authority and as governor of Galicia and of the territories of León, entrusting to him all the offices of the land.

King Pedro departed from Galicia, setting sail from La Coruña and making his way to San Sebastián, a town which he possessed in Guipúzcoa. With him he took his daughters and the treasure that he carried with him: just 36,000 *doblas* in gold coin, for all the rest he had left in the galley that was to be brought by his treasurer Martín Yáñez. However, King Pedro did have with him a great deal of jewellery with gold, pearls and precious stones.

Capitulo XIVº. Commo antes que el rrey don Enrrique llegasse a Seuilla fue tomada la galea del thesoro, que leuaua Martin Yañes de Seuilla.

Commo quier que deximos que el rrey quando llego a Alburquerque supiera nueuas que la galea de su thesoro era tomada, enpero mas por espeçial tornaremos a contar commo pasaron los fechos en Seuilla despues que el rrey don Pedro partio dende. E asi fue que despues que el rrey don Pedro partio de Seuilla con aquel murmullo e bolliçio que dicho auemos el almirante miçer Gil Boca Negra, que era ginoves, e otros de la çibdat armaron vna galea e algunos nauios e fueron en pos Martin Yañes de Seuilla, que yua en la galea do leuaua el tesoro del rrey, e alcançaronle en el rrio de Guadalquivir, ca avn non era mas arredrado, e tomaronle la galea con quanto ý leuaua.

E traxieron el almirante e los otros que lo tomaron todo el thesoro a Seuilla, e a Martin Yañes preso. E segun se sopo era el thesoro que leuaua Martin Yañes en la galea treynta e seys quintales de oro e muchas joyas. E el rrey don Enrrique cobro todo lo mas, e el dicho Martin Yañes finco con el. E despues dizian que fincara en la merçed del rrey don Enrrique con rreçelo que auia de yr al rrey don Pedro por que auia perdido el tesoro que le encomendo.

Capitulo XVº. Commo el rrey don Enrrique llego a la çibdat de Seuilla e commo fue rresçibido.

El rrey don Enrrique partio de Toledo e sopo en el camino commo el rrey don Pedro era partido de Seuilla e se yua para Portogal e dende que era su entençion de yr a Galizia e que leuara de Seuilla sus fijas

1366: CHAPTER XIV

How, before King Enrique reached Seville, the treasure galley under the charge of Martín Yáñez had already been captured.

Although we have already said that, on arriving at Alburquerque, the king had heard the news that his treasure galley had been captured, we shall now go back to recount in greater detail how events unfolded in Seville after King Pedro's departure. The fact is that, after the king had left amidst the disquiet and unrest that we mentioned, the Genoese Admiral Miçer Gil Boccanegra and other people from the city armed a galley and other ships. They then pursued Martín Yáñez de Sevilla, who was on board the galley carrying the king's treasure, and caught up with him in the River Guadalquivir, for he had reached no further than this. They then seized the galley with all that Martín Yáñez was carrying in it.

The admiral and the other men involved brought all the treasure to Seville, together with Martín Yáñez as a prisoner. As was then discovered, the treasure that he was transporting in the galley consisted of 36 *quintales* of gold together with a large number of jewels.[13] King Enrique took possession of most of it and Martín Yáñez pledged his allegiance to him; and afterwards it was said that he had gone over to King Enrique through his fear of returning to King Pedro because he had lost the treasure that the king had entrusted to him.

1366: CHAPTER XV

How King Enrique reached the city of Seville and concerning the reception that he received.

King Enrique left Toledo and during his journey he learned how King Pedro had set out from Seville and was heading for Portugal and how from there it was his intention to go on to Galicia. He also learned how

e todo lo que ý pudo leuar de su thesoro. E sopo commo la galea en que yua Martin Yanes, do leuaua grand parte de thesoro del rrey don Pedro, era tomada e commo la çibdat de Seuilla estaua por el, e ouo muy grand plazer e acuçio su camino quanto pudo para llegar a Seuilla. E fue por la çibdat de Cordoua do fue acogido con grand fiesta de todos los grandes e buenos dende e del conçejo de la çibdat.

E desque llego en Seuilla fue rresçebido con grand solepnidat en guisa que tan grandes eran las conpañas que de todas las comarcas alli eran uenidos para veer aquella fiesta, que maguer llego grand mañana çerca la çibdat, era mas de ora de nona quando llego a su palaçio. E desque el rrey don Enrrique cobro la çibdat de Seuilla e Cordoua, luego todas las villas de la frontera le obedesçieron, e el partio assy con los estranjeros que con el venian commo con los suyos en guisa que todos eran muy pagados e muy contentos del.

Otrosi el rrey Mahomad de Granada luego que sopo que el rrey don Enrrique auia cobrado los rregnos de Castilla e de Leon e toda el Andalozia, ouo muy grand temor del e enbiole luego sus mensajeros a el e firmo con el sus treguas commo quier que antes que esto fuesse, ouo alguna guerra entre los cristianos e los moros, e perdiosse vna villa que los cristianos tenian que dizian Yznaxar, que el rrey don Pedro ganara quando ouiera la guerra con el rrey Bermejo.

Otrossi el rrey don Enrrique enbio sus mensajeros al rrey don Pedro de Portogal e firmo con el sus pazes e amorios.

King Pedro had taken his daughters with him from Seville together with as much of his treasure as he could. And in addition he heard about the seizure of the galley in which Martín Yáñez was travelling and in which he was transporting a large part of King Pedro's treasure. He was told how the city of Seville had given him its support – at which he was delighted – and he hastened his pace in order to reach Seville as quickly as possible. He went by way of Córdoba, where he was welcomed with great celebration on the part of the great and good of the city and of its council.

Once King Enrique reached Seville he was welcomed with great ceremony: so great were the crowds that had flocked from all the surrounding districts to witness those celebrations that, although he arrived near the city early in the morning, it was past the hour of None when he reached his palace. Moreover, once King Enrique had taken possession of the cities of Seville and Córdoba, all the towns of the Frontier region were quick to give him their obedience. He rewarded both the foreigners accompanying him and his own men in such a way that all were content and satisfied with his actions.

In addition, when King Muhammad of Granada learned that King Enrique had taken control of the kingdoms of Castile and León and of all of Andalusia, he was filled with fear of him and quickly sent emissaries to the king and concluded a peace treaty. This was, however, not before there had been an outbreak of hostilities between Christians and Moors, involving the loss of a town called Iznájar which had been held by the Christians having been captured by King Pedro during the war with the Red King.

King Enrique also sent envoys to King Pedro of Portugal and they signed a treaty of peace and friendship.

Capitulo XVIº. Commo el rrey don Enrrique enbio algunas conpañas de las que con el vinieron de Françia e de Inglaterra para sus tierras.

Por quanto eran ý con el rrey don Enrrique muchas gentes de las conpañias que con el eran venidas assi françeses commo yngleses commo bretones e otros, e fazian grand daño en el rregno e grand costa, que de cada dia se contaua el sueldo que leuauan del rrey, e por tanto acordo de los enbiar los mas dellos e fizo en Seuilla su cuenta con ellos del tienpo que le auian seruido, e pagoles e enbiolos para sus tierras, e fueron todos muy contentos e muy pagados del.

Pero fincaron con el mossen Beltran de Claquin e los bretones que eran de su coñpania e mossen Hugo de Carualoy e algunos ingleses, que eran todos conpañias estranjeras, mil e quinientas lanças.

Otrossi el conde de la Marcha, que era vn grand señor del linaje del rrey de Françia, e el señor de Bea[ujeu], que eran parientes de la rreyna doña Blanca de Borbon, muger del rrey don Pedro, de la qual ya diximos, antes que se partiessen de Castilla para sus tierras, mandaron saber de vn vallestero que dizian Iohan Perez de Xerez, vallestero de maça, el qual matara a la rreyna doña Blanca, e traxieronlo preso a Seuilla al rrey don Enrrique e el mandogelo entregar a los dichos conde de la Marcha e señor de Beau[jeu] e mandaronlo enforcar, commo quier que fue pequeña emienda.

Pero estos dos señores de quien auemos dicho, el conde de la Marcha e el señor de Beau[jeu], non vinieron a Castilla con el rrey don Enrrique si non por seer contra el rrey don Pedro, por la muerte de la rreyna doña Blanca cuyos parientes eran.

1366: CHAPTER XVI

How King Enrique sent back to their lands some of the troops from France and England that had come with him.

Accompanying King Enrique there were many troops from the companies – both French and English, as well as Breton and of other nationalities – which had come with him, and they were doing great harm to the kingdom and causing considerable expense, for the salary that they were costing the king was accruing day by day. He resolved, therefore, to send most of them away and while he was in Seville he reckoned up his account with them for the period of service that they had given him. He made payment to them and sent them back to their lands, and they were all very well satisfied and pleased with his actions.

However, Monsieur Bertrand Du Guesclin remained with him, together with the Bretons who were members of his company and Sir Hugh Calveley and some Englishmen; all foreign troops, amounting to 1,500 lances.

In addition, the count of La Marche, a great lord and member of the family of the king of France, and the lord of Beaujeu – who were relatives of King Pedro's wife Queen Blanche of Bourbon, about whom we have already spoken –, before leaving Castile for their own lands, sought information about a royal guard by the name of Juan Pérez de Jerez. This man was a mace-bearing guard who had killed Queen Blanche and he had been brought as a prisoner to King Enrique in Seville. The king ordered him to be handed over to the count of La Marche and the lord of Beaujeu, and they had him hanged, although this was little by way of amends.

However, these two lords that we have mentioned – the count of La Marche and the lord of Beaujeu – had come to Castile with King Enrique for no other reason than to oppose King Pedro, on account of the death of their relative Queen Blanche.

Capitulo XVII °. Commo el rrey don Enrrique fue para Galizia.

El rrey don Enrrique moro en Seuilla el dia que llego ý fasta quatro meses e morara mas saluo que auia nueuas que el rrey don Pedro, desque llegara en Bayona de Gascueña, que se viera con el prinçipe de Gales e con el rrey de Nauarra e que auia fecho con ellos sus ligas e que cataua gentes de armas para tornar al rregno de Castilla.

Otrossi sopo el rrey don Enrrique commo don Ferrando de Castro era en Galizia e tenia la parte del rrey don Pedro e fazia mal e daño a los que tenian la su parte del rrey don Enrrique e por ende, partio de Seuilla e fue para Galizia.

E don Ferrando de Castro que era en Galizia, quando sopo de su venida del rrey don Enrrique, pusosse en la çibdat de Lugo, que es la mas fuerte que ay en toda Galizia. E el rrey don Enrrique llego alli e çercolo, pero non lo pudo tomar nin pudia assossegar mas en Gallizia, ca sabia ya commo el prinçipe de Gales juntaua muchas conpañas para venir con el rrey don Pedro.

Capitulo XVIII°. Commo fizo don Ferrando de Castro su pleytesia con el rrey don Enrrique.

El rrey don Enrrique touo çercado dos meses a don Ferrando de Castro en la çibdat de Lugo. E vino con el rrey el marques de Villena e el prior de Sand Iohan e el conde don Alfonso e tomaron todos los de Galizia boz del rrey don Enrrique. E don Ferrando de Castro ouo su pleytesia con el rrey en esta manera: que si el rrey don Pedro non lo acorriesse fasta el dia de Pascua de Resurreçion, que era fasta çinco meses, que don Ferrando le dexasse el rregno, e que todas las

1366: CHAPTER XVII

How King Enrique went to Galicia.

King Enrique remained in Seville for four months after his arrival and he would have stayed longer except that he received reports that King Pedro, having reached Bayonne in Gascony, had met with the prince of Wales and the king of Navarre, had entered into an alliance with them, and was recruiting troops with whom to return to the kingdom of Castile.

King Enrique also heard how Don Fernando de Castro was in Galicia and giving his backing to King Pedro and how he was inflicting harm and damage on the supporters of King Enrique. The king therefore left Seville for Galicia.

Don Fernando de Castro, who was in Galicia, when he learned that King Enrique was on his way, installed himself in Lugo, the most heavily fortified city in all of Galicia. King Enrique arrived there and laid siege to the city. However he could not take it and he was unable to linger there any longer, for he was now aware of how the prince of Wales was gathering a large force to accompany King Pedro.

1366: CHAPTER XVIII

How Don Fernando de Castro negotiated terms with King Enrique.

King Enrique besieged Don Fernando de Castro for two months in the city of Lugo. The marquis of Villena, the prior of Saint John and Count Alfonso were with the king, and all the people of Galicia declared their support for him.[14] Don Fernando de Castro then negotiated the following terms with the king: if King Pedro did not come to his aid by Easter Sunday, which allowed up to five months, Don Fernando was to leave the kingdom and surrender to King Enrique all the fortresses

fortalezas que tenia que las entregasse al rrey don Enrrique; pero sy don Ferrando de Castro quisiesse quedar en la merçed del rrey don Enrrique, que el rrey le dexasse el condado que el rrey don Pedro le auia dado, ca le diera a Castroxeriz por quanto dizia don Ferrando que aquella villa fuera de su linaje e que de aquel lugar se llamaban ellos 'de Castro', e del dia que el rrey don Pedro gela dio, se llamaua don Ferrando 'conde de Castro', e que fasta aquel plazo, que don Ferrando que non fiziesse mal ninguno a los que estauan por el rrey don Enrrique e que ellos non fiziessen guerra ninguna a don Ferrando nin a los que por el estudiesen.

E el rrey don Enrrique, esta pleytesia fecha, partio por todos santos de Lugo e fuesse para la çibdat de Burgos, ca ya auia nueuas commo el rrey don Pedro fallara grand esfuerço en el prinçipe de Gales e que se aparejaua para venir a Castilla con muchas gentes a dar batalla.

Otrossy en Galizia Iohan Perez de Nouoa que tenia boz del rrey don Enrrique, commo se fue de sobre Lugo el rrey, enbio a [tractar con] don Ferrando de Castro e tornosse suyo e entregole la puente de Orenes. E don Ferrando vino çercar otro cauallero de Galizia que dizian Iohan Rodriguez de Biedma, que estaua en Alariz, e los de la villa furtaronle dos torres de la villa e dieron la villa a don Ferrando de Castro. E Iohan Rodriguez dexo rrecabdo en el castillo de Alariz e vinosse para Monterrey. E don Ferrando touo çercado dos meses el dicho castillo e non lo pudo tomar, e junto todos los de la su parte e vinosse a el Aluar Perez de Castro e tornosse suyo.

E levo don Ferrando trezientos de cauallo e fue sobre Padron, do estaua Aluar Perez de Osorio, que tenia boz del rrey don Enrrique, e estudo ý ocho dias e non lo pudo tomar. E vinosse para Santiago a poner batalla al prior de Sand Iohan que dizian don Gomez Perez de Porres, e ouo ý con el sus tratos e treguas por dos meses.

E tornose don Ferrando luego a çercar a Monterrey e touo ý çercado a Iohan Rodriguez de Biedma un mes, e esto era ya en çima de enero. E dende leuantosse don Ferrando de sobre Monterrey e

that he held. However, if Don Fernando de Castro chose to give his allegiance to King Enrique, the king was to allow him to retain the county granted to him by King Pedro, who had given him Castrojeriz because Don Fernando claimed that this town had belonged to his family and that they called themselves 'de Castro' after it. Indeed, from the day that King Pedro had granted him the town Don Fernando had termed himself 'Count of Castro'. Moreover, until the expiry of the period of five months, Don Fernando was to do no harm to those who upheld King Enrique's cause and they were likewise to avoid any conflict with Don Fernando or his supporters.

Once these terms had been agreed, King Enrique left Lugo at All Saints and headed for the city of Burgos, for by now he had received reports of how King Pedro had found considerable support in the prince of Wales and was making ready to come to Castile with a large army in order to give battle.

Also in Galicia, as the king had abandoned the siege of Lugo, Juan Pérez de Novoa, who had declared his support for King Enrique, sent proposals to Don Fernando de Castro for an agreement by which he gave him his allegiance and handed over to him control of the bridge at Orense. Don Fernando then moved to besiege another Galician knight by the name of Juan Rodríguez de Biedma, who was in Allariz, and the townspeople occupied two of the town's towers and handed it over to Don Fernando de Castro. Juan Rodríguez left troops to defend the castle of Allariz and went on to Monterrey. Don Fernando besieged the castle for two months, but he was unable to take it. Álvar Pérez de Castro gathered together all his supporters and came to him, offering his allegiance.[15]

Don Fernando took 300 horsemen and launched an attack on Padrón, where King Enrique's supporter Álvar Pérez de Osorio was present. Don Fernando remained there for a week without being able to capture the town and he then moved on to Santiago. There he opened hostilities with Don Gómez Pérez de Porres, prior of Saint John, but negotiated with him the terms of a truce to last two months.

Don Fernando quickly went back to attack Monterrey, where he besieged Juan Rodríguez de Biedma for a month, and by now January was approaching. From there Don Fernando left the siege of

rrobole toda la tierra. E dexo fronteros en Alariz sobre el castillo que Iohan Rodriguez tenia, e don Ferrando fuesse camino de Çamora, por que ouo nueuas que el rrey don Enrrique enbiaua por el prior e por el conde don Alfonso e por Iohan Gonçalez de Baçan e por Pero Aluarez de Osorio, que estauan en la Curuña e en Santiago, que auian ya nueuas del prinçipe de Gales commo venia ya a ayudar al rrey don Pedro e a don Ferrando.

E llegaronle nueuas que Ferrand Alfonso de Çamora se alçara con la çibdat de Çamora, e don Ferrando fuesse para Çamora. E esto fue en el mes de febrero deste dicho año e moro ý en Çamora e en aquella tierra de Leon fasta que la batalla fue fecha. E tomo la boz del rrey don Pedro, Astorga e las otras villas todas de tierra de Leon.

Capitulo XIX°. Commo el rrey don Enrrique fizo cortes en Burgos.

El rrey don Enrrique, desque llego a la çibdat de Burgos, hordeno fazer sus cortes. E fueron ý llegados todos los mas honrrados e mayores del rregno e fizo ý jurar al infante don Iohan su fijo por heredero segund costunbre de España.

E commo quier que el rrey don Enrrique entrara en el rregno e ouiera estonçes muchos de los tesoros del rrey don Pedro, enpero era todo despendido, ca ouo de partir con muchos de los que le auien seruido e venido con el. E en estas cortes pidio ayuda al rregno e otorgaronle la dezena de todo lo que se vendiesse, vn dinero del marauedi, e rrindio aquel año diez e nueue cuentos. E este fue el primero año que esta dezena se otorgo.

Otrossi en aquellas cortes de Burgos fablo el rrey don Enrrique con todos los del rregno commo el rrey don Pedro entendia venir a le poner batalla con ayuda del prinçipe de Gales e de otras conpañas que venian con el e que les pidia consejo commo querian hordenar

Monterrey and plundered the whole area. He left field commanders in Allariz against the castle held by Juan Rodríguez and headed off towards Zamora, for he had received reports that King Enrique had sent for the prior and for Count Alfonso, Juan González de Bazán and Pero Álvarez de Osorio, who were in La Coruña and in Santiago: by now they had heard the news that the prince of Wales was already on his way to lend assistance to King Pedro and Don Fernando.

Reports also reached Don Fernando that Fernán Alfonso de Zamora had risen up with the city of Zamora, and so he made his way there. This was in the month of February of the year in question, and Don Fernando stayed there in Zamora and in the lands of León until the battle had taken place.[16] Astorga and all the other towns of the Leonese territories also declared their support for King Pedro.

1366: CHAPTER XIX

How King Enrique held *cortes* in Burgos.

Once he had arrived in the city of Burgos, King Enrique commanded that *cortes* be held. All the most honoured and senior figures of the kingdom had come together there and he had an oath of allegiance sworn to his son Don Juan as heir, according to Spanish custom.

Although King Enrique had invaded the kingdom and had then seized a large part of the treasure possessed by King Pedro, by now it had all been spent, as he had to make payment from it to many of those who had served and accompanied him. In these *cortes* he asked the kingdom for assistance and they granted him one tenth of the value of everything that was sold, one *dinero* in the *maravedí*, which in that year yielded him 19 million *maravedís*.[17] This was the first year in which this tax of a tenth part had been granted.

In those *cortes* which took place in Burgos King Enrique spoke with all the people of the kingdom about how King Pedro intended to come and wage war on him with the support of the prince of Wales and of other companies of troops that he was bringing with him; and he

que se fiziesse, ca el presto estaua para poner ý el su cuerpo por defendimiento del rregno. E todos le rrespondieron que fuesse çierto que todos ellos estauan muy prestos para le seruir e ayudar segund el lo veria por la obra quando cunpliesse.

E el rrey don Enrrique desque vio e entendio la buena voluntad de todos los suyos que mostrauan en lo seruir e ayudar si la dicha batalla fuesse, enbio luego por todas las conpañas que pudo, e de cada dia le venian e el los rresçibia muy bien. E partio con todos mucho algo e les fazia muchas honrras.

E en estas cortes dio el rrey a la çibdat de Burgos la villa de Miranda de Ebro por quanto se coronara en la çibdat de Burgos, e diogela en emienda de la villa de Briuiesca, que auia primero mandado a Burgos e agora la diera a Pero Ferrandez de Velasco.

Capitulo XXº. Commo don Tello conde de Vizcaya tomo vna muger que se dezia doña Iohana de Lara por su muger.

Estando el rrey don Enrrique en estas cortes fue dicho que vna dueña que estaua en Seuilla presa por mandado del rrey don Pedro, que se llamaua doña Iohana muger del conde don Tello, e el fizola traer a Burgos. E commo quier que don Tello dixo luego que era su muger e leuola a su casa, enpero dezia en su secreto que lo fazia por auer algund titulo a Lara e Vizcaya rreçelando que aquella muger se fuese a la partida del rrey don Pedro e que los vizcaynos, commo son omnes a su voluntad, tomassen con ella alguna emaginaçion por que don Tello perdiesse el señorio de Lara e Vizcaya; enpero era çierto don Tello que non era aquella su muger.

E algunos dias touola assy por su muger, enpero despues lo nego publica mente e fue fallado que non era ella, ca el rrey don Pedro

asked them to advise him on how they wished matters to proceed: for he was prepared to do battle in person in the defence of the kingdom. Their unanimous reply was that he should be in no doubt that they were all totally prepared to serve and support him, as he would see in practice when the need arose.

Once King Enrique had seen and understood the good will shown by all his people with regard to serving and supporting him if the battle took place, he lost no time in summoning all the forces that he could: more arrived each day and he welcomed them warmly. He paid them generously and heaped honours on them.

During these *cortes* the king granted the town of Miranda de Ebro to the city of Burgos, since he had been crowned in Burgos: he made this grant as compensation for the loss of the town of Briviesca, initially allocated to Burgos but which he had now given to Pero Fernández de Velasco.

1366: CHAPTER XX

How the count of Vizcaya, Don Tello, took as his wife a woman who called herself Doña Juana de Lara.

While King Enrique was at these *cortes*, a claim was made that a lady imprisoned in Seville at King Pedro's command and calling herself Doña Juana was the wife of Don Tello, and so he had her brought to Burgos. However, although Don Tello said at the time that she was his wife and took her to his home, he admitted in private that he did this in order to preserve his claim to Lara and Vizcaya. He also said he was afraid that the woman would associate herself with King Pedro's supporters and that the Vizcayans, being strong-minded men, would devise around her some scheme through which Don Tello would lose the lordship of Lara and Vizcaya. On the other hand, Don Tello was sure that she was not his wife.

For some days he presented her in this way as though she were his wife, although later he publicly denied it and it was concluded that

fiziera matar a la dicha doña Iohana muger del conde don Tello grand tienpo auia. E avn despues Martin Lopez de Cordoua quando fue preso en Carmona assi lo confeso e dixo que era muerta doña Iohana e mostro el lugar do estaua soterrada.

Capitulo XXI°. Commo los enbaxadores del rrey de Aragon venieron al rrey don Enrrique a la çibdat de Burgos.

El rrey don Enrrique estando en Burgos llegaron ý por mensajeros e enbaxadores del rrey don Pedro de Aragon, don Lope Ferrandez de Luna arçobispo de Çaragoça e don Iohan Ferrandez de Heredia castellan de Anposta, que es de la horden del Ospital de Sand Iohan en Aragon. E la su enbaxada e mensageria era que el rrey don Enrrique, quando partiera de Aragon para entrar en Castilla, oviera çiertos tractos jurados e firmados con el rrey de Aragon de çiertas cosas que le deuia dar de lo que se cobrasse en el rregno de Castilla, espeçial mente algunas çibdades e villas e quantia de moneda, por las cosas que el rrey don Pedro de Aragon fiziera quando las conpañas entraron con el rrey don Enrrique en Castilla e pasaron por Aragon, e por sueldo que les pagara.

E el rrey don Enrrique les rrespondio que el, que estaua en aquel tienpo que ellos veyan; ca sabian bien que el rrey don Pedro queria venir entrar en el rregno con esfuerço e poder del rrey de Inglaterra e del prinçipe de Gales su fijo, e que queria pelear e que non podria tener, sin grand escandalo, con el rrey de Aragon lo que era entre ellos tratado; ca si començasse a enajenar alguna cosa del rregno, toda la tierra seria contra el; pero que fiaua en Dios que si aquella batalla ouiesse de seer, que Dios le daria en ella buena ventura, e que el estaua presto para tener con el rrey de Aragon todo lo que con el pusiera e

she was not really the person that she claimed to be; for King Pedro had had Count Tello's wife Doña Juana killed a long time before. In addition, Martín López de Córdoba later admitted – when he was taken prisoner in Carmona – that this was the case, stating that Doña Juana was dead and pointing out the place where she was buried.

1366: CHAPTER XXI

How the king of Aragon's ambassadors came to King Enrique in the city of Burgos.

While King Enrique was in Burgos, he was approached by emissaries and ambassadors sent by King Pere of Aragon: the archbishop of Zaragoza Don Lope Fernández de Luna and Don Juan Fernández de Heredia, the castellan of Amposta, which belongs to the Order of the Hospital of Saint John in Aragon. Their mission and their message concerned the fact that King Enrique, on leaving Aragon to embark on his invasion of Castile, had sworn and put his signature to certain agreements with the king of Aragon with regard to certain things that he was to give to him from his gains in the kingdom of Castile. In particular, these included some cities and towns and a sum of money in return for what King Pere of Aragon had done when the Companies had gone with King Enrique into Castile and passed through Aragon, in addition to the salary that he had paid them.

King Enrique replied to them saying that they could see for themselves the position in which he found himself: they were well aware that King Pedro intended to enter the kingdom with support and forces provided by the king of England and his son the prince of Wales. King Enrique wished to give battle and could not meet the terms of his agreement with the king of Aragon without this causing a great furore: for, if he were to begin to hand over anything belonging to the kingdom, the whole land would oppose him. However, he trusted in God that if that battle took place He would grant him success in it; Enrique was prepared to meet all the terms that he had agreed with

el lo pudiesse conplir; ca le tenia en lugar de padre e rresçibiera del muchas ayudas en el tienpo que le ouo menester quando estudiera en el su rregno. E el castellan de Anposta con esta rrespuesta tornosse para el rregno de Aragon. E el arçobispo de Çaragoça finco con el rrey don Enrrique en Burgos.

Capitulo XXIIº. Commo se alço la çibdat de Çamora e por que rrazon.

Commo quiera que auemos dicho que don Ferrando de Castro tenia la boz del rrey don Pedro, era venido para Çamora. Pero queremos vos contar commo Çamora, que auia tomado boz del rrey don Enrrique, commo e por qual rrazon se partiera del.

E assi acaesçio estonçe en Burgos que vn cauallero que dizian Ferrand Alfonso de Çamora era uno de los mayores e mejores de la çibdat de Çamora e llegando a la camara del rrey don Enrrique rresçibio algund baldon de algunos porteros que lo derribaron e lo firieron sobre entrar en la camara del rrey, por lo qual fue dende mal contento por quanto algunos caualleros touieron la parte de los porteros e el rrey non ge lo estrañara. Partio luego de Burgos e fuesse, e desque llego en Çamora tomo la boz e parte del rrey don Pedro e fizo dende de la çibdat de Çamora mucha guerra estonçe e despues, segund adelante contaremos.

E el rrey don Enrrique enbio luego a la çibdat de Çamora a Gomez Carrillo, su camarero mayor, e al prior de Sand Iohan con conpañas; pero non pudieron ý fazer obra ninguna e tornaronse a Burgos al rrey don Enrrique.

the king of Aragon and he trusted that he would be in a position to do so. For he held King Pere in the place of a father and had received from him great assistance when he needed it during his stay in his kingdom. The castellan of Amposta returned with this reply to the kingdom of Aragon, while the archbishop of Saragossa remained with King Enrique in Burgos.

1366: CHAPTER XXII

How the city of Zamora rose up and for what reason.

Although we have already said that Don Fernando de Castro, who had declared his support for King Pedro, had come to Zamora, we also wish to tell you how and for what reason Zamora, which had taken the side of King Enrique, had then turned against him.

An event occurred at that time in Burgos involving a knight by the name of Fernán Alfonso de Zamora, one of the most distinguished and finest men of Zamora. On arriving at the king's chamber he suffered an affront at the hands of some doorkeepers who knocked him over, causing him injury, as he attempted to enter. He was annoyed that some knights had taken the side of the doorkeepers and the king had not rebuked them for it and so he promptly left Burgos and, once he arrived in Zamora, he gave his support and allegiance to King Pedro. As we shall relate in due course, both then and later he launched many attacks from the city of Zamora.

King Enrique lost no time in dispatching to Zamora his master chamberlain Gómez Carrillo and the prior of Saint John with companies of troops. However they were not able to achieve anything at all there and they returned to King Enrique in Burgos.

Capitulo XXIII°. Commo el rrey don Pedro llego a la çibdat de Vayona e fablo con el prinçipe de Gales e le dixo el prinçipe que le ayudaria.

Agora queremos tornar a contar commo fizo el rrey don Pedro despues que sallio del rregno de Castilla. Commo quier que auemos contado commo el rrey de Inglaterra e el prinçipe de Gales su fijo ayudauan al rrey don Pedro, pero agora tornaremos a contar commo el rrey don Pedro llego a Vayona e commo acaesçio. Assy fue que el rrey don Pedro llego a la çibdat de Vayona e non fallo ý al prinçipe de Gales, e luego a pocos dias llego el prinçipe a vn lugar çerca la canal de Bayona que dizen Cabreron. E el rrey don Pedro fue ally en vna galea e ally se vieron e finco asossegado que el prinçipe vernia luego a Bayona e anssi lo fizo.

E vino ý don Carlos rrey de Navarra e comieron con el rrey don Pedro. E assentaron al prinçipe en medio de la mesa, e el rrey don Pedro a la manderecha e el rrey de Nauarra a la otra mano. E desque alli llego el rrey don Pedro, fablo con el prinçipe commo auia mucho menester la ayuda del rrey de Ingla terra e la suya. E el prinçipe le dixo que fuesse çierto que el rrey de Ingla terra, su padre e su señor, e el estauan muy prestos para lo ayudar, e que sobre esta rrazon el enbiaua sus cartas al rrey de Ingla terra su padre, e tornosse para Burdeus.

E despues partio dende el rrey don Pedro e fuesse para Burdeus, e estando ý con el prinçipe algunos dias catando conpañas para venir a Castilla, e dende tornosse para Bayona. E avn despues otra vez partio de Vayona e fue a vna su villa, al prinçipe, que dizian Angulesma, e vio a la prinçesa su muger e diole muchas joyas. E el prinçipe fizo çierto al rrey don Pedro que el estaua presto con todo el poder del rrey de Ingla terra, su padre, de le ayudar e de le aconpañar para entrar a sus rregnos, e que todo esto el fiziera saber al rrey de Ingla terra, su padre e su señor, commo dicho es, e que era bien çierto que le plazeria

Chronicle of King Pedro

1366: CHAPTER XXIII

How King Pedro reached the city of Bayonne and spoke with the prince of Wales, and how the prince informed him that he would give him assistance.

Now we intend to return to the narrative of King Pedro's activities after leaving the kingdom of Castile. Although we have aready told of how the king of England and his son the prince of Wales were assisting King Pedro, now we shall go back and recount how King Pedro arrived in Bayonne and how events developed. The fact is that King Pedro arrived in the city of Bayonne but did not find the prince of Wales there, but then just a few days later the prince arrived at a place called Capbreton near to the Bayonne canal.[18] King Pedro travelled to Capbreton in a galley, and there they met. It was agreed that the prince would come to Bayonne very soon, and this he did.

King Carlos of Navarre also came to join them there and they ate together with King Pedro. The prince was seated at the centre of the table, King Pedro on his right and the king of Navarre on his left. Once King Pedro had taken his seat, he spoke with the prince of how he was badly in need of his aid and of that of the king of England. The prince told him to rest assured that his father and lord the king of England and he were entirely ready to give him their assistance and that he was writing to his father the king of England about this matter. He then returned to Bordeaux.

King Pedro later left Bayonne and likewise headed for Bordeaux, where he remained for some days with the prince, raising troops to come to Castile. From there he went back to Bayonne. Once again he set out from Bayonne and went to a town called Angoulême which belonged to the prince of Wales, and there he met his wife the princess and made her a gift of several jewels.[19] The prince assured King Pedro that he was ready with all the military force of his father the king of England to assist him and accompany him in his entry into his kingdoms. He also told him that he had informed his father and lord the king of England about all of this – as we have already said –

que el fuesse ayudado de todos los suyos. E el rrey don Pedro, desque sopo esta rrespuesta, ouo muy grand plazer, e ouieron alli su conssejo e acordaron commo auian de fazer.

E el prinçipe lo fizo saber al rrey de Ingla terra su padre, commo dicho auemos, en que le fizo saber todo lo que el rrey don Pedro le dixera e del menester en que estaua e commo era echado de su rregno e por quien e commo e que traya tesoros para pagas de las gentes que le auian de seruir e de ayudar.

E el rrey de Ingla terra le enbio sus mensageros al rrey don Pedro, otrossi sus cartas a su fijo el prinçipe, por las quales mostraua que le plazia de toda ayuda que le fuesse fecha por todos los suyos e enbiaua mandar al prinçipe su fijo e al duc de Alencastre, su fijo, que con sus cuerpos le fuessen ayudar. E esso mesmo enbio sus cartas a todos los grandes, condes e señores de Gujana e de Bretaña, e a todos los que el sabia que por le fazer plazer aconpañarian al prinçipe e al duc de Alencastre, sus fijos, en tal priesa commo esta, por las quales les enbio rrogar que fuessen con ellos.

E de alli adelante el prinçipe enbio catar todas las conpañas que pudo auer para esta caualgada e fallaua assaz dellas: lo vno por quanto el prinçipe estaua muy poderoso e señor de Gujana e auia pazes con Françia; otrossi por buenas pagas que el rrey don Pedro leuaua señalada mente en joyas de oro e de piedras preçiosas, sobre las quales el prinçipe acorria con grandes quantias.

E fizieron e acordaron el rrey don Pedro e el prinçipe de Gales todos sus tratos de lo que auian de auer todas las gentes de armas. E assi los pago el rrey don Pedro, dello en oro que leuaua, e el prinçipe le prestaua dello sobre joyas muy nobles e muy presçiadas que leuaua conssigo, segund la hordenança que el prinçipe fizo con todas las gentes de armas que auian de yr en esta caualgada.

and that he was in no doubt that the king would be pleased for all of his troops to assist King Pedro. Once he had heard this answer King Pedro was delighted, and they deliberated together and determined how they were to proceed.

As we have said, the prince informed his father the king of England about all that King Pedro had said to him, about the need in which the king of Castile found himself, about how and by whom he had been driven out from his realm, and about how he had brought treasure in payment for those who were to give him service and assistance.

The king of England sent envoys to King Pedro and also wrote to his son the prince, letting him know that he approved of any assistance given by his people and that he was instructing his sons the prince and the duke of Lancaster to go and assist him in person.[20] Likewise, he wrote to all the great nobles, the counts and lords of Guyenne and Brittany and to all of those that – as he knew – in order to please him would accompany his sons the prince and the duke of Lancaster in such a difficult enterprise as this, requesting that they go with them.

From that point on the prince sent out men to recruit as many troops as he could find for this campaign and he found a considerable number: on the one hand because at that time the prince held great power and because he was lord of Guyenne and was at peace with France; and also on account of the excellent remuneration which King Pedro was conspicuously bringing in the form of valuable articles of gold and of precious stones, on the strength of which the prince made available to him large sums of money.

King Pedro and the prince of Wales arranged and agreed every detail of what all the men-at-arms were to receive; and so they were paid by King Pedro partly in gold that he had brought with him and partly from what the prince lent him on the strength of the very fine and valuable jewels that the king had in his possession. Payment was made according to the agreement reached by the prince with all the men-at-arms who were to take part in this campaign.

Capitulo XXIIII°. Commo el rrey don Pedro dio al prinçipe la tierra de Vizcaya e la villa de Castro Durdiales, e otras cosas que acaesçieron.

En estos tratos que fizieron puso el rrey don Pedro de dar al prinçipe de Gales la tierra de Vizcaya e la villa de Castro Durdiales, e a mossen Iohan Chandos, conde estable de Gujana, que era vn buen cauallero e priuado del prinçipe, de le dar la çibdat de Soria.

Otrossi puso con el prinçipe que fasta que el cunpliesse todas sus debdas pagadas de lo que ouiessen de auer el prinçipe e las gentes que con el venian por el tienpo que estudiessen en Castilla, que en tanto firmassen en Bayona, por manera de arrehenes, las fijas del rrey don Pedro e de doña Maria de Padilla, las quales eran doña Beatriz e doña Costança e doña Ysabel, que llamauan infantas.

E finco todo esto acordado e el rrey don Pedro tornosse para Bayona. E el prinçipe finco en Angulesma e alli estudo esperando las conpañas que con el auian de yr a Castilla.

1366: CHAPTER XXIV

How King Pedro granted the prince the territory of Vizcaya and the town of Castro Urdiales, and concerning other events which occurred.

As part of their agreement, King Pedro undertook to grant the prince of Wales the territory of Vizcaya and the town of Castro Urdiales, and to the constable of Guyenne Sir John Chandos, who was a fine knight and a close adviser of the prince, he promised to give the city of Soria.

He also agreed with the prince that, until he had settled all his debts arising from the payment due to the prince and the troops in his company for the time that they were in Castile, the daughters of King Pedro and Doña María de Padilla – Doña Beatriz, Doña Constanza and Doña Isabel, who were known as princesses – were to remain in Bayonne as a guarantee.

All of this was confirmed and then King Pedro returned to Bayonne. The prince remained in Angoulême where he awaited the troops that were to go with him to Castile.

AÑO SEGUNDO

que el rrey don Enrrique rregno, que fue año del Señor mill e trezientos e sessenta e siete, e de la era de Çesar mill e quatroçientos e çinco e era AÑO DIEZ E OCHO que el rrey don Pedro rregnara.

Capitulo primero. De las pleytesias que el rrey don Enrrique e el rrey de Nauarra fizieron.

En el segundo año que el sobre dicho rrey don Enrrique rregno, que fue en el año diez e ocho que el rrey don Pedro auia rreynado, e fue en el año del Señor mill e trezientos e sesenta e siete, e de la era de Çesar mill e quatroçientos e çinco, e del Criamiento del mundo segund la cuenta de los ebreos, en çinco mil e çiento e veynte e siete años, e de los alarabes en sieteçientos e sesenta e nueue años. E luego al comienzo del año, el rrey don Enrrique traya sus pleytesias con el rrey de Nauarra don Carlos por quanto aquellas conpañas que auian de venir con el rrey don Pedro e con el prinçipe de Gales non auian otro paso tan bueno commo por los puertos de Ronçes valles, e eran del rregno de Nauarra e son en tal manera que se non podrian pasar los dichos puertos contra voluntad de los que estudiessen en esta otra parte de Nauarra.

E vieronse los rreyes don Enrrique e el rrey don Carlos de Nauarra en vna villa del rrey de Castilla que es frontera de Nauarra, que dizen Santa Cruz de Canpeço. E fizieron ý juras sobre el cuerpo de Dios e pleytos e omenajes, estando ý presentes don Lope Ferrandez de Luna arçobispo de Çaragoça e don Gomez Manrrique arçobispo de Toledo e don Alfonso marques de Villena e mosen Beltran de Claquin e muchos otros grandes señores. E finco que el rrey de Nauarra non daria el paso de los puertos de Ronçes valles al rrey don Pedro e al prinçipe de Gales e a los que con ellos venian e que por su cuerpo

YEAR TWO (1367)

of the reign of King Enrique, which was the year of the Lord 1367 and, counting from the era of Caesar, 1405; and THE EIGHTEENTH YEAR of the reign of King Pedro.

1367: CHAPTER I

Concerning the negotiations between King Enrique and the king of Navarre.

These events occurred in the second year of the reign of King Enrique – the eighteenth year of the reign of King Pedro – which was the year of the Lord 1367; in 1405, counting from the era of Caesar; 5,127 years from the creation of the world by the reckoning of the Hebrews; and, according to that of the Arabs, it was in the year 769. Right at the beginning of the year, King Enrique began negotiations with King Carlos of Navarre, as there was no other route through for the companies of troops coming with King Pedro and the prince of Wales as good as that which crossed the pass of Roncesvalles. This pass belonged to the kingdom of Navarre and its nature is such that it would not be possible to cross it against the will of the people on the Navarrese side.

King Enrique and King Carlos of Navarre met together in a town belonging to the king of Castile called Santa Cruz de Campezo, which stood on the frontier with Navarre. There they swore on the body of Christ, gave their undertakings and made their vows of fidelity in the presence of the archbishop of Saragossa Don Lope Fernández de Luna, the archbishop of Toledo Don Gómez Manrique, the marquis of Villena Don Alfons, Monsieur Bertrand du Guesclin and many other great lords. It was agreed that the king of Navarre would not allow King Pedro and the prince of Wales and those accompanying them to cross

seria en la batalla con todo el poder que ouiesse, en ayuda del rrey don Enrrique. E para esto ser firme finco que daria el rrey de Nauarra al rrey don Enrrique en arrehenes el castillo de La Guardia, que lo touiesse don Lope Ferrandez de Luna arçobispo de Çaragoça, que era vn perlado que amaua al rrey don Enrrique, e que daria el castillo de Sand Viçente, que lo touiesse mosen Beltran de Claquin, que era vn cauallero de Françia que ayudaua al rrey don Enrrique, e que daria el castillo de Buradon, que lo touiesse don Iohan Remirez de Arellano, que maguera era cauallero de Nauarra, amaua seruir al rrey don Enrrique e era con el en esta guerra.

Otrossi el rrey don Enrrique auia a dar al rrey de Nauarra por que el cunpliese lo que auia prometido de defender el puerto de Ronçes valles al rrey don Pedro e al prinçipe de Gales e que fuesse con el rrey don Enrrique en la batalla, la villa de Logroño, que el rrey don Pedro le prometiera por esta tal ayuda que el rrey de Nauarra fiziesse a el.

E esto fecho el rrey de Nauarra se fue para Panplona e estudo alli. E fizo otros tratos con el rrey don Pedro e con el prinçipe de Gales en esta manera: que el rrey de Nauarra les diesse el paso por el puerto de Ronçes valles e que el fuesse con ellos por su cuerpo en la batalla e que el rrey don Pedro le daria las villas de Logroño e Vitoria. E el rrey de Nauarra pensando commo el poder del rrey don Pedro e el prinçipe de Gales que trayan, era mayor que el poder que traya el rrey don Enrrique, otorgo al rrey don Pedro e al prinçipe de Gales de les desenbargar los puertos de Ronçes valles e de seer con ellos en la batalla por su cuerpo. E dexo pasar libre mente el puerto al rrey don Pedro e al prinçipe de Gales con todas sus conpañas. E despues que sopo commo eran pasados, rreçelo mucho de seer en la batalla por su cuerpo e non los quiso atender en Panplona; pero dexo ý vn rrico omne de su tierra, que dizian don Martin Enrriquez, su alferez, con tresçientas lanças, que se fuesse con ellos.

E el rrey de Nauarra fue para vna su villa que dizen Tudela, que es çerca de Aragon. Por non seer por su cuerpo en la batalla, trato con vn cauallero breton, primo de mosen Beltran de Claquin, al qual dizien

the pass of Roncesvalles, and that he would do battle in person and with the whole of the army at his disposal in support of King Enrique. As assurance for the agreement, it was determined that the king of Navarre would hand over to King Enrique the castle of Laguardia as a guarantee; it was to be held by the archbishop of Saragossa Don Lope Fernández de Luna, a prelate who was an ally of King Enrique. He was also to cede the castle of San Vicente to Monsieur Bertrand du Guesclin, a French knight assisting King Enrique; and the castle of Buradón was to be handed over to Don Juan Ramírez de Arellano who, although he was a Navarrese knight, was loyal to King Enrique and was supporting him in this war.

In return for the king of Navarre fulfilling his promise to defend the pass of Roncesvalles against King Pedro and the prince of Wales and to take part in the battle at his side, King Enrique was to give him the town of Logroño. This had also been promised to the king of Navarre by King Pedro for similar assistance that he was to give to him.

Once this meeting had taken place, the king of Navarre went to Pamplona and remained there. He negotiated another agreement with King Pedro and the prince of Wales with the following terms: the king of Navarre was to allow them to enter by the pass of Roncesvalles and was to be at their side in person in the battle, and King Pedro would hand over to him the towns of Logroño and Vitoria. The king of Navarre, considering that the army being brought by King Pedro and the prince of Wales was greater than that of King Enrique, conceded to them that he would allow them to cross the pass of Roncesvalles without obstruction and accompany them in person in the battle. And he did indeed allow King Pedro and the prince of Wales to cross the pass unhindered with all their troops. Subsequently, however, once he knew that they had crossed, in his great fear of taking part in the battle in person he was not willing to await them in Pamplona; but he did leave in the city his commander-in-chief, a magnate of his kingdom called Don Martín Enríquez, who was to accompany them with 300 lances.

The king of Navarre went to a town in his territory called Tudela, which is situated near to Aragon. In order not to take part in person in the battle, he came to an arrangement with a Breton knight called

mosen Oliuer de Ma[u]ny, el qual cauallero tenia a Borja, vn castillo e villa de Aragon, que el rrey de Aragon diera al dicho mosen Beltran por heredad e por le fazer merçed quando entraran con el rrey don Enrrique en Castilla.

E la pleytesia fue esta: que el rrey de Nauarra andaria a caça çerca de la villa e castillo de Borja, que es a quatro leguas de Tudela, que el dicho mosen Oliuer salliesse a el e le prendiesse e lo touiesse preso en el dicho castillo de Borja fasta que la batalla del rrey don Pedro e del prinçipe de Gales con el rrey don Enrrique fuesse pasada, e anssy podria auer escusa que non pudiesse seer por su cuerpo en la batalla, e que el rrey de Nauarra le daria por heredat al dicho mossen Oliuer vn castillo e villa que el rrey de Nauarra auia en tierra de Normandia en Françia, que dezian Gabray, con tres mill francos de oro de rrenta. E desto fizieron sus juras e sus pleytos. E anssy fue que el rrey de Nauarra fue vn dia a caça e sallio a el el dicho mossen Oliuer e prendiolo e leuolo al castillo de Borja e touolo alli fasta que la pelea del rrey don Enrrique con el prinçipe e con el rrey don Pedro fue fecha.

Capitulo segundo. Commo el rrey don Enrrique se torno de las vistas del rrey de Nauarra e commo se partio del vn cauallero de Inglaterra que era con el.

Agora tornaremos a contar commo fizo el rrey don Enrrique despues que el rrey de Nauarra se partio del en Santa Cruz de Canpesço. E despues destas vistas tornosse el rrey don Enrrique para Burgos teniendo que en todas maneras que por aquella partida de los puertos de Ronçes valles non pasarian el rrey don Pedro nin el prinçipe de Gales nin aquellas conpañas que con ellos venian, ca ge lo pudia muy bien defender el rrey de Nauarra.

E desque el rrey don Enrrique llego en la çibdat de Burgos, luego partio dende e vinose para Haro e estudo ý algunos dias ordenando sus gentes para la batalla.

Monsieur Olivier de Mauny. This man was Monsieur Bertrand du Guesclin's cousin and he held the Aragonese castle and town of Borja, which the king of Aragon had granted in perpetuity and as a token of gratitude to Monsieur Bertrand when they had entered Castile with King Enrique.

What was agreed was as follows: the king of Navarre would go out hunting near to the town and castle of Borja, situated four leagues from Tudela; then Monsieur Olivier would set out and capture him and hold him prisoner in the castle of Borja until the battle between King Pedro and the prince of Wales and King Enrique was over; and thus there could be an excuse for him not taking part in the battle in person. In return the king of Navarre would grant Monsieur Olivier possession in perpetuity of a castle and town called Gavray which he owned in the territory of Normandy in France, with an income of 3,000 gold francs. Oaths were sworn and an agreement settled to this effect. And so it was that one day the king of Navarre went out hunting and Monsieur Olivier set out after him, captured him and took him to the castle of Borja, where he held him until King Enrique's battle with the prince and King Pedro was over.

1367: CHAPTER II

How King Enrique returned from his meeting with the king of Navarre and how an English knight in his company left his service.

Now we shall return to the account of what King Enrique did after the king of Navarre left him at Santa Cruz de Campezo: after the meeting had taken place, King Enrique returned to Burgos believing that in no way would it be possible for King Pedro or the prince of Wales or the troops coming with them to cross that part of the pass of Roncesvalles, for the king of Navarre was well able to defend it against them.

Then, once he reached the city of Burgos, King Enrique promptly set off again for Haro, where he remained for a number of days

E mossen Hugo de Carualoy, que era vn cauallero ingles, con quatroçientos de cauallo de su conpañia que tenia consigo de Inglaterra, partio del rrey don Enrrique e fuesse para Nauarra por quanto su señor el prinçipe de Gales venia de la otra parte e el non podria seer contra el. E el rrey don Enrrique, commo quier que sopo commo el dicho mossen Hugo partia del e le pudiera el rrey fazer algund enojo, non lo quiso fazer teniendo que el dicho mossen Hugo fazia su debdo de se yr seruir a su señor el prinçipe, que era fijo de su señor el rrey de Inglaterra.

Capitulo III°. Commo el rrey don Enrrique sopo commo el rrey don Pedro e el prinçipe de Gales auian ya pasados los puertos de Ronçes valles e commo se venian para la batalla.

Otrossi desque el rrey don Enrrique sopo commo el rrey don Pedro e el prinçipe de Gales pasaran los puertos de Ronçes valles e que el rrey de Nauarra non les puso enbargo ninguno en ello nin curara dello, antes, desque supo que el rrey don Pedro e el prinçipe de Gales venian, se partio de la çibdat de Panplona e se fue para la villa de Tudela de Ebro, que estaua mas arredrada, e commo fuera preso por su arte, e sopo el rrey don Enrrique commo el rrey don Pedro e el prinçipe de Gales e todas aquellas conpañas eran ya llegadas en la cuenca de Panplona e estauan ý todos ayuntados.

E el rrey don Enrrique desque esto sopo, ayunto sus conpañas e fue para tierra de Rioja e puso su rreal çerca de Santo Domingo de la Calçada en vn enzinar muy grande que alli esta, que dizen de Vañares, e estudo ý algunos dias e fizo alarde de las gentes que ý eran con el.

E estando en el dicho enzinar de Vañares sopo commo el rrey don Pedro e el prinçipe de Gales e aquellas gentes suyas querian entrar en

organizing his forces in readiness for the battle.

An English knight by the name of Sir Hugh Calveley, who had 400 horsemen in the company that he had brought with him from England, left the service of King Enrique and departed for Navarre, since his lord the prince of Wales was on the opposing side and it would not be possible for him to fight against him. Although he was aware of how Sir Hugh was leaving his service and he could have taken some measure against him, King Enrique was unwilling to do so, considering that Sir Hugh was fulfilling his obligation in leaving in order to serve his lord the prince, the son of his lord the king of England.

1367: CHAPTER III

How King Enrique learned that King Pedro and the prince of Wales had now crossed the pass of Roncesvalles and that they were coming to do battle.

In addition, King Enrique learned of how King Pedro and the prince of Wales had crossed the pass of Roncesvalles. He also became aware of how the king of Navarre had not obstructed them or made any effort to do so; and he heard how, instead of doing this, on learning of the approach of King Pedro and the prince of Wales, King Carlos had left the city of Pamplona and headed for the town of Tudela de Ebro, which was further away, and had been taken captive through his own scheming. Moreover, King Enrique learned that King Pedro and the prince of Wales and all their troops had already reached the Basin of Pamplona, where they were all assembled.

On discovering this, King Enrique assembled his forces and headed for the territories of La Rioja, establishing his encampment near to Santo Domingo de la Calzada in a very extensive wood of holm oaks in that area, known as Bañares. There he remained for a number of days, reviewing the troops that he had at his disposal.

While he was encamped in the wood at Bañares he heard how King

Alaua. E partio de alli e paso a Ebro e puso su rreal çerca vna aldea que dizen Añastro, que es aldea de la villa de Treuiño de Yuda. E estando alli sopo commo fasta seysçientos de cauallo castellanos e ginetes, que el auia enbiado por cobrar la villa de Agreda, que estaua contra el, eran todos pasados al rrey don Pedro. E por esto todo el rrey don Enrrique non curo si non cada dia hordenar sus gentes para batalla. E de los estranjeros que con el estauan, eran estos de Aragon: estaua ý don Alfonso, fijo del infante don Pedro e nieto del rrey don Jaymes de Aragon, el qual era conde de Denia e de Riba gorça, e el rrey don Enrrique lo fiziera marques de Villena, e don Felipe de Castro, que era vn rrico omne de Aragon e casado con doña Iohana, hermana del rrey, e lo auia el rrey heredado en Castilla, ca le diera a Medina de Rio Seco e a Paredes de Naua e Otordehumos. E don Iohan Martinez de Luna e don Pero Buyl e don Pero Ferrandez d'Yxar e don Pero Jordan d'Vrres e otros.

E estauan otros muchos buenos caualleros de França, ca era ý mossen Beltran de Claquin, que era breton, muy buen cauallero, e el mariscal de [Audenan], que era mariscal de França, e el vegue de Villanes, que despues el rrey fiziera conde de Ribadeo, e otros caualleros e escuderos de França.

E del rregno de Castilla e de Leon eran ý todos los señores e rricos omnes e caualleros fijos dalgo saluo el maestre de Santiago don Gonçalo Mexia e don Iohan Alfonso de Guzman, que fue despues conde de Niebla, que el rrey dexara en Seuilla por guardar la tierra del Andalozia. E estauan con el don Tello conde de Vizcaya, señor de Lara, e don Sancho conde de Alburquerque, que eran sus hermanos, e el conde don Alfonso su fijo del rrey, e don Pedro conde de Trastamara, su sobrino, fijo del maestre don Fadrique su hermano, e el maestre de Calatraua don Pero Moñiz e el prior de Sand Iohan don Gomez Perez de Porres e otros señores e caualleros de Castilla e de Leon.

Pedro and the prince of Wales with their troops were intending to enter Álava. He set off, crossed the Ebro and established his camp near Añastro, a village belonging to the town of Treviño de Ibda. While he was there he heard news concerning a force of some 600 Castilian horsemen and light cavalry that he had sent to take the town of Ágreda which was opposed to him: they had all gone over to King Pedro. In the light of all of this King Enrique concentrated each day on organizing his troops for battle. Among the foreigners in his company were the following men from Aragon: Don Alfons, son of Prince Pere and grandson of King Jaume, who was count of Denia and Ribagorza and had been created marquis of Villena by King Enrique; Don Felipe de Castro, an Aragonese magnate married to the king's sister Dona Juana, and to whom the king had given lands in Castile, granting him Medina de Rioseco, Paredes de Nava and Tordehumos; and also Juan Martínez de Luna, Don Pere Boïl, Don Pedro Ferrándiz d'Ixar, Don Pero Jordan d'Urries and others.

Also present were many fine French knights: these included Monsieur Bertrand du Guesclin, a Breton and a knight of great quality, the marshal d'Audrehem, a marshal of France, Le Bègue de Villaines, whom the king later created count of Ribadeo, and other French knights and squires.[1]

From the kingdom of Castile and León had come all the lords, magnates and knights of noble standing, with the exception of the master of Santiago Don Gonzalo Mejía and Don Juan Alfonso de Guzmán, who later became count of Niebla; for the king had left these men in Seville to defend the territory of Andalusia. With King Enrique were his brothers, the count of Vizcaya and lord of Lara Don Tello and the count of Alburquerque Don Sancho, the king's son Count Alfonso, his nephew Count Pedro of Trastámara – son of the king's brother the master Fadrique –, the master of Calatrava Don Pero Muñiz, the prior of Saint John Don Gómez Pérez de Porres and other lords and knights of Castile and León.

Capitulo IIIIº. Commo el rrey don Enrrique hordeno su batalla.

El rrey don Enrrique ouo su conssejo e dixeronle que pues los contrarios todos venian a pie, que era bueno tener esta hordenança. E hordeno su batalla en esta guisa: puso que estudiessen de pie en la delantera mossen Beltran de Claquin e el mariscal de [Audenan] e el vegue de Villanes e otros caualleros de Françia. Otrossi hordeno que de los caualleros de Castilla, estudiessen a pie con el su pendon de la Vanda estos que aqui dira: el conde don Sancho su hermano e Pero Manrrique adelantado mayor de Castilla, e Pero Fernandez de Velasco e Gomez Gonçalez de Castañeda e Pero Ruyz Sarmiento e Ruy Diaz de Rojas e Sancho Sanchez de Rojas e Iohan Rodriguez Sarmiento e Ruy Gonçalez de Çisneros e Sancho Ferrandez de Touar e Suer Perez de Quiñones e Garçi Laso de la Vega e don Iohan Remirez de Arellano e don Garçi Aluarez, maestre que fuera de Santiago, e Pero Lopez de Ayala, que leuaua el pendon de la Vanda, e Iohan Gonçalez de Auellaneda e Men Xuarez clauero de Alcantara e Garçi Gonçalez de Ferrera e Gonçalo Bernal de Quiros e otros que pudian seer todos fasta mill omnes de armas los que estauan a pie.

E puso el rrey en la ala de a manisquierda de la batalla, do estauan los que yuan de pie, que fuessen a cauallo, y eran estos: el conde don Tello su hermano e don Gomez Perez de Porres prior de Sand Iohan e muchos caualleros fijos dalgo e con ellos fasta mill de cauallo, en los quales auia muchos caualleros armados.

E en la otra parte, a la manderecha de los que yuan de pie, puso el rrey don Enrrique estos otros, que yuan todos a cauallo: el marques de Villena que dezian don Alfonso, fijo del infante don Pedro de Aragon e nieto del rrey don Jaymes de Aragon, que era conde de Denia e de Riba gorça, e era agora marques de Villena e el maestre de Calatraua don Pero Moñiz de Godoy e los comendadores mayores de Santiago que eran de Leon, don Ferrand Osores, e de Castilla, don Pero Ruyz de Sandoual. E eran en esta batalla mill de cauallo e muchos caualleros armados.

1367: CHAPTER IV

How King Enrique organized his troops.

King Enrique consulted his counsellors and was told that, since his opponents were all going to be on foot, it was advisable to adopt the same strategy. He drew up his forces as follows: in the vanguard he placed Monsieur Bertrand du Guesclin, the marshal d'Audrehem, Le Bègue de Villaines and other French knights, all on foot. He also determined that the following Castilian knights would be on foot bearing the banner of *La Banda*: his brother Count Sancho, the governor general of Castile Pero Manrique, Pero Fernández de Velasco, Gómez González de Castañeda, Pero Ruiz Sarmiento, Ruy Díaz de Rojas, Sancho Sánchez de Rojas, Juan Rodríguez Sarmiento, Ruy González de Cisneros, Sancho Fernández de Tovar, Suer Pérez de Quiñones, Garci Laso de la Vega, Don Juan Ramírez de Arellano, Don Garci Álvarez – who had been master of Santiago –, the bearer of the banner of *La Banda* Pero López de Ayala, Juan González de Avellaneda, the keybearer of Alcántara Men Suárez, Garci González de Ferrera, Gonzalo Bernal de Quirós and other men-at arms, up to a thousand in all, who fought on foot.[2]

On the left flank of his army, next to the men fighting on foot, the king placed the following, who were to be mounted: his brother Count Tello, the prior of Saint John Don Gómez Pérez de Porres and numerous knights of noble birth, together with some 1,000 horsemen including many knights in full armour.[3]

On the other flank – on the right of the men on foot – King Enrique positioned these other troops, all of them mounted: the marquis of Villena Don Alfons – son of Prince Pere of Aragon and grandson of King Jaume of Aragon, the man who had been count of Denia and Ribagorza and was now marquis of Villena –; the master of Calatrava Don Pero Muñiz de Godoy and the commanders major of Santiago, Don Fernán Osórez for León and Don Pero Ruiz de Sandoval for Castile. On this flank of the army there were 1,000 horsemen with many knights in full armour.

En la otra batalla de en medio destas dos batallas, yua el rrey don Enrrique e con el, el conde don Alfonso su fijo e el conde don Pedro su sobrino, fijo del maestre don Fadrique, e Yñigo Lopez de Horozco e Pero Gonçalez de Mendoça e don Aluar Garçia de Albornoz e don Ferrand Perez de Ayala e Pero Gonçalez de Aguero e miçer Anbrosio Boca Negra almirante e don Alfonso Perez de Guzman e don Iohan Alfonso de Haro e Gonçalo Gomez de Çisneros, e muchos otros fijos dalgo caualleros e escuderos de Castilla e de Leon e muchos rricos omnes e fijosdalgo de Aragon que pudian seer en esta batalla mill e quinientos de cauallo.

Assi que tenia el rrey don Enrrique aquel dia desta batalla, con su conpaña de los que yuan de cauallo e de pie, quatro mill e quinientos de cauallo. Otrossi tenia el rrey don Enrrique de las montañas de Guipuzcoa e Vizcaya e Asturias, muchos escuderos de pie; pero aprouecharon muy poco en esta batalla, ca toda la pelea era en los omnes de armas.

Capitulo V°. Commo el rrey don Pedro e el prinçipe de Gales hordenaron su batalla.

Otrossi de la parte del rrey don Pedro fue hordenada la batalla en esta guisa. Ellos todos vinieron a pie: en la auanguarda venia el duc de Alencastre, hermano del prinçipe, que dezian don Iohan, e mossen Iohan Chandos, que era conde estable de Gujana por el prinçipe, e mossen Ruberte Canoles e mossen Hugo de Carualoy e mossen Oliuer señor de Clison e otros muchos caualleros e escuderos de Ingla terra e de Bretaña, que eran tres mill omnes de armas muy buenos e muy husados de guerra.

Otrossi en la vna ala de la su manderecha, venian el conde de Armiñac e el señor de Lebret e sus parientes e el señor de Moxidan e el conde de Rosen e otros grandes caualleros e escuderos de Gujana fasta dos mill lanças. E de la otra ala de la su mano esquierda venia el cabtal de Buche e muchos caualleros e escuderos de Gujana del

King Enrique formed part of another batallion, in between these two flanks, and with him were his son Count Alfonso, his nephew Count Pedro, son of the master Don Fadrique, Íñigo López de Orozco, Pero González de Mendoza, Don Álvar García de Albornoz, Don Fernán Pérez de Ayala, Pero González de Agüero, Admiral Miçer Ambrosio Boccanegra, Don Alfonso Pérez de Guzmán, Don Juan Alfonso de Haro, Gonzalo Gómez de Cisneros and numerous other noble knights and squires of Castile and León together with many magnates and nobles of Aragon who in this batallion numbered altogether about 1,500 mounted troops.

Thus on the day of the battle King Enrique had, among his combined company of men on horseback and footsoldiers, 4,500 cavalry. He also had many men on foot, squires from the mountain areas of Guipúzcoa, Vizcaya and Asturias. However they proved of very little value in this battle, for the whole encounter centred on the men-at-arms.

1367: CHAPTER V

How King Pedro and the prince of Wales drew up their troops for battle.

Moreover, on the side of King Pedro the army was drawn up as follows, with the whole army fighting on foot: in the vanguard were John duke of Lancaster, the prince's brother; Sir John Chandos, who served the prince as constable of Guyenne; Sir Robert Knoles; Sir Hugh Calveley and Monsieur Olivier, lord of Clisson, and many other knights and squires from England and Brittany, altogether 3,000 very fine men-at-arms who were highly experienced in warfare.

Also on one flank of their army, on the right, were the count of Armagnac, the lord of Albret and his relatives, the lord of Mucidan, the count of Rosen and other great knights and squires of Guyenne numbering up to 2,000 lances. On the other flank, on the left of the army, were the captal de Buch, many knights and squires from Guyenne

vando e partida del conde de Fox e Senesorgas de Alemaña e Espiota e muchos capitanes e conpañias fasta dos mill omnes de armas.

E en la batalla postrimera venia el rrey don Pedro e el rrey de Napol, que era fijo del rrey que fuera de Mallorcas, que dixeron Jaymes, e el prinçipe de Gales e el pendon del rrey de Nauarra con rricos omnes caualleros e escuderos suyos fasta trezientos omnes de armas, e muchos otros caualleros de Ingla terra, e eran en esta batalla tres mill lanças. Assi que eran todos estos diez mill omnes de armas e otros tantos frecheros.

E estos omnes de armas eran estonçe la flor de la caualleria de la christiandad, ca era estonçe paz entre França e Ingla terra e todo el ducado de Guiana estaua por el prinçipe. E assi venian con el todos los buenos del dicho ducado assi foxencos commo armiñaques. Otrossy todos los rricos omnes e caualleros de Bretaña e toda la caualleria de Ingla terra. Otrossi venian con el rrey don Pedro de los suyos fasta ochoçientos omnes de armas castellanos e ginetes. E desta manera que auedes oydo fueron hordenadas las batallas de cada vna partida para el dia de la pelea.

Capitulo VI°. Del consejo que ouo el rrey don Enrrique sy pelearia o non.

Estando el rrey don Enrrique en el dicho enzinar de Vañares do tenia ayuntadas sus conpañas, ouo cartas e mensageros del rrey don Carlos de França por las quales le enbio rrogar e consejar que non peleasse e escusasse aquella batalla, ca el le fazia çierto que con el prinçipe de Gales venia la flor de la caballeria del mundo e que desmanase aquella pelea e fiziesse su guerra en otra guisa, ca el prinçipe e aquellas conpañas non podrian mucho durar en Castilla e que se tornarian. E sobre esto mossen Beltran e el mariscal de [Audenan], que estauan

belonging to the contingent of the count of Foix, Johan Hazenorgue from Germany, Espiote and many captains with companies altogether consisting of up to 2,000 men-at-arms.

In the rearguard were King Pedro, the king of Naples – Jaume, son of the late king of Majorca –, the prince of Wales, the standard of the king of Navarre with magnates, knights and squires from his kingdom – some 300 men-at-arms – and many other English knights.[4] In this batallion there were 3,000 lances. Altogether, therefore, there were 10,000 men-at-arms and the same number of archers.

These men-at-arms were at that time the flower of Christendom's knighthood, for France and England were currently at peace and the whole of the duchy of Guyenne was giving its allegiance to the prince. Thus he was accompanied by all the finest men of the duchy, including supporters of both the count of Foix and the count of Armagnac, all the magnates and knights of Brittany and all the chivalry of England. In addition, of his own forces King Pedro had with him some 800 men-at-arms, both Castilian knights and light cavalry. This, just as you have heard, was how the forces of the two sides were drawn up on the day of the battle.[5]

1367: CHAPTER VI

Concerning the advice that King Enrique was given with regard to whether or not he should do battle.

While he was encamped at the holm-oak wood at Bañares, where he had assembled all his forces, King Enrique received envoys with a letter from King Charles of France, requesting and advising him not to fight but rather to avoid doing battle. King Charles assured him that the prince of Wales was accompanied by the flower of the world's chivalry and that he should not take part in that encounter but find another way of conducting his campaign: the king and those companies would not endure for long in Castile before withdrawing. Monsieur Bertrand and the marshal d'Audrehem, knights who were

con el rrey don Enrrique, eran caualleros vasallos del rrey de Françia e fablaron con el rrey don Enrrique de partes del rrey de Françia todas estas rrazones que le enbiaua dezir e mandaua a ellos que fablassen con el por tal manera que la batalla non se fiziesse, ca el rrey de Françia e todo su consejo eran en esto. E el rrey don Enrrique les rrespondio que le paresçia que esta rrazon tal que la deurian poner en su consejo, que se fablasse secreta mente, e fizieronlo assi.

E todos los que de su consejo eran e amauan su serviçio le dizian que si el pusiesse alguna dubda en esta batalla que fuesse çierto que todos los mas del rregno se partirian del e se yrian para el rrey don Pedro, e eso mesmo farian çibdades e villas. Ca tenian todos grand miedo del rrey don Pedro e si viessen que non auia quien defendiesse el campo, podrian dexar a el e tener con el rrey don Pedro; pero si viessen que el queria pelear, que todos esperauan la ventura de la batalla e que fiauan en la merçed de Dios que le daria victoria. E el rrey don Enrrique acogiosse a este consejo e dio rrespuesta a los caualleros de Françia commo le seria grand peligro sola mente mostrar nin fazer muestra de non querer pelear nin defender tantas çibdades e villas e señorios que tomaron su partida e pues assi era, que lo ponia todo en la mano de Dios.

E el rrey Enrrique estando alli en el enzinar de Bañares, sopo commo el rrey don Pedro e el prinçipe de Gales e el rrey de Napol e las otras conpañas que eran con ellos partian de la cuenca de Panplona e entrauan por Alaua e que la villa de Salua tierra de Alaua, que es en aquella comarca, se diera al rrey don Pedro e lo acogieran. E el rrey don Enrrique era en el enzinar de Bañares e desque sopo commo el rrey don Pedro e el prinçipe e las otras conpañas suyas eran entradas en Alaua, partio del enzinar de Bañares e fuesse para aquella tierra do el rrey don Pedro era, e puso su rreal en vna sierra alta que esta sobre Alaua, do esta vn castillo del rrey que dizen Çaldiaran. E estaua el su rreal en lugar do los que eran con el rrey don Pedro e con el prinçipe non podian pelear con ellos por la grand fortaleza que aquel asentamiento del rreal tenia. E aquel dia cobraron los ingleses e las otras conpañas del rrey don Pedro e del prinçipe grand esfuerço por

fighting in the service of King Enrique but who were vassals of the king of France, passed on to King Enrique all the arguments against the battle taking place that the French monarch had communicated to them and commanded them to put forward. For the king of France and all his council were of this opinion. King Enrique replied to them that he considered that this argument should be put to his own council to be discussed privately, and this was done.

All of the members of his council, his loyal supporters, said that if he showed any hesitation over going to battle he could be sure that most of his subjects would abandon his cause and transfer their support to King Pedro, and that towns and cities would do likewise. For they were all in great fear of King Pedro and, if they saw that there was nobody to defend them on the field of battle, they might well abandon him and give their allegiance to King Pedro. On the other hand, if they saw that King Enrique was ready to fight, they all expected him to be successful in battle and trusted in the mercy of God to give him victory. King Enrique was persuaded by this advice and replied to the French knights that it would be highly dangerous for him to give any sign or indication of being unwilling to do battle or give protection to so many cities, towns and lordships which had given him their support; and, since this was the case, he was placing all his trust in God.

While King Enrique was in his camp at the wood at Bañares, he heard how King Pedro, the prince of Wales, the king of Naples and the other forces accompanying them were leaving the Pamplona Basin and making their entry through Álava, and that the town of Salvatierra de Álava in that area had surrendered to King Pedro and welcomed him in. Then, once King Enrique, in that camp in the wood at Bañares, learned how King Pedro, the prince and the rest of their army had entered Álava, he set off for the area where King Pedro was now to be found and established his encampment on a high range of hills rising over Álava, in the vicinity of a castle called Zaldiaran which belonged to the king. His camp occupied a site which did not allow the supporters of King Pedro and the prince to do battle with them on account of the great strength of its position. That day the English and the other troops of King Pedro and the prince took great heart since

quanto vieron que el rrey don Enrrique se pussiera en aquella sierra e non desçendia a lo llano do ellos estauan prestos para dar la batalla.

Capitulo VIIº. Commo el rrey don Enrrique enbio algunas gentes a buscar algunas conpañas de los ingleses que eran entrados en Alaua a catar viandas e andauan derramados por la tierra.

El rrey don Enrrique sopo commo muchos de los de la conpañia del rrey don Pedro e del prinçipe se tendian por la tierra de Alaua a buscar viandas e dixeronle que si enbiasse alla algunas de sus gentes que les podrian enpeesçer ca los fallarian derramados. E el rrey don Enrrique fizo lo assi e enbio alla a don Alfonso conde de Denia, fijo del infante don Pedro de Aragon e nieto del rrey don Jaymes de Aragon, que era marques de Villena, e don Tello su hermano del rrey, que era conde de Vizcaya e señor de Aguilar e de Castañeda, e Pero Gonçalez de Mendoça e a don Pero Moñiz maestre de Calatraua e don Iohan Ramirez de Arellano e los comendadores mayores de Santiago de Castilla e de Leon que eran don Pero Ruiz de Sandoual e don Ferrand Osorez e muchos otros caualleros e escuderos de Castilla. Otrossi enbio al mariscal de [Audenan], que era mariscal de Françia e el vegue de Villanes, que eran françeses.

E todos estos fueron para Alaua e fallaron ý pieça de gentes ingleses e gascones, que andauan a catar viandas e posauan por las aldeas, e tomaron los. Otrossi fallaron dozientos omnes de armas e otros tantos frecheros, e quando los vieron las gentes de los contrarios, pusieronse en vn otero asaz pequeño a pie çerca vn aldea que dizian Arinis. E en tal guisa se hordenauan los ingleses que los de cauallo non los podian desbaratar en ninguna manera nin entrar entrellos. E quando esto vieron el vegue de Villanes e el mariscal de [Audenan] e don Iohan Ramirez de Arellano apearonse para yr a ellos. E Pero Gonçalez

they could see that King Enrique had taken up a position there on the heights rather than coming down onto the plain where they were ready to give battle.

1367: CHAPTER VII

How King Enrique sent forces to hunt down some companies of English troops who had entered Álava in search of provisions and were scattered over the region.

King Enrique received reports that many men from the army of King Pedro and the prince were spreading out over the region of Álava foraging for provisions, and he was told that if he sent some of his forces there they would be able to inflict losses on them as they would find them widely scattered. King Enrique did so, dispatching Count Alfons of Denia – son of Prince Pere and grandson of King Jaume of Aragon, and marquis of Villena –, his own brother Don Tello – count of Vizcaya and lord of Aguilar and Castañeda –, Pero González de Mendoza, the master of Calatrava Don Pero Muñiz, Don Juan Ramírez de Arellano, the commanders major of Castile and León Don Pero Ruiz de Sandoval and Don Fernán Osórez, and many other Castilian knights and squires. With them he also sent the marshal d'Audrehem, who was a marshal of France, and Le Bègue de Villaines, both of whom were French.

These men headed for Álava, where they found a good number of English and Gascon troops engaged in searching out provisions and staying in the villages, and they took them prisoner. They also encountered 200 men-at-arms and a similar number of archers, and when their enemies caught sight of them they positioned themselves on foot on a relatively small hill near to a village called Aríñez. Moreover, the English organized themselves in such a way that the horsemen could not drive them back or get in amongst them. So, when they saw this, Le Bègue de Villaines, the marshal d'Audrehem and Don Juan Ramírez de Arellano dismounted in order to attack

de Mendoça e otros caualleros que estauan a cauallo acometieron los en guisa que los desbarataron. E morio ý el dicho mossen Guillen de Feleron e otros caualleros que ý eran con el, e los otros fueron presos. Otrossi tomaron esse dia muchos omnes de armas e frecheros de la conpañia del prinçipe, que andauan a catar viandas.

Capitulo VIIIº. Commo el rrey don Pedro e el prinçipe fizieron aquel dia e commo fue cauallero el rrey don Pedro.

El rrey don Pedro e el prinçipe de Gales estauan allende la villa de Bitoria quando sopieron que aquellas gentes del rrey don Enrrique eran en la tierra de Alaua e fazian daño en los que fallauan que andauan a catar viandas: pensaron que el rrey don Enrrique era, que venia a la batalla, e pusieronsse todos en vn otero que es allende de la villa de Bitoria que dizen Sant Roman e ally reglaron su batalla.

E alli se armo el rrey don Pedro cauallero aquel dia, de mano del prinçipe e se armaron otros muchos caualleros. E los del rrey don Enrrique que alli eran venidos non cataron de fazer mas e tornaronsse para el rreal que tenia el rrey don Enrrique e non ouo aquel dia mas.

Capitulo IXº. Commo el rrey don Pedro e el prinçipe de Gales partieron de Alaua e se fueron para Logroño.

Despues que el rrey don Pedro e el prinçipe de Gales vieron que el rrey don Enrrique non desçendia de aquella sierra a lo llano e que

them. Pero González de Mendoza and other mounted knights then launched an assault on the English of such force as to throw them into disarray. Sir William Felton died in this encounter together with some other knights who were accompanying him, and the remainder were taken prisoner. Also captured that day were numerous men-at-arms and archers from the prince's company, men who had been foraging for provisions.

1367: CHAPTER VIII

How King Pedro and the prince reacted that day, and how King Pedro was knighted.

King Pedro and the prince of Wales had advanced beyond the town of Vitoria when they heard that some of King Enrique's troops were in the territory of Álava and inflicting losses on the men that they found foraging for provisions. They thought that it was King Enrique who was coming to do battle and so they positioned themselves on a hill called San Román on the far side of the town of Vitoria, and there they drew up their army.

This was where on that day King Pedro was knighted by the prince along with many other men. The members of King Enrique's army who been drawing near sought to do no more and withdrew to the king's encampment. Nothing more ocurred that day.

1367: CHAPTER IX

How King Pedro and the prince of Wales left Álava and headed for Logroño.

King Pedro and the prince of Wales saw that King Enrique was not coming down from the heights to the plain and that they could only do

ellos non podian pelear con el si non a grand su peoria nin pasar para yr a Castilla por alli, ca les tenia los puertos de aquella comarca, partieron de Alaua e fueronsse para la villa de Logroño, que estaua por el rrey don Pedro. E ha en ella sobre Ebro vna grand puente e buena, e pasaron por ally el rrey don Pedro e el prinçipe de Gales e todas sus conpañas. E fizieron su cuenta que el rrey don Enrrique les vernia a la pelea o que entrarian por el rregno de Castilla.

Capitulo X°. Commo el rrey don Enrrique partio de Çaldiaran e se fue para Najara e de las cartas que ouo del prinçipe de Gales.

El rrey don Enrrique desque sopo que el rrey don Pedro e el prinçipe de Gales e los que con ellos eran auian tomado el camino de Logroño e yuan alla por pasar por alli el rrio de Ebro, partio dende e fuesse para Najara. E puso su rreal aquende la villa en guisa que el rrio de Najarilla estaua entre su rreal e el camino por do el rrey don Pedro e el prinçipe auian de venir a pasar a Rioja e tomar su camino para Burgos.

E el rrey don Pedro e el prinçipe e las otras conpañas partieron de Logroño e venieron para Nauarrete. E de alli enbio el prinçipe al rrey don Enrrique vn su araute con vna carta, el tenor de la qual es este:

'Eduarte fijo primo genito del rrey de Ingla terra prinçipe de Gales e de Gujana, duc de Cornoalla e conde de Çestre, al noble poderoso prinçipe don Enrrique, conde de Trastamara. Sabed que en estos dias passados el muy alto e muy poderoso prinçipe don Pedro, rrey de Castilla e de Leon, nuestro muy caro e muy amado pariente, llego en las partidas de Gujana do nos estauamos e nos fizo entender que quando el rrey don Alfonso su padre morio, que todos los de los rregnos de Castilla e de Leon paçifica mente le rresçibieran e tomaran por su rrey e señor, entre los quales vos fuestes vno dellos que asi le obedesçieron

battle with him at a great disadvantage, and they also realized that, as he was blocking all the passes in the area, by that route they could not find a way through to Castile. So they left Álava and headed towards the town of Logroño, which had declared its support for King Pedro. In Logroño there is a fine, large bridge which crosses the Ebro and it was over this that King Pedro and the prince of Wales passed with their whole army. They reckoned that King Enrique would come and do battle with them or that otherwise they would enter the kingdom of Castile.

1367: CHAPTER X

How King Enrique left Zaldiaran for Nájera, and concerning the letter that he received from the prince of Wales.

Once King Enrique learned that King Pedro and the prince of Wales had set off with their army and were heading towards Logroño with the intention of crossing the river Ebro at that point, he too set out for Nájera. He established his encampment on the near side of the town so that the River Najerilla flowed between his camp and the road by which King Pedro and the prince had to come in order to cross into La Rioja and follow the route towards Burgos.

King Pedro and the prince with the rest of the army set off from Logroño and headed for Navarrete. From there the prince sent a herald to King Enrique bearing a letter, the content of which was as follows:[6]

'Edward, first-born son of the king of England, prince of Wales and of Guyenne, duke of Cornwall and count of Chester, to the noble and redoubtable Prince Enrique, count of Trastámara. You should be aware that in the recent past the illustrious and redoubtable King Pedro of Castile and León, our dear and beloved relative, came to us in the territory of Guyenne.[7] He explained to us how, on the death of his father King Alfonso, he had been peacefully welcomed and accepted as king and lord by all the people of the kingdoms of Castile and León; and among them you were one of those who gave him their

e estudistes gran tienpo en su obediençia. E diz que despues desto, agora puede auer vn año, que vos con gentes e conpañias de diversas nasçiones, que llegastes e entrastes en el su rregno e gelo ocupastes e llamastes vos rrey de Castilla e de Leon, e le tomastes los sus thesoros e las sus rrentas e le tenedes forçado e tomado asi su rregno e dezides que lo defenderedes del e de los que le quisieren ayudar, de lo qual somos mucho marauillado que vn tan noble omne commo vos, fijo de rrey, fiziessedes cosa que vos sea vergoñosa de fazer contra vuestro rrey e vuestro señor.

E el rrey don Pedro enbio mostrar todas estas cosas a mi señor e mi padre el rrey de Ingla terra e le rrequirio, lo vno por el grand debdo e linaje que las casas de Ingla terra e Castilla ouieron en vno: otrossi por las ligas e confederaçiones que el dicho rrey don Pedro tiene fechas con el rrey de Ingla terra mi padre e mi señor e comigo, e que le quisiesse ayudar a tornar al su rregno e cobrar lo suyo. E el rrey de Ingla terra mi padre e mi señor veyendo que el rrey don Pedro su pariente le enbiaua pedir justiçia e derecho e cosa rrazonable a que todo rrey deue ayudar, plogole de lo fazer assi. E enbio nos mandar que con todos sus vasallos e valledores e amigos que el ha, que nos le viniessemos a ayudar e confortar segund cunple a su honrra, por la qual rrazon nos somos aqui e estamos oy en el lugar de Nauarrete que es en los terminos de Castilla.

E por que si voluntad fuesse de Dios que se pudiesse escusar tan grand derramamiento de sangre commo podria contesçer de christianos si batalla ouiesse, de lo qual sabe Dios que a nos pesara mucho dello, por ende vos rrogamos e rrequerimos de parte de Dios e con el martil Sand Jorge, que si vos plaze, que nos seamos buen medianero entre el dicho rrey don Pedro e vos, que nos lo fagades saber e nos trabajaremos commo vos ayades en los sus rregnos e en la su buena graçia e merçed, grand parte, por que muy honrrada mente podades bien pasar e tener vuestro estado, e si algunas otras cosas ouiere de librar entre el e vos, nos con la merçed de Dios entendemos poner las en tal estado commo vos seades bien contento. E si desto

allegiance, remaining loyal to him for a long time. He asserts that, since then, about a year ago, you came with troops and companies from various nations, invaded and occupied his kingdom and called yourself King of Castile and León. He also says that you have taken from him his treasure and his income, that you have seized and stolen his kingdom from him in this way and are declaring that you will defend it against him and from those who may seek to give him assistance. It causes us great surprise that so noble a man as yourself, son of a king, should have committed an act which is so shameful against your king and your lord.

King Pedro sent an explanation of all these matters to my lord and father, the king of England, and he appealed to him to be willing to assist him to return to his kingdom and regain possession of what was his. He asked this partly on account of the close family bond and connection between the ruling houses of England and Castile but also because of the treaties and agreements which King Pedro has made with my father and lord, the king of England, and with me. My father and lord the king of England, seeing that his relative King Pedro was sending him an appeal for what was just and right, a reasonable request which any king should grant, agreed to do what was asked of him. He sent us a command that, together with all his vassals, supporters and allies, we should come to give King Pedro assistance and backing in keeping with his honourable standing; and it is for this reason that we have come and today are here in the town of Navarrete within the borders of Castile.

Moreover, so much Christian blood might be shed if the battle took place, which God knows would cause us great distress. And so, in the hope that it is God's will for this to be avoided, we beg and appeal to you in the name of God and that of the martyr Saint George, that, if you are willing, we may serve as a fitting intermediary between King Pedro and yourself. We ask you to inform us if this is the case, and we will work to ensure that you will share fully in his kingdoms and in his grace and his favour, in such a way that you may enjoy honourable access to and possession of your estates. And if there are other matters to be resolved between King Pedro and yourself, it is our intention, with God's mercy, to settle them to your full satisfaction. However,

non vos plaze e queredes que se libre por batalla, sabe Dios que nos desplaze mucho dello, pero non podemos escusar de yr con el dicho rrey don Pedro nuestro pariente por el su rregno. E si algunos quisieren enbargar los caminos a el, nos que con el ymos faremos mucho por le ayudar con la ayuda e graçia de Dios. Escrita en Nauarrete, villa de Castilla, primero dia de abril.'

Capitulo XI°. De la rrespuesta que el rrey don Enrrique enbio al prinçipe.

El rrey don Enrrique desque vio la carta que el prinçipe le enbiaua, rresçibio muy bien el su haraute e diole de sus paños de oro e de sus doblas. E ouo su consejo commo rresponderia al prinçipe por que algunos ý eran que dizian que por que el prinçipe non le llamaua rrey en su carta que le deuia escreuir por otra manera; pero despues fue acordado que el deuia escreuir cortes mente, ca avn entre los henemigos bien paresçe seer omne cortes e bien rrazonado.

E mando luego fazer su carta de rrespuesta para el prinçipe, la qual leuo el dicho haraute que traxo esta carta del prinçipe de que auemos dicho, la qual carta dizia assi:

'Don Enrrique por la graçia de Dios, rrey de Castilla e de Leon al muy alto e poderoso prinçipe don Eduarte, fijo primo genito del rrey de Ingla terra, prinçipe de Gales e de Gujana, duque de Cornoalla e conde de Çestre. Resçibi por vn haraute vna carta vuestra, en la qual se contenian muchas rrazones que vos fueron dichas por parte de ese nuestro adversario que ý es, e non nos paresçe que vos auedes seydo bien enformado commo esse nuestro adversario, en los tienpos que touo estos rregnos, los rrigio en tal manera que todos los que lo saben e oyen se pueden dello marauillar por que el haya tanto a seer sofrido en el señorio que touo. E todos los de los rregnos de Castilla

if you do not agree to this and you wish the dispute to be decided by battle – and God knows that we have no desire for this – we have no choice but to accompany our relative King Pedro into his kingdom. If there is an attempt on the part of anyone to block his way, we who are in his company, with the help and grace of God, will make every effort to assist him. Written in the Castilian town of Navarrete on the first of April.'

1367: CHAPTER XI

Concerning the reply that King Enrique sent to the prince.

King Enrique, on seeing the letter sent to him by the prince, gave a very warm welcome to his herald and made him gifts of cloths of gold and payment in *doblas*. He consulted his advisers with regard to how he would reply to the prince because there were some present who said that, as the prince had not addressed him as King in his letter, King Enrique should write to him in different terms from these. However, it was subsequently agreed that King Enrique should address the prince with courtesy, as even between adversaries it is right to appear a polite and well-spoken man.

He lost no time in drawing up his reply to the prince, which was taken to him by the same herald who had brought the prince's letter of which we have already spoken. King Enrique's letter read as follows:

'Don Enrique, by the grace of God king of Castile and León, to the worthy and redoubtable Prince Edward, first-born son of the king of England, prince of Wales and of Guyenne, duke of Cornwall and count of Chester. I received from a herald a letter of yours, in which there appeared many arguments that had been put to you on behalf of our enemy there present. However, it does not seem to us that you have been well informed with regard to how that enemy of ours, during the time when he possessed these kingdoms, ruled over them in such a way that those who know about or hear of it may well wonder that he had to be tolerated for so long in his position of lordship. All the

e de Leon, con muy grand trabajo e daño e peligros de muertes e de manzillas, sostouieron lo que el fizo fasta aqui e non las pudieron mas encobrir nin sofrir, las quales cosas serian luengas de contar: Dios por su merçed ouo piedat de todos los de estos rregnos por que non fuesse este mal cada dia mas, e non le faziendo omne de todo su señorio ninguna cosa, saluo obediençia, e estando todos con el para le ayudar e seruir e para defender los dichos rregnos en la çibdat de Burgos, Dios dio su sentençia contra el que el de su propia voluntad los desanparo e se fue.

E todos los de los rregnos de Castilla e de Leon ouieron dende muy grand plazer teniendo que Dios les auia enbiado su misericordia para los librar de su señorio tan duro e tan peligroso commo tenian. E todos los de los dichos rregnos de su propia voluntad vinieron a nos e nos tomaron por su rrey e por su señor assi perlados commo caualleros e fijos dalgo e çibdades e villas, e por tanto entendimos por estas cosas sobre dichas que esto fue obra de Dios. E por ende pues por voluntad de Dios e de todos los del rregno nos fue dado, vos non auedes rrazon alguna por que nos destoruar, e si batalla ouiere de seer, sabe Dios que nos desplaze dello; pero non podemos escusar de poner nuestro cuerpo en defender estos rregnos, a quien tan tenudo somos, contra qualquier que contra ellos quiera seer. Por ende vos rrogamos e rrequerimos con Dios e con el apostol Santiago que vos non querades entrar assi poderosa mente en nuestros rregnos faziendo en ellos daño alguno, ca faziendolo non podemos escusar de los non defender. Escrita en el nuestro rreal çerca de Najara, segundo dia de abril.'

E despues que el prinçipe ouo esta carta e la mostro al rrey don Pedro, fue ý dicho que estas rrazones non eran sufiçientes para se poder escusar la batalla; pero que todo esto era en la voluntad de Dios e commo fuesse la su merçed de fazer, e que non auia otro rremedio si non ponerlo a batalla luego.

Chronicle of King Pedro 153

people of the kingdoms of Castile and León, suffering great trials and great harm and danger of death and dishonour, have endured his actions until now, but they have been unable either to disguise them or to suffer them any longer; and the account of these matters would be long indeed. God in his mercy took pity on all the people of these realms so that this ill would not continue to grow greater day by day: although none of King Pedro's subjects showed him anything other than loyalty and they were all gathered with him in the city of Burgos ready to give him help and support and to defend the kingdoms of Castile and León, God pronounced his sentence on the man who, of his own free will, abandoned them and left.

All the people of Castile and León took great pleasure in this, considering that God had granted them his mercy to free them from such harsh and dangerous lordship as they were enduring. All those who dwelt in those realms – prelates as well as knights, noblemen and the people of the cities and the towns – turned to us of their accord and took us as their king and lord. Therefore, from these events that we have described, we understood it to be the work of God, and so, since the throne was given to us through the will of God and of all the people of the kingdoms, you have no reason at all to stand in our way. If there has to be a battle God knows that it gives us no pleasure, but we have no choice other than to risk our own person in the defence of these kingdoms, to which we are so devoted, against anyone who sets himself against them. For this reason we, with God and the Apostle Saint James, ask and appeal to you not to seek to enter our realms with such a display of force and not to inflict any harm on them; for if you do so we cannot justify failing to defend them.[8] Written in our royal encampment near to Nájera on the second day of April.'

After the prince had received this letter and had shown it to King Pedro, the conclusion was reached that these arguments were not sufficient for them to avoid battle but that rather all of this was in the hands of God and depended on what was His will: there was no alternative but to settle the affair by battle without delay.

Capitulo XII°. En que cuenta commo la batalla fue ayuntada por amas las partidas e commo acaesçio aquel dia.

El rrey don Enrrique segund dicho auemos, tenia el su rreal asentado en guisa que el rrio de Najarilla estaua entre [el e] el lugar por do auian de venir el rrey don Pedro e el prinçipe. E el ouo su acuerdo de pasar el rrio e poner la batalla en vna grant plaça que es contra Nauarrete por do los otros venian e fizolo assi. E desto peso a muchos de los que con el estauan, ca tenian primero su rreal a mayor auentaja que despues lo asentaron; pero el rrey don Enrrique era omne de muy grand coraçon e de muy grand esfuerço e dixo que en todas las guisas queria poner batalla en plaça llana syn auantaja alguna.

E el rrey don Pedro e el prinçipe e sus conpañas partieron de Nauarrete sabado por la mañana en la hordenança que auemos contado que hordenaron sus batallas, e apearonsse todos grand pieça antes que llegassen do los de la partida del rrey don Enrrique estauan.

E el rrey don Enrrique hordeno su batalla eso mesmo en aquella manera que suso auemos contado que lo tenia hordenado. E luego antes que las batallas se ayuntassen, algunos ginetes e el pendon de Santesteuan del Puerto con los del dicho lugar que alli estauan con el rrey don Enrrique pasaronsse a la otra parte del rrey don Pedro. E luego mouieron los vnos contra los otros. E el conde don Sancho, hermano del rrey don Enrrique, e mossen Beltran de Claquin e los caualleros que estauan con el pendon de la Vanda e todos aquellos caualleros que deximos que el rrey don Enrrique hordenara que estudiessen de pie fueron juntar con la auan guarda de la otra parte, do venian el duc de Alencastre e el conde estable de Gujana e mossen Iohan Chandos e otros muchos muy buenos caualleros. E los de la partida del rrey don Pedro e el prinçipe de Gales trayan por señal los escudos e sobre señales blancas e con cruzes bermejas por Sand Jorge. E todos los de la partida del rrey don Enrrique leuauan esse dia vandas en las sobre señales. E tan rrezio se juntaron los vnos con los otros que a los de la vna parte e de la otra, cayeron las lanças en tierra e juntaronsse

1367: CHAPTER XII

Which relates how battle was joined by both sides and tells of the events of the day.

As we have already said, King Enrique had positioned his encampment in such a way that the River Najerilla separated it from the route by which King Pedro and the prince had to come. He had resolved to cross the river and fight the battle in a large open area outside Navarrete through which his enemies would pass, and this is what he did. Many of those with him were unhappy about this, for the initial position of their camp was more advantageous than the one that they subsequently occupied. However, King Enrique was a man of great spirit and very strong will and he said that in any case he wished to do battle on level ground without having any advantage.

King Pedro and the prince moved out from Navarrete on the Saturday morning with their forces organized just as we set out above, and they all dismounted a considerable distance before they came near to the position of King Enrique's troops.

King Enrique likewise drew up his army in precisely the way in which we have already set out. Then, shortly before battle was joined, some light cavalry and the men accompanying the banner of Santisteban del Puerto, who were part of King Enrique's army, went over to King Pedro's side.[9] Rapidly the two forces moved together. King Enrique's brother Count Sancho, Monsieur Bertrand du Guesclin and the knights accompanying the banner of *La Banda*, together with all those knights that – as we explained – King Enrique had instructed to fight on foot: all of these troops closed with the vanguard of the opposing army, which included the duke of Lancaster, the constable of Guyenne Sir John Chandos and many other very fine knights. The men in the army of King Pedro and the prince bore as their emblem shields and surcoats of white with the red cross of Saint George. And that day all the men of King Enrique's army wore the emblem of the sash of *La Banda* on their surcoats. So violent was the clash between the two sides that the lances of both fell to the ground and the men

cuerpos con cuerpos, e luego se començaron de ferir de las espadas e hachas e dagas llamando los de la parte del rrey don Pedro e del prinçipe de Gales por su apellido: '¡Gujana! ¡San Jorge!', e los de la partida del rrey don Enrrique: '¡Castilla! ¡Santiago!'

E los de la auanguarda del prinçipe rretrayeronsse vn poco quanto vna pasada en manera que los de la auanguarda del rrey don Enrrique cuydaron que vençian, e llegaronse mas a ellos e començaronse otra vez a ferir. E don Tello, hermano del rrey don Enrrique e señor de Lara e de Vizcaya, que estaua de caualo a la mano esquierda de la auanguarda del rrey don Enrrique, non mouia para pelear. E los de la ala derecha del prinçipe que eran el conde de Arminac e los de Lebret e otros muchos que venian en aquella haz aderesçaron a don Tello e el e los que con el estauan non los esperaron e mouieron del canpo a todo rronper fuyendo.

E los de aquella haz que yuan a don Tello quando vieron los de caualo fuyr e que non los podian alcançar nin enpeesçer, tornaron sobre las espaldas de los que estauan de pie en la auanguarda del rrey don Enrrique que peleauan con la auanguarda del prinçipe, do estaua el pendon de la Vanda, e firieronlos por las espaldas e començaron apriessa de matar dellos. E eso mesmo fizo la otra haz de la mano siniestra de la auanguarda del prinçipe: despues que non fallaron gentes de los de caualo que auian de pelear con ellos, firieron en los que estauan de pie en la auanguarda del rrey don Enrrique en guisa que luego fueron todos los de la dicha auanguarda del rrey don Enrrique que estauan de pie, muertos e presos, ca ninguno non les acorria e ellos estauan de cada parte çercados de los henemigos.

E el rrey don Enrrique llego dos o tres vezes en el su caualo armado de lorigas por acorrer a los suyos que estauan de pie teniendo que assi lo farian todos los suyos que estauan con el de caualo. E llegando veya quel pendon de la Vanda estaua alto, que avn non era derribado. E quando el rrey don Enrrique llego do era la priessa de la batalla e vio que los suyos non peleauan, ouo de boluer, ca non pudo sofrir los henemigos que eran ya muy esforçados. E assi fizieron los de caualo que con el eran: partieron todos del canpo, e los ingleses e gascones e bretones los siguieron fasta la villa de Najara.

Chronicle of King Pedro

came together in hand-to-hand combat, setting about each other with swords, axes and daggers. The troops of King Pedro and the prince shouted out their war cry 'Guyenne! Saint George!' and King Enrique's supporters cried 'Castile! Santiago!'

The men at the fore of the prince's army withdrew by just a short distance in such a way that King Enrique's vanguard, believing that they were gaining victory, pushed closer to them, and then they began to strike each other again. However, King Enrique's brother Don Tello, lord of Lara and Vizcaya, who was on horseback to the left of King Enrique's vanguard, did not move forward to fight. So the men on the right flank of the prince's army – the count of Armagnac, the lord of Albret and his company and many others who made up that batallion – made straight for Don Tello. He and those with him did not wait to engage with them but drew back and set off in headlong flight.

The body of troops who were making for Don Tello, on seeing the cavalry take flight and realizing that they could not catch or harm them, turned to attack the backs of the men on foot in King Enrique's vanguard who were engaging the prince's vanguard – where the banner of *La Banda* was flying – and, striking them from behind, they rapidly began to inflict deaths. The flank to the left of the prince's vanguard did likewise and, once they did not come up against men on horseback to fight against them, they directed their attack against those who were fighting on foot in King Enrique's vanguard. In consequence it was not long before the members of that vanguard, fighting on foot, were either killed or taken prisoner, for nobody came to their assistance and they found themselves completely surrounded by their enemies.

King Enrique rode forward on his armoured horse two or three times to assist those of his men who were on foot, believing that the mounted troops accompanying him would all do the same. As he drew near, he could see that the banner of *La Banda* was still flying and had not yet been brought down. And when King Enrique arrived in the thick of the battle and saw that his men were putting up no fight, he was forced to turn back, for he could no longer resist the attacks of his enemies, whose morale was now very high. The cavalry who were with him did likewise, all fleeing the field of battle with the English, Gascons and Bretons giving pursuit as far as the town of Nájera.

E los de cauallo de la partida del rrey don Enrrique, desque boluieron las espaldas, non pudian sallir de la villa de Najara con la priessa, ca por alli era el camino que ellos tomauan para fuyr de los henemigos, e alli fueron muchos muertos e presos.

E de los de la auanguarda que el rrey don Enrrique mandara estar de pie con el su pendon de la Vanda e con el conde don Sancho su hermano e con mossen Beltran de Claquin fueron muertos estos que aqui diremos: Garçi Laso de la Vega, Suer Perez de Quiñones, Sancho Sanchez de Rojas, Iohan Rodriguez Sarmiento, [Furtado Diaz de] Mendoça, Ferrand Sanchez de Angulo e otros fasta quatroçientos omnes de armas. E fueron presos, de los que estauan a pie en la dicha auanguarda, el conde don Sancho, hermano del rrey don Enrrique, e mossen Beltran de Claquin e el mariscal de [Audenan], que era mariscal de Françia e el vegue de Villanes e don Felipe de Castro e Pero Ferrandez de Velasco e don Garçi Aluarez de Toledo, que fuera maestre de Santiago e Pero Ruyz Sarmiento e Gomez Gonçalez de Castañeda e Iohan Diaz de Ayllon e Iohan Gonçalez de Avellaneda e el clauero de Alcantara que dizian Melen Suarez e Garçi Gonçalez de Ferrera e Pero Lopez de Ayala e Sancho Ferrandez de Touar e Iohan Remirez de Arellano e otros.

Otrossi de los de cauallo de la parte del rrey Enrrique fueron presos el conde de Denia, que el rrey don Enrrique fiziera marques de Villena, e el conde don Alfonso e el conde don Pedro e don Pedro Moñiz maestre de Calatraua e Men Rodriguez de Biedma e don Aluar Garçia de Albornoz e don Beltran de Guiuara e Iohan Furtado de Mendoça e Pero Gonçalez de Mendoça e don Pedro Tenorio, arçobispo que fue despues de Toledo, e don Iohan Garçia Palomeque, obispo de Vadajoz, e Pero Gonçalez Carrillo e don Pero Boyl e don Iohan Martinez de Luna e don Pero Ferrandez Dixar e don Pero Jordan Dures e don Ferrand Osores comendador mayor de tierra de Leon de la horden de Santiago, e Garçi Jufre Tenorio e Sancho Sanchez de Moscoso e Gomez Carrillo de Quintana, camarero mayor del rrey don Enrrique, e muchos otros caualleros e escuderos de Castilla e de Leon e de Aragon.

Otrossi morio esse dia Yñigo Lopez de Horozco, que mato el rrey don Pedro teniendole preso vn cauallero del prinçipe. Otrossi despues de la batalla fizo matar el rrey don Pedro a Gomez Carrillo

On account of the crush, once they had turned to flee, the cavalry of King Enrique's army could not make their way out of the town of Nájera – which was the route that they took to escape from their enemies – and there many of them suffered death or captivity.

Of the members of the vanguard that King Enrique had instructed to fight on foot under the banner of *La Banda* and alongside his brother Count Sancho and Monsieur Bertrand du Guesclin, the following were killed: Garci Laso de La Vega, Suer Pérez de Quiñones, Sancho Sánchez de Rojas, Juan Rodríguez Sarmiento, Hurtado Díaz de Mendoza, Fernán Sánchez de Ángulo and up to 400 other men-at-arms. Of those who were on foot in the vanguard the following were taken prisoner: King Enrique's brother Count Sancho, Monsieur Bertrand du Guesclin and the marshal d'Audrehem, who was a marshal of France, Le Bègue de Villaines, Don Felipe de Castro, Pero Fernández de Velasco, Don Garci Álvarez de Toledo, who had been master of Santiago, Pero Ruiz Sarmiento, Gómez González de Castañeda, Juan Díaz de Ayllón, Juan González de Avellaneda, the keybearer of Alcántara Melén Suárez, Garci González de Herrera, Pero López de Ayala, Sancho Fernández de Tovar, Juan Ramírez de Arellano and others.

In addition, of those of King Enrique's troops who were fighting on horseback the following were taken prisoner: the count of Denia, whom King Enrique had created marquis of Villena, Count Alfonso, Count Pedro, the master of Calatrava Don Pedro Muñiz, Men Rodríguez de Biedma, Don Álvar García de Albornoz, Don Beltrán de Guevara, Juan Hurtado de Mendoza, Pero González de Mendoza, Don Pedro Tenorio who later became archbishop of Toledo, the bishop of Badajoz Don Juan García Palomeque, Don Pere Boïl, Don Juan Martínez de Luna, Don Pedro Ferrándiz d'Ixar, Don Pero Jordan d'Urries, Don Fernán Osórez, commander major of the Order of Santiago for the territories of León, Garci Jofré Tenorio, Sancho Sánchez Moscoso, King Enrique's master chamberlain Gómez Carrillo de Quintana, and many other knights and squires of Castile, León and Aragon.

Also among those who died that day was Íñigo López de Orozco, killed by King Pedro whilst being held prisoner by one of the prince's knights. In addition, after the battle King Pedro ordered the death of

de Quintana, fijo de Ruy Diaz Carrillo, que era camarero mayor del rrey don Enrrique. E fizo matar a Sancho Sanchez de Moscoso, comendador mayor de la orden de Santiago. E despues desto mato a Garçi Jufre Tenorio, fijo del almirante don Alonso Jufre, que fuera preso aquel dia de la batalla.

Capitulo XIII°. Commo fueron otro dia despues de la batalla traydos delante del rrey don Pedro e el prinçipe todos los que fueron presos e commo el mariscal de [Audenan] se escuso de lo que el prinçipe le acusaua.

Otro dia domingo, despues de la batalla, fueron traydos delante del prinçipe todos los caualleros que eran presos, por quanto el rrey don Pedro dizia que auia trato con el prinçipe que algunos dellos contra quales el pasara por sentençia, que le deuian seer entregados para fazer dellos justiçia. E entre todos los presos fueron ý traydos les estrangeros que acaesçieron en la batalla de la parte del rrey don Enrrique, entre los quales fue ý traydo el mariscal de [Audenan], que era françes de Picardia, muy buen cauallero, que fue preso en esta batalla e era mariscal de França. E quando el prinçipe vio al mariscal llamole traydor e fementido e que meresçia muerte. E el mariscal le rrespondio: 'Señor, sodes fijo de rrey e non vos rrespondo tan conplida mente commo debo en este caso; pero non so traydor nin fementido.' E el prinçipe dixo al mariscal si queria estar a juyzio de caualleros con el sobre esto e que el gelo prouaria que era asi. E el mariscal dixo: 'Si'.

E desque el prinçipe ouo comido, pusieron doze caualleros: quatro ingleses e quatro de Gujana e quatro bretones por juezes. E el mariscal fue ý traydo e dixole el prinçipe: 'Mariscal de [Audenan], vos sabedes bien que en la batalla de Piteus, que yo vençi e fue preso el rrey don Iohan de França, vos fuestes prisionero e vos toue en mi poder e vos

King Enrique's master chamberlain Gómez Carrillo de Quintana, son of Ruy Díaz Carrillo; and also that of Sancho Sánchez de Moscoso, commander major of the Order of Santiago. Moreover, after this he killed Garci Jofré Tenorio, son of Admiral Don Alfonso Jofré, who had been taken prisoner in that day's battle.

1367: CHAPTER XIII

How on the day following the battle all those who had been taken prisoner were brought before King Pedro and the prince, and how the marshal d'Audrehem defended himself against the prince's accusations.

On the day following the battle, which was a Sunday, all the knights who had been taken prisoner were brought before the prince, because King Pedro claimed that he had made an agreement with him that some of these men, whom he had already formally condemned, were to be handed over in order for him to dispense justice. Among all the prisoners brought to him were the foreigners who had taken part in the battle on King Enrique's side. They included the marshal d'Audrehem, a Frenchman from Picardy, a marshal of France and a very fine knight, who had been captured in the battle. When the prince saw the marshal, he declared him a traitor and a perjurer and said that he deserved to die. 'My lord,' the marshal replied, 'you are the son of a king and therefore I will not reply as forcefully as I should on this matter: but I am neither a traitor nor a perjurer'. The prince then asked the marshal if he wished to have the dispute between them tried by knights and told him that if he did he would prove to him that the accusation was true. 'Yes, I do', replied the marshal.

When the prince had eaten, 12 knights were nominated as judges: four English, four from Guyenne and four Bretons. Then the marshal was brought forward and the prince addressed him as follows: 'Marshal d'Audrehem, you are well aware that in the battle of Poitiers which I won and in which King Jean of France was taken prisoner,

puse a rrendiçion e me fezistes pleyto e omenaje so pena de traydor e de fementido que, si non fuesse con el rrey de Françia vuestro señor o con algunos de su linaje de la flor de lis, que vos non armariedes contra el rrey de Ingla terra, mi padre e mi señor, nin contra mi persona fasta que toda vuestra rrendiçion fuesse pagada, la qual fasta aqui non es pagada. E oy non fue en esta batalla el rrey de Françia vuestro señor, nin alguno de su linaje de la flor de lis, e veo vos armado de todas vuestra armas contra mi e non auedes avn pagado vuestra rrendiçion, segund lo posistes comigo. E por tanto digo que vos auedes falsado el omenaje que me fezistes por lo qual sodes caydo en mal caso. Otrossi auedes falsado la fe por la qual sodes fementido, pues non conplistes lo que prometistes sobre vuestra fe en esta rrazon segund dicho he.'

E a muchos caualleros de los que ý estauan les pesaua temiendo que el mariscal tenia su pleyto mal e non se podia escusar la muerte, e todos le querien bien; ca era muy buen cauallero e lo fuera sienpre, e era en hedat de sesenta años o mas. E desque el prinçipe ouo dicho su rrazon delante los doçe caualleros juezes deste pleyto, dixo el mariscal de [Audenan] assi al prinçipe: 'Señor con humil rreuerençia vos pregunto si vos plaze dezir mas contra mi desto que auedes dicho delante estos caualleros que vos hordenastes en este pleyto.' E el prinçipe dixo que non. Estonçe el mariscal dixo assi: 'Señor yo vos suplico que vos non ayades enojo de mi por yo dezir de mi derecho pues este fecho toca en mi fama e en mi verdad.' E el prinçipe dixo que segura mente lo dixiesse que esto era fecho de caualleros e de guerra e era rrazon cada vno de defender su verdat e su fama. E estonçe dixo el mariscal al prinçipe assi: 'Señor, verdad es que yo fuy vuestro preso en la batalla de Piteus, do mi señor el rrey de Françia fue preso, e verdad es señor que yo vos fize pleito e omenaje e vos di mi fe aquel dia que me non armasse contra el rrey de Ingla terra nin contra vos fasta que toda mi rrendiçion fuesse pagada, la qual yo avn non he pagado, saluo si me armasse con el rrey de Françia mi señor,

you were captured, I held you in my power and I freed you in return for the payment of a ransom. You gave me a sworn undertaking that, on pain of being condemned as a traitor and perjurer, unless it were in the service of your lord the king of France or of some member of the line of the *fleur-de-lis*, you would not take up arms against my father and lord the king of England or against my own person until your ransom had been paid in full. So far it has not been paid. Today your lord the king of France was not present in the battle, nor was any member of his line of the *fleur-de-lis*. I see you there fully armed to fight against me although you have not yet paid your ransom as you undertook to do. I declare, therefore, that you have broken the bond of trust into which you entered with me, which means that you are guilty of a misdemeanour. You have also broken your word, and so you are a perjurer as you did not keep to the promise that you made in this respect on your word of honour, as I have already explained.'

Many of the knights who were present were concerned, fearing that the marshal did not have a strong case and that he would not be able to avoid death. He was very popular with everyone, since he was, and always had been, a very fine knight and he was 60 years old or more. Once the prince had set out his argument before the 12 knights who were judging the case, the marshal d'Audrehem replied to him as follows: 'My lord, with humble reverence I would like to ask you if it is your wish to say any more against me on this matter of which you have spoken before these knights that you nominated as judges of the case.' The prince said that it was not, and then the marshal continued: 'My lord, I beg you to show no anger towards me for asserting my right, for this matter concerns my reputation and my integrity.' The prince told him to speak out with confidence, for this affair concerned knights and war and it was right that any man should defend his integrity and his reputation. Then the marshal addressed the prince thus: 'My lord, it is true that I was your prisoner in the battle of Poitiers, in which my lord the king of France was made captive, and it is also true that on that day I gave a sworn undertaking and made a vow that I would not take up arms against the king of England or against you until my ransom was paid in full – and this has indeed not yet been done – unless it were in the service of my lord the king of

viniendo por su cuerpo o con alguno o algunos de su linaje de la flor de lis. E, señor, yo veo bien que mi señor el rrey de Françia non es aqui nin ninguno de su linaje de la flor de lis; pero, Señor, con todo esto yo non soy caydo en mal caso nin fementido, ca yo non me arme oy contra vos, que vos non sodes oy aqui el cabo desta batalla, ca el capitan e cabo desta batalla es el rrey don Pedro e a sus gajes e a su sueldo commo asoldado e gajero venides vos aqui el dia de oy e non venides assi commo mayor de la hueste. E assi, señor, pues vos non sodes cabo desta batalla saluo gajero e asoldado, yo non fize yerro en me armar el dia de oy, pues non me arme contra vos saluo contra el rrey don Pedro, que es el capitan mayor de vuestra partida e cuya es la rrequesta desta batalla.'

E los doze cuaalleros juezes que el prinçipe hordenara para oyr e librar este pleyto segund dicho auemos, entendieron que el mariscal dizia rrazon e se defendia segund cauallero, e dixeron luego al prinçipe que el mariscal le rrespondia bien e con derecho e dieronlo por quito de la acusaçion que el prinçipe le fazia. E al prinçipe e a todos los otros cualleros plogo mucho que el mariscal touiera rrazon para se escusar, por que era buen cauallero. E fue muy notada la rrazon que el mariscal le dizia. E por esta sentençia se librauan despues pleitos quales quier semejante desto en las partidas do auia guerra e acaesçia caso semejante.

Otrossy esta batalla ya desbaratada, el rrey don Pedro e el prinçipe de Gales e las otras conpañas fueron para Burgos, ca la batalla fuera el sabado antes del domingo de Lazaro, e el domingo estudieron en el canpo e el lunes partieron dende todos para Burgos.

France, present in person, or of one or more members of his line of the *fleur-de-lis*. Moreover, I recognize that my lord the king of France is not present here and that likewise there is no member of his line of the *fleur-de-lis*. However, my lord, I am guilty of no misdemeanour, nor am I a perjurer, for today I did not take up arms against you, as you are not here as the head of this army: its captain and the man who heads it is King Pedro and you are present today receiving payment and salary, contracted by him and in his employ; you are not here as the leader of the army. Thus, my lord, since you are not the man commanding these troops but a paid soldier and a mercenary, I did no wrong by taking up arms on this day, as I did so not against you but against King Pedro, who is the commander-in-chief of your forces and who sought this battle.'

The 12 knights nominated as judges by the prince to hear and decide this case, as we have explained, understood that the marshal was right in what he said and was defending himself as befitted a knight. They quickly told the prince that the marshal had given him a fitting response and had right on his side and they declared him innocent of the misdemeanours of which the prince had accused him. The prince and all the other knights took great pleasure in the fact that the marshal had justified himself sufficiently to merit acquittal, for he was a fine knight. Good note was taken of the argument that he put to the prince and subsequently this ruling served to decide any similar disputes in areas where there was conflict and cases of this kind arose.

Furthermore, once this battle had been settled, King Pedro, the prince of Wales and the rest of their forces headed for Burgos: the encounter had taken place on the Saturday before Lazarus Sunday.[10] On the Sunday they had still been on the field of battle and on the Monday they all left for Burgos.

Capitulo XIIII°. Commo fizo el rrey don Enrrique despues que la batalla fue vençida.

Agora tornaremos a contar que fue del rrey don Enrrique despues que partio de la batalla. Asi acaesçio que el rrey don Enrrique aquel dia estaua en vn cauallo grande rruçio castellano e armado de lorigas, e quando todos los suyos fueron vençidos e partidos del canpo, el fue para la villa de Najara: commo quier que es asaz çerca enpero non pudia el caualло leuar, que andaua cansado. E vn escudero su criado, que dizian Ruy Ferrandez de Gaona, natural de tierra de Alaua, estaua en vn caualло ginete e llego al rrey don Enrrique e dixole: 'Señor, tomad este caualло, ca esse vuestro non puede mouerse.' E el rrey fizolo assi, e caualgo en el ginete e sallio de la villa de Najara e tomo camino de Soria para Aragon. E yua con el don Ferrand Sanchez de Touar, que fue despues almirante, e don Alfonso Perez de Guzman e miçer Anbrosio fijo del almirante miçer Gil Boca Negra e otros.

E otro dia llegando çerca vna aldea de tierra de Soria que dizian Borouia, sallieron a el algunos de caualло desque vieron assi yr omnes por el camino apresurados. E algunos dellos conosçieron lo e quisieran lo matar o tomar preso, por auer la graçia del rrey don Pedro. E desque los vio estar assi dubdando llegosse a ellos e peleo con ellos e desbaratolos, e mato a aquel que le queria prender o matar.

E dende aporto en Aragon çerca Calatayud en vn lugar de don Iohan Martinez de Luna, que dizen Yllueca, e ally fallo a don Pedro de Luna, que fue despues papa Benedito, e el lo guio e fue con el fasta fuera del rregno de Aragon. E llego a los puertos de Jaca e de alli fue para Ortes, vna villa del conde de Fox, e llego ý, commo quier que al conde le pesara mucho por que el rrey don Enrrique fuera vençido. Enpero eso mesmo le peso por que aporto en su casa, ca veya que el prinçipe era estonçe vno de los mayores omnes del mundo entre los christianos e auia rresçelo que se fallaria mal con el por que lo non

1367: CHAPTER XIV

What King Enrique did after the battle had been decided.

Now we shall return to our account of what happened to King Enrique after he had left the field of battle. The fact is that on that day King Enrique was mounted on a large grey Castilian charger protected by chain-mail and, when all his troops had been defeated and had left the field, he rode off towards the town of Nájera. Although this town is not situated far away, his exhausted horse could no longer carry him. A squire from his household, a native of the lands of Álava by the name of Ruy Fernández de Gaona, who was mounted on a light-cavalry horse, rode up to King Enrique. 'My lord,' he said, 'take this horse, for yours is too tired to move.' The king did so, mounting the horse, leaving the town of Nájera and taking the Soria road towards Aragon. He was accompanied by Don Fernán Sánchez de Tovar, later to become admiral, Don Alfonso Pérez de Guzmán, Miçer Ambrosio, son of Admiral Miçer Gil Boccanegra, and others.

The next day, as he drew near to a village called Borobia in the area of Soria, some horsemen, on seeing men hurrying along the road, rode out towards them. Some of them recognized him and would have liked to kill him or take him prisoner in order to win the favour of King Pedro, but, once he had seen them hesitating in this way, King Enrique rode up to them, confronted them and put them to flight, killing the man who had wanted to bring about his death or his capture.

From there he rode as far as a village called Illueca which belonged to Don Juan Martínez de Luna, situated in Aragon near to Calatayud. There he found Don Pedro de Luna, later to become Pope Benedict, who went with him as his guide until he left the kingdom of Aragon.[11] He reached the pass of Jaca, and from there he went on to Orthez, a town belonging to the count of Foix.[12] He entered the town, in spite of the fact that the count had been troubled by the defeat suffered by King Enrique and, indeed, because the king had come to stay in his household: he was well aware that at that time the prince was one of the most important men in Christendom and he feared that he would

prendiera, pues lo tenia en su casa. Enpero el rresçibio muy bien al rrey don Enrrique e diole cauallos e dineros e omnes suyos que fueron con el fasta Tolosa.

E estudo ý algunos dias e dende fue para Villa Nueua çerca de Aviñon, ca era ý estonçe el duc de Angeos, que era hermano del rrey de Françia e su lugar teniente en Lenguadoc, e alli estudo con el librando lo que le cunplia, en el qual fallo muchas buenas obras e le dio de sus dineros con muy buena voluntad.

E el papa Urbano quinto, que estonçe era en Aviñon, queria bien al rrey don Enrrique, e por su conseio se trato que el dicho duc de Angeos lo ayudasse e confortasse. Enpero el rrey don Enrrique non vio al papa, ca todos se temian de fazer enojo al prinçipe de Gales, tan poderoso le veyan estonçe.

Capitulo XV°. Commo fizo don Tello desque sallio de la batalla de Najara e commo la rreyna e sus fijos los infantes partieron de Burgos.

Agora tornaremos a contar commo fizo don Tello, hermano del rrey don Enrrique despues que partio de la batalla de Najara. E assi fue que despues que partio de la batalla de Najara, don Tello segund dicho auemos, luego fue para Burgos, pero non se detovo ý e tomo su camino para Aragon.

E el arçobispo de Toledo don Gomez Manrrique e el arçobispo de Çaragoça don Lope Ferrandez de Luna, que eran ý e auian fincado con la rreyna doña Iohana e los infantes, desque supieron que la batalla era desbaratada, partieron de Burgos con muy grand priessa e leuaron de Burgos a la rreyna doña Iohana muger del rrey don Enrrique e al infante don Iohan e a la infanta doña Leonor sus fijos del rrey don

find himself in difficulty with him for having sheltered King Enrique in his household without taking him prisoner. Nevertheless, the count welcomed King Enrique warmly, made him gifts of horses and money and gave him some of his men to go with him as far as Toulouse.

King Enrique remained there for some days, and from there he went on to Villeneuve near Avignon, where the duke of Anjou, brother of the king of France and his lieutenant in Languedoc, was to be found. He spent some time with him, coming to a decision about how it was best for him to proceed. From this King Enrique achieved much that was to his benefit and the duke made King Enrique gifts from his own wealth with great generosity.

Pope Urban V, who was currently in Avignon, was giving his backing to King Enrique and on his advice it was agreed that the duke of Anjou should give the king help and support. Nevertheless, King Enrique did not see the Pope, for everybody was afraid of angering the prince of Wales, so powerful did he seem at that time.

1367: CHAPTER XV

What Don Tello did after leaving the battlefield of Nájera, and how the queen and her son and daughter, the prince and princess, left Burgos.

Now we shall go back to our account of what King Enrique's brother Don Tello did after he left the battlefield of Nájera. The fact is that, after fleeing from the field of battle, Don Tello – as we have already related – headed immediately for Burgos. However he did not stop there but set off for Aragon.

The archbishop of Toledo Don Gómez Manrique and the archbishop of Saragossa Don Lope Fernández de Luna, who had been waiting there with Queen Juana and the prince and princess, on hearing that the battle had been lost set off from Burgos in very great haste. With them they took King Enrique's wife Queen Juana, Prince Juan and Princess Leonor, the son and daughter of King Enrique and Queen

Enrrique e de la dicha rreyna doña Iohana e a la infanta doña Leonor, fija del rrey de Aragon, que ý era por esposa del infante don Iohan, e fueron camino de Çaragoça. E yuan con grand miedo por aquel camino, e yuan ý muchas dueñas e donzellas, e llegaron a Çaragoça con muy grand miedo e con muy grandes trabajos e alli fueron acogidos e assosegaron ý.

E de cada dia llegauan ay muchas conpañas de los que escapauan de la dicha batalla.

Capitulo XVIº. Commo fizo el rrey de Nauarra despues de la batalla, el qual estaua preso en Borja.

Segunt dicho auemos el rrey don Carlos de Nauarra auia prometido e jurado al rrey don Enrrique, quando se vio con el en Santa Cruz de Canpesço, que non daria pasada por los puertos de Ronçes valles al rrey don Pedro e al prinçipe de Gales nin a los que con ellos venian. E desto dio al rrey don Enrrique en arrehenes los castillos de Laguardia e a Sant Viçente e Buradon. E avn le asseguro, si estas gentes pasassen, que seria con el en la batalla con todo su poder. E despues segund suso auemos contado, commo quier que dio los dichos castillos, dexo el paso del puerto de Ronçes valles al rrey don Pedro e al prinçipe, por do pasaron, e avn los aseguro que seria con ellos en la batalla, de la su partida. Otrossi auemos contado commo el rrey de Nauarra por non seer en la batalla, trato con mossen Oliuer de Mauni que le prendiesse e le touiesse en Borja, segund mas larga mente es contado. E agora despues de la batalla los dichos castillos de Laguardia e Sand Viçente luego fueron tomados por los nauarros saluo el castillo de Buradon, que tenia Iohan Ramirez de Arellano, que se non pudo tomar.

E el rrey de Nauarra despues desta batalla estando en el castillo de

Juana, and also Princess Elionor, daughter of the king of Aragon, who was there because she was betrothed to Prince Juan. They set off for Saragossa, full of anxiety as they made that journey, accompanied by several noble ladies and ladies-in-waiting, and they arrived in Saragossa deeply apprehensive and after enduring great difficulties. There they were given a warm welcome and they rested.

Day by day there arrived large numbers of troops who were escaping from the battle.

1367: CHAPTER XVI

What the king of Navarre, who was being held captive in Borja, did after the battle.

As we have already explained, King Carlos of Navarre had sworn an oath to King Enrique when he met with him in Santa Cruz de Campezo that he would not allow King Pedro and the prince of Wales, or the men that they were bringing with them, to cross the pass of Roncevalles. Moreover, as surety he had handed over to King Enrique the castles of Laguardia, San Vicente and Buradón, and in addition he had assured him that, if those troops did manage to get through, he would be at his side in the battle with his whole army. Subsequently, as we have related above, although he had handed over these castles to King Enrique, he allowed King Pedro and the prince access over the pass of Roncevalles, by means of which they did make their entry; and he even gave them an assurance that he would be with them in the battle, fighting on their side. We have also told of how the king of Navarre, in order not to take part in the battle, arranged with Monsieur Olivier de Mauny for him to take him prisoner and hold him in Borja, as has been related at greater length. Now, after the battle, those castles of Laguardia and San Vicente were quickly seized back by the Navarrese, although they were unable to take the castle of Buradón which was being held by Juan Ramírez de Arellano.

After the battle, the king of Navarre, who was in the castle of Borja

Borja commo dicho auemos, trato con mossen Oliuer de Morni que el pornia en arrehenes por si en el dicho castillo de Borja a su fijo el infante Pedro, que era el su fijo segundo, e que mossen Oliuer lo traxiesse a la villa de Tudela, que es en el rregno de Nauarra, e que alli le faria rrecabdo de lo que con el pusiera segund auemos contado. E mossen Oliuer fizolo assy e pusieronlo en el dicho castillo de Borja al infante don Pedro fijo del rrey de Nauarra, e mossen Oliuer vino con el rrey de Nauarra a la villa de Tudela.

E despues que alli llegaron el rrey de Nauarra mando prender a mossen Oliuer e a vn su hermano, e el hermano salto por vnos tejados cuydando escapar. E mataronlo e prendieron a mossen Oliuer fasta que dio el infante don Pedro fijo del rrey, que tenia en el castillo de Borja. E assy en esta pleytesia perdio mossen Oliuer su hermano. E el rrey de Nauarra non le dio la villa e castillo de Gabray en Normandia con los tres mill francos de oro de rrenta, que le prometiera segunt suso dicho es.

Capitulo XVIIº. Commo el rrey de Aragon tomo su fija la infanta doña Leonor e commo trato su paz con el prinçipe de Gales e de otras cosas que estonçes acaesçieron.

El rrey don Pedro de Aragon estaua muy quexado diziendo que el rrey don Enrrique non cunpliera luego que cobrara el rreyno de Castilla algunas cosas que eran acordadas entre el rrey de Aragon e el. Otrossi por quanto estaua el prinçipe muy poderoso e el rrey don Pedro. E por estas cosas non fallaron en el rrey de Aragon la rreyna doña Iohana, muger del rrey don Enrrique, e sus fijos tan buen acogimiento commo cuydaron, antes tomo luego el rrey de Aragon a la infanta doña Leonor su fija e dixo que la non daria por muger al infante don Iohan fijo del rrey don Enrrique, pues non le cunpliera lo que con el pusiera e que non queria estar por el dicho casamiento.

– as we have already said –, arranged with Monsieur Olivier de Mauny that he would leave in his own place as surety in the castle Prince Pedro, his second son, and that Monsieur Olivier was to accompany him to the town of Tudela, in the kingdom of Navarre, where King Carlos would make good what – as we have related – had been settled between them. Monsieur Olivier agreed to this: the king of Navarre's son, Prince Pedro, was placed in the castle of Borja and Monsieur Olivier accompanied the king of Navarre to the town of Tudela.

Then, once they had arrived there, the king of Navarre ordered the arrest of Monsieur Olivier and of a brother of his, who tried to escape by leaping over the rooftops. They killed the brother and took Monsieur Olivier prisoner, holding him until he handed over King Carlos's son Prince Pedro, who was being held by him in the castle of Borja. Thus, through these dealings, Monsieur Olivier lost his brother and the king of Navarre failed to hand over to him the town and castle of Gavray in Normandy with the income of 3,000 gold francs, which – as was stated above – he had promised him.

1367: CHAPTER XVII

How the king of Aragon took back his daughter Princess Elionor and how he made peace with the prince of Wales; and concerning other events which occurred at that time.

King Pere of Aragon was deeply aggrieved, arguing that King Enrique, on winning the throne of the kingdom of Castile, had failed to fulfil some obligations which had been agreed between the the two of them. Moreover, since the prince and King Pedro were very powerful, King Enrique's wife Queen Juana and his son and daughter did not find in the king of Aragon as warm a welcome as they had expected, but instead King Pere promptly took back his daughter princess Elionor, saying that he would not give her in marriage to King Enrique's son Prince Juan, as King Enrique had not honoured the commitments that he had made to him, on account of which he was not willing to favour the union.

Otrossi el prinçipe de Gales enbio luego al rrey de Aragon por mensagero a mossen Hugo de Ca[uar]lay, vn cauallero de Inglaterra a tratar con el sus amistades, e esso mesmo fizo el rrey don Pedro. E esto todo se fazia por que el rrey don Enrrique non fallaua acogimiento ninguna en la casa de Aragon.

E la rreyna doña Iohana, muger del dicho rrey don Enrrique, e sus fijos estudieron en Çaragoça algunos dias, ca non sabian del rrey don Enrrique a do aportara nin en que tierra era despues que partiera de la batalla.

E ouo estonçe en la casa del rrey de Aragon grandes vandos, ca el infante don Pedro, tio del rrey de Aragon, hermano del rrey don Alfonso su padre, e el conde de Anpurias e el arçobispo de Çaragoça don Lope Ferrandez de Luna e don Iohan Martinez de Luna e otros muchos tenian la parte del rrey don Enrrique e consejauan al rrey de Aragon que sostuuiesse la parte del rrey don Enrrique. E consseiauan al rrey de Aragon esto diziendo que en sus menesteres de guerras que ouiera con Castilla sienpre lo fallara buen ayudador e leal amigo e que en tal tienpo commo este gelo deuia agradesçer. E avn diziendo que si el rrey don Pedro fincasse asossegado en el rregno de Castilla, que tornaria a le fazer guerra a el e al rregno de Aragon commo primero fazia.

E otros auia ý, los quales eran la rreyna de Aragon e el conde de Vrgel e el conde de Cardona e el obispo de Lerida, que eran priuados, e estos eran contrarios al rrey don Enrrique: los vnos diziendo que non touiera con el rrey de Aragon lo que prometiera de le dar en Castilla quando la cobrasse, e otros algunos destos non le querian bien por la muerte del infante don Ferrando, diziendo que fuera con el rrey de Aragon en aquel consejo, e otros auia ý grandes en la corte del rrey de Aragon que non se ponian en los vandos e eran commo medianeros, pero bien les plazia que el rrey de Aragon ouiesse paz con todos. E assi eran los fechos de la corte del rrey de Aragon partidos.

In addition, the prince of Wales lost no time in sending an English knight, Sir Hugh Calveley, as his emissary to the king of Aragon to negotiate a peace agreement, and King Pedro did likewise. All of this was being done because King Enrique was now finding no acceptance in the House of Aragon.

King Enrique's wife Queen Juana and his son and daughter remained in Saragossa for some days as they did not know the whereabouts of King Enrique or in what land he had been since leaving the field of battle.

At that time in the household of the king of Aragon there were sharply divided factions. Prince Pere, uncle of the king of Aragon – a brother of his father King Alfons –, together with the count of Ampurias, the archbishop of Saragossa Don Lope Fernández de Luna, Don Juan Martínez de Luna and many others took the side of King Enrique and advised the king of Aragon to continue to support him. They gave this counsel to the king of Aragon arguing that when in need in time of war with Castile he had always found him quick to help and a loyal ally and that at such a time as this he should show him gratitude; and in addition they said that, if King Pedro were to be firmly established on the throne of Castile, he would once again make war on King Pere and on the kingdom of Aragon as he had done previously.

There were others – namely the queen of Aragon, the count of Urgel, the count of Cardona and the bishop of Lleida, the king's close advisers – who were opponents of King Enrique. Some of them argued that he had not kept his promises to the king of Aragon with regard to concessions that he would make to him in Castile on gaining the throne. Others of them were hostile to King Enrique on account of the death of Prince Ferran, saying that he had been involved in devising the plan with King Pere. And there was another group of prominent figures in the court of the king of Aragon who did not form part of any faction and had a role similar to that of mediators: they were very keen for King Pere to be at peace with everybody. In this way opinions in the court of the king of Aragon were divided.

Capitulo XVIII°. Commo mossen Beltran de Claquin fue preso en esta batalla e commo fue rrendido e lo que sobre esto acaesçio.

En esta batalla fue preso mossen Beltran de Claquin, vn cauallero muy grande e bueno, que era de Bretaña e viniera con el rrey don Enrrique quando entrara en Castilla, segund que ya auemos contado. E en esta batalla estaua de pie en vno con el conde don Sancho. E commo quier que al prinçipe pluguiera que el moriera en la batalla por quanto era vn cauallero muy guerrero; pero despues que fue preso, fizole mucha honrra e quando partio de Castilla, leuolo conssigo a Burdeus.

E estando alli mossen Beltran de Claquin fizo dezir al prinçipe que fuesse su merçed de lo mandar poner a rrendiçion, ca non cunplia a su seruiçio estar el anssi en la prision e que mejor era leuar del lo que pudiesse pagar. E el prinçipe ouo su conssejo que por quanto mossen Beltran era muy buen cauallero que era mejor, durando la guerra de Françia e de Ingla terra, que estudiesse preso e que mas valia perder cobdiçia de lo que podia montar su rrendiçion que librarlo. E fizo le dar esta rrespuesta al dicho mossen Beltran. E quando mossen Beltran lo oyo, dixo assi al cauallero que esto le dixo de partes del prinçipe: 'Dezid vos assi a mi señor el prinçipe que yo tengo que me faze Dios, e el, muy grand graçia, entre otras muchas honrras que yo oue en este mundo de caualleria: que mi lança sea tan temida que yaga yo en prision durante las guerras entre Françia e Ingla terra e non por al, e pues assi es, yo tengo por honrrada la mi prision mas que la mi deliberaçion. E que sea çierto que yo gelo tengo en merçed señalada, ca todos aquellos que gelo oyeren e sopieren ternan que rresçibo dende muy grand honrra, e el bien e el prez de caualleria en esto va, ca la vida ayna pasa'.

1367: CHAPTER XVIII

How Monsieur Bertrand du Guesclin, who had been taken prisoner in the battle, was ransomed, and what happened in this respect.

Monsieur Bertrand du Guesclin had been taken prisoner in the battle of Nájera. He was a very great and very fine knight from Brittany, who had accompanied King Enrique when he had entered Castile, as we have already related. In the battle he had fought on foot alongside Count Sancho. Although the prince would have preferred him to die in the battle since as a knight he was highly skilled in the arts of war, once he had been captured he treated him with great respect and, when he left Castile, he took him with him to Bordeaux.

Finding himself in this position, Monsieur Bertrand du Guesclin sent a request to the prince that it be his will to give instructions for him be ransomed, for it did not do the prince credit for him to be held in prison in this way and it would be better for him to take from him what he could afford to pay. After consultation, the prince reached the conclusion that, since Monsieur Bertrand was a very fine knight, it would be preferable for him to remain a prisoner as long as the war between France and England lasted, and that it was better to give up the desire for what could be gained from his ransom than to set him free. He gave instructions for this reply to be communicated to Monsieur Bertrand, who, on hearing it, spoke as follows to the knight who had given it to him on the prince's behalf: 'Tell my lord the prince that I consider that both God and he have treated me with very great favour – which is among many other honours that I have gained in this world of chivalry – in that my lance should be so feared that I lie in prison throughout the wars between France and England for this and for no other reason. And, since this is the case, I hold my imprisonment to bring me greater honour than I would gain by being set free. The prince can be certain that I view this as an act of conspicuous generosity, for all of those who hear and learn of this will consider that I am very greatly honoured by it, and in this lies the worth and the splendour of chivalry, for life quickly passes.'

E el cauallero dixole al prinçipe todas estas rrazones que mossen Beltran dixera. E el prinçipe penso en ello e dixo: 'Verdad dize; yd e tornad a el e dezilde que a mi plaze de lo poner a rrendiçion e que la quantia que el dara por si sea tanta quantia quanta el quisiere e mas non le demandare. E si vna paja sola prometiere por si, por tanto le otorgo su deliberaçion'. E la entençion del prinçipe era esta: que si mossen Beltran dixiesse que por çinco francos queria sallir de prisión, que mas non le demandase, ca por quanto menos salliesse, menos honrra leuaua, e que entendiesse mossen Beltran que non le detenia el prinçipe por otro themor que del ouiesen los ingleses e que el pudia bien escusar sus dineros.

E el cauallero del prinçipe torno a mossen Beltran e dixole: 'Mi señor el prinçipe vos enbia dezir que su voluntad es que vos seades delibre de la prision e que vuestra fiança sea tanta la quantia quanta vos quisieredes e dixeredes, e que mas non pagaredes avnque mas non prometades de vna paja de las que estan en tierra, e que esto sea luego'. E mossen Beltran entendio bien la entençion del prinçipe e dixo: 'Yo le he en merçed a mi señor el prinçipe lo que me enbia decir, e pues assi es, yo quiero nonbrar la quantia de mi fiança'. E todos cuydauan que se pornia en alguna pequeña quantia, ca mossen Beltran non auia en el mundo si non el cuerpo. E dixo mossen Beltran assi: 'Pues que mi señor el prinçipe es assi franco contra mi e non quiere de mi saluo lo que yo nonbrare de fiança, dezid le vos que maguer so pobre cauallero de quantia de oro e de moneda, enpero con esfuerço de mis amigos, yo le dare çient mill francos de oro por mi cuerpo, e que desto le dare buenos rrecabdos'.

E el cauallero del prinçipe torno a el muy marauillado e dixole: 'Señor, mossen Beltran es rrendido a su voluntad e ha nonbrado su fiança.' E el prinçipe le pregunto que quantia. E el cauallero le dixo: 'Señor, mossen Beltran dize que vos tiene en merçed todo lo que le

Chronicle of King Pedro

The knight reported all of Monsieur Bertrand's words to the prince, who gave the matter thought and then replied, 'He is speaking the truth. Go back to him and inform him that I agree to ask a ransom in return for his freedom. Moreover, I am satisfied for the ransom asked to be a figure that he himself sets: I will not ask him for more. And if he promises just a single straw, that will be enough for me to grant him his freedom.' The prince's intention was as follows: that if Monsieur Bertrand said that he wished to be freed from his imprisonment in return for five francs, he would demand no more from him, for the less Monsieur Bertrand paid the less he would gain in terms of honour. Monsieur Bertrand should understand that the prince was not keeping him captive out of any further fear that the English had of him and that he could well do without his money.

The prince's knight went back to Monsieur Bertrand. 'My lord,' he said to him, 'the prince sends you word that it is his will that you be released from your imprisonment and that the ransom asked for you should be exactly the sum that you choose to name. You will pay no more than that, even if what you promise amounts to just one of the pieces of straw which lie on the ground. And this is to happen without delay.' Monsieur Bertrand understood clearly the prince's purpose. 'I am grateful to my lord the prince for the message that he has sent me', he said, 'and since this is the case I wish to specify the size of my ransom.' Everybody anticipated that he would name some small amount, for in the whole world Monsieur Bertrand possessed no more than his own body. 'Since my lord the prince is so generous in his treatment of me,' said Monsieur Bertrand, 'and since for my ransom he demands only the sum that I specify, inform him that, although I am a poor knight in terms of gold and coin, nevertheless with the support of my friends I will give him 100,000 gold francs in return for the freedom of my person and that I will provide him with ample security for this amount.'

The prince's knight returned to him in amazement and said to him, 'My lord, Monsieur Bertrand is to be set free in return for a sum of his choice and he has stated the size of the ransom.' The prince asked him how much this was. 'My lord,' the knight said, 'Monsieur Bertrand says that he is grateful to you for all that you communicated to him

enbiastes dezir en rrazon de su fiança, e dize que commo quier que el sea pobre cauallero en oro e en moneda, enpero que con esfuerço de sus parientes e amigos, el vos dara çient mill francos de oro por su persona e que desto vos dara buenos rrecabdos'.

E el prinçipe fue marauillado: primera mente del grand coraçon de mossen Beltran, otrossi donde podria el auer tanta quantia. E dixo al cauallero que pues el fecho era a esto llegado, que le plazia. E dixo al cauallero que le diesse rrecabdo de çient mill francos de oro, pues los auia nonbrado. E el cauallero torno a mossen Beltran e dixole que el prinçipe su señor era contento de la quantia de los çient mill francos que el nonbrara e prometiera por si, e pues asy era que diese rrecabdo dellos e que seria libre de prision.

E mossen Beltran enbio luego a Bretaña a grandes señores varones e caualleros sus amigos a les fazer saber commo el era rrendido por quantia de çient mill francos, que auia a dar por su deliberança al prinçipe de Gales, e que les rrogaua que quisiessen fazer e dar rrecabdo por el al dicho prinçipe en guisa que el fuesse contento de las pagas que le prometiera, e que fiaua en Dios e en la merçed del rrey de Françia su señor, que quando el fuesse delibre de la prision, el los quitaria de lo que por el prometiessen e diessen.

E los señores varones e caualleros de Bretaña a quien el dicho mossen Beltran enbio sus cartas luego le enbiaron dezir que todos ellos estauan prestos para se obligar en la quantia que el quisiesse por su rrendiçion en tal que el fuesse delibre de la prision. E por que el fuesse çierto de sus voluntades quales eran, que cada vno dellos le enbiaua vn su escudero que leuaua su sello e poder para le obligar en la quantia que mossen Beltran quisiese e al plazo que quisiese. E en Françia e en Inglaterra la mayor obligaçion que cauallero a omne de linaje puede dar es su sello; ca dizen que por poner omne su nonbre es asaz, pero en el sello va el nonbre e las armas, que son honrra del cauallero.

with regard to his ransom and that, even though he is a poor knight in terms of gold and coin, nevertheless with the support of his relatives and friends he will give you 100,000 gold francs in return for the freedom of his person and he will provide you with ample security for this amount.'

The prince was amazed, firstly at the nobility of spirit shown by Monsieur Bertrand but also at the question of where he could obtain such a sum. He told the knight that, since the discussion had reached this point, he was in agreement. He told the knight that Monsieur Bertrand should provide him with security for 100,000 gold francs, since this was the sum that he had named. The knight went back to Monsieur Bertrand and informed him that his lord the prince was satisfied with the sum of 100,000 gold francs that he had named and promised for his liberty, and since this was the case Monsieur Bertrand should provide surety for it and he would then be freed from his imprisonment.

Immediately Monsieur Bertrand sent word to his friends among the great lords, barons and knights of Brittany to let them know how he was being ransomed for the sum of 100,000 francs, which he was to pay to the prince of Wales in return for his release, and that he requested that they be willing to contribute to this and send security to the prince such that he would be content that he would receive the promised payments. He added that he trusted in God and in the mercy of his lord the king of France that, when he was free of his imprisonment, the king would make good to them what they had promised and paid on his behalf.

The lords, barons and knights of Brittany to whom Monsieur Bertrand had written lost no time in replying to him that they were willing to commit themselves with regard to the sum that he sought for his ransom in order to be freed from imprisonment. Moreover, so that he might be certain of their intention, each one of them was sending him a squire bearing his seal and legal authorization committing him to pay whatever amount Monsieur Bertrand wished by whatever date he indicated. In France and England the greatest commitment that a knight can give to a man of noble birth is his seal: they say that it is enough for a man to sign his name, but the seal bears the name and the arms, which represent the knight's honour.

E los escuderos de los señores e varones e caualleros de Bretaña sus amigos de mossen Beltran llegaron a el a Burdeus e dixeronle commo aquellos señores e varones e caualleros de Bretaña lo saludauan e le enbiauan sus sellos para que el los pudiesse obligar en tanta quantia commo el quisiesse e para el tienpo que le fuesse demandado. E mossen Beltran desque vio los escuderos que trayan los sellos de aquellos sus amigos de Bretaña, fizo sus rrecabdos con el prinçipe e hordeno cada sello por quanta quantia lo dexaua e a que tienpo se auia de pagar la rrendiçion a conplimiento de los çient mill francos que le prometiera.

E fue luego mossen Beltran delibre de la prision e partio de alli e fuesse para el rrey don Carlos de Françia, e quando ý llego, el rrey lo rresçibio muy bien e le plogo con el; pero vn dia le pregunto que quanta fiança prometiera por sy, e mossen Beltran le dixo que çient mill francos e contole todo lo que le contesçiera con el prinçipe en rrazon de su deliberança, segund dicho es. E el rrey de Françia le dixo: 'Yo so bien çierto que vos estos çient mill francos non los prometistes saluo en mi esfuerço, e yo quiero pagarlos por vos estos çient mill francos'. E mando a vn su thesorero que diesse a mossen Beltran luego rrecabdo de mercadores de Paris commo pagassen los çient mill francos a los que ouiessen de auer rrendiçion de mossen Beltran e quitassen los sellos de los señores e varones e caualleros de Bretaña. Otrossi mando al su thesorero que diesse a mossen Beltran treynta mill francos para se apostar e encaualgar e armar. E assy fue todo fecho e conplido.

E acordamos de poner este fecho en este libro commo passo e por que acaesçio assi a este cauallero que fue preso en esta batalla de Najara. Otrossi por contar los grandes fechos e nobles que los buenos fazen, ca el prinçipe de Gales todo lo que fizo en este fecho fizo commo grande: primera mente en poner a rrendiçion a mossen Beltran por que non dixiessen que auian rresçelo los ingleses a vn solo cauallero; otrossi fizo bien en le dexar la fiança en aluedrio de mossen Beltran e non mostro cobdiçia. Otrossy fizo bien mossen Beltran en

The squires of the lords, barons and knights of Brittany who were Monsieur Bertrand's friends came to him in Bordeaux and told him that they brought him greetings from those lords, barons and knights and that they had sent him their seals so that he could commit them to pay whatever sum he wished and by whatever deadline was set. Then, once Monsieur Bertrand saw that the squires had brought the seals of his friends in Brittany, he made his reckoning with the prince and determined what sum of money corresponded to each seal that he was leaving with him and by when the ransom was to be paid on the basis of the 100,000 francs that he had promised him.

It was not long before Monsieur Bertrand was freed from his imprisonment and he set off to join King Charles of France. On his arrival, the king gave him a very warm welcome and took pleasure in his company. However, one day he asked him how much he had undertaken to pay as a ransom. Monsieur Bertrand told him that it was 100,000 francs and informed him about all that had happened between the prince and himself with regard to him gaining his freedom – as has been explained. 'I am quite certain,' the king of France said to him, 'that you did not promise those 100,000 francs other than for my benefit, and so I wish to pay them for you.' He instructed one of his treasurers to lose no time in giving to Monsieur Bertrand guarantees from Paris merchants that they were to pay the 100,000 francs to those due to receive the knight's ransom and so recover the seals of the lords, barons and knights of Brittany. He also instructed his treasurer to give Monsieur Bertrand 30,000 francs for him to buy clothing and equip himself with a horse and armour. All of this was put into full effect.

We resolved to include in our book an account of how this episode took place and why this knight who had been taken prisoner in the battle of Nájera was treated in such a way. Moreover, we did so in order to illustrate the great and noble deeds performed by good men, for all the actions of the prince of Wales in this affair were those of a person of greatness. In the first place this was in ransoming Monsieur Bertrand lest it be said that the English were afraid of one single knight; but he also acted fittingly in leaving the size of the ransom to the choice of Monsieur Bertrand instead of acting out of greed.

todo lo que dixo: assi en lo primero, que se tenia por honrrado en le tener el prinçipe antes preso que deliberarle, diziendo que era omne que pudia fazer enojo a los ingleses; otrosi fuele contado a bien a mossen Beltran en se poner en grand cuenta de rrendiçion, pues que la rrendiçion del prinçipe era que por pequeña valia lo dexaria e que lo non preçiaria mas. Otrossi fue e es grand rrazon de seer contada la rrazon de la grandeza e nobleza del rrey de Françia en la dadiua que fizo en dar a mossen Beltran çient mill francos para su rrendiçion e treynta mill francos para se apostar. E por estas rrazones se puso aqui este cuento, ca las franquezas e noblezas e dadiuas de los rreyes grand rrazon es que finquen en memoria e non sean oluidadas; otrossi las buenas rrazones de cauallerias.

Capitulo XIX°. Commo pasaron los fechos despues de la batalla entre el rrey don Pedro e el prinçipe de Gales.

Agora tornaremos a contar commo fizieron en Burgos el rrey don Pedro e el prinçipe desque llegaron. Deuedes saber que luego que la batalla fue vençida aquel dia, e dende adelante siempre, ouo entre el rrey don Pedro e el prinçipe de Gales poca abenençia, e las rrazones por que era, son estas: Primera mente el dia de la batalla fue preso vn cauallero que dezian Yñigo Lopez de Horozco, de vn cauallero gascon, e teniendolo preso llego ý el rrey don Pedro, que caualgara ya en vn cauallo, e mato al dicho Yñigo Lopez. E el cauallero que lo perdiera vinosse luego a querellar al prinçipe, que el teniendo aquel cauallero preso que el rrey don Pedro llegara e que lo matara. E non sola mente se quexaua de la perdida que el fiziera en el su prisionero, mas que se sentia por muy desonrrado de le matar vn cauallero que a el era

Monsieur Bertrand also showed good judgement in all that he said, firstly in affirming that he considered himself honoured that the prince should keep him as his prisoner rather than freeing him, asserting that he was a man who could prove to be a thorn in the side of the English; and it was also held in Monsieur Bertrand's favour that he set a high value on his own ransom, since the prince's intention in ransoming him was to free him for a small amount and thus no longer hold him in high esteem. Another point, and it is an important one to include, is the greatness and nobility of spirit shown by the king of France in giving Monsieur Bertrand 100,000 francs for his ransom and 30,000 francs to re-equip himself. It is for these reasons that this account was included here: there is very good cause for the acts of generosity and noble deeds performed by kings and the gifts that they make, and likewise great acts of chivalry, to remain in the memory and not be forgotten.

1367: CHAPTER XIX

How, after the battle, events developed between King Pedro and the prince of Wales.

Now we shall return to the narrative of what King Pedro and the prince did in Burgos after their arrival there. You should know that as soon as the battle had been won on that day, and constantly from that point on, there was little agreement between the two of them, and the reasons for this were as follows: firstly, on the day of the battle a knight called Íñigo López de Orozco was taken prisoner by a Gascon knight; and, while he was being held captive, King Pedro appeared, already mounted, and killed Íñigo López. The knight who had lost him immediately went to make his complaint to the prince that, while Íñigo López de Orozco had been in his custody, King Pedro had ridden up and killed him. His grievance concerned not only the loss that he had suffered in terms of the value of his prisoner but also the fact that he felt deeply dishonoured at the killing of a knight who had

rrendido e lo tenia en poder. E el prinçipe dixo al rrey don Pedro que non fiziera en ello bien, ca bien sabia el que, entre las otras cosas que estauan entre ellos acordadas e firmadas e juradas, era este capitulo vno de los prinçipales, que el rrey don Pedro non matasse a caualleros ningunos de Castilla nin omne de cuenta estando ý el prinçipe fasta que fuesse juzgado por su derecho, saluo si fuesse alguno de los que sentençiara antes de todo esto, e que aquel cauallero Yñigo Lopez non era de aquellos. E que bien paresçia que non era su voluntad de le guardar lo que con el auia puesto, e entendia que assi le guardaria todas las otras cosas que entre ellos estauan acordadas commo esta. E el rrey don Pedro se escuso lo mejor que pudo; pero non fincaron el rrey e el prinçipe bien contentos aquel dia.

Otro dia de la batalla el rrey don Pedro pidio al prinçipe que todos los caualleros e escuderos de cuenta que eran naturales de Castilla, e fueran presos en aquella batalla, que le fuessen a el entregados e que los apreçiasse vn preçio rrazonable e que el lo pagaria a los que los tenian presos e para esto, que el prinçipe los fiziesse seguros de las pagas a los caualleros e omes de armas que tenian los tales presos, que el rrey don Pedro faria su obligaçion al prinçipe por las quantias que montasen. E dizia el rrey don Pedro que si estos caualleros el cobrasse, que el guisaria con ellos e fablaria en tal manera por que fincassen suyos e de su parte. E si de otra manera se delibrassen por sus rrendiçiones o fuxessen de la prision en donde los caualleros que los auian tomado los tenian, que sienpre serian sus contrarios e en su deserviçio. E en este punto se afirmo mucho el rrey don Pedro otro dia de la batalla, que era domingo, e la batalla fue el sabado de quaresma antes de Lazaro a [tres] dias de abril.

E el prinçipe de Gales dixo al rrey don Pedro que sabia su rreal majestad que non dizia nin pidia rrazon, ca aquellos señores e caualleros e omnes de armas que alli eran en su serviçio e del, auian trabajado por la honrra, e si algunos prisioneros tenian, que eran suyos e que

surrendered to him and was his prisoner. The prince told King Pedro that he had not acted correctly in this matter, for he was well aware that, among other matters on which they committed themselves to a signed agreement confirmed with an oath, this was one of the most important: that King Pedro was not to kill any of the knights of Castile or any man of account, as long as the prince was present, without this person having previously been tried in accordance with his legal rights. This was unless he was one of the men sentenced before the campaign began, and this knight Íñigo López was not one of those. The prince told King Pedro that he appeared to have had no intention of observing the pact which the two of them had made and that he expected him to adhere to all other such points which they had agreed. King Pedro made his excuses as best he could, but that day he and the prince did not remain on good terms with each other.

On the day following the battle King Pedro made a request to the prince concerning all the knights and squires of account who were natives of Castile and had been captured in the battle: that they be handed over to him and that the prince fix a reasonable price, which King Pedro would pay to the men who were holding them. He also asked that, in this matter, the prince provide security for the payments to the knights and men-at-arms holding the prisoners, and said that he would undertake to repay him the total amount. King Pedro claimed that, if he had those knights in his power, he would negotiate with them and discuss matters in such a way that they would remain on his side and loyal to him; whilst if, on the other hand, they achieved their freedom through the payment of a ransom or escaped from the captivity in which they were being held by the knights who had captured them, they would always be his enemies and would remain disloyal towards him. King Pedro made this point insistently on the day following the battle, which was a Sunday: the battle had taken place on the Saturday in Lent before Lazarus Sunday, the 3rd of April.

The prince of Wales told King Pedro that his Royal Majesty was well aware that neither what he said nor what he asked was reasonable, for those lords, knights and men-at-arms who were there in the service of both of them had fought for the sake of honour and, if they had prisoners, they were theirs; and, moreover, such was the

tales eran los caualleros que los tenian que por dineros del mundo, avnque fuesse mill tanto que valiesse el prisionero, que touiesse que lo non venderian a el por quanto pensarian que los conpraua para los matar. E quanto en esto, que non se trabajase, que non era cosa que el pudiesse librar. Enpero si tales caualleros fuessen presos de los contra quales el pasara por sentençia antes desta batalla, que gelos faria entregar.

E estonçe dixo el rrey don Pedro al prinçipe que si estas cosas assi auian de pasar, que mas perdido tenia agora el rregno que lo tenia primera mente, que todos aquellos que eran presos eran los que le auian fecho perder el rregno, e que pues aquellos assi auian de escapar o non seer entregados a el para traer con ellos sus pleytesias para que fincassen suyos, que non fazia cuenta que le auia ayudado el prinçipe, mas tenia que espendiera sus thesoros de balde.

E el prinçipe fue sañudo estonçes por estas rrazones que el rrey don Pedro assi le dixo e rrespondiole en esta manera: 'Señor pariente, a mi paresçe que vos tenedes maneras mas fuertes agora para cobrar vuestro rregno que touistes quando teniades vuestro rregno en posesion e lo rregistes en tal guisa que lo ouistes a perder. E yo vos consejaria çesar de fazer estas muertes e de buscar manera de cobrar las voluntades de los señores e caualleros e fijos dalgo e çibdades e pueblos de vuestro rregno, e si de otra manera vos gouernades segund primero lo faziades, estades en grand peligro para perder el vuestro rregno e vuestra persona e llegarlo a tal estado que mi señor e mi padre el rrey de Ingla terra nin yo, avn que quisiessemos, non vos podriamos valer'. E assi pasaron aquel dia estas rrazones entre el rrey don Pedro e el prinçipe. E aquel dia domingo, otro dia despues de la batalla, estudieron alli en el canpo, e otro dia lunes partieron el rrey don Pedro e el prinçipe del lugar donde fue la batalla e tomaron su camino para Burgos. E el rrey don Pedro llego primero a Burgos e los de la çibdad lo rresçibieron muy bien e fue luego apoderado en la çibdad e en el castillo. E hordeno que el prinçipe posasse en el monesterio de Las Huelgas, que es vn monesterio de dueñas muy noble, çerca la çibdad, que fundaron los rreyes de Castilla, e el duc de

nature of the knights who were holding them that, for all the money in the world, even if the amount were 1,000 times more than the value of the prisoner, King Pedro could expect them not to sell them to him given that they believed him to be buying them in order to kill them. In this respect, the king should not persevere in his arguments, as it was not something that the prince could make happen. On the other hand, if among the prisoners there were knights that King Pedro had already condemned before this battle took place, he would have them handed over to him.

Then King Pedro told the prince that, if this was the case, his realm was now more totally lost to him than it had been previously, for all the men being held captive were those who had caused him to lose the kingdom; and that, since these men were to escape in this way or not to be handed over to him so that he could persuade them to transfer their loyalty to him, he did not reckon that the prince had lent him any assistance but rather that he had spent his treasure in vain.

The prince was then moved to anger by how King Pedro had spoken these words to him. 'My lord and kinsman,' he said, 'it seems to me that you have an even rougher approach now towards recovering your kingdom than you had when you held it in your possession and ruled it in such a way that you came to lose it. I would advise you to cease inflicting these deaths and to seek a way of winning the hearts of the lords, knights, noblemen, cities and towns of your kingdom; and, if you once again govern as you did previously, you are in serious danger of losing both your kingdom and your life and of bringing matters to a point such that neither my lord and father the king of England nor I, even if we wished to do so, would be able to help you.' Such were the words that were exchanged that day between King Pedro and the prince. That Sunday, which was the day after the battle, they remained there on the field and on Monday, the following day, King Pedro and the prince left the place where the battle had taken place and set off for Burgos. King Pedro was the first to arrive there and, warmly greeted by the people of the city, he quickly took possession of Burgos and its castle. He instructed that the prince was to be lodged in the renowned convent of las Huelgas which had been founded for ladies by the royal house of Castile and stood near to the

Alencastre su hermano del prinçipe, que posasse en el monesterio de Sant Pablo, çerca la çibdad. E por algunas posadas que auia fuera de la çibdad, posaron los suyos del prinçipe, e los otros por las comarcas enderredor de la çibdad fasta çinco leguas.

E el prinçipe llego despues que el rrey don Pedro llegara en Burgos, dos dias, e poso en aquel monesterio de Las Huelgas do el rrey don Pedro hordenara, e los suyos enderredor del en posadas que eran ý çerca dellos, en las aldeas mas allegadas a la çibdad. E el duc de Alencastre su hermano del prinçipe poso en el monesterio de Sant Pablo, que es de la horden de Santo Domingo, segund dicho auemos.

Otrossi fallo el rrey don Pedro en la çibdat de Burgos al arçobispo de Braga, que era françes e dezianle don Iohan Cardellaquo, e era letrado e grand sabidor, e pariente del conde de Armiñac, e estaua con el rrey don Enrrique, e prendiolo e leuolo preso al castillo de Alcala de Guadayrea e alli estudo en vn silo fasta que se vençio la pelea de Montiel. E despues lo saco de alli el rrey don Enrrique e fue despues arçobispo de Tolosa e patriarca.

Capitulo XXº. Commo fizieron el rrey don Pedro e el prinçipe de Gales en Burgos desque ý llegaron.

Desque alli llegaron en la dicha çibdat de Burgos, el rrey don Pedro e el prinçipe de Gales començaron a tratar sus fechos. E el prinçipe fizo dezir al rrey don Pedro por algunos caualleros del su consejo, que bien sabia en commo el llegara en la çibdat de Vayona con muy grand menester que auia de buscar acorro para cobrar sus rregnos de Castilla e de Leon, de los quales su henemigo le auia echado e desapoderado, e le rrequiriera e fiziera rrequerir que, por los grandes

city, and that the prince's brother, the duke of Lancaster, was to stay in the convent of San Pablo, also close to the city. The prince's retainers were allocated quarters outside the city, and the remainder throughout the surrounding area at a distance of up to five leagues.

The prince arrived in Burgos two days after King Pedro and was accommodated in the convent of las Huelgas as King Pedro had arranged, whilst his retainers lodged in the surrounding area, in the villages situated closest to the city. As we have already said, his brother the duke of Lancaster stayed in the convent of San Pablo, which belongs to the Order of Saint Dominic.

Moreover, in the city of Burgos King Pedro found the archbishop of Braga, who was a Frenchman by the name of Jean de Cardaillac, a scholar and man of great learning and a relative of the count of Armagnac. The archbishop was a supporter of King Enrique, and King Pedro seized him and took him off as a prisoner to the castle of Alcalá de Guadaíra, where he remained in a dungeon until the battle of Montiel was decided. King Enrique then freed him from this prison and he went on to become archbishop of Toulouse and a patriarch.

1367: CHAPTER XX

Concerning what King Pedro and the prince of Wales did on their arrival in Burgos.

On their arrival in the city of Burgos, King Pedro and the prince of Wales began their discussions. The prince communicated to King Pedro through some knights who were members of his council that he, the king, was well aware of how he had arrived in the city of Bayonne in desperate need of assistance in the recovery of his kingdoms of Castile and León, his enemy having driven him out and seized power. King Pedro had appealed to the prince and he had caused him in turn to appeal to the king of England on his behalf. He had requested, on account of the close family bonds which had always existed between the royal houses of Castile and England and likewise in view of the

debdos que las casas de Castilla e de Ingla terra ouieran sienpre en vno, otrossi por las ligas e confederaçiones que auian nueua mente fechas con el rrey de Ingla terra, su padre e su señor, e con el, que le ayudassen a tornar e cobrar su rregno, del qual le auian echado, e tomado sus thesoros todos e rrentas. Otrossi bien sabia commo el rrey de Ingla terra veyendo que le demandaua rrazon, que le plogo dello e que enbiara mandar al dicho prinçipe su fijo que viniesse con el con todas las conpañas e gentes suyas, las mas e mejores que pudiesse auer, e que el asi lo fiziera.

E que era verdat que por quanto por venir tanta gente e tan grandes omnes commo aquellos que vinieron con el, que el non los pudiera auer sin grandes despensas, fue hordenado a voluntad del rrey don Pedro que pagasse las gajes e estados e sueldo al prinçipe e a todos los otros señores e caualleros e gentes de armas e arqueros que en este viaje venieran en su ayuda. E commo quier que el rrey don Pedro pagara algunas de las dichas gajes e sueldo al prinçipe e a los que con el venieran antes que partiessen de la çibdat de Vayona, pero que fincaua el dicho prinçipe avn en grandes debdas a algunos señores e caualleros e omnes de armas de los que con el venieran, para les fazer pago assi de sus estados commo de sus gajes e sueldo que auian de auer, segund el tienpo que auian seruido e segund las abenençias que con ellos fiziera. E que el assi los auia asegurados e fecho sobre ello muy grandes rrecabdos assi de juramentos commo de obligaçiones e omenajes, con acuerdo e consejo e voluntad del rrey don Pedro, e que le rrogaua que fuesse su mesura e touiesse por bien de le dar rrecabdo, pues estaua en su rregno, de las dichas quantias que eran assi deuidas a los dichos señores e caualleros e omnes de armas por que ellos fuessen pagados e el prinçipe touiesse la verdat que con ellos pusiera asegurandolos que en las dichas pagas de gajes non auia falta.

Otrossi le fizo dezir que bien sabia el rrey don Pedro commo por su voluntad le prometiera, quando era en Vayona, que le daria grandes tierras en el rregno de Castilla assy de çibdades e villas commo castillos

treaties and alliances recently established with the prince's lord and father the king of England and with the prince himself, that they help him to go back and regain his realm. For he had been driven out from this kingdom and all his treasure and his income had been seized. King Pedro was also well aware of how the king of England, seeing that his requests were being rightfully made, had agreed to them and had sent a command to his son that he should accompany King Pedro with all his forces and all the troops at his disposal – as many and of as high a quality as he could assemble –, and the prince had done so.

The prince added that it was not possible to have the services of so large an army and men so distinguished as those that he had brought without incurring considerable expenses, and therefore it had been established, with King Pedro's agreement, that he would pay the allowances, maintenance and salary of the prince and of all the other lords, knights, men-at-arms and archers who had come to assist him in this campaign. Although King Pedro had paid some of those allowances and some of the salary to the prince and those accompanying him before their departure from the city of Bayonne, the prince was still left owing large sums to some of the lords, knights and men-at-arms who had come with him, to cover both their expenses and the allowances and salaries that were due to them, according to the period of time that they had served and to the agreements that he had made with them. The prince had given them assurances in this respect and also solemn guarantees, expressed in terms both of oaths and of formal pledges and binding covenants, with the agreement, counsel and approval of King Pedro. He now requested of the king, giving the matter his considered judgement, that he see fit to give him surety – since he was in his own kingdom – for those sums which were owed to those lords, knights and men-at-arms, in order that they might receive payment. In this way the prince would keep the promise that he had made to them when he assured them of the wages being paid without fail.

He also directed that King Pedro be reminded that he was aware of how, of his own free will, he had promised him – when he had been in Bayonne – that, if he recovered the kingdom of Castile with the prince's assistance, he would give him extensive possessions there, in the form of cities and towns and also of castles and incomes. It was to be pointed

e rrentas si el dicho rregno cobrasse e el le ayudasse a ello, e que el prinçipe ge lo agradesçiera mucho e dixera que lo non tomaria, ca sin ninguna cobdiçia el estaua presto de le ayudar por el debdo e linaje que auia con el. Otrossi por las ligas e confederaçiones que entre el rrey de Ingla terra, su padre e su señor, e el, con el rrey don Pedro, eran, por lo qual el rrey de Ingla terra su padre le enbiara espeçial mente mandar que le veniesse ayudar con todos sus valedores e amigos. E que el rrey don Pedro le dixera en la çibdad de Vayona que en todas las guisas del mundo era su voluntad que el prinçipe ouiesse alguna tierra en el rregno de Castilla, e que el estonçe quando viera que su voluntad era assi, que le dixo que le plazia de tomar lo que el le diesse e por bien touiesse, e pues assi era su voluntad que el non queria mas çibdades nin villas en Castilla saluo que le diese la tierra e señorio de Vizcaya e la villa de Castro de Vrdiales, e que pues estaua ya, loado fuesse Dios, en el su rregno e su enemigo vençido e desterrado e todas las çibdades e villas de sus rregnos eran ya a su obediençia, que le rrogaua e pidia que cunpliesse esto que le auia assi prometido de le dar, de lo qual tenia sus cartas e rrecabdos que le fiziera en Vayona antes que de alli partiesse.

Otrossi fizo dezir el prinçipe al rrey don Pedro que pues el estaua en su rregno, que non le cunplia tener muy grandes costas e despensas con el nin tener tantas conpañas, e que seyendo çierto destas cosas que le auia a conplir el rrey don Pedro, e auiendo rrecabdo dello, que le cunplia partir de Castilla e tornarsse para su tierra; lo vno por le non fazer costa al rrey don Pedro nin le dañar la tierra con tantas gentes; otrosi por que auia nueuas que los françeses començauan fazer guerra en el ducado de Gujana por manera de conpañias.

E el rrey don Pedro desque oyo estas rrazones que el prinçipe le fizo dezir, rrespondio muy bien a los que le dixeron las dichas rrazones e enbio con ellos a algunos del su consejo rrespondiendo al prinçipe que

out to him that the prince had said that he was very grateful for this but that he would not accept, for, without any question of desire for gain, he was ready to help him on account of their family links and the common lineage that they shared; and also because of the treaties and alliances which existed between his father and lord the king of England and himself and King Pedro; for it was as a result of this that his father the king of England had sent the prince the specific command that he come with all his supporters and allies to help King Pedro. Nevertheless, King Pedro had told him while in the city of Bayonne that, come what may, it was his wish that the prince should possess some land in the kingdom of Castile and that, when he saw that this really was the king's wish, he had then told him that he agreed to take whatever he gave him and judged to be appropriate, since this was what the king desired. The prince of Wales wished to receive no cities or towns in Castile except the lordship of Vizcaya and the town of Castro Urdiales.[13] However, since – thanks be to God! – King Pedro was now in his own kingdom, with his enemy defeated and driven out of the land and with all the cities and towns obeying his command, the prince now requested and entreated him to fulfil his promise to grant him this land: and in this respect he possessed written documents and formal undertakings that King Pedro had made to him in Bayonne before his departure.

The prince of Wales also had the point made to King Pedro that, since he was now installed in his own kingdom, it was not appropriate for the prince to sustain considerable costs and incur such great expense on his account or to keep such a large army; and that, once he was certain that King Pedro would fulfil his obligations towards him and once he had received surety, it was right for him to leave Castile and return to his own land. In part this was in order to avoid causing King Pedro expense and so as not to inflict damage on his land through the presence of so many troops, but it was also because there were reports that the French were beginning to wage war on the duchy of Guyenne by means of companies of mercenaries.[14]

On hearing the arguments that the prince had instructed his representatives to put to him, King Pedro gave them a firm response. He then sent some members of his council to accompany them back to the prince. He replied to him that he agreed to observe and adhere to

le plazia de tener e guardar todo lo sobre dicho, ca assi era verdat que pasara todo entre el e el dicho prinçipe. E los caualleros que el rrey don Pedro hordeno para tratar en este fecho estudieron por muchas vegadas con el prinçipe e por mandamiento del rrey don Pedro rrespondieron assi: primera mente a lo que le dezia el prinçipe que le fiziesse pagar el rrey don Pedro algunas quantias que fincauan por pagar assi a el commo a los señores e caualleros e omnes de armas e frecheros de sus estados e de sus gajes, de lo que ouieron de auer para venir con el a su rregno, por lo qual el dicho prinçipe era e fincaua a ellos obligado segund la hordenança que el fiziera en Vayona sobre esto. E a esto rrespondia el rrey don Pedro que bien sabia el prinçipe commo el estando en Vayona, que es çibdat del rrey de Ingla terra, su padre, e en su tierra, pagara de sus tesoros que conssigo leuara a algunos caualleros e frecheros asi de lo que auian de auer por sus estados commo por sus gajes, dello en dobles e en moneda de oro e dello en rreales e moneda de plata e de aljofar e piedras preçiosas, en lo qual el fuera muy agrauiado, ca la tomauan e rresçibian en las dichas pagas la moneda de oro e de plata a muy grand menospreçio. Otrossi las joyas de oro e de plata e de aljofar e piedras preçiosas, por la meatad menos de lo que valian, e que muchas vegadas gelo fizo saber al prinçipe e dezir por sus thesoreros que fazian las dichas pagas, e nunca pudiera auer rremedio en ello, e que en este fecho touiesse por bien de mandar a algunos de los suyos que se ayuntassen con los sus thesoreros e viessen los libros de las pagas que se fizieron e que moneda de oro e de plata e joyas se dieran por los dichos preçios, e si algund engaño o agrauios el rresçibiera, que lo el mandasse descontar; e de lo al que fincaua por pagar, lo que el cuydaua que seyendo todo esto puesto en buena cuenta, que le non deuia mas de lo que auia pagado; enpero si algo fincasse, que el estaua presto para lo pagar.

Otrossi rrespondio a lo segundo de lo que el prinçipe dizia, que el

Chronicle of King Pedro

all that had been set out, for it was indeed true that all of this had taken place between himself and the prince. The knights that King Pedro nominated to take part in these negotiations paid several visits to the prince and at the king's command gave the following reply: firstly, with regard to how the prince had said that King Pedro should ensure that settlement was made of certain debts which still remained to be paid, both to him and to the lords, knights, men-at-arms and archers for their maintenance and their pay, which they were due to receive in return for accompanying King Pedro to his kingdom; and with regard to the prince's argument that the king remained under a firm obligation to them in accordance with the terms that he had agreed in Bayonne, King Pedro's response to this was that the prince was well aware of how, when he was in Bayonne, a city which belonged to the prince's father the king of England and which was situated in his territory, he had made payment to some knights and archers out of the treasure that he had taken with him, in order to cover both the costs due to them and their pay, partly in *doblas* and in gold coin and partly in *reales*, silver coin, pearls and precious stones.[15] In this he had lost out badly, for in these payments the gold and silver coin was accepted and received but given an excessively low value. Likewise, the jewellery of gold, silver, pearl and precious stones was valued at half of its true worth: several times he had brought this to the prince's attention and had it pointed out by his treasurers who were making the payments, but he had never been able to have the matter put right. He asked the prince to see fit to command that some of his treasurers meet with those of King Pedro to inspect the books of accounts for the payments made and see what amount of gold and silver coin and jewels had been exchanged at the specified rates; and if the king had suffered any act of dishonesty or any wrong then the prince should instruct that it be discounted from the total owed. And of the remainder that was still to be paid, King Pedro believed that, once all of this had been put in good order, the total sum owing was no greater than what he had actually paid. However, if anything was outstanding, then he was ready to make the payment.

He also responded to the second point made by the prince: that of his own free will King Pedro had told him that he wished to hand over

rrey don Pedro de su voluntad le dixera que el le queria dar tierras en el señorio de Castilla e que le daria çibdades e villas e grandes tierras si las el quisiera auer, pero que el non lo quisiera, saluo con su afincamiento; que le dixera pues assi era su voluntad, que le diesse la tierra de Vizcaya e la villa de Castro de Vrdiales. A esto dixo el rrey don Pedro que assi era todo verdad e que a el plazia de gelo dar e de gela mandar luego entregar la dicha tierra de Vizcaya e la dicha villa de Castro de Vrdiales. Otrossi a lo que dizia el prinçipe que pues el rrey don Pedro estaua en su rregno e su henemigo era fuera del e todo el rregno estaua a su obediençia, que le non cunplia tener tantas gentes commo el tenia ally, lo vno por le non fazer costas tan grandes nin dañar la tierra, lo qual non se podia escusar por la grand conpaña que alli era.

Otrossi por las nueuas que el prinçipe auia cada dia, que algunos françeses en nonbre de conpañias le fazian guerra e enojo en el ducado de Gujana, e que por todo esto le cunplia partir assi de Castilla e yrse para su tierra, que le rrogaua que le pluguiesse dello. E a esto dixo el rrey don Pedro que le plazia e gelo agradesçia, pero si su voluntad fuesse de dexarle mill lanças a su despensa e a sus gajes e sueldo del dicho rrey don Pedro fasta que todo fuesse bien assossegado, que gelo agradesçeria.

E desque el prinçipe de Gales ouo oydo todas las rrazones de la rrespuesta que el rrey don Pedro le enbiaua sobre las rrazones que le el fizo dezir por sus mensageros, rrespondio a la primera rrazon: que el rrey dizia lo que su merçed era e lo que por bien tenia, que quanto atañia a las pagas que el fizo en Vayona a el e a los señores e cauallleros e omnes de armas e frecheros que con el venian, ninguno non le auia culpa, ca los sus thesoreros del rrey don Pedro fizieron las pagas a su voluntad, assi de las monedas de oro e de plata commo de las joyas de aljofar e piedras presçiosas. E avn sobre ello los señores e cauallleros e omnes de armas dizian que fueran en ello mucho agrauiados, ca ellos

to him lands which were under Castilian lordship and that he would give him cities, towns and extensive estates if he wished to have them. The prince asserted that he had not wished to accept this offer, except when he had been urged to do so by King Pedro, at which point he had asked him – since this was what he wished – to give him the territory of Vizcaya and the town of Castro Urdiales. King Pedro replied that this was indeed all true and that he agreed to give the prince the said territory of Vizcaya and the town of Castro Urdiales and to instruct them to be handed over immediately. In addition, he replied to what the prince had said to him about how, now that he was installed in his own kingdom, his enemy had been driven out of it and the whole realm was now obeying his command, it was not appropriate for the prince to keep as many troops there as he had at present, partly so as not to cause the king such great expense or inflict such damage on his territory, which was inevitable on account of the large army which was being kept there.

This was also in view of the reports being received by the prince each day that French troops under the name of mercenary companies were raiding and causing him trouble in the duchy of Guyenne: for all of these reasons it was right for him to leave Castile and return to his own territory, and he was asking King Pedro to give his agreement. In response King Pedro said that he did indeed agree, but he requested that the prince see fit to leave him 1,000 mounted troops, which he would pay for at his own expense, taking responsibility for their pay and their allowances until all was well settled. He would be grateful if this were done.

Once the prince of Wales had listened to all the points made by King Pedro in response to those that he had put to him through his intermediaries, he gave his reply to the first item. He said that in his response the king had spoken according to his will and said what he considered right. However, with regard to everything concerning the payments made in Bayonne to the prince himself and to the lords, knights, men-at-arms and archers accompanying him, none of them were at fault in their dealings with King Pedro as his treasurers had made their payments freely, both those in gold and silver coin and those made with jewellery containing pearls and precious stones. Moreover, on this

auian menester moneda llana para seer bien pagados e conplir lo que auian menester, e les daua joyas e aljofar e piedras, que eran cosas que les non cunplian, ca les fuera mejor tomar monedas que aljofar para conprar armas e cauallos e otras cosas que auian menester, ca la joyas vendian a menos presçio e dellas tenian avn que non se podian aprouechar dellas. Otrossy que bien sabia el rrey don Pedro que commo quier que con el venieran tantas buenas conpañas, non venieran por aquellas pagas que les fizo el, saluo por el gran afincamiento e trabajo que el prinçipe pusiera en los fazer contentos e pagados, e por seer algunos amigos del e otros, vasallos del rrey de Ingla terra, su padre, e por le fazer placer. E quanto en esto, si su merçed era, non deuia sola mente fazer memoria dello, ca fuesse bien çierto que las gentes de armas perdieron en ello asaz en tomar las dichas joyas en pago e que en lo que fincaua que ellos auian de auer de sus pagas, touiesse por bien de fazer manera commo fuessen pagados e contentos.

Otrossi a lo que dizia el rrey don Pedro que le daria a Vizcaya e a Castro de Vrdiales segund gelo auia prometido, que gelo agradesçia mucho e que pidia e rrogaua que le mandasse dar luego sus cartas e sus rrecabdos commo gelo fiziessen luego entregar. Otrossi a lo que dizia que si su voluntad era de partir de Castilla, que le dexasse mill lanças a sus despensa e a sus gajes fasta que todo el rregno fuesse sosegado, a esto le rrespondio el prinçipe que le plazia de fazer todo lo que el mandasse e viesse que era su prouecho, mas que esto que pidia que fincassen las gentes de armas en Castilla, non le rrespondia luego de presente, ca las gentes de armas que en Castilla ouiessen a quedar con el, queria primero veer commo los omnes de armas eran pagados de lo que auian seruido.

Sobre estas cosas pasaron en Burgos muchas muchos tratos e muchas rrazones entre el rrey don Pedro e el prinçipe de Gales, pero despues acordaron que se fiziessen las cuentas de las gentes que con

point the lords, knights and men-at-arms argued that they had lost out heavily, for they needed money in cash in order to be properly paid and in order to meet their needs, whilst the prince was giving them jewellery with pearls and gems, which were not appropriate: it would have been better for them to receive coins than pearls in order to buy arms and horses and their other requirements, for they sold the jewels below their true value and they still had some of them in their possession of which they could not make use. The prince also argued that, as King Pedro was well aware, although an army of such size and quality had accompanied him, the troops had not come on account of the payment made to them by the king but rather through the hard work and effort which the prince had put into leaving them satisfied and content. Moreover, there were some who had come because of their friendship with him, and others, as vassals of his father the king of England, in order to please him. In view of this, if such was his will, King Pedro should not only bear this fact in mind – for he should be in no doubt that the soldiers had lost a good deal of money by accepting the jewels in payment – but, with regard to the outstanding part of what was due to them, he too should see fit to act in such a way as to leave them content and satisfied.

In addition the prince gave a reply to King Pedro's statement that he would give him Vizcaya and Castro Urdiales as he had promised, expressing his gratitude and earnestly requesting him to give instructions for him to receive without delay the letter of authorization together with surety for the rapid transfer of ownership. And also in response to King Pedro's request that, if it was his wish to leave Castile, he should leave him – until order was restored throughout the kingdom – 1,000 mounted troops, for which he would pay expenses and wages, the prince replied that he agreed to do all that the king commanded and considered to be to his benefit; but he could not give an immediate reply to this request with regard to troops remaining with him in Castile, as first he wished to see how the men-at-arms received payment for the service that they had given.

A great deal of negotiation and discussion on these matters took place in Burgos between King Pedro and the prince of Wales, but finally they agreed that the accounts were to be drawn up for the payment already received by the troops who had come with King

el rrey don Pedro vinieran e lo que ouieran de pagas e lo que les fincaua de pagar, que el rrey don Pedro ge lo pagasse o el prinçipe les asegurasse por ello a los que las tales pagas auian de auer, faziendo el rrey don Pedro rrecabdo dello al prinçipe en guisa que fuesse contento. Otrossi dixo el prinçipe al rrey don Pedro que para el seer seguro que cobraria lo que pagasse a las gentes de armas, que el rrey don Pedro le diesse veynte castillos de su rregno quales el prinçipe quisiesse e nonbrasse en arrehenes por las dichas pagas conplir. E el rrey don Pedro dixo que le plazia de le fazer entregar a Vizcaya e a Castro de Vrdiales al prinçipe segund lo auia prometido. Otrossi dixo que las mill lanças non le cunplia que fincassen en el rregno nin las queria. Otrossi en rrazon de los veynte castillos que el prinçipe demandaua en arrehenes de las dichas pagas, rrespondio el rrey don Pedro que a esto, de presente, non dizia mas fasta que viesse que debdas fincauan por pagar. E esto acordado e asossegado el prinçipe mando a mossen Iohan Chandos su conde estable e a los sus mariscales e contadores que supiessen por todas las conpañas que con el vinieran en Castilla, que tienpo auian seruido e quanto les era pagado de lo que deuian auer, assi por sus estados commo por sus gajes e por quanto les era deuido. E mossen Iohan Chandos conde estable e los mariscales e contadores del prinçipe lo fizieron e mandaron a los thesoreros e contadores que fiziessen dello cuenta, los quales assi lo fizieron e monto todo muy grand quantia e de lo que dende se sopo, fizieron lo saber al prinçipe su señor.

E el prinçipe demandaua toda via los veynte castillos en arrehenes por aquellas quantias que fallaua que le deuia e que estos castillos fuessen quales el nonbraria e fincassen en arrehenes por lo que era tenudo el rrey don Pedro de pagar a los señores e caualleros e omnes de armas e frecheros que venieran en aquella caualgada en su seruiçio.

Otrossi mossen Iohan Chandos demandaua al rrey don Pedro que le fiziesse entregar la çibdad de Soria, la qual le auia prometido por cartas publicas de gela dar quando estaua en Vayona.

E el rrey don Pedro a lo que el prinçipe demandaua de los veynte castillos por arrehenes de la deuda que era tenudo a la gente de armas de gajes, e dixo que en ninguna manera del mundo non los pudia

Pedro and for what remained to be paid to them, and that King Pedro should make payment to them or the prince should give assurances to those due to be paid, with King Pedro providing the prince with such guarantees as would leave him satisfied. The prince also told King Pedro that, in order for him to be certain of being reimbursed the sum that he had paid to the men-at-arms, the king should hand over to him 20 castles in his kingdom, which the prince was to specify and name, as surety for the settlement of the payments. King Pedro stated that he agreed to have Vizcaya and Castro Urdiales handed over to the prince, as he had promised. He also said that he had no need for the 1,000 mounted troops to remain in the kingdom, nor did he desire them. Moreover, with regard to the 20 castles which the prince was requesting as surety for the payments, King Pedro's response was that he would say no more at present until he saw what debts remained to be settled. Then, once this had been agreed and settled, the prince sent his constable Sir John Chandos and his marshals and stewards round all the bodies of troops that had come with him to Castile, to find out what their period of service had been and how much they had been paid for their living expenses and their wages and all that was due to them. The constable John Chandos and the prince's marshals and stewards acted in accordance with the prince's instructions and the treasurers and stewards were ordered to draw up accounts. They did so: the money owing added up to a large sum and the information that had been collected was passed on to their lord the prince.

The prince was still asking for the 20 castles as surety for the amounts that he discovered to be owed to him by the king. He demanded that these castles be ones that he specified and that they should serve as a guarantee for what King Pedro was bound to pay to the lords, knights, men-at-arms and archers who had taken part in this campaign in his service.

In addition, Sir John Chandos was demanding that King Pedro have the city of Soria handed over to him, given that the king had made this promise to him in a letter patent when he was in Bayonne.

With regard to the prince's demand for the 20 castles as surety for the amount which he was bound to pay to the troops in wages, King Pedro said that there was no way in the world that he could give him

dar a los dichos castillos, ca si lo fiziese, todos los del rregno ternian que queria dar la tierra a otras gentes estrañas e por ventura que se leuantarian contra el. Otrossy a lo que dizia de la çibdat de Soria en la dar a mossen Iohan Chandos conde estable dixo que le plazia, e sobre todo esto ouo muchos debates.

E el prinçipe bien entendia que el rrey don Pedro dizia buena rrazon de non poder entregar los veynte castillos que le demandaua; pero dizia que queria saber que rrecabdo podria auer por que aquellas conpañas fuessen pagadas de lo que auian de auer e el fuesse quito de las obligaçiones que les fiziera por esta rrazon. E el rrey don Pedro le fizo dezir que el luego enbiaua por todo su rregno sus cartas e omnes de rrecabdo a demandar ayuda al rregno todo para pagar estas debdas atales e luego que el pudiesse auer la moneda, luego gela daria. Otrossi por lo al que fincasse, que el prinçipe sabia bien que el tenia en la çibdat de Vayona tres fijas suyas, las infantas doña Beatriz e doña Costança e doña Ysabel, e que las touiesse en arrehenes fasta que el cunpliesse todo lo que el deuia a el e a aquellas conpañas en este caso de las pagas.

E desque vio el prinçipe que el rrey don Pedro non pudia al fazer, dixole que le plazia e fizieron luego desto sus rrecabdos en esta manera: que el rrey don Pedro fasta vn dia çierto diesse al prinçipe la meatad de la paga en dineros. Otrossi que por la otra meatad, que las tres infantas sus fijas, doña Beatriz e doña Costanza e doña Ysabel, que estauan en Vayona, las touiesse el prinçipe en arrehenes fasta que fuesse pagado.

Otrossi diole el rrey al prinçipe sus cartas que le entregassen la tierra de Vizcaya e la villa de Castro de Urdiales. E enbio luego el prinçipe para las rresçibir e tomar la posession de la tierra de Vizcaya e de la villa de Castro de Urdiales a vn su cauallero que dizian el señor de Poyana e vn letrado su mensagero que dizian el jugue de Burdeu. E el rrey don Pedro enbio por su parte para gela entregar a don Ferrand Perez de Ayala e que estudiesse con los de la tierra de Vizcaya; enpero

those castles, for, if he were to do so, all the people of his kingdom would believe that he intended to give territory to other foreigners and they might rise up against him. He also replied to what the prince said about handing over the city of Soria to the constable John Chandos, stating that he agreed to do so. There was a great deal of discussion over all these matters.

The prince understood clearly that King Pedro was right when he said that he could not hand over the 20 castles for which he had asked him. However, he said that he wanted to know what guarantee he could have that the members of those companies would be paid what was due to them and also that he, the prince, would receive payment to cover all his commitments to them in this respect. King Pedro communicated to him that he was, without delay, sending letters and dispatching his agents throughout his realm to ask all the people of the kingdom to contribute to the payment of debts of such a size; and that as soon as he could obtain the money he would pay it over to the prince. Moreover, with regard to the outstanding amount, the prince was well aware that he was holding in the city of Bayonne three daughters of King Pedro – princesses Doña Beatriz, Doña Constanza and Doña Isabel – and he should continue to hold them as hostages until the king had met all his obligations to him and to the companies in this matter of the payments.

Once the prince realized that there was no more that King Pedro could do, he told him that he was in agreement and they lost no time in drawing up the following terms: by a specified date, King Pedro was to make payment in cash to the prince of half of the amount due, whilst the prince was to hold his daughters the princesses – Doña Beatriz, Doña Constanza and Doña Isabel – who were in Bayonne, as a guarantee until the other half was paid.

The king also gave the prince his letters of authorization for the territory of Vizcaya and the town of Castro Urdiales to be handed over to him; and the prince immediately sent two men to receive and take possession of them: a knight in his service called the lord of Poyanne and a lawyer whose title was the lord justice of Bordeaux, acting on his behalf. For his part, King Pedro sent Don Fernán Pérez de Ayala to be responsible for the transfer, with instructions for him to remain with the people of the territory of Vizcaya. However, it was not the

non era voluntad del rrey de lo conplir assy nin de dar la dicha tierra al prinçipe, e assi se fizo que el prinçipe non ouo la dicha tierra por quanto los de la dicha tierra sabian que non plazia al rrey don Pedro que fuesse aquella tierra del prinçipe. E avn dizian los de Vizcaya e de Castro de Urdiales que el rrey don Pedro enbiaua sus cartas a las villas e castillos de Vizcaya sobre esta rrazon: que en ninguna manera non se diesse al prinçipe. E maguera los enbaxadores suso dichos fueron a Vizcaya nunca pudieron lybrar con los de la tierra que les entregassen la possesion, e fizieronlo saber asi al prinçipe.

Otrossi a lo que mossen Iohan Chandos conde estable del prinçipe demandaua que la çibdat de Soria le fuesse entregada, dixo el rrey que le plazia e mandole dar sus cartas para que gela entregassen; pero vn su chançeller del rrey don Pedro, que dizian Matheos Ferrandez de Caçeres, pidiole por chançelleria, por la carta, diez mill doblas e el conde estable non le quiso tomar la dicha carta teniendo que non le pidian chançelleria assy tan grande saluo por non le dar la dicha çibdat de Soria.

Capitulo XXI°. Commo el rrey don Pedro e el prinçipe de Gales fizieron sus juramentos en la yglesia de Santa Maria de Burgos.

Assy pasaron estas cosas commo auedes oydo, pero el prinçipe, por dar logar que el rrey don Pedro non se touiesse de mal contento del, dixo que le plazia atender algunos dias en Castilla fasta que el touiesse mejor assosegado el rregno para librar mejor estas cosas, que por auentura non osaua el rrey don Pedro, por rresçelo de los del rregno, mandar las conplir e entregar las tierras que le mandara, e despues que el touiesse mas afirmado su fecho e estouiesse mas asossegado en el

king's intention to carry this through or to hand the territory over to the prince; and so it was brought about that the prince did not in fact take possession of Vizcaya, as its people were aware that King Pedro was not in agreement with it falling into his hands. The people of Vizcaya and Castro Urdiales even claimed that King Pedro wrote to the towns and castles of the region saying that in no way should they be handed over to the prince. Moreover, although the aforementioned ambassadors went to Vizcaya, they were never able to complete the arrangements with the people of the territory for the transfer of possession, and they informed the prince of this.

In addition, with regard to the demand made by the prince's constable Sir John Chandos that the city of Soria be handed over to him, the king expressed his agreement and intructed that Sir John be given a letter of authorization for this to happen. However, one of the king's chancellors, called Matheos Fernández de Cáceres, asked him to pay chancery fees of 10,000 *doblas* in return for the letter. The constable was not willing to accept it, as he considered that they were only charging him such a high fee in order to avoid handing over the city of Soria.

1367: CHAPTER XXI

How King Pedro and the prince of Wales swore their oaths in the church of Santa María in Burgos.

These events took place just as you have heard, but, in order to avoid King Pedro feeling dissatisfied with his conduct, the prince declared that he would agree to remain in Castile for a few days until the king had his realm more fully under control, in order that he could carry out all of these undertakings more effectively. The prince did this because he considered that perhaps King Pedro, fearful of the people of his kingdom, would not dare to fulfil what he had agreed and hand over the territories that he had allotted to him. He hoped that once the king's position had been strengthened and he was more settled in the

señorio del rregno, que le pagaria las quantias que le deuia. Otrossi que le faria entregar a Vizcaya e Castro de Urdiales segund gelo auia prometido, e eso mesmo a mossen Iohan Chandos a Soria, e para esto que el rrey le fiziesse juramento de conplir todo lo que les era prometido. E el rrey don Pedro dixo que le plazia. E acordaron commo este juramento se fiziese e hordenaron que el prinçipe, que posaua en el monesterio de Las Huelgas, veniesse a la yglesia de Santa Maria la mayor de la çibdat de Burgos e el rrey viniesse alli e publica mente viessen todas las escrituras entre ellos hordenadas e se jurassen en el altar mayor de la dicha iglesia sobre la cruz e los Santos Euangelios.

E el prinçipe por seer mas seguro, demando que le diesen vna puerta de la dicha çibdat en que ouiesse vna torre, para do el pusiesse conpaña de armas que estudiessen ally en guarda de la puerta en quanto el estudiesse en la çibdat. E el rrey don Pedro le mando dar vna puerta con su torre en vna plaça que dizen Conparada. E el prinçipe mando poner en la torre omnes de armas e frecheros. E yuso a la puerta en vna grand plaça que auia contra dentro de la çibdat, puso el prinçipe mill omnes de armas e partida de frecheros. E fuera de la çibdat en un monesterio do el prinçipe posaua que dizian las Huelgas, enderredor del dicho monesterio, estauan las mas conpañas que venieron con el, armadas.

E el prinçipe entro dentro en la çibdat por la puerta que auemos dicho que le dieran, do tenia sus omnes de armas e frecheros en guarda. E el prinçipe fuesse para la yglesia de Santa Maria e con el yuan quinientos omnes de armas e muchos de los capitanes que con el eran. E yuan todos a pie enderredor del prinçipe, que yua en vn coser, pero non armado, e yua ý con el, el duc de Alencastre, su hermano, en otro cauallo. E el rrey don Pedro llego alli a aquella iglesia de Santa Maria la mayor, do era hordenado que se ayuntassen e se auia de fazer la jura de lo que era e fuesse tratado e afirmado.

E desque entro el rrey don Pedro en la iglesia, seyendo presentes todos los mas capitanes, leyeron las escrituras publica mente en guisa que todos podian bien oyr. E era commo el rrey don Pedro era tenudo

lordship of his kingdom he would pay him the sums that he owed; and that he would also see that Vizcaya and Castro Urdiales were handed over as he had promised, and likewise that Soria was given to Sir John Chandos. He asked the king to swear an oath undertaking to fulfil all his promises to them, and King Pedro said that he was willing to do so. They agreed on how this oath was to be sworn, and they arranged that the prince, who was staying in the convent of las Huelgas, was to come to the church of Santa María la Mayor in the city of Burgos, and that the king was to do likewise. They were to review publicly all the agreements drawn up between them and their oaths were to be sworn on the church's high altar, on the cross and on the Holy Gospels.

In order to enjoy greater security, the prince asked to be given charge of a city gate where there was a tower in which he could install a company of troops to guard the gateway during the time that he spent in the city. King Pedro instructed that the prince be given a gateway with a tower which stood in a square called the Plaza de la Comparada, and the prince ordered men-at-arms and archers to be posted in the tower. Moreover, below the gateway, in a large square which faced into the city he stationed 1,000 men-at-arms and a substantial body of archers; and outside the city around the convent of las Huelgas, where the prince was lodged, most of the troops who were accompanying him were drawn up in full armour.

The prince entered the city through the gateway which, as we have already mentioned, had been allocated to him and where he had posted his men-at-arms and his archers to stand guard. The prince went to the church of Santa María, accompanied by 500 men-at-arms and many of the commanders of the companies who were with him. They were all on foot surrounding the prince, who was mounted on a courser but not in full armour, and alongside him rode his brother the duke of Lancaster. Then King Pedro arrived at the church of Santa María la Mayor, where it had been arranged that they would meet and the oath was to be sworn on what had been, and what was to be, agreed and confirmed.

Once King Pedro had entered the church, and in the presence of most of the commanders, the text of the formal agreement was read aloud in such a way that all those present could hear clearly. It set out how King Pedro was legally bound to pay the prince of Wales

al prinçipe de Gales e a çiertos señores e caualleros capitanes que ally eran, de çierta suma e quantia de moneda, la qual deuia por gajes e estados e sueldo que ellos auian de auer del por çierto tienpo que le auian seruido en esta venida e caualgada que fizieron en España e a su rregno. E por quanto de presente non podia auer la dicha suma o quantia para les pagar, que el se obligaba de pagar la meytad de la dicha quantia de aquel dia que alli eran ayuntados fasta quatro meses dentro en Castilla, al prinçipe de Gales o a los sus thesoreros, en los quales quatro meses ellos auian de atender en el rregno de Castilla. Otrossi se contauan sus gajes destos quatro meses en la cuenta sobre dicha, e la otra meatad de la dicha suma que gela daria fasta vn año en Vayona de Ingla terra. E por aquella suma e quantia que fincaua en Vayona de pagar, que el prinçipe touiesse en tanto en prendas e en arrehenes, tres fijas suyas, las quales eran doña Beatriz e doña Costança e doña Ysabel, que llamauan las Infantas. Otrossi juro aquel dia el rrey Pedro que faria entregar la tierra e señorio de Vizcaya al prinçipe, e la villa de Castro de Urdiales, segund gelo auia prometido. Otrosi que faria entregar la çibdat de Soria a mossen Iohan Chandos conde estable de Gujana, segund lo tenia prometido. E este juramento fecho, el rrey fue para su palaçio e el prinçipe se fue para el monesterio de Las Huelgas do el posaua.

Capitulo XXIIº. Commo el rrey don Pedro enbio sus cartas a vn moro de Granada, que era vn grand sabidor, commo el auie vençido e commo el era en Castilla, e demandauale consejo de algunas cosas.

Asi fue que el rrey don Pedro despues que la pelea de Najara fue vençida, enbio sus cartas a vn moro de Granada de quien el fiaua e era su amigo, e era grand sabidor e grand filosofo e consegero del

and certain lords and commanders there present a specified sum, an amount of money which he owed in allowances, expenses and salary as payment for a determined period of time during which they had served him in the course of this campaign and of this foray into Spain and into his kingdom. However, since at the present time he could not raise the said sum or amount with which to pay them, the king undertook to pay half of the amount in question to the prince of Wales or his treasurers and to do this in Castile within four months of this day on which they were all assembled there. During these four months they were to wait in the kingdom of Castile, and their pay for this time was likewise to be included in the said account. King Pedro was then to pay the other half of the amount within a year in the English city of Bayonne, and to cover that amount of money which remained to be paid in Bayonne, it was agreed that the prince was to hold as surety and as a guarantee the three daughters of the king: Doña Beatriz, Doña Constanza and Doña Isabel, known as the princesses. That day, King Pedro also swore that he would see that the territory and lordship of Vizcaya and also the town of Castro Urdiales were handed over to the prince, as he had promised him; and he also undertook to have the city of Soria placed in the possession of Sir John Chandos, constable of Guyenne, as he had promised to do. Then, once this oath had been sworn, the king returned to his royal apartments and the prince went back to the convent of las Huelgas where he was staying.

1367: CHAPTER XXII

How King Pedro wrote to a Moor in Granada, who was a man of great wisdom, about how he had been victorious and was in Castile, and asking him for advice about certain matters.

So it was that King Pedro, after his victory in the battle of Nájera, wrote to a Moor in Granada, his friend in whom he trusted and who was a man of great wisdom, a great philosopher and a counsellor of

rrey de Granada, el qual auia nonbre Benahatin, en que le fizo saber commo auia vençido en pelea a sus henemigos e commo estaua ya en su rregno muy aconpañado de muchas gentes nobles e estrañas que le vinieron ayudar. E el moro despues que rresçibio las cartas del rrey, enbiole rrespuesta en castigos çiertos e buenos, de la qual el traslado es este:

'Las graçias sean dadas a Dios, Criador de todo. A vos el grand rrey publicado e noble, allegue vos Dios a la tierra del mundo finable e a la ventura del mundo durable. E acuerde vos commo El sea seruido de vos e la salud sea sobre vos. Sabed que yo so en parte del Andalozia faziendo saber a las gentes el vuestro poder e el poder del que en vuestro nonbre es entitulado e amo, sabelo Dios, aderesçar el vuestro derecho segund el mi pequeño poder, que non podria segund el vuestro alto estado, que si vos de tal commo yo demandades que cunpla los vuestros conplimientos commo atal commo a vos pertenesçe, seria a mi muy graue sin alguna dubda, de mas que non so mio nin puedo auer apartamiento para estudiar, e muchos otros negoçios que me enbargan. E sobre todo esto el saber del omne tal commo yo, que es pobre para alcançar cosa conplida, e digo en conparaçion que el que alcanzo vna de las cosas del mundo en conplida manera, es fallesçido en otras muchas. Otrossi en su casa omne con su conpaña non alcança lo que querria, mas en las cosas del mundo, que lo formo Dios en diuersas maneras e sentençio en el sus juizios commo la su merçed fue, e otras cosas que enbargan al omne de alcançar su voluntad. E ssy cataredes con derecho mis rrazones e me rresçibieredes mis escusas, con ello me alegrare. E pido a Dios que vos alegre en todas cosas que le a El plazen assi del dicho commo del fecho.

A lo que me demandastes de mi, que vos faga saber de lo que me paresçe en los vuestros grandes fechos e fieles, rrey alto, sabed que los males son en caso semejante de las melezinas amargas e pesadas para el que las beue, e son aborridas del, enpero el que las puede

the king of Granada. This man was called Benahatin, and in his letter King Pedro told him how he had defeated his enemies in battle and was now in his kingdom in the company of a large number of noble foreign troops who had come to give him assistance.[16] The Moor, after receiving the king's letter, sent him a reply expressing good and sound advice, the translation of which is as follows:

'May God, the creator of all things, be praised. And may God guide you, great, illustrious and noble king, to material wealth in the ephemeral world and the blessings of the enduring world. May He direct you just as He is served by you and may you be granted health. I want you to know that I am in a region of Andalusia proclaiming your power and that of the man who in your name bears the title of ruler, and, as God knows, it gives me great pleasure to guide your path as best my limited ability permits.[17] However, I could not do this in the way in which your high standing merits, for if you ask a man such as myself to fulfil what you require of me in a manner which befits you, it will without any doubt prove a very difficult task, all the more so as my time is not my own, I do not have the opportunity to be free to study, and many other affairs stand in my way. Over and above all of this, the wit of a man such as myself is too feeble to achieve anything of such consequence. I can say in comparison that a man who has fully achieved one thing in the world falls short in many others. Also if a man in his own household with his own family cannot achieve what he would have wished, how much more is this the case in the affairs of the world, created by God in a variety of forms and in which He has passed his judgements according to His will, and where there are other considerations which prevent a man from achieving his desires? So, if you look fairly on my words and accept my pleas, this will give me pleasure. I ask of God that He grants you happiness in all things that are pleasing to Him, both in word and in deed.

In reponse to your request that I give you my opinion on your great and faithful deeds, illustrious king: you should be aware that misfortunes bear a similarity to medicines which are bitter and unpleasant for the person taking them, who strongly dislikes them; for, in spite of this, someone who endures and puts up with them and

sofrir e atender e penar el su mal sabor esta a esperança del bien e de la salud; pero non sufren las tales amarguras saluo aquellos que son pertenesçientes de auer lo que por las sofrir se alcança, e yo me adelante, que vos fize sabidor de algunas cosas atales e vistes las sus verdades, e commo quier que a las vuestras puertas aya buenos e sabios a quien non sean encubiertos los tales fechos. Pero cada vno despiende de lo que tiene segund la parte que Dios le dio, e el vuestro conplimiento encubre las menguas e non culpara por cosa de lo que por culpa meresçe, e lo que yo fablare de lo de vuestra fazienda ençierrasse en dos casos: el vn caso es en lo que tañe en vuestra fazienda e en el semejante vuestro e del vuestro titulo, que es el vuestro enemigo, e el segundo caso es en lo que atañe a los fechos de la gente estraña que venieron con vos de otra tierra.

E digo en el primero caso que atañe a vuestra fazienda: bien sabedes que los christianos que fizieron contra vos vergoñosa cosa, que sea suma obra de dezir e fazer en guisa que non se pueda lauar sy non despues de grand tienpo, e non la ouieron de fazer por mengua de vuestra fidalguia nin por vos non seer pertenesçiente a señorio rreal; mas ocasion dello fueron cosas que pasaron, que vos sabedes, fasta que se fizo lo que vistes. E agora que Dios vos acorrio e vos torno a ellos, se catan e se veen por pecadores, non a manera de los penitençiar, ca non pueden seer conosçidos los del vuestro estado rreal syn ellos, pues, señor, obrad contra ellos al rreues de las maneras porque vos aborresçieron, ca mucho mas breue les es agora arredrarse de vos que la primera vez. E semejante es desto quien quiso alçar vna cosa pesada e quebrose su braço, e guaresçio e torno a prouar de alçar otra vez ante que fuesse bien asoldada la quebradura e mucho mas aparejada estaua de se quebrar que ante, pues dad a las cosas sus pertenençias e comunal guisa e asossegat los coraçones espantados de vos, e dad a gostar a las gentes pan de paz e de sossiego e apoderad los e ensseñoread los en sus algos e en sus villas e en sus fijos que assaz paso por ellos premias e afincamientos en cosas que non ouistes dello sy non conplir voluntad.

Chronicle of King Pedro

who copes with their bad taste has a hope of achieving recovery and health. On the other hand, the only people able to tolerate such bitter medicines are those who are really bent on achieving the goal which enduring them makes possible. I have ventured to make you aware of some such matters and you have seen the truth of them. Although at your own door there are good and wise men to whom such affairs as these are no mystery, each person makes use of what he has according to what was allotted to him by God, and your courtesy conceals shortcomings and will not attribute blame where it is due. What I will say about your affairs is summed up in two points: one is with regard to your way of governing and to your rival for your position and your title – and this man is your enemy – and the second concerns the actions of the foreigners who have come with you from abroad.

With regard to the first point, which concerns the way in which you govern: you are well aware that the Christians acted so shamefully towards you – amounting to actions of word and deed of a kind that can only be erased after a very long time – and that they did not do so through any lack of noble origins on your part or because you did not belong to the royal line. Rather, this was the result of a series of developments which, as you know well, culminated in the events that you witnessed. Now that God had come to your aid and returned you to them, they look into their hearts and see themselves as sinners. However this does not mean that they should have penance imposed on them, for your royal standing cannot be recognised without them. So, my lord, act towards them in a manner which is contrary to that which made them hate you, for it would now take much less to make them reject you than it did the first time. This is similar to the case of a person who, having broken his arm by trying to lift a heavy object and having recovered, again tried to lift the object before the break was properly mended: the arm was now much more likely to break than before. So give allowance where due and, acting with moderation, bring calm to the hearts which you have filled with terror, allowing the people to taste the bread of peace and tranquillity. Offer them security and authority over their possessions, their towns and their children, since for them they endured no small trials and hardships in matters in which you did nothing other than to pursue your own desires. Ensure that all the things

E todas las cosas por que vos aborresçieron sean trocadas con las sus contrallas e mostradles el arrepentimiento de todo lo pasado e honrrad a los grandes e guardad vos de las sangres e de los algos de vuestros subditos, sy non con derecho e justiçia, e alegrad el rrostro e abrid la mano e cobraredes la bien querençia.

E non auantagedes a los que non touieron con vos en vuestros menesteres sobre los que touieron con vos a la dicha sazon, por que la enbidia non aya logar. E dad los ofizios a los que les pertenesçen, puesto que los non querades bien, e non los dedes a los que non son pertenesçientes a ello, puesto que los bien querades, e bien podedes fazer otros bienes a los que bien queredes. E guardat vos de los honrrados que enfanbreastes e de los de pequeño estado que fartastes, e rreparad en el rregno lo que se estruyo por que oluiden las gentes los yerros e quiten de sus coraçones lo que vos ensañaron e afincaron, e abenid vos con vuestros comarcanos en tal sazon commo agora estades, ca las llagas son avn frescas e con esto faredes çerca entre vos e vuestros henemigos syn costa. E guardad vuestros algos en lo que cunple e criarsse han vuestras gentes: que las aues sossiegan e se fartan con lo poco en el tienpo del inuierno, e el vuestro henemigo es biuo e el curso del mundo non es durable e non sabedes que acaesçera. E Castilla es ya follada e despresçiada de gentes estrañas e muchos de los grandes de vuestro rregno son finados en las guerras e los algos fallesçidos. E tal fazienda menester ha grand rremedio, e non otro rremedio saluo el conorte e el sossiego e cobrir lo que se decubrio de la vergueña. E dixo vn sabidor consejando al honrrado que oluide los yerros que le son fechos. E dixo otro sabidor: 'Si ouiesse entre mi e las gentes un cabello, non se cortaria: quando ellos trauasen, yo afloxaria, e quando ellos afloxassen, yo trauaria.' E rresçibid sienpre los desculpamientos de los vuestros, puesto que sepades que son mentirosos, e es mejor que descobrir las verdades. E sienpre agradesçed a los que bien fazen, puesto que a vos non faze menester, e non se escusaran de seruir vos a la ora de vuestro menester.

which caused them to hate you are reversed, show them repentance for all that happened in the past, honour the great families and do not spill the blood of your subjects or take away their possessions, unless it is with right and justice. Brighten your countenance and open your hand in generosity, and you will reap the affection of your people.

So that there may be no cause for envy, do not confer advantage on those who did not stand by you in your times of need over those who did. Bestow office on those to whom it rightly belongs, even if you are not on good terms with them. On the other hand, do not do so on those who are not appropriate, even though you hold them in high regard: there are other benefits that you can bestow on those that you favour. Be careful of the men of noble rank on whom you inflicted hardship and those of low estate to whom you gave plenty. Make good what was destroyed in your kingdom so that the people will forget the wrongs done and remove from their hearts the anger towards you that became rooted there. At a time like the present you should make your settlement with those around you, for the wounds are still fresh and in this way you will form a bond with your enemies without cost. Take care over your wealth as is befitting and the number of your supporters will grow, for in the winter birds are settled and are satisfied with little. Your enemy remains alive, the course of the world fluctuates and you do not know what will happen. Castile is downtrodden and despised by foreign troops, many of the great nobles of your realm have died in the wars and its wealth is exhausted. Such a situation is in urgent need of a solution, and this can be achieved only by bringing solace and calm and covering over the ignominy which had been exposed. A man of learning advised a man of honour that he should forget the wrongs done to him. 'If there were a hair between me and other people,' said another wise man, 'it would not be cut: when they pulled harder I would lessen my effort and when they pulled less hard I would make more effort.' Always accept an apology made by your people, even if you know that they are being deceitful, for it is better to do this than to uncover the truth. Always show gratitude to those who do good to you, even if there is no necessity for you to do so, and then they will not hold back from assisting you in your hour of need.

You should be aware that there are many causes for the affairs of

E sabed que las ocasiones de los dañamientos de las faziendas de los rreyes son muchas, pero nonbrare algunas dellas. E la prinçipal es tener las gentes en poco, e la segunda es auer grand cobdiçia en allegar los algos, e la terçera es querer conplir su voluntad, e la quarta es despreçiar los omnes de la ley, [e] la quinta es vsar de crueldad. E el primero caso que es de tener las gentes en poco es grand locura manifiesta, que en los omnes ay muchos de los malos saberes e de los malos comedimientos, e verter las sangres syn meresçimientos e muerte dellos e de las profetas, fizieron muchos de los males en el mundo desfaziendo todas las posturas e mandamientos que fueron dende [Adan] fasta hoy. E esto forço a los grandes maestros e sabidores de fazer libros de leyes e de hordenamientos por guardar a las gentes de sus daños este corto tienpo de la vida, e aprouecharonsse de seer llamados conpaña de Dios e sus rrequeridos e sus amados, e amuestran les carrera e pone[n] en ellos saber para se guardar de los pecados e perdonarles los fechos. E sabed que la vmildança de los omnes que es por fuerça, non es durable e la que es por voluntad e por grado, es propia e durable, e quando se dañan sus voluntades, mueuen se los coraçones e los ojos e las lenguas e las manos, e puesto que vos non temades de sus juntamentos, deuedes vos temer de sus maldiçiones e de pensamientos de sus coraçones, que quando se juntan las voluntades de los coraçones, sobre qual quier cosa son oydos en los çielos, commo se prueua quando se detienen las aguas en los grandes menesteres. E puesto que non temades de lo vno nin de lo otro, deuedes temer de la vuestra nonbradia en la vida, e en la muerte, de lo que pueden dezir, ca la buena nonbradia es vida segunda e muchos de los buenos rreligiosos aborresçieron la vida e amaron la muerte por cobrar la nonbradia despues de la muerte. E publico es que non pueden escusar los rreyes a los omnes e es en dubda si se podria dezir el contrario, e en los escusar non es cosa que seer pueda. E dizen que vn rrey estaua en su palaçio e los suyos le vinieron demandar cosas que a ellos cunplian, e afincauanle por ello e esperauan su rrespuesta a la puerta de su alcaçar. E el rrey ensañosse e dixo a su alguazil: 'Ve e diles que non me cunple.' E yendo el alguaçil con la rrespuesta tornose del camino e dixo al rrey: 'Señor, mostrad me que rrespuesta

kings coming to harm, but I will list some of them. The first of these is setting little value on people, the second is displaying great greed in the acquisition of wealth, the third is pursuing their own impulses, the fourth is showing contempt for men of the law, and the fifth is acting with cruelty. The first case – setting little value on people – is conspicuous madness, for in men there is much knowledge of evil and great excess; and shedding without due cause the blood of men and of the prophets has caused many of the ills of the world, going against all the principles and commandments established from the time of Adam until today. It was this which obliged the great masters and scholars to produce books of laws and precepts to keep people from harm during life's brief span. Benefitting from being known as the companions of God and the object of His love and affection, they show the people the paths to follow in life and give them the knowledge to guard themselves from sin and to gain pardon for their actions. You should know that the submission of men that is imposed by force is not lasting but that which is given freely and willingly is sincere and enduring; and when men are harmed in mind, the heart, eyes, tongue and hands are all affected, and, even if you do not fear their coming together, you should be afraid of their curses and of the thoughts that they hold in their hearts, for, when the desires felt in the heart on any matter are united, they are heard in the heavens, as is demonstrated when the rains cease to fall in times of great need. And even if you fear neither the one nor the other, you should fear for your name both in life and in death and for what men may say of you, for a man's good name is his second life: many good men of religion have felt a hatred of life and a love of death, in order that they might be held in high esteem after their death. It is well known that kings cannot exempt men from blame and it is doubtful whether the converse could be said; for absolving kings from fault is not something that can be done. They say that once a king was in his royal apartments and his people came to ask him for some things that were in their interest. They were insistent and they waited for his answer at the door to his palace. The king grew angry and said to his constable, 'Go and tell them that it is not in my interest.' As the constable was on his way to take them this answer, he turned back. 'My lord,' he said to the king,

les dare sy me dizen "nin nos a el".' Estonçe callo el rrey vn rrato e dixo: 'Ve e diles que quiero fazer lo que me demandan.'

E la segunda ocasion del dañamiento del rrey es grand cobdiçia en allegar los algos quando salle de rregla e esta es ocasion de muchos dañamientos. E los algos de los rreyes son vsados a las guerras commo se vsaron las creençias en las leyes, e si de golpe pujassen en las creençias, non lo cunplirian los omnes. E los algos son mandados a los omnes por seer decolgada la honrra en ellos, e ay omnes que presçian sus algos mas que sus honrras. E el rrey que quiere aderesçar sus rregnos con algos de sus gentes semeja al que quiere labrar sus camaras con los çimientos de sus palaçios. E fuerça es de fazer sin razon el que se acuçia a allegar algo, e dizen los antigos que puede durar la descreençia e non la sin rrazon. E la manera del rrey con sus gentes es semejada al pastor con su ganado. Sabida cosa es el vso del pastor con su ganado: la gran piedad que ha en el, que anda a buscar la mejor agua e el buen pasto e la grand guarda de los contrarios assi commo los lobos, trasquilar la lana desque apesga e hordeñar la leche en manera que non faga daño a la vbre nin apesgue sus carnes nin fanbriente sus fijos. E dixo vn omne a su vezino: 'Fulano, tu cordero leuo un lobo e eche en pos el e tomegelo.' E dixole: '¿Pues que es del o do esta?' E dixole: 'Degollelo e comilo.' E dixole: 'Tu e el lobo vno sodes.' E si el pastor vsa desta guisa con el ganado, lieua mala vida o dexara de seer pastor, quanto mas deue seer el rrey con sus subditos e naturales.

E la terçera ocasion del dañamiento del rrey es el que quiere conplir su talante, e tal commo este fazesse siervo aunque sea rrey, e apoderasse sobre el su apetito e con su voluntad fazele su catiuo e su sieruo, e tira del su nobleza e su propiedat e quitale el espiritu que ha de mejoria sobre las bestias. E el que non se sabe apoderar sobre su voluntad non podra apoderarse sobre su enemigo e es fea cosa el que quiere que sean los omnes sus catiuos e fazesse el catiuo del que

'let me know what answer I give them if they tell me, "Nor is he in ours." The king was silent for a while and then he said, 'Go and tell them that I am willing to do what they ask.'

The second cause of harm befalling a king is when greed to acquire wealth exceeds reasonable limits, and this does indeed cause a great deal of harm. The wealth of kings is used for wars just as beliefs were used in laws, and if suddenly they hesitated in their beliefs men would not obey. Wealth is entrusted to men as a means of displaying their honour but there are men who value their wealth more than their honour. The king who desires to enhance his realm using the wealth of his subjects resembles one who wishes to build his palace halls using the material from their foundations. The man who hungers to acquire wealth inevitably acts without reason: the ancients say that lack of belief can last but not lack of reason. The role of the king with regard to his subjects is similar to that of the shepherd towards his sheep. The way that the shepherd treats his flock is well known: the great concern that he shows, seeking out the best water and fine pasture, providing safe protection against enemies such as wolves, shearing the sheep once its wool becomes too thick and milking it in such a way as not to damage the udder, do harm to its flesh or leave its lambs hungry. A man said to his neighbour, 'So-and-so, your lamb was being carried off by a wolf and so I went after them and took the lamb away from it.' So the neighbour said to him, 'Well what happened to the lamb and where is it?' 'I cut its throat and ate it,' the man replied. The neighbour said, 'You are just the same as the wolf.' And if a shepherd treats his flock in this way, he will lead a hard life or he will give up being a shepherd: so how much more must this be the case for the king in his dealings with his subjects and the people of his kingdom?

The third cause of harm befalling a king relates to the one who pursues his own impulses, for such a man as this becomes a slave even though he is a king: he is taken over by appetites and his desire, which turn him into their captive and their slave, depriving him of his nobility and his true character and robbing him of the spirit which raises him among the beasts. The man who does not know how to control his own desires will not be able to overcome his enemy, and it is not pleasant to behold a man who wants to hold others captive

non deue: e la peor de las voluntades es la forniçion por quanto el que se enbeueçe en ello le nasçen muchos daños e perdida el anima e el seso e el entendimiento e los sentidos e cobra mala nonbradia e daña sus generaçiones e tal omne commo este es semejado a las bestias. E el dios que dizen los sabidores de los christianos que se vistio en carne e en figura de omne por los saluar, e non ouo ninguno que mas arredrado fuesse deste pecado que el, e fue en el tienpo que el fue paresçido en carne. E el buen omne sabidor faze mucho en quanto puede en semejar a su Dios e entiende de alcançar mucho en ello, cuanto mas el rrey que es por El, e su teniente lugar en la tierra. E las ocasiones que acaesçieron a los rreyes por el forniçio publicos son. E vna dellas fue quando el conde don Yllan metio los moros al Andalozia por lo que el rrey fizo a su fija.

Quanto a la quarta ocasion del dañamiento del rrey, que es el despreçiamiento a los omnes de la ley, tal commo este es ponçoña mortal, que la ley es cosa general e es la ley verdadera e el rrey su siervo e su guarda, e el que la despreçia tienen los omnes que el faze a ellos desuiar e despreçiarle. E non ha menester la ley sy non es guardada de auer pena en este mundo e la yra de Dios en el otro. Ca escrito es e amonestamiento sin dubda, e por tanto lo tienen las gentes por menguado e despreçiado al rrey que la su ley despreçia e non fian en su jura nin en su omenaje, que el rrey non ha juez que lo juzgue, saluo su omenaje e su ley, e, quando non fian del, non podra rregir su rregno.

E quanto a la quinta ocasion del dañamiento del rrey, es la crueldad e la mengua de piedad. E el el rrey que dellas husa rrecresçera entre el e los suyos grand escandalo, e fuyran del commo los ganados de los lobos por natura e por aborrençia, e escusaran el su prouecho e buscaran manera para ello. E el rrey que faze justiçia por cosas que el non se puede saluar dellas e defiende cosas que a el podrian escusar

but himself becomes the captive of one into whose hands he must not fall. The worst kind of desire is fornication since the man who becomes enmeshed in it starts to suffer great ills, losing his soul, his mind, his understanding and his senses, gaining an evil reputation and bringing harm upon his lineage: such a man resembles the beasts. The god that, according to the wise men among the Christians, assumed flesh and the form of a man in order to save them, in the time when he appeared as flesh, held back more than any other from this sin. So, if the man of goodness and wisdom does all that he can to resemble his god and understands that in this way he achieves much, the king who stands in his place and is God's lieutenant on earth should seek to do so all the more. The examples of harm that has befallen kings through fornication are well known, and one of them occurred when Count Julian introduced the Moors into Andalusia as a result of what the king did to his daughter.

With regard to the fourth cause of harm befalling a king, which is showing contempt for men of the law, such an error is a deadly poison, for the law applies to all men and is indeed the true law. The king is its servant and its guardian, and if a ruler treats it with scorn he is held by men to be turning them aside from their natural course and causing them to treat him in turn with scorn. The sole purpose of the law is to provide protection from affliction in this world and from the anger of God in the next. For it has been set down as an unequivocal warning, and therefore the people view as a diminished and despised figure any king who treats their law with contempt and they have no trust in his word or in the vow of allegiance which binds them: the king has no judge to pronounce a verdict on him, except for his feudal bond and his law, and when he is not trusted he will be unable to rule his kingdom.

With regard to the fifth cause of harm suffered by a king, this is cruelty and failure to act with sufficient compassion. In the case of a ruler who has these failings, great trouble will arise between him and his people, who through abhorrence and by their very nature will flee from him like flocks from wolves: they will hold back from acting to his benefit and will seek out ways of doing so. In the case of the king who administers justice for actions of which he cannot himself be considered free of guilt and who defends things of which he might

por ello, e podria seer que oye aquel mal dezir de omne que non le quiere dar la vida e deue temer a Dios quando da pena al pecador e sepa commo es omne commo el, e llegale su yerro e su pecado a este mal estado, e sea justiçiado por lo que es forçado de la ley e de la justiçia de los rreyes. E señor, estas palabras en esta rrazon son pocas de muchas que se podrian dezir en esto, e si començasse a fablar en ello es commo la mar que non ha cabo.

E en rrazon de las gentes estrañas dañosas, son las gentes estrangeras que con vusco venieron, sabed que vuestro consejo e su amigança es ya fecha. E el aperçebido es el que se guarda de la cosa antes que contesca, e el orgulloso, el que piensa commo salga de la cosa despues que nasçe, e la su ayuda de la tal gente es tal commo la propiedad de las ponçoñas, que se beuen por escusar otra cosa mas peor que ellas. E vuestra manera paresçe con ellos al omne que criaua vn leon e caçaua con el las animalias e aprouechauasse del, e vn dia fallesçio de comer al leon e comio a vn fijo que tenia aquel que lo criaua, e el desque vido aquello que le auia fecho, mato al leon e dixo: 'Este es el que non cata su pro quanto su daño.' E es verdad que dizen desta gente que han grand poder, commo dezides e prouecho dellos, es semejante al fuego, que si se oluida, quema todo quanto alcança. E pues ellos son commo dezides grand gente e mucha e començaron a tener en poco a los de Castilla e vençieron sus gentes e catiuaron sus grandes e mataron sus omnes, e son christianos e non mudaron su ley, e el que de tal guisa es muy ligero terna de cobrar todos los rregnos e pasar los assy. E de las cosas que vos deuedes aperçebir es que tienen en su poder muchos presos de los grandes de vuestros rregnos e sus gentes de los presos en vuestras çibdades e villas, quexados de vos, e les mostraran e fiuzaran de lo vuestro deque vean vuestras villas e fortalezas e cubdiçiar las han: e deuedes guardar que non se apoderen en algunas dellas e acogeran conpaña que las pueblen, e de mas si fueren villas en la rribera de la mar, e podra seer que las contentaran

himself be accused, it may be that he hears that curse of the man whom he is unwilling to allow to live: he must fear God when he passes sentence on the sinner and he should be aware that he is a man like him who has been brought by his error and his sin into this wretched situation and is to be judged according to what is determined by the law and the justice of kings.[18] My lord, these words on this matter are just a few of the many that could be spoken about it, and if I were to begin to discuss the subject it would be like the sea which has no end.

Regarding foreign troops, the men that came with you from abroad bring destruction, but you must know that your decision has been taken and your alliances with them have already been formed. The prudent man is the one who takes precautions against something before it happens, whilst the arrogant man thinks about how he can escape from a situation after it has come about. The help of such people is similar to the nature of poisons which are drunk in order to avoid something which is worse than they are. Your attitude to them resembles that of the man who reared a lion and made use of it to hunt other animals, until one day the lion ran out of food and ate the man's own son. Once he had seen what it had done, the man killed the lion. 'This', he said, 'is one who seeks to bring himself not so much good as harm.' It is true that these people are said to be very powerful, as you argue; but the benefit that you gain from them is similar to the fire which, if it is not watched over, burns everything within range. And since, as you say, they are formidable men and great in number, they began to look down on the people of Castile: they defeated their troops, took their nobles prisoner and killed their men. They are Christians and yet they have not changed their way of acting: for such people it will be a rapid affair to take possession of all kingdoms and treat them in this manner. Among the things of which you should take note is the fact that they are holding as their prisoners many of the great lords of your realms and that the supporters of those captives in your cities and towns, out of resentment towards you, will give them information and encouragement with regard to your possessions. Then once they see your towns and fortresses they will wish to possess them, and you must guard against them seizing some of them. They will bring in people to populate them, all the more so if they are coastal towns. It may be that they will make

e apaziguaran, e vuestros enemigos ayudar los han e auran en estas tales villas rregnado e guerra asentada e durable contra vos. E muchas de las cosas tales han acaesçido e nonbraria alguna dellas sy non por non alongar.

Oy dezir que tomades algos de vuestros comunes por fuerça e dades gelos a ellos por les pagar lo que les deuedes de la venida que convusco fazen a esta guerra. E en esto ha tres daños: primera mente la henemistad de los comunes, que, commo quier que sean vsados de pechar, non querrian que fuesse todo para el rrey sola mente saluo cosa que aprouechasse a ellos e a las villas do moran los pecheros, que los de la tierra dan al rrey otra vez los dineros e tornasse a ellos e aprouechansse dende, mas que lo que dieredes a los estraños en oro e en plata, que assi lo querrian leuar a sus tierras. E la segunda cosa del daño sobre dicho es que enflaquesçedes los vuestros e esforçades conpaña estranjera, que a primera vista paresçe el poco cabdal que en vos e en los vuestros ha. E la terçera cosa es que rrecresçe la cobdiçia en los estraños veyendo el mucho algo que les dan. E el mi consejo es que les mostredes que estades en grand menester e el fallesçimiento del algo que es en vuestro rregno, e que sodes forçado de conleuar las gentes vuestras e que non las podedes agora apremiar agora commo soliades: las llagas son frescas e la tierra poblada de henemigos, e deuedes enbiar gelo fazer saber todo esto con los grandes perlados de vuestro rregno, de quien auran verguença e creeran sus dichos, e con esto asossegaran e quedaran desfiuzados e allegaredes tienpo. E con esto faran vna de dos cosas: o tornarsse han a sus tierras, e es lo mas çierto, o se enflaquesçera el poder que han sy mucho tardan en la vuestra tierra. Otrossy en les dar algos luego e la enemistad non tirada fasta que vayades cobrando los mas de los comunes por vos, entre vos e ellos seeria peligro, e assi alongad.

them settled and peaceful. Moreover, your enemies will assist them and in such towns they will hold sway and possess a firmly established and lasting base for waging war against you. Many events of this nature have already taken place and I would mention them specifically but for the fact that it would make this account too lengthy.

I have heard that you forcibly seize wealth from your common people and hand it over to the foreigners in payment of what you owe them for coming with you to wage this war. This does harm in three ways. Firstly it provokes hostility among the common people who, even though they may be accustomed to paying tax, would not wish all that they pay to go to the king alone but rather would want it to be used for their benefit and for that of the towns where the taxpayers reside; for the people of the land once again make payment to the king but it comes back to them and they take benefit from it, whilst on the other hand the intention of the foreigners would be to take back to their own lands what you hand over to them in gold and silver. The second way in which it causes harm is by weakening your people and increasing the strength of the foreign forces, for the shortage of resources possessed by you and your nation is apparent at first sight. And the third way is that the greed of the foreigners is increased by seeing the great wealth that they receive. My advice is that you make them aware that you are in great need, that there is a shortage of wealth in your country and that you are obliged to give support to your people and cannot now impose the burden on them that they used to bear. The wounds are fresh and the land is overrun by enemies, and you should have all of this communicated to them by the great prelates of your realm, who will make them feel a greater sense of shame and whose words they will believe. In this way they will be placated and become less assured, and you will gain time. In consequence they will do one of two things: either they will return to their own lands – and this is the most probable outcome – or, if they stay for a long time on your territory, they will become less powerful. Moreover, if you were to make prompt payment to the foreigners, before the hostility has been overcome and you have won over to you the majority of the common people, a dangerous situation would develop between you and them. So take your time over it.

E este es mi consejo si son los fechos assy commo suenan. E el que esta presente vee mas desto que, si el fecho non es assi o a los del rregno non les pesa dar de sus algos, es otra demanda. Pero el consejo desto es acuçiar por que salgan de vuestra tierra e si pelear quisieren con vos, non es de creer despues que vos ayudaron. Si omnes de bien fueran non vendieran lo que vos fizieron por presçio e prendas, e deuierales abondar lo que rrobaron en vuestra tierra e la rrendiçion de los prisioneros que tomaron de los vuestros e los algos de los vuestros comunes e armas de las vuestras gentes. E los fechos de los rreyes e de los grandes son contrarios de los fechos de los mercadores, e ellos non deuen mostrar cobdiçia, pues son rreyes e non mercadores. Sabed que el que hoy demandare pelea con vos, veyendo vuestra bien querençia con los moros vuestros vezinos e auiendo quanta gente e nobles tenedes, seria vençido con ayuda de Dios. E prouado lo auedes la su grand querençia de los moros con vos e la enemistad con vuestros enemigos, lo que vos non fallastes en los de vuestros grandes e de vuestros criados. E esta es cosa que vos non fezistes por vuestras manos, mas fizolo Dios que puso entre vos e entre su rrey grand amigança e bien querençia, que non podria seer mayor manera en coraçones de hermanos e de parientes. Pues gradesçed a Dios por ello e guardad esta cosa e esta grand amistad.

E la cosa por que me escuso de vos dezir lo que querria es el açidente por que acaesçio lo que fasta aqui acaesçio, es presente e el henemigo, biuo e los vuestros que fizieron lo que non deuian, biuos. E el mundo, que es tal commo quien juega con las gentes asi commo juega el enbaydor con sus juegos, e non es durable, e el tienpo que ha menester, corto. E es menester el sosiego mas que el fervor, e tener pagados a los vuestros mucho mejor que a los estraños, que non ay dubda que non eran despagados, e non vos cunple arreziarles e ayudarles ca non auredes poder de los quitar de lo que quisieren, e

This is my advice if the situation is indeed as it sounds to be. The person who is actually present can see more than this, for if things are otherwise or the people of the kingdom are not bothered by giving up some of their wealth, it is a different question. However, the advice in this case is to encourage the foreigners to leave your land quickly. It is difficult to believe that, having given you their help, they would want to do battle with you. If they were men of honour, they would not ask a price in terms of payment or possessions in return for what they did on your behalf: they should have sufficient with what they have stolen from your lands, the ransom payments for the prisoners that they have taken from your subjects, the wealth of your common people and the arms of your soldiers. The dealings of kings and of great lords run counter to those of merchants and they must not act out of greed, for they are indeed kings and not merchants. I tell you that any man who today seeks conflict with you, in view of your friendship with your neighbours the Moors and of the number of troops and nobles that you have at your disposal, would be defeated with God's help. You have seen the proof of the Moors' great affection for you and of their hostility towards your enemies, something which you did not find in your great lords or in the members of your own household. This is something which you did not achieve for yourself, but rather it was brought about by God who created between you and the king of the Moors great friendship and affection, such as could not be surpassed in the hearts of brothers and family members. So give thanks to God for it and preserve this bond and this great friendship.

The reason why I hold back from saying to you what I would have wished is the fact that the cause of what has happened is still present and the enemy remains alive, as do those of your subjects who did what they should not have done. And the world, which resembles somebody playing with people just like a trickster with his games, is ephemeral and time, which is necessary, is short. Calm is needed more than zeal, and it is better to keep your own people contented than it is to give satisfaction to foreigners: for there is no doubt that the foreigners were not left discontented and it is not in your interest to strengthen and assist them, as then you will not have the power to keep them from achieving their desires. They will have power over

ellos auran el poder sobre vos e despresçiaran a los vuestros e seran ocasion de vos dañar con aquellos que vos guardan syn por que.

Sabed que toda cosa tiene tienpo que le pertenesçe, e a este tienpo pertenesçe sossiego. E yo por Dios e leal de voluntad, a vos e a quantos de mi demandan dare leal consejo e a otro ninguno non dare lo que yo dixe saluo a su rrey que el crio, e yo fare por vos lo que fare por el seyendo amos vnos, e el seso adebda quanto vos he dicho e por la prueua paresçera.

E podra seer que me sean juzgadas algunas menguas de parte del trasladador desta carta que vos enbio e non de mi parte. E yo vos pido por merçed que me conoscades quanto he dicho e perdonad me lo que contra vuestra voluntad dixe atreuiendo me a la vuestra merçed e a la vuestra bien querençia. E sodes grand rrey e segund vuestra grandeza deuen seer contadas vuestras noblezas e el vuestro poder. E Dios vos de el bien que El por bien touiere e vos lieue adelante la ventura e vos mantenga a su seruiçio e vos esfuerçe del su esfuerço.'

E el rrey don Pedro ouo esta carta e plogole con ella; enpero non se allego a las cosas en ellas contenidas, lo qual le touo grand daño.

Capitulo XXIIIº. Commo el rrey don Pedro dixo al prinçipe de Gales que queria yr por el rregno por auer dineros para pagar.

Agora tornaremos a contar commo el rrey don Pedro se partio del prinçipe de Gales e fue en esta manera. El rrey don Pedro fue vn dia a ueer al prinçipe a su posada de Las Huelgas e dixole commo el auia enbiado muchos omnes por todo el rregno a demandar seruiçio

you and will treat your people with contempt; and thus they will cause you to suffer harm among those who protect you without good reason.

I tell you that everything has its own due time and at the present time what is appropriate is calm. I, in the name of God and as a man loyal in heart, will give loyal advice to you and to others who ask it of me, but to no other will I say what I have said to you, except to the king in whose court I have lived.[19] I will do for you the same as for him, the two of you being as one. My understanding requires me to say all that I have told you, and the proof of it will become apparent.

It may be that I am held to blame for some failings on the part of the translator of this letter that I am sending you which are not of my making. I beg you to accept all that I have said and to forgive me for points that I have made which were not to your liking and for daring to go against your wishes and against your affection. You are a great king and among the signs of your greatness must be counted your nobility and your authority. May God grant you the blessings which indeed He counts as blessings, may He bring you success and preserve you in His service, and may His aid give you sustenance.'

King Pedro received this letter and was pleased by it. However he did not address the matters contained in it, and this was to bring him great harm.

1367: CHAPTER XXIII

How King Pedro informed the prince of Wales that he wished to travel round his kingdom in order to obtain the money with which to pay him.

Now we shall return to the account of how King Pedro took his leave of the prince of Wales. This occurred as follows: one day the king went to call on the prince in his lodgings in las Huelgas and told him how he had sent out many men throughout the kingdom to demand the payment of a financial contribution and the provision of assistance,

e ayuda que le fiziessen, espeçial mente para la primera paga de los quatro meses que le auia de fazer, e que por tener mayor acuçia, que el mesmo queria partir de Burgos e yr por el rregno, e que entendia luego auer mejor rrecabdo. E el prinçipe dixo al rrey que lo fazia bien e que gelo agradesçia e que le rrogaua que pusiesse en ello grande acuçia: lo vno por tener su verdad e juramento que fiziera a el e a las conpañas que venieran con el e le siruieran muy bien segund el sabia. Otrossy por que el e las conpañas muchas que eran con el se partiessen ayna del rregno de Castilla a do non pudian estar syn fazer mucho enojo en comer las viandas e gastar la tierra.

Otrossy le dixo el prinçipe aquel dia al rrey don Pedro que le dizian que el enbiaua sus cartas e aperçibimientos para los de la tierra de Vizcaya e de Castro de Urdiales, que le non tomassen por señor e que el non pudia creer la tal cosa e que le rrogaua que le fiziesse entregar la dicha tierra e villa segund lo tenia prometido e jurado. E esso mesmo le rrogaua por la çibdat de Soria, que la deuia auer el conde estable mossen Iohan Chandos. E a todo esto dixo el rrey don Pedro que el nunca tales cartas enbiara e que le queria darle e otorgarle la dicha tierra e villa e çibdat de Soria, e que le plazia e que en todo, el pornia buen rremedio en este espaçio de los dichos quatro meses. E assi se partio el rrey don Pedro de Burgos e se fue para Aranda sobre Duero e ally estudo algunos dias doliente. E el prinçipe partio de Burgos e fuesse para vn lugar que dizen Hamusco e sus gentes posaron por estas comarcas de entre Burgos e Hamusco.

especially towards the first instalment that he had to pay after four months. He explained that, in order to achieve this with greater speed, he intended to leave Burgos and travel round the kingdom in person and that he expected in this way to collect a larger sum very quickly. The prince told the king that he was right to do this and that he thanked him for it, and he asked him to do so with urgency. This was partly in order that King Pedro might keep his word and observe the oath that he had sworn to the prince and the companies of troops who had come with him and who, as King Pedro was well aware, had served him well. However, it was also so that the prince and the large number of troops with him might be able to leave the kingdom of Castile quickly, for they could not remain there without causing considerable trouble by consuming the provisions and laying waste the land.

That day the prince of Wales also told King Pedro that he had been informed about how he had written to warn the people of the lands of Vizcaya and of Castro Urdiales that they should not accept him, the prince, as their lord. He added that he could not believe such a thing and that he now requested that the king hand over the territory and the town as he had promised and sworn to do. He also asked him for the same to be done in the case of Soria, which was to become the property of the constable Sir John Chandos. In reply to all of this, King Pedro said that he had never sent such letters and that it was his wish to grant and hand over to him the territory of Vizcaya, the town of Castro Urdiales and the city of Soria. He confirmed that he agreed to do so and stated that he would deal fully with all these matters during the coming period of four months. With this, King Pedro left Burgos for Aranda de Duero, where he remained for some days suffering from illness. The prince left Burgos for a village called Amusco and his troops were billeted throughout the area which lies between Burgos and Amusco.

Capitulo XXIVº. Commo el rrey don Pedro partio de Aranda e fue para Toledo e a Cordoua e a Seuilla, e lo que fizo en las dichas çibdades.

El rrey don Pedro despues que partio de Aranda fue su camino para la çibdat de Toledo e antes que ý llegase auia enbiado mandar de Burgos que matassen vn cauallero e otro omne bueno de la çibdat, que estauan presos en el alcaçar. E al cauallero dizian Ruy Ponçe Palomeque e era de los buenos dende. E al omne bueno llamauan Ferrand Martinez del Cardenal e era un omne honrrado, e fizolo matar por quanto andudiera con el rrey don Enrrique despues que entrara en el rregno.

Otrossi demando el Rey don Pedro en Toledo a los de la çibdat asy caualleros e omnes buenos del comun, que le diessen arrehenes que leuasse consigo a Seuilla e seer seguro dellos. E ouo sobre esto en la çibdat de Toledo muy gran rrebuelta, ca non querian dar las arrehenes. Enpero el rrey tanto se afirmo en ello que gelas dieron e leuolas conssigo a Seuilla. E dexo en Toledo por mayores para guardar la çibdat, caualleros naturales dende, a Ferrand Aluarez de Toledo, su alguazil mayor de la çibdat, e a Tel Gonçalez Palomeque, alcalde mayor de la çibdat e otros.

E dende partio e fue para la çibdat de Cordoua e a dos dias que ally llego, vna noche a la media noche pasada armosse con çiertas conpañas e andudo por la çibdat por casas çiertas e fizo matar diez e seys omnes de la çibdat, que eran omnes de honrra, diziendo que quando el rrey don Enrrique llegara ý, que ellos fueran los primeros que le fueran rresçibir. E esto fecho dexo en Cordoua por capitan mayor a Martin Lopez de Cordoua, maestre de Calatraua, que fiziera despues que don Diego Garçia de Padilla, maestre que fuera de Calatraua, se partiera del.

E el rrey fuese para Seuilla e antes que ý llegase fizo matar, ca estauan ý presos desque sopieran las nueuas commo la batalla de

1367: CHAPTER XXIV

How King Pedro left Aranda and went to Toledo, Córdoba and Seville, and what he did in those cities.

After leaving Aranda King Pedro headed for the city of Toledo, and before he arrived there he had already sent instructions from Burgos for the execution of a knight and another leading citizen of the city who were being held prisoner in the *alcázar*. The knight was called Ruy Ponce Palomeque and he was one of the principal figures in the city. The name of the other citizen was Fernán Martínez del Cardenal: he was a man of honour and the king had him killed because he had accompanied King Enrique after his entry into the kingdom.

While King Pedro was in Toledo he also demanded of the people of the city, both knights and leading citizens among the common people, that they give him hostages to take with him to Seville as a guarantee of the conduct of the people of Toledo. This caused considerable unrest in Toledo, whose citizens did not want to provide hostages. Nevertheless, the king's insistence was such that the hostages were handed over to him and he took them with him to Seville. In Toledo he left in overall charge some knights who were natives of the city: his chief constable for Toledo, Fernán Álvarez de Toledo, Tel González Palomeque, the city's chief judge, and a number of others.

From there the king set off for the city of Córdoba and two days after his arrival there, after midnight, he made ready with a body of troops and went round the city raiding a number of houses and ordering the death of 16 honourable men, saying that when King Enrique had arrived in the city they had been the first to go and welcome him. And once he had done this he left in Córdoba as his principal commander the master of Calatrava Martín López de Córdoba, whom he had appointed after the previous master of Calatrava, Don Diego García de Padilla, had severed his bond of allegiance to him.

The king travelled on to Seville and before his arrival he ordered the execution of a number of men, for they had been held there as prisoners since the news had arrived of the outcome of the battle

Najara era desbaratada, a miçer Gil Boca Negra e a don Iohan, fijo de don Pero Ponçe de Leon señor de Marchena, e otro escudero que dizian Alfonso Arias de Quadros, e otro que tenia las taraçanas, que dizian Alfonso Fernandez, fijo del ama de don Tello, e otros de la çibdat

Capitulo XXVº. Commo Martin Lopez de Cordoua maestre de Calatraua fablo con algunos caualleros de Cordoua algunos fechos que dizia que el prinçipe fablara con el.

Martin Lopez de Cordoua maestre de Calatraua, que tenia la partida del rrey don Pedro e estudiera en Vayona, se rresçelaua del rrey; enpero Martin Lopez era apoderado e tenia muchas gentes e muchos dineros e non lo podia el rrey tan ayna desatar assy.

E Martin Lopez por poner escandalo entre el rrey e los de la çibdat de Cordoua, dixoles vn dia a algunos de los mayores que el prinçipe de Gales non se pagaua de las maneras del rrey e que fablara e tratara con el que seria bien que vn rregno tamaño commo el de Castilla non se perdiesse e que se pusiesse en ello algund rremedio e que fuesse este. Primera mente que el rrey don Pedro estudiesse en la çibdat de Toledo e que lo casassen con alguna noble muger donde pudiesse auer fijos herederos. Otrossy que el prinçipe fuesse rregidor e gouernador mayor de los rregnos de Castilla e de Leon e de las otras tierras e señorios del rrey, e que Martin Lopez fuesse gouernador por el prinçipe del Andalozia con el rregno de Murçia, e don Ferrando de Castro, del rregno de Leon con Galizia, e Diego Gomez de Castañeda, gouernador de Castilla, e Garçi Ferrandez de Villodre, del rregno de Toledo e Estremadura.

at Nájera. These were Miçer Gil Boccanegra, Don Juan, son of the lord of Marchena Don Pero Ponce de León, another squire by the name of Alfonso Arias de Quadros, and another man called Alfonso Fernández who was in charge of the shipyards and was the son of the lady responsible for Don Tello's household, and other men of the city.

1367: CHAPTER XXV

How the master of Calatrava Don Martín López de Córdoba spoke with some knights from Córdoba about matters that he said the prince had discussed with him.

The master of Calatrava Martín López de Córdoba, although he was a supporter of King Pedro and had been in Bayonne, was in fear of the king. However, Martín López was a powerful figure, had many troops at his disposal and possessed considerable wealth, and the king could not rid himself of him with such ease.

One day, in order to cause trouble between the king and the people of Córdoba, Martín López told some of the leading citizens that the prince of Wales was not happy with the ways of the king and had talked with him and discussed with him how it would not be right for a kingdom of the importance of Castile to go to ruin. He had suggested that a solution for this be put in place, and this was as follows: firstly that King Pedro should remain in the city of Toledo and a marriage should be arranged for him with some noble lady who could give him heirs to inherit the throne; and secondly that the prince should become overall governor with supreme authority over the kingdoms of Castile and León and the other lands and lordships of the king. Martín López should be governor on the prince's behalf of Andalusia, together with the kingdom of Murcia; Don Fernando de Castro should have responsibility for the kingdom of León with Galicia; Diego Gómez de Castañeda was to be governor of Castile, and Garci Fernández de Villodre would be responsible for the kingdom of Toledo together with Extremadura.

E los de Cordoua que esto oyeron, plogoles mucho del desabenimiento que entendieron que era entre el rrey e el prinçipe, e otrossi por saber la voluntad del maestre Martin Lopez; enpero si esto era assy o non, non se sabe, saluo que algunos caualleros de Cordoua dixeron al rrey don Enrrique despues que Martin Lopez fablara con ellos, todo esto.

Capitulo XXVI°. Commo Martin Lopez maestre de Calatraua dixo a algunos caualleros de Cordoua que el rrey don Pedro le mandara que matasse a algunos dellos e commo el non lo quiso fazer e lo que acaesçio sobre esto.

Don Martin Lopez de Cordoua maestre de Calatraua despues que finco en la çibdad de Cordoua, dixo a algunos caualleros naturales dende que el rrey le auia mandado que matasse en Cordoua a don Gonçalo Ferrandez de Cordoua e a don Alfonso Ferrandez señor de Monte Mayor e a Diego Ferrandez, alguazil mayor de la dicha çibdat. E don Martin Lopez maestre de Calatraua dixo que commo quier que el rrey gelo mandara assi fazer, que lo non queria fazer. E dende a dos dias, el dicho don Martin maestre de Calatraua conbido a comer a los dichos don Alfonso Ferrandez e don Gonçalo Ferrandez e Diego Fernandez e desque ouieron comido, mostroles vn aluala del rrey commo le mandaua que les cortasse las cabeças e dixoles que el les daua la vida por que entendia que faria mal en los matar seyendo el natural de la çibdat de Cordoua, fechura e criança de su linaje dellos, e rrogoles que touiessen este fecho en secreto.

E el rrey don Pedro desque pasaron algunos dias, sopo que Martin Lopez de Cordoua maestre de Calatraua non fiziera lo que le mandara en rrazon de la muerte destos caualleros e fue muy mal contento del e fablo con vn freyre de la horden de Alcantara que dizian Pero Giron

The citizens of Córdoba who heard this took great pleasure in the disagreement that they understood to exist between the king and the prince and also in finding out about the wishes of the master Martín López. However, whether or not what he said was true is not known, except that some knights from Córdoba, after Martín López had spoken with them, reported all of it to King Enrique.

1367: CHAPTER XXVI

How the master of Calatrava Martín López told some knights from Córdoba that King Pedro had commanded him to kill some of them and that he had been unwilling to do so, and what happened about this.

After staying for some time in the city of Córdoba, the master of Calatrava Martín López de Córdoba informed some knights from the city that the king had commanded him, during the time that he was there, to kill Don Gonzalo Fernández de Córdoba, Don Alfonso Fernández, lord of Montemayor and Diego Fernández, the chief constable of the city. The master of Calatrava Don Martín López said that, even though the king had ordered him to commit this act, he was unwilling to do so. Two days later, the master of Calatrava Don Martín López invited Don Alfonso Fernández, Don Gonzalo Fernández and Diego Fernández to eat with him, and after they had finished their meal he showed them an official letter from the king instructing him to have them beheaded. He told them that he was allowing them to live as he understood that he would be doing wrong in killing them, given that he was a native of the city of Córdoba, where their families had their origin and they had grown up. He asked them to keep this matter secret.

Once a few days had passed, King Pedro learned that the master of Calatrava Martín López de Córdoba had not carried out his command to have these knights executed and he was highly displeased with him. He spoke with a brother of the Order of Alcántara called Pero

e fizieralo el rrey fazer maestre de Alcantara, e dixole que se fuesse para Martin Lopez maestre de Calatraua e andudiesse con el, e sy lo pudiesse matar, que le daria el maestradgo de Calatraua. E el Pero Giron partio luego del rrey e fuesse para Martin Lopez maestre de Calatraua e andudo con el.

E el Martin Lopez ya se rresçelaua del rrey e non quiso estar en Cordoua e fuesse para vn lugar de la horden de Calatraua que es en su comarca, que dizen Martos, e yua con el el cauallero Pero Giron, que diximos que el rrey enbiara para lo matar, e andudo catando manera para ello e non se le guisaua. E desque llegaron a Martos, el dicho Pero Giron prendio al dicho Martin Lopez de Cordoua maestre de Calatraua e a otro freyre de Calatraua que dizian Iohan Ferrandez de Lago. E esto pudia bien fazer Pero Giron por quanto tenia el castillo por Martin Lopez, e Martin Lopez entrara en el castillo con pocas gentes e fiandose del Pero Giron.

E el dicho Pero Giron quisiera los luego enbiar presos al rrey don Pedro. E sopolo el rrey de Granada, que queria bien al maestre don Martin Lopez, e enbio luego sus mensageros al rrey don Pedro, por los quales le enbio dezir que fuesse çierto que si non soltasse luego al dicho Martin Lopez, que el seria en su destoruo. E el rrey con rreçelo que ouo del rrey de Granada, ca tenia grand esfuerço en su ayuda, mandolo soltar.

Capitulo XXVIIº. Commo el rrey don Pedro fizo matar en Seuilla a doña Urraca de Osorio, madre de don Iohan Alfonso de Guzman.

El rrey don Pedro, segund auemos contado, quando partio de la çibdat de Seuilla el año que el rrey don Enrrique entrara en Castilla, e ouo ý gran bolliçio por que don Iohan Alfonso de Guzman, que despues fue conde de Niebla, non se llego al rrey nin se partio de Seuilla quando el rrey fue para Portogal e era el rrey querelloso del.

Girón, whom he had created master of Alcántara, and instructed him to go to the master of Calatrava Martín López and remain with him; and if he was able to kill him he would give him the mastership of Calatrava.[20] Pero Girón lost no time in taking his leave of the king and he went to the master of Calatrava and kept his company.

Martín López was already suspicious of the king and did not wish to remain in Córdoba, and so he went to a place called Martos which belonged to the Order of Calatrava and was situated in the Order's territory. He was accompanied by the knight Pero Girón, whom, as we have already said, the king had sent to kill him and who had been looking in vain for an opportunity to do so. Then, once they reached Martos, Pero Girón seized Martín López de Córdoba and another brother of Calatrava called Juan Fernández de Lago. Pero Girón was able to do this easily as he was holding the castle on behalf of Martín López, who entered it with just a small number of troops and trusting in Pero Girón.

Pero Girón would have liked to send them immediately as prisoners to King Pedro. However, the king of Granada, who was a good friend of the master Martín López, heard about this and at once sent envoys to King Pedro to tell him to be sure that, if he did not release Martín López, he would make matters difficult for him. The king, concerned about the reaction of the king of Granada on whose support he relied heavily, ordered the release of the master.

1367: CHAPTER XXVII

How King Pedro ordered the death in Seville of Doña Urraca de Osorio, the mother of Don Juan Alfonso de Guzmán.

As we have already related, when King Pedro left the city of Seville in the year of King Enrique's invasion of Castile, there was considerable agitation there because Don Juan Alfonso de Guzmán, later to become count of Niebla, did not come to join the king or leave the city when the king went to Portugal, and the king was extremely annoyed with him.

Otrossi quando el rrey partio de Seuilla para yr a Galizia e desque fue a la batalla de Najara, el dicho don Iohan Alfonso finco en Seuilla en vno con el maestre de Santiago don Gonçalo Mexia, que el rrey don Enrrique dexara en Seuilla por capitan. E quando las nueuas llegaron commo la batalla de Najara vençieran el rrey don Pedro e el prinçipe, partieron el dicho maestre don Gonçalo Mexia e don Iohan Alfonso de Guzman de Seuilla e fueronsse para Alburquerque, que lo tenia Garçi Gonçalez de Herrera por el conde don Sancho, hermano del rrey don Enrrique. E quando el rrey don Pedro torno a Seuilla despues de la batalla vençida, fallo ý a doña Vrraca de Osorio, madre del dicho don Iohan Alfonso de Guzman, e con grand saña que auia de su fijo, fizola prender e matola muy cruel mente e mandole tomar todos sus bienes que ella e su fijo auian.

E otrossy antes que el rrey don Pedro llegasse a la çibdat de Seuilla, tenian ya tomada su partida del, e don Gonçalo Mexia maestre de Santiago e don Iohan Alfonso de Guzman e todos los otros caualleros que ally estauan por la partida del rrey don Enrrique, commo quier que algunos dias porfiaron de estar ally, enpero despues non pudieron sofrirlo e partieron dende.

E en este tienpo don Gil Boca Negra almirante de Castilla e don Iohan Ponçe de Leon señor de Marchena e otros caualleros que touieran la partida del rrey don Enrrique, antes que el rrey don Pedro llegasse a Seuilla, por su mandado fueron muertos.

Capitulo XXVIIIº. Commo el rrey don Pedro fizo matar en Seuilla a Martin Yañes su tesorero que fuera.

Otrosi segund auemos contado, Martin Yañes thesorero mayor del rrey don Pedro, que fue tomado con la galea en que leuaua el thesoro e despues sienpre andudo con el rrey don Enrrique, ca non osaua yr al rrey don Pedro por la galea que perdiera con el thesoro, e acaesçio

Moreover, when King Pedro left Seville for Galicia and once he had gone to take part in the battle of Nájera, Don Juan Alfonso remained in Seville together with the master of Santiago Don Gonzalo Mejía, whom King Enrique had left in charge of the city. Then, when the news arrived of how the battle of Nájera had been won by King Pedro and the prince, the master Don Gonzalo Mejía and Don Juan Alfonso de Guzmán left Seville for Alburquerque, which was being held by Garci González de Herrera on behalf of King Enrique's brother Count Sancho. When King Pedro returned to Seville following his victory in the battle, he found Doña Urraca de Osorio in the city. Doña Urraca was the mother of Don Juan Alfonso de Guzmán and, out of the anger that he felt towards her son, the king had her arrested and put to death with great cruelty, ordering the seizure of all her possessions and of those of her son.[21]

Indeed, by the time that King Pedro had reached the city of Seville, its people had already declared their support for him. The master of Santiago Don Gonzalo Mejía, Don Juan Alfonso de Guzmán and all the other knights who were supporters of King Enrique, although they had persisted in remaining there for some days, eventually had been unable to cope with the situation and had abandoned the city.

During this period before King Pedro reached Seville, the admiral of Castile Don Gil Boccanegra, the lord of Marchena Don Juan Ponce de León and other knights who had declared their support for King Enrique were put to death at the king's command.

1367: CHAPTER XXVIII

How King Pedro had Martín Yáñez, who had been his treasurer, executed in Seville.

Moreover, as we have already related, King Pedro's chief treasurer Martín Yáñez, who had been captured with the galley on which he was transporting the treasure, from that time on remained on the side of King Enrique, not daring to approach King Pedro on account of

con el rrey don Enrrique en la batalla de Najara, e despues que fue vençida, fuesse con don Gomez Perez de Porras prior de Sand Iohan, que escapo de la batalla, e fueronsse para Trasmiera, que es çerca de Asturias de Santillana. E vn escudero de la tierra, que dizien Martin Velez de Rada, prisole al Martin Yañes e leuogelo al rrey don Pedro a Seuilla por mar. E el rrey luego que lo vio mandolo matar en Seuilla diziendo que por el auia perdido su thesoro. E Martin Yañes dixo que non fuera perdido a su culpa, ca el quisiera conplir lo que el rrey le mandara, pero tal bolliçio era en la gente de Seuilla que armaran vna galea e otros nauios, de los quales non se pudiera defender.

Capitulo XXIX°. Commo la rreyna doña Iohana, muger del rrey don Enrrique, que estaua en Aragon, ouo su consejo con aquellos que amauan seruiçio del rrey don Enrrique si estaria en Aragon o sy se yria para Françia do estaua el rrey don Enrrique su marido.

Agora tornaremos a contar commo fizo la rreyna doña Iohana despues que llego a la çibdat de Çaragoça. Assi fue que la rreyna doña Iohana, muger del rrey don Enrrique, estando en Çaragoça, non sabia commo auia de fazer, ca en Aragon non osaua estar por quanto auia muchos grandes en el rregno que non querian bien al rrey don Enrrique su marido, assi commo era la rreyna de Aragon e el conde de Vrgel e el conde de Cardona e otros. E otrossy non sabia adonde yria, ca el rrey don Enrrique estaua muy desbaratado en Françia e non fallaua las ayudas assy commo le cunplian por quanto era paz entre el rrey de Françia e el rrey de Ingla terra.

E ouo la rreyna su consejo con algunos grandes señores e caualleros de Aragon que querian bien el seruiçio del rrey don Enrrique, los quales eran el infante don Pedro, tio del rrey de Aragon e el conde

having lost the treasure galley. He took part with King Enrique in the battle of Nájera and, after its outcome had been decided, he rode off with the prior of Saint John Don Gómez Pérez de Porras, who escaped from the field of battle, and they headed for Trasmiera, near to Asturias de Santillana.[22] A squire from that region by the name of Martín Vélez de Rada captured Martín Yáñez and took him by sea to King Pedro in Seville. As soon as he saw him the king ordered him to be put to death in that city, saying that he was to blame for the loss of his treasure. Martín Yáñez argued that the treasure had not been lost through his fault, for he had sought to carry out the king's command but there was such disturbance among the people of Seville that they had armed a galley and other ships, against which he had been unable to defend himself.

1367: CHAPTER XXIX

How King Enrique's wife Queen Juana, who was in Aragon, consulted the loyal supporters of King Enrique as to whether she should remain in Aragon or leave to join her husband King Enrique in France.

Now we shall return to our account of what Queen Juana did after her arrival in the city of Saragossa. The situation was that King Enrique's wife Queen Juana, now that she was in Saragossa, did not know what she should do, for she did not dare to remain in Aragon as there were numerous people of importance in the kingdom who had no love for her husband King Enrique, including the queen of Aragon, the count of Urgel, the count of Cardona and others. Moreover, she did not know where she would go, for King Enrique was in a very difficult position in France and was failing to find the kind of assistance that he needed, as the kings of France and England were at peace.

Queen Juana consulted some great lords and knights of Aragon who were loyal to King Enrique: Prince Pere, uncle of the Aragonese king, the count of Ampurias, the archbishop of Saragossa, Don Pedro de

de Anpurias e el arçobispo de Çaragoça e don Pedro de Luna e otros señores e caualleros, e dixoles la quexa en que estaua e pidioles consejo. E el infante don Pedro, tio del rrey de Aragon e padre del marques de Villena, que era conde de Denia, dixo assy: 'Señora yo fuy criado en las cunas de los rreyes e conozco e se bien las maneras de las sus cortes, e non puedo mas declarar. Mas mi consejo es que luego partades de aqui e vos vayades a Françia do esta el rrey don Enrrique vuestro marido e non vos detengades en este rregno de Aragon.' E todos los otros que querian bien al rrey don Enrrique fueron en este consejo e fue bueno: ca segund las maneras e tratos que andauan entre el rrey de Aragon e el prinçipe de Gales, pudiera auer peligro en la estada de la rreyna.

E assi partio luego la rreyna de Çaragoça e fuesse para Françia, do estaua el rrey don Enrrique su marido. E fallolo en vna villa que dizen Seruian, que es en Lengua doc.

Capitulo XXX°. Commo fizo el rrey don Enrrique despues que fue en Françia.

Agora tornaremos a contar lo que fizo el rrey don Enrrique despues que llego en Françia a Villa Nueua çerca de Aviñon, do diximos que llegara despues que partiera de la batalla. E assi fue que quando el rrey don Enrrique llego a Villa Nueua çerca de Aviñon, que es del señorio del rrey de Françia, e era ý don Luys duque de Angeu, hermano del rrey de Françia e su lugar teniente en Lenguadoc, que es vna grand partida del rregno de Françia. E commo quier que segund diximos rresçibio muy bien al rrey don Enrrique e partio con el de su tesoro, enpero non le plogo con el, ca estonçe el rrey de Françia e el rrey de Ingla terra auian fecho sus pazes e auian entregado el ducado de Gujana al prinçipe e estaua el prinçipe muy apoderado. E rresçelauasse el duque de Angeu por la vista e acogimiento que el fazia al rrey don Enrrique,

Luna and other lords and knights. She explained to them the difficulty in which she found herself and asked them for advice. Prince Pere, uncle of the king of Aragon and father of the marquis of Villena, who was also count of Denia, spoke out as follows: 'My lady, I was brought up in the birthplace of kings and I understand and know well the ways of their courts – I can say no more about this. However, my advice is that you leave here without delay and that you go to France to join your husband King Enrique without remaining any longer in this kingdom of Aragon.' And all the others who were loyal to King Enrique agreed with this counsel, which was sound; for in view of the relationship and dealings between the king of Aragon and the prince of Wales there could have been danger if the queen had stayed in Aragon.

And so the queen left Saragossa for France to join her husband King Enrique. She found him in a town called Servian in Languedoc.

1367: CHAPTER XXX

What King Enrique did once he was in France.

Now we shall return to our account of what King Enrique did after arriving in France, in Villeneuve near to Avignon, where, as we have already said, he had come after leaving the field of battle. The fact is that, when King Enrique reached Villeneuve, which is situated close to Avignon and is under the lordship of the king of France, Duke Louis of Anjou was present there. Duke Louis was a brother of the king of France and his lieutenant in Languedoc, which makes up a substantial area of the kingdom of France. Although, as we have said, he gave a warm welcome to King Enrique and gave him part of his treasure, on the other hand he was not pleased that he had come, for at that time the kings of France and England were at peace and had placed the duchy of Guyenne in the hands of the prince, who was in a position of considerable power. The duke of Anjou was uneasy about meeting with King Enrique and giving him such a welcome,

que non le plazeria al rrey de Françia, cuyo hermano el era, por que el prinçipe non entendiesse que el rrey de Françia auia voluntad de boluer la guerra e dixiesse que el acogia a los onbres que el non queria bien, espeçial mente tan grande omne commo el rrey don Enrrique; ca commo quier que el rrey don Enrrique auia seydo desbaratado e era fuera del rregno de Castilla, pero era muy buen cauallero e de grand esfuerço e muy amado en el rregno de Castilla. E el prinçipe avn se rresçelaua del. E el duque de Angeu escusose quanto pudo por lo non veer e desque vio que se non podia escusar de veerlo, hordeno que diessen por posada al rrey don Enrrique la torre de la puente de Auiñon que es de la parte del rrey de Françia, e alli secreta mente vino la primera vez que lo vio el duc de Angeu al rrey don Enrrique. E fue su consejo que enbiasse contar al rrey de Françia su fazienda e pidirle ayuda e conssejo sobre lo que ouiesse de fazer. E estonçe era Papa Vrbano quinto, el qual estaua en Auiñon.

E el rrey don Enrrique fizo segunt el conssejo del duc de Angeu e enbio sus mensageros al rrey don Carlos de Françia a do el estaua en Paris, a le contar commo el era venido a su rregno de Françia despues que fuera desbaratado en la batalla de Najara, e que le rrogaua que le quisiesse ayudar e confortar en aquella manera que el viesse que le conplia, ca la casa de Françia era la mayor de los christianos e non deuia fallesçer a los que tal caso commo el auian auido, espeçial mente que el rrey de Françia sabia bien que el rrey don Pedro era aliado con el rrey de Ingla terra e con el prinçipe su fijo e non queria bien a la casa de Françia maguer que de presente estauan en paz.

E el rrey de Françia luego que ouo sus mensageros e cartas del rrey don Enrrique, enbiole muy buenas cartas de rrespuesta e mando al duc de Angeu, su hermano e su lugar teniente en Lenguadoc, que le diesse al rrey don Enrrique çinquenta mill francos de oro, los quales le fueron pagados en la çibdat de Narbona, e avn por el estar mas seguro, pues tenia ally en su rregno la rreyna su muger e los infantes sus fijos, diole vn castillo que era en aquella comarca do el estaua, que dizian Piera Pertusa, que era muy fuerte e era del rrey de Françia, en frontera de Aragon. Otrossy le mando dar vn condado en Lenguadoc, que llaman

which would not please his brother the king of France. The king did not want the prince to draw the conclusion that he intended to restart the war and accuse him of harbouring his opponents, especially a man of such standing as King Enrique: for, although King Enrique had been defeated and was in exile from the kingdom of Castile, he was nevertheless a fine and courageous knight, much loved in Castile. The prince was still uneasy about him. So the duke of Anjou did all that he could to avoid meeting with King Enrique and then, once he saw that he could not help doing so, he instructed that he be lodged in the tower of the bridge of Avignon on the side belonging to the king of France, and the duke of Anjou came there in secrecy the first time that he met with him.[23] The duke's advice was that Enrique should send envoys to tell the king of France about his position and to ask him for help and advice as to how he should act. At that time the Pope, who was in Avignon, was Urban V.

King Enrique followed the advice of the duke of Anjou and sent emissaries to King Charles of France in Paris to tell him how he had come to his kingdom following his defeat in the battle of Nájera. He requested that King Charles agree to give him assistance and support in whatever manner he considered fitting; for the royal House of France was the greatest in Christendom and should not fail those who had suffered a setback such as his, especially since the king of France was well aware that King Pedro was an ally of the king of England and of his son the prince and that he was no friend of the House of France, even though at present they were at peace.

As soon as the king of France had received King Enrique's emissaries bearing his letter, he wrote to him very warmly in reply and instructed the duke of Anjou, his brother and his lieutenant in Languedoc, to give King Enrique 50,000 gold francs, which were paid over to him in the city of Narbonne. Moreover, in order to give King Enrique greater security – since he had there with him in the kingdom of France both his wife the queen and his children, the prince and the princess, – he gave him a castle situated in the area in which he was currently staying. This was a strongly fortified castle called Peyrepertuse which belonged to the king of France and stood on the frontier with Aragon. King Charles also commanded that King Enrique be given a county in Languedoc, known

el condado de Sezeno, en que ha tres villas, la vna llaman Tesan, otra Seruian e a la otra Sesenon. E commo quier que este condado le ouiera dado al rrey don Enrrique el rrey don Iohan de Françia quando el rrey don Enrrique era con el e le seruia en las guerras que ouiera con Ingla terra, pero despues que ouiera enpeñado el rrey don Enrrique el dicho condado al dicho rrey de Françia, nunca lo quitara. E agora este rrey don Carlos que agora rreynaua, quando lo vio assy en grand menester al rrey don Enrrique, tornogelo.

E el rrey don Enrrique desque vio los rrecabdos que el rrey de Françia le enbiaua, assy de los buenos esfuerços que en el fallo commo de los francos que le acorrio, e otrossi el castillo e el condado que le desenbargo, fue muy alegre e contento. E luego el duc de Angeu le fizo dar los çinquenta mill francos de oro, e diole de lo suyo otros çinquenta mill, e fizole entregar el dicho condado de Sesenon. Otrossy le fizo dar el dicho castillo de Piera Pertusa e entregogelo vn cauallero muy bueno, que era senescal de Carcaxona por el rrey de Françia, que dizian mossen Arnao de España.

E el rrey don Enrrique estudo algunos dias en vna villa que dizen Tesan, del dicho condado de Sesenon e despues en otra que dizen Servian, e despues se fue para el castillo de Piera Pertusa, e lleuo alli la rreyna doña Iohana su muger e sus fijos, el infante don Iohan e la infanta doña Leonor. E enbio a Aviñon a conprar muchos arneses de armas, ca de cada dia le venian caualleros e escuderos e otras gentes de Castilla e se aparejauan para tornar a ella.

Capitulo XXXI°. Commo el rrey don Enrrique auia nueuas de Castilla que los señores e caualleros que tenian su partida se esforçauan de cada dia.

En este tiempo auia el rrey don Enrrique, de cada dia, nueuas de Castilla commo el rrey don Pedro e el prinçipe non se abinian bien e commo algunos caualleros de los que fueran presos en la batalla

as the county of Cessenon, which includes three towns: Thézan, Servian and Cessenon.[24] Although King Enrique had previously been granted this county by King Jean of France while he had been in his service, fighting on his side during his wars with England, he had subsequently handed it over to the French monarch as security for a loan and had never redeemed it. At this point King Charles, who was now on the throne, on seeing King Enrique in such great need, returned it to him.

When he saw the support that the king of France was giving him, in terms of both warm encouragement and financial assistance, and also with regard to the castle and the county that were restored to him, King Enrique was delighted and filled with satisfaction. The duke of Anjou lost no time in arranging for him to receive the 50,000 gold francs and he gave him another 50,000 on his own account, as well as having the county of Cessenon made over to him. In addition, he arranged for the castle of Peyrepertuse to be given to King Enrique and it was handed over to him by Monsieur Arnaud d'Espagne, a very fine knight who was seneschal of Carcassonne on behalf of the king of France.

King Enrique stayed for a few days in the town of Thézan in the county of Cessenon and then in the town called Servian, and from there he went on to the castle of Peyrepertuse, taking with him his wife Queen Juana and his children, Prince Juan and Princess Leonor. He sent to Avignon to buy a large number of sets of armour, for each day he was being joined by knights, squires and other troops from Castile and they were making ready to set off back to their kingdom.

1367: CHAPTER XXXI

How King Enrique received reports from Castile that the lords and knights who supported him were becoming more emboldened by the day.

During this period King Enrique was receiving daily reports from Castile about how King Pedro and the prince were falling out and how some of the knights who had been taken prisoner had now regained

eran ya delibres e estauan en los castillos que primero tenian e fazian dellos guerra al rrey don Pedro, los quales eran estos: del castillo de Peñafiel e del castillo de Curiel e del castillo de Gormaz e del castillo de Atiença e del alcaçar de Segouia, e assi en partidas de otros logares. E sopo del rrey don Pedro despues que fiziera su pleytesia e juramento con el prinçipe de Gales en Burgos, se fuera para Seuilla, e maguer el prinçipe le auia atendido los quatro meses que le pusiera de le pagar la primera paga de lo que deuia a el e a sus gentes que con el vinieran, assy de sus estados commo de las gajes que les eran deuidas, que nunca ouiera dende rrecabdo nin entregara al prinçipe a Vizcaya nin a Soria a mossen Iohan Chandos, e que el prinçipe se queria partir de Castilla e tornarsse a su tierra desabenido del rrey don Pedro.

E ouo cartas el rrey don Enrrique de algunos caualleros ingleses, sus amigos, que fueran en su seruiçio en la entrada que el fiziera en Castilla quando se llamara rrey e andauan en la conpañia del prinçipe agora, que le consejauan que fasta que el prinçipe salliesse de Castilla, que el non fuesse alla; pero que luego que sopiesse que era partido, que non se detouiesse e fuesse çierto que el prinçipe era del todo mal contento del rrey don Pedro e que non tornaria a ayudarle nin las conpañas que con el venieran, por quanto non les pagara.

Otrossi sopo el rrey don Enrrique commo don Gonçalo Mexia maestre de Santiago e don Iohan Alfonso de Guzman, que fue despues conde de Niebla, e otros caualleros que dexara en Seuilla, partieran dende, por que toda la tierra tomaua la boz del rrey don Pedro con grand miedo que del auian, e que eran en Alburquerque e en esa comarca, e que ya yuan llegando a tierra del maestradgo de Santiago e eran mucha conpaña e fazian guerra al rrey don Pedro. Otrossy sopo commo todos los caualleros e escuderos suyos que fueron presos en la batalla eran libres e fuera de prision, e se yuan en caualgando e armando, e se ponian en villas e castillos e fortalezas, e fazian guerra contra el rrey don Pedro, e todos estauan por el. E sopo el rrey don Enrrique commo la çibdat de Segouia, por quanto el alcaçar estaua por el, era ya en su obediençia.

their freedom and once again were occupying the castles that they had held previously. Moreover, some of them were waging war on King Pedro from these castles, namely those of Peñafiel, Curiel, Gormaz, Atienza and the *alcázar* of Segovia, as well as a number of other places. King Enrique learned how after giving his solemn pledge to the prince of Wales in Burgos King Pedro had left for Seville and how, although the prince had waited for the four months that he had allowed for the king to pay the first part of what he owed to him and to the troops in his company, to cover both their expenses and the pay owing to them, none of it had ever been received; nor had King Pedro handed over Vizcaya to the prince or Soria to Sir John Chandos. King Enrique also heard that the prince intended to leave Castile and return to his own land, at odds with King Pedro.

King Enrique received letters from some English knights who were his allies and had been in his service at the time when he had entered Castile and taken the title of King. These men, who were now accompanying the prince, advised King Enrique that he should not return to Castile as long as the prince remained there, but that as soon as he learned that he had left he should not delay in making his entry; and they told him to rest assured that the prince was thoroughly displeased with King Pedro and that neither he nor the troops who had accompanied him would assist the king again, since he had failed to pay them.

King Enrique also heard how the master of Santiago Don Gonzalo Mejía, Don Juan Alfonso de Guzmán, later to become count of Niebla, and other knights that he had left in Seville, had abandoned that city, as the whole region was declaring its support for King Pedro out of the fear that they felt for him, and how those men were in Alburquerque and in the surrounding area; they were gathering in the territory of the Order of Santiago and made up a considerable force which was waging war on King Pedro. Moreover, King Enrique learned how all those of his knights and squires who had been captured in the battle were now free and out of prison, how they were equipping themselves with horses and armour, occupying castles and fortresses and campaigning against King Pedro.They had all given their support to King Enrique. And in addition King Enrique heard how the city of Segovia − since the *alcázar* had given him its support − was now loyal to him.

Otrossi sopo el rrey don Enrrique commo estos logares tenian por el e tenian su boz, a saber: los castillos de Peñafiel e Curiel e Atiença e Gormaz e Ayllon e la villa de Valladolid e la çibdat de Palençia e la çibdat de Auila e toda Vizcaya e otras muchas villas e logares e comarcas. Otrossi sopo commo estaua por el Guipuzcoa, saluo dos villas, las quales eran Sand Sebastian e Guetaria, que eran en Guipuzcoa, e assy de cada dia auia muchas nueuas con que se esforçaua.

Otrossy en el ducado de Gujana andauan algunos capitanes de conpañas, que fazian guerra al prinçipe, los quales eran: Lymosin e Perrin de Saboya e otros, e de cada dia se yua descubriendo mas la guerra entre Françia e Ingla terra.

Capitulo XXXII°. Commo el rrey don Enrrique se vio con el duc de Angeu, hermano del rrey de Françia en Aguas Muertas e con el cardenal de Boloña, e commo se fizieron alli ligas suyas con la casa de Françia.

Estando el rrey don Enrrique en el castillo de Piera Pertusa, commo dicho auemos, hordenandosse de cada dia para partirsse dende e yrsse para Castilla, fue tratado que el se viesse con el duc de Angeu, hermano del rrey de Françia e su lugar teniente en Lenguadoc, en vna villa del rrey de Françia que dizen Aguas Muertas. E fue el rrey don Enrrique para alla e fallo ally en Aguas Muertas al duc de Angeu e al cardenal de Boloña, que dizien don Guido, que era fijo del conde de Boloña e pariente del rrey de Françia, e era omne de grand linaje e de la casa de Françia. E alli fue el rrey don Enrrique muy bien rresçibido e ouieron su consejo muy secreto, ca bien sabian que el prinçipe era partido de Castilla e se venia para Gujana con entençion de fazer guerra a Françia. E fizieron sus tratos el duc de Angeu e el cardenal de Boloña e sus abenençias por el rrey de Françia, con el rrey don Enrrique las mas firmes que pudieron alli hordenar e firmaron las con

King Enrique also heard how the following places were on his side and had declared their support for him: the castles of Peñafiel, Curiel, Atienza, Gormaz and Ayllón, the town of Valladolid, the cities of Palencia and Ávila, all of Vizcaya and many other towns, villages and districts. He also heard that Guipúzcoa had given him its support, with the exception of two of its towns: San Sebastián and Guetaria. And thus each day he received many reports which gave him heart.

Moreover, in the duchy of Guyenne some captains of the Companies – Limousin, Perrin of Savoie and others – were actively waging war on the prince, and with each day that passed the approach of war between France and England was becoming more apparent.

1367: CHAPTER XXXII

How in Aigues-Mortes King Enrique met with the duke of Anjou, brother of the king of France, and with the cardinal of Boulogne; and how an alliance was formed between King Enrique and the royal House of France.

While King Enrique was in the castle of Peyrepertuse, as we explained, devoting every day to preparations for his departure for Castile, it was arranged that he would meet with the duke of Anjou, brother of the king of France and his lieutenant in Languedoc, in a town called Aigues-Mortes which belonged to the French king. On arriving in Aigues-Mortes, King Enrique found the duke of Anjou and Cardinal Guy de Boulogne. Cardinal Guy was the son of the count of Boulogne and a relative of the king of France; he was a man of high birth and a member of the royal House of France. King Enrique was given a warm welcome, and their discussions took place in great secrecy, for they were well aware that by now the prince had left Castile and was on his way to Guyenne intending to wage war on France. On behalf of the king of France, the duke of Anjou and the cardinal of Boulogne carried out their negotiations and concluded agreements with King Enrique which were as firm as it was possible to make them under

juramento entre ellos. E dio el duc de Angeu al rrey don Enrrique pieça de moneda de oro para yr a Castilla.

E partio el rrey don Enrrique de Aguas Muertas mediado el mes de agosto deste dicho año e tornose para el castillo de Piera Pertusa, donde auia dexado la rreyna doña Iohana su muger e los infantes sus fijos, e de alli enbio buscar conpaña para que fuessen con el en Castilla. E el tenia consigo estonçe fasta dozientas lanças e fallo otras dozientas, de las quales eran capitanes el conde de la Ylla e don Bernal conde de Osona e el bastardo de Bearne e mossen Berni de Villamur, que fuera preso en la batalla de Najera e era ya suelto. E venieron con el rrey, el vegue de Villanes, commo quier que las mas conpañas destas tenia el bastardo de Bearne, que fue despues conde de Medina Çeli en Castilla.

Capitulo XXXIIIº. Commo el rrey don Enrrique torno a Castilla e commo el rrey de Aragon le queria destoruar el camino e la pasada por su rregno si pudiera.

El rrey don Enrrique hordeno de partir para Castilla e leuo consigo la rreyna doña Iohana su muger e el infante don Iohan su fijo e dexo en el castillo de Piera Pertusa la infanta doña Leonor su fija e otras dueñas e donzellas con ella. E el rrey de Aragon, que auia fecho su abenençia con el prinçipe de Gales, desque sopo que el rrey don Enrrique tornaua para Castilla e auia de passar por su rregno, enbiole dezir con vn su cauallero gouernador de Rossellon que le rrequeria que non pasasse por su rregno, ca el era amigo del prinçipe e non le queria fazer enojo, e si el al quisiesse fazer, que non dexaria de gelo defender. E el rrey don Enrrique le rrespondio al cauallero que el se marauillaua mucho del rrey de Aragon de le enbiar dezir tal cosa, ca

those circumstances, and they confirmed them by the swearing of oaths. The duke of Anjou gave King Enrique a substantial sum in gold coin for his return to Castile.

King Enrique left Aigues-Mortes in mid-August of the year in question and went back to the castle of Peyrepertuse, where he had left his wife Queen Juana and his children the prince and the princess, and from there he sent out a call for troops to accompany him into Castile. At that time he had with him some 200 lances and he acquired another 200, whose captains were the viscount of Illa, Count Bernat of Osona, the Bastard of Béarn and also Monsieur Bernard de Villemur, who had been taken prisoner in the battle of Nájera but had by now been released.[25] Le Bègue de Villaines also went with King Enrique, although it was the Bastard of Béarn, later to become count of Medinaceli in Castile, who contributed most of these troops.

1367: CHAPTER XXXIII

How King Enrique returned to Castile and how it was the intention of the king of Aragon, if he could, to block his way and prevent him from passing through his kingdom.

King Enrique made arrangements for his departure for Castile. He took with him his wife Queen Juana and his son Prince Juan, but he left his daughter Princess Leonor in the castle of Peyrepertuse, together with other noble ladies and ladies-in-waiting. The king of Aragon – who had reached an agreement with the prince of Wales –, on learning that King Enrique was on his way back to Castile and needed to pass through his kingdom, sent word with one of his knights, the governor of Roussillon, forbidding him to do so: the knight told King Enrique that the king of Aragon was an ally of the prince and did not wish to cause him displeasure, and that if King Enrique chose to go against his wishes he would most certainly stand in his way. King Enrique replied to the knight that he was highly surprised that the king of Aragon had sent him such a message, for King Pere was

sabia el muy bien que en el tienpo que a el cunpliera en sus guerras, que nunca le fallesçiera. Otrossi por la su entrada que el fiziera en Castilla, le fiziera cobrar çiento e veynte villas e castillos que el rrey don Pedro le tenia ganados; enpero que el auia de yr a Castilla e que non pudia escusar de pasar por su rregno de Aragon, e que si el quisiesse tener el camino e destoruarle, que faria en ello su voluntad; pero que el non pudia al fazer e que de qualquier destoruo que le quisiese fazer, que el se defenderia muy bien.

E auia muchos del rregno, segund ya deximos, que tenian la parte del rrey don Enrrique e lo amauan, los quales eran el infante don Pedro, padre de don Alfonso conde de Denia que el rrey don Enrrique fiziera despues marques de Villena, e estaua el marques estonçe en poder de los ingleses, que fuera preso en la batalla de Najara, segund ya deximos. Otrossy eran de la parte del rrey don Enrrique, que tenian en la corte del rrey de Aragon su vando: el conde de Anpurias, que era de la casa rreal, fijo del infante don Remon Berenguel, que fuera fijo del rrey don Jaymes de Aragon, e el arçobispo de Çaragoça, que dizian don Lope Ferrandez de Luna, e don Pedro de Luna e don Iohan Martinez de Luna e otros grandes señores. E el infante don Pedro, de quien diximos, que era tio del rrey don Pedro de Aragon, hermano del rrey don Alfonso su padre, enbio al rrey don Enrrique vn escudero que era de su casa, que le guiase por su tierra, que dizian de Ribagorça.

E el rrey don Enrrique partio de Piera Pertusa donde estaua e vino por toda la tierra de Aragon pasando por vnas sierras de Val de Andorra muy fuertes e con grand enojo de muchas gentes de tierra del rrey de Aragon, que de cada dia le tenian los caminos e le fazian quanto destoruo pudian, pero que lo non atendian a batalla. E llego el rrey don Enrrique con grant trabajo a vna villa de Ribagorça que era del señorio del infante don Pedro, que dizen Arenes, e ally estudo el rrey don Enrrique e los que con el venian dos dias descansando.

E despues partio el rrey don Enrrique de aquel lugar de Arenes continuando su camino para Castilla, e fallo al infante don Pedro en otro su logar que dizen Abennauarra e fizole dar viandas e todo

well aware that the king of Castile had never failed him when he had needed his help in his wars. In addition, as a result of his invasion of Castile, he had enabled the king of Aragon to recover 120 towns and castles which King Pedro had won from him. Nevertheless, he informed him that he needed to go to Castile and that he could not avoid passing through the kingdom of Aragon. If King Pere chose to bar the road to him and stand in his way, he must do just as he wished, but King Enrique could not follow any other course and he would defend himself vigorously against any attempts to bar his path.

As we have already pointed out, there were many people in the kingdom of Aragon who were supporters of King Enrique and who were loyal to him. These included Prince Pere, father of Count Alfons of Denia whom King Enrique had subsequently created marquis of Villena and, having been captured during the battle of Nájera – as we have already explained – was currently in the hands of the English. Other supporters of King Enrique, constituting a faction in the court of the king of Aragon, were the count of Ampurias, who was of royal lineage – the son of Prince Remón Berenguer, whose father had been King Jaume of Aragon – the archbishop of Saragossa Don Lope Fernández de Luna, Don Pedro de Luna, Don Juan Martínez de Luna and other great lords. Prince Pere, who, as we have said, was uncle to King Pere of Aragon, being the brother of his father King Alfons, sent a squire from his household to guide King Enrique across his lands, known as Ribagorza.

King Enrique set off from Peyrepertuse and crossed the territory of Aragon, making his way over a very high range of mountains bordering the Valley of Andorra.[26] This was much to the annoyance of many inhabitants of the king of Aragon's territories who day after day obstructed King Enrique's route and did all that they could to prevent him from passing but without engaging him in battle. With great difficulty the king reached a town in Ribagorza called Arén which was under the lordship of Prince Pere, and here he and his company halted for two days to rest.

After that King Enrique set off from Arén, continuing on his way towards Castile, and he found Prince Pere in another town in his territory which was called Benabarre. Prince Pere ensured that the king and all those accompanying him were supplied with provisions

lo que ouo menester, e a los que con el venian. E dende partio el rrey don Enrrique e vinosse por el rregno de Aragon a otro lugar que dizen Estadilla, que era de don Phelipe de Castro, vn rrico omne de Aragon, que era casado con vna su hermana del rrey don Enrrique que dizian doña Iohana. E estonçe estaua don Phelipe preso en el castillo de Burgos en poder del rrey don Pedro, ca fuera preso en la batalla de Najara. E despues que el rrey don Enrrique llego en el lugar de Estadilla, ouo nueuas commo el rrey de Aragon mandara a todos los suyos que salliessen al camino a pelear con el e que eran partidos los pendones del rrey de Aragon e muchas gentes con ellos fuera de la çibdat de Çaragoça.

E el rrey don Enrrique partio esse dia del dicho lugar de Estadilla e fue dormir essa noche a vna villa que dizen Valuastro, del rrey de Aragon. E alli sopo commo el rrey de Aragon era en Çaragoça e que tenia ý conpañas ayuntadas e las auia mandado pasar la puente que es sobre Ebro, e que estaua ya fuera de la çibdat el su pendon del rrey de Aragon do se auian de ayuntar las conpañas para que fuessen a tomar el camino al rrey don Enrrique; pero los de Aragon non lo fazian todos de buen talante, ca todos los mas querian bien al rrey don Enrrique e non querian partir de la çibdat de Çaragoça para yr contra el en ninguna guisa. E el rrey don Enrrique partio otro dia de Valuastro e fue por Huesca continuando su camino para Castilla. E paso por el rregno de Nauarra e llego a la çibdat de Calahorra que es en la frontera de Castilla. E los de Calahorra rresçibieron lo muy bien e acogieron lo en la çibdat con todos los que traya. E enbio luego el rrey don Enrrique conpañas al camino por do venia de Çaragoça don Gomez Manrrique arçobispo de Toledo e algunos caualleros e vasallos suyos del rrey e muchas dueñas e donzellas e otras conpañas suyas que eran en la çibdat de Çaragoça, que eran alli ayuntados despues que la pelea de Najara fuera desbaratada. E atendiolos el rrey en Calahorra fasta que venieron todos e ally estudo fasta que los rrecogio a todos.

and everything that they needed. King Enrique then set off again and travelled through the kingdom of Aragon as far as another small town called Estadilla, which belonged to Don Felipe de Castro, an Aragonese magnate married to Doña Juana, King Enrique's sister. At that time Don Felipe was being held prisoner in Burgos castle by order of King Pedro, having been captured in the battle of Nájera. Then, once King Enrique had reached Estadilla, he received reports of how the king of Aragon had issued a command that all of his subjects were to go and do battle with him – King Enrique – and of how a large body of troops accompanying the standards of the king of Aragon had set off from the city of Saragossa.

That same day King Enrique left Estadilla and went to spend the night in a town called Barbastro which belonged to the king of Aragon. There he learned that the king of Aragon was in Saragossa, where he had assembled troops and instructed them to cross the bridge over the Ebro. King Pere's standard had now been raised outside the city, and this was where his forces were to assemble ready to march against King Enrique. On the other hand King Enrique learned that not all the people of Aragon were doing this willingly, for most of them supported him and in no way did they want to move out from Saragossa to attack him. King Enrique left Barbastro on the following day and continued his journey towards Castile by way of Huesca. He crossed the kingdom of Navarre, reaching the city of Calahorra on the Castilian frontier. The people of Calahorra gave him a warm reception and welcomed him into the city together with all of his company. King Enrique promptly sent troops out to the road along which Archbishop Gómez Manrique of Toledo was travelling from Saragossa together with some knights and vassals of the king, numerous noble ladies and ladies-in-waiting and others of his supporters who had gathered in the city of Saragossa after the defeat in the battle of Nájera. The king waited for them in Calahorra until they had all arrived and remained there until he had gathered them all together.

Capitulo XXXIVº. Commo fizo el rrey don Enrrique despues que llego a la çibdat de Calahorra e commo enbio saber la voluntad de los de la çibdat de Burgos sy lo acogerian en ella.

El dia que el rrey don Enrrique fue a vista de la çibdat de Calahorra, donde fuera acogido bien segund auemos contado, antes que llegasse a la çibdat armo cauallero en vn canpo çerca del rrio de Ebro a don Bernal de Bear[n]e, que fizo despues el rrey conde de Medina Çeli, que venia con el. E otrossy esse dia pregunto el rrey don Enrrique a los que venian con el si estaua ya en los terminos de Castilla e ellos le dixeron que sy. E el estonçe descaualgo de vn cauallo en que venia e finco los ynojos en tierra e fizo vna cruz en vn arenal que estaua çerca del rrio de Ebro e beso en ella e despues dixo assy: 'Yo lo juro a esta significança de cruz que nunca en mi vida, por menester que aya, salga del rregno de Castilla e antes espere ý la muerte o la ventura que me viniere.' E esto dizia el rrey don Enrrique por que salliera del rregno de Castilla despues de la pelea de Najara e fallara asaz graues todas las cosas que ouo de librar con sus amigos e con los que le auian de ayudar. Otrossy armo cauallero otro escudero que le diera el conde de Fox quando paso por su casa el rrey don Enrrique despues de la batalla de Najara, que dizian el escudero Dolet.

E llegaron al rrey don Enrrique en la çibdat de Calahorra caualleros e omnes de armas de Castilla, que tenian su parte e andauan por el dicho rregno de Castilla fasta seysçientas lanças, los quales eran don Iohan Alfonso de Haro e don Iohan Remirez de Arellano e don Melen Suarez teniente lugar de maestre de Alcantara e otros muchos caualleros e escuderos de Castilla e bretones que fueron en la batalla de Najara de la parte del rrey don Enrrique e eran ya armados e encabalgados. E el rrey don Enrrique los rresçibio mucho bien e le plugo mucho con ellos.

E estudo el rrey don Enrrique fasta que llegaron ý en Calahorra el arçobispo de Toledo don Gomez Manrrique e algunos caualleros

1367: CHAPTER XXXIV

Concerning what King Enrique did after arriving in the city of Calahorra and how he sent envoys to enquire whether it was the will of the citizens of Burgos to admit him into their city.

On the day that King Enrique came within sight of Calahorra, where – as we have already related – he had previously been given a warm welcome, and before making his entry into the city, in a field near the River Ebro, he knighted Don Bernard de Béarn who was accompanying him and whom he later created count of Medinaceli. Also that day the king asked the people with him if he was now within the frontiers of Castile and they informed him that he was. At this he dismounted, knelt down and, marking a cross in a stretch of sand near the river Ebro, he kissed it and then said, 'I swear by this image of the Cross that never in my lifetime, whatever may be my need, will I leave the kingdom of Castile. Rather than doing so, I will remain there to await either my death or whatever fortune befalls me.' King Enrique uttered these words because, having left the kingdom of Castile after the battle of Nájera, he had encountered considerable difficulty in all the negotiations that were necessary with his allies and with those who had to give him their support. He also knighted another squire called Dolet who had been assigned to him by the count of Foix during the king's stay in his household after the battle of Nájera.[27]

In the city of Calahorra King Enrique was joined by knights and men-at-arms from Castile who were his supporters and were roaming the kingdom in a company of some 600 lances: Don Juan Alfonso de Haro, Don Juan Ramírez de Arellano and Don Melén Suárez, lieutenant master of the Order of Alcántara, and many other knights and squires from Castile and Brittany. These men had taken part in the battle of Nájera on the side of King Enrique and were now equipped with mounts and with armour. King Enrique gave them a very warm welcome and took great pleasure in their presence.

King Enrique remained in Calahorra until the arrival of Archbishop Gómez Manrique of Toledo. The archbishop was accompanied by a

e muchas dueñas e donzellas que estauan en Aragon despues que acaesçio la batalla e se fueran para alla, segund dicho auemos. E el rrey don Enrrique auia enbiado por ellos, e despues que llegaron estas conpañas en Calahorra, tomo el rrey su camino para Burgos e paso por la villa de Logroño, que tenia la parte del rrey don Pedro, e pelearon los suyos ý en las barreras e non la pudo cobrar.

E dende fue para Burgos e antes que llegasse a ella, enbio saber la voluntad de los de la çibdat que querian fazer e que si lo acogerian ý. E a todos los de la dicha çibdat de Burgos plogo mucho con la venida del rrey don Enrrique e enbiaron luego a el sus mensageros a vn lugar que dizen Çalduendo, que es a quatro leguas de la çibdat, e dixeronle que todos los que eran en la dicha çibdat eran de acuerdo de lo acoger en ella e que les plazia mucho con la su venida e que le pidian por merçed que otro dia entrasse en la dicha çibdat, ca todos estauan prestos para lo rresçibir con aquella rreuerençia que deuian; enpero que el rrey don Pedro dexara ý quando dende partio, en el castillo de la çibdat por alcayde a vn su vezino que dizian Alfonso Ferrandez, el qual estaua en el castillo, e estauan con el, de gente de fuera de la çibdat, fasta dozientos omnes.

Otrossy sopo el rrey que estaua en el castillo de Burgos el rrey de Napol. E este rrey de Napol era fijo del rrey de Mallorcas que dizian don Jaymes e casara con doña Iohana la rreyna de Napol e por ella se llamaua rrey de Napol. E este rrey de Napol se pusiera en el castillo de Burgos quando supiera que el rrey don Enrrique venia, ca el venia en ayuda del rrey don Pedro e se acaesçiera con el en la batalla de Najara, segund suso auemos dicho. Otrossy enbiaron dezir los de la çibdat de Burgos al rrey don Enrrique que la juderia de la çibdat estaua rrebelde e que los judios tenian con Alfonso Ferrandez alcayde del castillo, mas despues que el rrey don Enrrique entrasse en la çibdat, que todo aquello cobraria e vernia a la su merçed.

E el rrey don Pedro agradesçio mucho a los de la çibdat lo que le enbiauan dezir por sus mensageros, enpero en antes que el rrey ý llegasse estauan fasta seysçientas lanças, que posauan enderredor de la çibdat por los monesterios que son enderredor della e peleauan cada dia con los de la çibdat, ca los que eran en la çibdat amauan seruiçio

number of knights and many noble ladies and ladies-in-waiting who had been in Aragon since the battle had taken place and had made their way there, as we have already related. King Enrique had sent for them to come to him, and then, once they had arrived in Calahorra, he went on his way to Burgos. He passed by the town of Logroño, which was on the side of King Pedro, but although his troops fought there at the ramparts he did not succeed in capturing the town.

From there he went on to Burgos but, before arriving, he sent envoys to find out the will of the people and to discover whether they would allow him to enter the city. All the citizens of Burgos were delighted at King Enrique's approach and lost no time in sending their envoys to him in a place called Zalduendo, situated four leagues from the city. They informed him that all of the people in the city were agreed that they should allow him to enter and that they were greatly pleased at his arrival. Moreover, they beseeched him to make his entry into the city on the following day, for they were all ready to welcome him with due reverence. This was in spite of the fact that on his departure King Pedro had left as the governor of the city's castle Alfonso Fernández, one of its citizens, who was in the castle together with some 200 men who were not natives of Burgos.

The king also learned that the king of Naples was in Burgos castle. He was the son of King Jaume of Majorca and had married Queen Giovanna of Naples, through whom he took the title of King of Naples. He had taken refuge in the castle on learning of King Enrique's approach, for he had come in support of King Pedro and had fought alongside him in the battle of Nájera, as we related above. The citizens of Burgos also sent word to King Enrique that the Jewish community had rebelled and that the Jews were in alliance with the governor of the castle, Alfonso Fernández, although once King Enrique had made his entry into the city all of this would be brought under control and the king's will would be obeyed.

King Enrique gave warm thanks to the citizens for what they had sent their messengers to tell him. However, before the king reached the city there were as many as 600 mounted troops billeted in the convents situated around it who each day fought with its people. For the people of Burgos were loyal to King Enrique, although, as we have already

del rrey don Enrrique e non se osauan descobrir fasta que vieron al rrey don Enrrique llegado, segund dicho auemos.

Capitulo XXXV°. Commo el rrey don Enrrique entro en la çibdat de Burgos e çerco el castillo e ouo por su prisionero al rrey de Napol.

Despues que el rrey don Enrrique ouo rrespuesta de los de la çibdat de Burgos commo lo acogerian de buena voluntad, partio de aquel lugar do estaua e fuesse para la çibdat de Burgos. E el obispo e toda la clerezia e todos los honrrados e buenos omnes de la çibdat lo rresçibieron con grand solepnidat, commo quier que del castillo e de la juderia tirauan truenos e saetas.

E estando el rrey en la çibdat antes que tomasse el castillo e la juderia, llegaron al rrey otros muchos caualleros e omnes de armas, que eran de su partida e andauan por el rregno faziendo guerra. E luego hordeno el rrey commo se fiziessen minas e cauas a la juderia e al castillo, e commo les armassen engeños e assy fue fecho. E mando combatir la juderia, e los judios desque vieron que non se podian defender pleytearon con el rrey e fincaron con todo lo suyo e en su merçed saluos e seguros, e seruieronle con vn cuento.

E Alfonso Fernandez alcayde del castillo estudo algunos dias porfiando e defendiendo el castillo; pero desque sopo que las cauas eran fechas e los engenios que de cada dia ponian, pleyteo con el rrey don Enrrique e vino a la su merçed e diole el castillo e entregole al rrey de Napol, que veniera a la batalla de Najara en ayuda del rrey don Pedro e estaua en el dicho castillo segund dicho auemos. E el rrey don Enrrique enbio al rrey de Napol al castillo de Curiel e despues fue rrendido por ochenta mill doblas que pago la rreyna doña Iohana de Napol por el.

related, they did not dare to show their support openly until they had witnessed the arrival of the king.

1367: CHAPTER XXXV

How King Enrique made his entry into the city of Burgos, laid siege to the castle and took the king of Naples prisoner.

Once king Enrique had received a reply from the citizens of Burgos informing him that they would willingly grant him entry, he set off towards the city. The bishop, all the clergy and all the good and honourable men of Burgos received him with great ceremony, although there was cannon and crossbow fire coming from the castle and the Jewish quarter.

During the time that the king was in the city but before he took the castle and the Jewish quarter, he was joined by numerous other knights and men-at-arms who had given him their support and were roaming the kingdom raiding the land. The king then instructed that the walls of the castle and the Jewish quarter be attacked by mining and tunnelling and that siege engines be put in position, and all of this was done. He then ordered an assault on the Jewish quarter, and once the Jews saw that they were unable to put up sufficient resistance they came to terms with the king: they kept all of their possessions, threw themselves on his mercy – remaining safe and unharmed – and paid a levy to the value of a million *maravedís*.

For some days Alfonso Fernández, the governor of the castle, continued in his struggle to defend it, but once he saw that the tunnels had been dug and day by day siege engines were being put in place, he negotiated terms with King Enrique. He swore loyalty to him, surrendered the castle to him and handed over the king of Naples, who had come to take part in the battle of Nájera on the side of King Pedro and, as we have already explained, was now in this castle. King Enrique sent the king of Naples to the castle at Curiel, and subsequently he was ransomed for the sum of 80,000 *doblas* which Queen Giovanna of Naples paid in return for his freedom.

Otrossy fallo el rrey don Enrrique en el castillo de Burgos a don Phelipe de Castro, natural de Aragon, que era casado con su hermana doña Iohana, e estaua preso en poder del rrey don Pedro, ca fuera preso en la batalla de Najara, e fue suelto. E diole el rrey a el e a doña Iohana, su muger, por heredat a Paredes de Naua e a Medina de Rio Seco e a Tordehumos.

Capitulo XXXVI°. Commo el rrey don Enrrique ouo nueuas commo la çibdat de Cordoua auia tomado su boz.

Estando el rrey don Enrrique en la çibdat de Burgos ouo nueuas commo la çibdat de Cordoua estaua ya por el e todos los caualleros e escuderos que en ella biuian eran de su parte e que enbiaron por don Gonçalo Mexia maestre de Santiago e por don Iohan Alfonso de Guzman, que fue despues conde de Niebla e por don Alfonso Perez de Guzman alguazil mayor de la çibdat de Seuilla e por otros muchos caualleros que tenian la parte del rrey don Enrrique, que estauan en Llerena e en otros lugares de aquellas comarcas e los acogieron en la çibdat de Cordoua.

Otrossi el rrey don Enrrique ouo nueuas commo el rrey don Pedro era en Seuilla e basteçia de cada dia la villa de Carmona, e ouo muy grand plazer con estas nueuas. E enbio luego a Cordoua a don Pero Moñiz maestre de Calatraua, que estaua con el, para les contar commo era ya venido de Françia e estaua en el rregno de Castilla e seria ayna con ellos. E estudo el rrey don Enrrique en Burgos algunos dias catando dineros para las gentes que con el venian por que fuessen pagados de lo que deuian auer de sus gajes e su sueldo.

Otrossi acordo de enbiar de alli de Burgos para tierra de Toledo a la rreyna doña Iohana su muger e al infante don Iohan su fijo, ca tenia en esa comarca muchos lugares que estauan por el, los quales

In Burgos castle, King Enrique also found Don Felipe de Castro, a native of Aragon, who was married to the king's sister Doña Juana and was being held prisoner by King Pedro, having been captured in the battle of Nájera. He was now set free. The king endowed Don Felipe and his wife Doña Juana with Paredes de Nava, Medina de Rioseco and Tordehumos.

1367: CHAPTER XXXVI

How King Enrique heard the news that the city of Córdoba had declared its support for him.

While King Enrique was in Burgos he heard the news that the city of Córdoba had now given him its support and that all the knights and squires who lived there were on his side. He also learned that they had sent for the master of Santiago Don Gonzalo Mejía, Don Juan Alfonso de Guzmán, who later became count of Niebla, Don Alfonso Pérez de Guzmán, head constable for the city of Seville, and numerous other knights who were supporters of King Enrique and who were in Llerena and other places in that area. They had, moreover, welcomed all of these men into the city of Córdoba.

King Enrique also heard reports of how King Pedro was in Seville and day by day was equipping the town of Carmona with supplies ready to resist attack. He took great delight in this news. He promptly sent the master of Calatrava Don Pero Muñiz, who was present in Burgos with him, to inform the people of Córdoba he had now arrived from France and was in the kingdom of Castile, and also to tell them that he would very soon be with them. King Enrique then remained for a few days in Burgos in order to raise money to ensure that the troops in his company were paid what was due to them to cover their allowances and salary.

He also decided to send his wife Queen Juana and his son Prince Juan from Burgos to the lands of Toledo, for in that area he had a large number of places which had given him their support: Guadalajara,

eran Guadalfajara e Sepuluega e Segouia e Auila e Ayllon e Yllescas e Atiença e Olmedo e Medina del Canpo e Salamanca e Toro e Valladolid e Palençia e Carrion e Areualo e Madrigal e Coca e otros muchos lugares.

E la rreyna e el infante fueronsse para Guadalfajara e estudieron ý algunos dias e dende fueronsse para Yllescas. E fue con la rreyna e con el infante, don Gomez Manrrique arçobispo de Toledo e don Gutierre obispo de Palençia e Pero Gonçalez de Mendoça e don Ferrand Gomez de Albornoz comendador de Montaluan de la horden de Santiago e otros cauallleros castellanos e françeses.

Capitulo XXXVIIº. Commo el rrey don Enrrique fue çercar la villa de Dueñas.

El rrey don Enrrique despues que ouo enbiado la rreyna e el infante para tierra de Toledo, partio de Burgos e fue çercar la villa e castillo de Dueñas, ca estaua ý Rodrigo Rodriguez de Torquemada, el qual dexara el rrey don Pedro por su adelantado mayor en Castilla. E estaua aquella villa e castillo en el camino de Burgos a Valladolid e fazian mucho daño e destoruo los que ý estauan en todas las comarcas. E el rrey don Enrrique desque ý llego, fizola çercar e fizo poner muchos engeños en derredor della e estudo ý vn mes. E Rodrigo Rodriguez desde que vio que non auia acorro alguno, fizo su pleytesia con el rrey don Enrrique e enbio enplazar el castillo de Dueñas al rrey don Pedro. E pasados los dias de plazo, entrego el castillo e la villa de Dueñas al rrey don Enrrique e a quien el mando. E finco Rodrigo Rodriguez e los que con el estauan en la merçed del rrey don Enrrique.

Sepúlveda, Segovia, Ávila, Ayllón, Illescas, Atienza, Olmedo, Medina del Campo, Salamanca, Toro, Valladolid, Palencia, Carrión, Arévalo, Madrigal, Coca and numerous others.

The queen and the prince travelled to Guadalajara, where they stayed for a few days before moving on to Illescas. They were accompanied by Archbishop Gómez Manrique of Toledo, Bishop Gutierre of Palencia, Pero González de Mendoza, Don Fernán Gómez de Albornoz, commander of Montalbán for the Order of Santiago, and other Castilian and French knights.

1367: CHAPTER XXXVII

How King Enrique went to lay siege to the town of Dueñas.

After sending the queen and the prince into the lands of Toledo, King Enrique set off from Burgos and went to lay siege to the town and castle of Dueñas, as Rodrigo Rodríguez de Toledo, appointed by King Pedro as his governor general for Castile, was to be found there. This town and castle stood on the road from Burgos to Valladolid and the troops based there were causing a great deal of damage and disruption throughout the region. Once King Enrique arrived, he besieged the town and its castle, encircling it with siege engines, and he remained there for a month. Once Rodrigo Rodríguez saw that he had no hope of being relieved, he negotiated an agreement with King Enrique and sent to King Pedro a request that he come to the aid of the castle at Dueñas. And when the deadline had passed, he handed the castle and the town over to King Enrique and to the person that he designated. Rodrigo Rodríguez and those with him gave their allegiance to King Enrique.

Capitulo XXXVIII°. De las cosas que en este año acaesçieron en la corte de Roma.

En este año que fue año del Señor mill e trezientos e sesenta e siete, el papa Urbano quinto leuo la corte a Roma e fueron todos los cardenales con el mucho contra su voluntad.

Otrossy en este año morio en Ytalia el cardenal don Gil, que era legado del papa e auia conquistada mucha tierra de la que estaua rrebelde contra la Iglesia. E fue este cardenal don Gil natural de Castilla, del obispado de Cuenca, de los Albornoz, e fuera primero arçobispo de Toledo e fue muy noble omne e de muy grand valor. E mandosse traer a Castilla e que lo enterrassen en la iglesia de Santa Maria de Toledo, do fuera primero arçidiano de Calatraua e despues arçobispo de Toledo. E yaze alli en la capilla que dizen de Sant Alifonso.

1367: CHAPTER XXXVIII

Concerning the events which occurred during this year in the court of Rome.

During this year, which was the year of the Lord 1367, Pope Urban V transferred the court to Rome and all of the cardinals moved with him much against their will.[28]

Also during this year the death occurred in Italy of Cardinal Gil, who had been a papal legate and had conquered much of the territory that was in rebellion against the Church.[29] Cardinal Gil was a native of Castile, from the diocese of Cuenca, and a member of the Albornoz family. He had previously been archbishop of Toledo and was a man of great nobility and fine qualities. His instructions were that his body should be brought to Castile to be interred in the church of Santa María in the city of Toledo where he had served first as archdeacon of Calatrava and subsequently as archbishop. He lies there in the chapel which bears the name of Saint Ildefonsus.

AÑO TERÇERO

del rrey don Enrrique, que fue año del Señor de mill e trezientos e sesenta e ocho e de la era de Çesar mill e quatroçientos e seys años. AÑO DIEZ E NUEUE del rrey don Pedro.

Capitulo primero. Commo el rrey don Enrrique çerco la çibdat de Leon e la tomo.

En el año terçero que el sobre dicho rrey don Enrrique rregno e año diez e nueue que el rrey don Pedro rregnara, e andaua en el año del Señor en mill e trezientos e sesenta e ocho, e de la era de Çesar en mill quatroçientos e seys años, e del Criamiento del mundo segund los ebreos en çinco mill e çiento e veynte e ocho, e de los alarabes en sieteçientos e setenta, el rrey don Enrrique, despues que tomara la villa e castillo de Dueñas, partio dende luego, e esto fue en el comienzo deste año en el mes de enero. E fue para tierra de Leon, ca la çibdat de Leon estaua por el rrey don Pedro e los caualleros fijos dalgo de la tierra estauan por el rrey don Enrrique, e llego alla e çerco la çibdat de Leon e fizole vna bastida en el monesterio de los predicadores, que dizen de Santo Domingo, ca estaua muy allegado a vna torre de la villa en guisa que los de la torre non pudian defenderla, tan apoderados estauan en la bastida que fizieron en el dicho monesterio, e ouieron de pleytear con el rrey don Enrrique en guisa que le dieron la çibdat de Leon e fincaron en la su merçed los que estauan dentro en ella.

Otrosi todas las conpañas de las montañas de Asturias e de Ouiedo fueron en su obediençia saluo muy pocos e estos ouieron entre sy muchas peleas; pero toda via la partida del rrey don Enrrique se apoderaua mas.

E el rrey don Enrrique partio de Leon despues que la cobro e fue

YEAR THREE (1368)

of the reign of King Enrique, which was the year of the Lord 1368 and, counting from the era of Caesar, 1406; and THE NINETEENTH YEAR of the reign of King Pedro.

1368: CHAPTER I

How King Enrique besieged the city of León and captured it.

These events occurred in the third year of the reign of King Enrique – the nineteenth year of the reign of King Pedro – which was the year of the Lord 1368; in 1406, counting from the era of Caesar; 5,128 years from the creation of the world by the reckoning of the Hebrews; and, according to that of the Arabs, it was in the year 770. After capturing the town and castle of Dueñas, King Enrique lost no time in setting off again; and this was right at the beginning of the year, in the month of January. He headed for Leonese territory, as the city of León was on the side of King Pedro whilst the knights of noble birth of the region supported King Enrique. On his arrival the king laid siege to the city, establishing a siege tower in the convent of Santo Domingo, which belonged to the preaching friars. This was situated very close to one of the city's towers in such a way that it was not possible for the tower to be defended, so strong was the position of the men in the siege tower that had been constructed in the convent. As a result of this, the defenders had to negotiate with King Enrique terms by which the city of León was handed over to him and those within it submitted themselves to his authority.

Moreover, all the contingents from the mountain areas of Asturias and Oviedo had given him their allegiance, with the exception of just a few – and among these there were numerous internal conflicts. The supporters of King Enrique continued to gain the upper hand.

Having seized control of León, King Enrique set off for Tordehumos,

para Tordehumos, que estaua alçada contra el e fizola conbatir e dieronsele. E mataron ý al conde de Osona, que auia venido con el rrey e fue fijo de don Bernal vizconde de Cabrera, vn grand señor del rregno de Aragon. E tomo el rrey aquel camino a Medina de Rioseco e algunos otros lugares que estauan contra el. E acordo de yr a Yllescas, do estaua la rreyna doña Iohana su muger e el infante don Iohan su fijo. E es aquella villa a seys leguas de Toledo e paso por Buytrago, que la tenian çercada los suyos e non la pudo auer; pero a pocos dias se dio.

Otrossy el rrey paso por Madrid e fallo que la auian cobrado los suyos e estaua por el, e plogole mucho por que vna villa tan buena e tan abastada e en tal comarca era suya. E fuera tomada Madrid en esta guisa: gentes e caualleros del rrey don Enrrique la touieron mucho tienpo çercada e vn aldeano que estaua dentro, que dizian Domingo Muñoz de Leganes, dioles vn dia dos torres que el tenia e sus parientes a la puerta que dizen de moros e por alli se cobro Madrid; pero fue rrobada.

Capitulo segundo. Commo el rrey don Enrrique fue para tierra de Toledo e çerco a Toledo.

El rrey don Enrrique despues que llego a Yllescas, estudo alli algunos dias e ouo muchos consejos preguntando a todos que le cunplia fazer o sy yria o andaria por el rregno o si çercaria a Toledo. E sobre esto ouo alli muchos acuerdos, ca todos los que estauan por el en la çibdat de Cordoua querian, e assi ge lo enbiauan dezir, que fuesse al Andalozia; pero por quanto el non tenia dineros assi para pagar a las gentes de

which had risen up against him. He launched an attack on the town and it was surrendered to him. At Tordehumos the death occurred of the count of Osona – son of Viscount Bernat of Cabrera, a great lord of the kingdom of Aragon – who had come to Castile accompanying the king. King Enrique then headed towards Medina de Rioseco and some other places which were opposed to him. He decided to go to Illescas to meet up with his wife Queen Juana and his son Prince Juan. Illescas is situated six leagues from Toledo and his route towards it took him by Buitrago, which was being besieged by his forces. So far they had not been able to capture it but it did surrender a few days later.

The king's journey also took him by way of Madrid and he found that it had fallen to his supporters and was now loyal to him. He was delighted that so fine and so rich a town, situated in such an area, was now in his hands. Madrid was captured after a lengthy siege by the knights and troops of King Enrique: one day a villager by the name of Domingo Muñoz de Leganés who was inside the town handed over to them two towers standing at what is known as the Gate of the Moors, which were held by himself and his family. It was by means of that gateway that Madrid was taken, but, nevertheless, the town was looted.

1368: CHAPTER II

How King Enrique went to the lands of Toledo and laid siege to that city.

Having arrived in Illescas, King Enrique remained there for some days and consulted widely, asking all his supporters what would be the right way for him to proceed: whether he should leave and move around his kingdom or whether he should lay siege to Toledo. On this question there were various schools of thought, for all of King Enrique's supporters in the city of Córdoba wanted him to come to Andalusia, and they sent envoys to tell him this. However, as he had

armas e por quanto en la comarca de Toledo auia muchas viandas, acordo de çercar a Toledo e assy lo fizo.

E puso su rreal de partes de la vega a treynta dias de abril deste año e eran con el rrey don Enrrique fasta mill omnes de armas e en la çibdat de Toledo, fasta seysçientos de cauallo e mucha gente de pie, e commo quier que auia en ella grandes caualleros e fijos dalgo; pero los que tenian la carga de la çibdat eran estos: Ferrando Aluarez de Toledo, que era ý alguazil mayor e tenia sienpre cuydado de gouernar las gentes de armas e era muy buen cauallero; otrossi era ý, que entrara por mandado del rrey, otro cauallero que dizian Garçi Ferrandez de Villodre, el qual traxo alli de vasallos del rrey e de los suyos, trezientos de cauallo e pieça de ballesteros, e estauan otros caualleros naturales de la çibdat, que todos auian grand voluntad de la defender. E el rrey don Enrrique para apoderarse mas para çercar la çibdat de Toledo, fizo luego fazer çerca su rreal e en el rrio de Tajo, vna puente de madera e mando a çiertas gentes de armas de los suyos pasar allende e posauan ý.

E desque çerco la çibdat de Toledo, enbio a la rreyna doña Iohana su muger e al infante don Iohan su fijo a Burgos por que touiesen lugar en Castilla de sossegar e guardar muchas çibdades e villas e caualleros que tenian la su parte. E teniendo çercada la çibdat de Toledo, cobro el rrey don Enrrique estos lugares: Cuenca e Villa Real e Ucles e Talauera e el castillo de Mora e el castillo de Hita e el castillo de Consuegra. E auia en el rreal muchas viandas de la comarca e grand acorro de dineros, ca Segouia e Auila e Valladolid e otros muchos lugares de Castilla e de Leon que estauan por el rrey don Enrrique acorrian a el e a los suyos con quanto pudian auer.

Otrossy estauan estonçes por el rrey don Pedro: Soria e Berlanga e Bitoria e Logroño e Salua tierra de Alaua e Santa Cruz de Canpesço e Sand Sebastian e Guetaria e Çamora. E de Gallizia todo lo mas dello estaua por el rrey don Pedro saluo algunos caualleros que estauan por

no money to pay his troops and the area around Toledo offered a rich supply of provisions, he determined to lay siege to the city and proceeded to do so.

King Enrique established his encampment in the area of the flood plain on the 30th of April of the year in question. In his company there were up to 1,000 men-at-arms, whilst in the city of Toledo there were as many as 600 mounted troops together with a large number of men on foot. Although in the city there were knights and noblemen of high standing, those who had authority over it were: Fernán Álvarez de Toledo, who was the head constable and a very fine knight who had permanent responsibility for the organization of the men-arms; and also another knight called Garci Fernández de Villodre, who had come to the city at the command of King Pedro and had brought with him some vassals of the king and some of his own, 300 horsemen together with a substantial number of crossbowmen. There were also other knights who were citizens of Toledo, all of whom were determined to defend the city. In order to strengthen his position for the siege, King Enrique promptly gave instructions for the construction of a wooden bridge over the River Tagus near to his encampment. He then commanded a number of his troops to cross to the other side of the river where they remained in position.

Once he had laid siege to the city of Toledo, he sent his wife Queen Juana and his son Prince Juan to Burgos so as to have a base in Castile from which to settle and keep secure the numerous cities, towns and knights that had given him their support. Moreover, while he was besieging the city of Toledo, King Enrique captured Cuenca, Villa Real, Uclés, Talavera and the castles of Mora, Hita and Consuegra. In his encampment he now had a large stock of provisions taken from the surrounding area and a considerable amount of money, as Segovia, Ávila, Valladolid and many other places in Castile and León which were on his side were assisting him and his army with as much money as they could raise.

At that time there were also places which had declared their support for King Pedro: Soria, Berlanga, Vitoria, Logroño, Salvatierra in Álava, Santa Cruz de Campezo, San Sebastián, Guetaria and Zamora. In addition, most of Galicia was on his side, with the exception of a

el rrey don Enrrique. E el rregno de Murçia e Seuilla e Carmona e Xerez e Vbeda estauan por el rrey don Pedro.

Otrossy el rrey don Enrrique desque puso su rreal sobre la çibdat de Toledo, ouo su consejo donde auria dineros para pagar las gentes que alli tenia, e non fallaron otro acorro saluo labrar moneda. E estonçe mando fazer vna moneda nueua, que llamauan sezenes e valia vno seys dineros, e desta moneda labrauan en la çibdat de Burgos do estaua la rreyna e el infante. Otrossi labrauan en la villa de Talauera desta dicha moneda e con esta moneda ouo acorrimiento el rrey don Enrrique para las pagas de las gentes que alli tenia; pero despues tornaron a labrar otras monedas segund adelante contaremos.

Capitulo III°. Commo fazia el rrey don Pedro en Seuilla desque sopo que el rrey don Enrrique cobrara la çibdat de Burgos e de Leon.

Agora tornaremos a contar commo fizo el rrey don Pedro despues que sopo que el rrey don Enrrique era ya en el rregno. Assi fue que el rrey don Pedro estando en Seuilla sopo commo el rrey don Enrrique era llegado a la çibdat de Burgos e commo fuera rresçibido e que çercara el castillo e la juderia e lo cobrara todo e que partiera dende e tomara la villa e castillo de Dueñas. E que Rodrigo Rodriguez de Torquemada su adelantado mayor de Castilla, que tenia la dicha villa e castillo de Dueñas, pleyteara con el e era con el rrey don Enrrique, e commo despues fuera para la çibdat de Leon e la çercara e la cobrara, e commo era venido a Toledo por la cobrar e cobrara a Madrid e a Otordehumos e Medina de Rioseco e Buytrago e otros lugares, e ouo

number of knights who were partisans of King Enrique; and King Pedro also had the backing of the kingdom of Murcia and of Seville, Carmona, Jerez and Úbeda.

Having established his encampment outside the city of Toledo, King Enrique also took advice with regard to where he could obtain money to pay the troops that he had there with him, and the only solution that could be found was to mint money. He then ordered the issue of a new coin called the *seisén*, worth six *dineros*.[1] These coins were produced in the city of Burgos, where the queen and the prince were residing, and also in the town of Talavera, and this provided King Enrique with a way of making payment to the troops who were accompanying him. However, as we shall relate in due course, they subsequently went back to minting other kinds of coin.[2]

1368: CHAPTER III

How King Pedro reacted in Seville on learning that the cities of Burgos and León had fallen to King Enrique.

Now we shall return to the account of how King Pedro reacted on hearing that King Enrique was now in the kingdom. The fact is that while King Pedro was in Seville he heard how King Enrique had reached Burgos and had been welcomed into the city, how he had laid siege to the castle and to the Jewish quarter and how all parts of the city had fallen into his hands, and how he had gone on from Burgos and captured the town and castle of Dueñas. He also learned about how Rodrigo Rodríguez de Torquemada, his senior governor for Castile, who had held the town and castle of Dueñas, had been negotiating with King Enrique and had now gone over to his side; how King Enrique had then moved on to the city of León, laying siege to it and capturing it; how he had gone to Toledo with the intention of taking possession of the city, and how he had captured Madrid, Tordehumos, Medina de Rioseco, Buitrago and other places. He was deeply saddened by all of this. It was still his intention to prepare

dende grand pesar e toda via su entençion era de basteçer a Carmona, e assi lo fazia sienpre lo mas que pudia.

E don Gonçalo Mexia maestre de Santiago era partido de Alburquerque e don Iohan Alfonso de Guzman, que fue despues conde de Niebla, e don Alfonso Perez de Guzman alguazil mayor de Seuilla e otros muchos cavalleros que tenian la parte del rrey don Enrrique eran llegados a Llerena e a la comarca de Seuilla, e çercaran vna fortaleza pequeña que auia en vn lugar de Seuilla que dizen Caçalla de la sierra, e eran fasta quinientos de cauallo.

E el rrey don Pedro non se partia de Seuilla, antes estaua ay quedo, ca nin se fiaua de los de la çibdat nin de los que con el estauan, e traya sus pleytesias con el rrey de Granada para que le ayudasse.

Capitulo IIII°. Commo el rrey don Pedro traxo conssigo al rrey de Granada sobre Cordoua e commo acaesçio.

El rrey don Pedro desque vio que la çibdat de Toledo estaua çercada, trato con el rrey Mahomad de Granada que le quisiesse ayudar e venir a se juntar con el para yr sobre la çibdat de Cordoua. E el rrey de Granada fizolo assi e vino con mucha gente de cauallo, que eran siete mill de cauallo, ginetes, e de pie ochenta mill, los doze mill ballesteros. E el rrey don Pedro tenia mill e quinientos de cauallo e seys mill omnes de pie. E el rrey don Pedro e el rrey de Granada juntaronsse en vno e vinieron sobre Cordoua.

E estauan en Cordoua don Gonçalo Mexia maestre de Santiago e don Pero Moñiz maestre de Calatraua e don Iohan Alfonso de Guzman, que fue despues conde de Niebla. E de la çibdat de Cordoua estauan cavalleros: don Alfonso Ferrandez de Monte Mayor adelantado mayor de la frontera e don Gonçalo Ferrandez de Cordoua, que fue despues

Carmona for a siege and he constantly put as much effort as he could into doing so.

The master of Santiago Don Gonzalo Mejía, together with Don Juan Alfonso de Guzmán – later to become count of Niebla –, Don Alfonso Pérez de Guzmán, head constable for Seville, and numerous other knights who were supporters of King Enrique, had left Alburquerque and advanced as far as Llerena and the area around Seville. Here they had laid siege to a small fortress which stood in a village belonging to Seville and was called Cazalla de la Sierra. Altogether they amounted to some 500 mounted troops.

King Pedro chose to remain in Seville rather than leaving the city, for he trusted neither its people nor those in his own company, and he negotiated an agreement by which the king of Granada would come to his aid.

1368: CHAPTER IV

How King Pedro brought the king of Granada to join him in an attack on Córdoba, and concerning the events which occurred.

Once he realized that the city of Toledo was under siege, King Pedro arranged for King Muhammad of Granada to come to his aid and join him in an attack on the city of Córdoba. The king of Granada did as he had requested and brought with him a large force of light cavalry – numbering 7,000 – and 80,000 footsoldiers including 12,000 crossbowmen. King Pedro had 1,500 horsemen and 6,000 footsoldiers. The two kings brought their armies together and moved against Córdoba.

The master of Santiago Don Gonzalo Mejía, the master of Calatrava Don Pero Muñiz and Don Juan Alfonso de Guzmán, subsequently count of Niebla, were all present in Córdoba. There were also the following knights from the city: Don Alfonso Fernández de Montemayor, governor general of the Frontier region, Don Gonzalo Fernández de Córdoba, who subsequently became lord of Aguilar, his

señor de Aguilar, e Diego Ferrandez, su hermano, alguazil mayor de Cordoua e otros muchos buenos.

E don Alfonso Perez de Guzman estaua en vn castillo cerca de Cordoua, que dizian Hornachuelos, e fazia grand guerra a todos los que tenian la parte del rrey don Pedro, de aquel lugar, e quando sopo que los moros tenian su rreal con el rrey don Pedro sobre la çibdat de Cordoua, partio de Hornachuelos e fuesse para alla. E los moros cuydando que eran de sus gentes, non cataron por ellos e el, con muy grand peligro fuesse dentro de la çibdad por la ayudar a defender.

E el rrey don Pedro e el rrey de Granada llegaron çerca la çibdat de Cordoua e los de la çibdat, que eran muchos e buenos, teniendo que pelearian con ellos por las barreras de la çibdat, non estauan aperçebidos de poner rrecabdos en los muros, e los moros eran muchos e llegaron muy fuerte mente a la çibdat en guisa que vn señor de moros que ý venia, que le dizian Abenfaluz, que fue despues rrey de Marruecos, con la grand ballesteria que traya, llegaron a vna coracha que dizian 'la Calahorra' e tan de rrezio la conbatieron que la cobraron e la tomaron e al alcaçar viejo fizieron en el seys portillos e subieron suso pieça dellos con sus pendones.

E ouo grand desmayo en los de la çibdat, que cuydaron que eran entrados. E las dueñas e donzellas que ý eran, que eran muchas e muy buenas, sallieron ha andar por las calles, todas en cabellos, pidiendo merçed a los señores e caualleros e omnes de armas que ý eran en la çibdat, que ouiessen duelo dellas e non quisiessen que fuessen ellos e ellas en catiuerio de los moros enemigos de la fe de Ihesu Christo. E tales lagrimas e palabras fazian e dizian que todos los que lo oyan cobraron grand esfuerço e luego adresçaron para las torres e el muro del alcaçar viejo, que los moros auian entrado: pelearon con ellos muy de rrezio commo muy buenos en guisa que mataron pieça dellos e a los otros fizieron los sallir fuera de la çibdat, e dellos saltaron por ençima de las torres e tomaron los sus pendones que ellos auian

brother Diego Fernández, head constable of Córdoba, and many other men of great qualities.

Don Alfonso Pérez de Guzmán was in a castle by the name of Hornachuelos which was situated near to Córdoba and from there was engaging in bitter conflict with all the supporters of King Pedro. When he learned that the Moors had set up their encampment together with King Pedro outside the city of Córdoba, he left Hornachuelos and set off in that direction. The Moors, believing that his men were part of their own army, were taken unawares, and, facing considerable danger, he entered the city to assist in its defence.

King Pedro and the king of Granada approached Córdoba and the people defending the city, although they were numerous and good fighters, in the belief that they would do battle with the enemy forces at the outworks of the city, had not had the foresight to place additional support on the walls. The Moors had a large army and attacked the city with such force that, together with his large company of crossbowmen, a Moorish nobleman called Abū Yaflūsin, later to become king of Morocco, reached an outlying part of the fortifications known as 'la Calahorra' and so ferocious was their assault on it that it fell to them and they took possession of it.[3] They made six breaches in the wall of the old *alcázar* and a considerable number of them climbed up to the top of it with their banners.

Such trepidation ran through the people of Córdoba that they believed that the Moors had already entered the city. The numerous ladies and maidens who were there, women of great nobility, went out into the streets with their hair loose begging the lords, knights and men-at-arms in the city to take pity on them and not allow either men or women to become captives of the Moors, who were enemies of the faith of Jesus Christ. So bitter was their weeping and so powerful were their words that all those who heard them were filled with great courage and at once made straight for the towers and the wall of the old *alcázar* into which the Moors had made their entry. They fought with them so furiously and to such effect that they killed a good number of their enemy and drove the remainder back from the city. Some of them jumped up onto the towers, seizing the banners that the Moors had put in place, and they pursued them across the outworks,

puesto e sallieron con ellos por las barreras matando e firiendo en ellos en tal manera que los arredraron dende grand pieça.

E en tanto que los moros se tiraron afuera, luego los maestres e los otros caualleros e señores fizieron aderesçar los muros muy hordenada mente, por que sabian bien que otro dia los moros prouarian lo que pudiessen fazer por cobrar aquella çibdat. E toda aquella noche fueron fechas por la çibdat muchas danças e alegrias, e todos tenian grand esfuerço, ca fiauan en la merçed de Dios que darian buena cuenta de la çibdat en guisa que los enemigos de la fe non los podrian enpeesçer.

E el rrey de Granada e todos los moros tenian que [en] esta çibdat de Cordoua era la su eglesia mayor, que fuera la cabeça de toda su ley por quanto aquella es la mas fermosa iglesia que en su tienpo fue mezquita e sienpre la rrazonauan por lugar santo. Otrossi el rrey don Pedro tenia grand saña desta çibdat por quanto estauan en ella muchos de los que le auian fecho guerra. Otrossy tenia grand quexa de los caualleros de la çibdat por que se partieran del e en todas las guisas le plazia que los moros cobrassen la çibdat e la destruyessen. Enpero Dios quiso acorrer a los de su fe.

E otro dia llegaron los moros e los que eran con el rrey a la çibdat, mas fallaron la hordenança de otra manera que non el primero dia, e non la pudieron enpeesçer e tiraronse afuera.

Capitulo Vº. Commo el rrey de Granada tomo la çibdat de Iahen e la destruyo, e commo el rrey don Pedro e el rrey de Granada tornaron otra vez sobre Cordoua e commo el rrey de Granada destruyo a Ubeda.

Despues desto estudieron el rrey don Pedro e el rrey de Granada en sus reales çerca de Cordoua algunos dias e dende tornosse el rrey de Granada para su tierra y el rrey don Pedro para Seuilla. E despues

inflicting death and attacking with such force as to drive them back a considerable distance.

As the Moors had retreated from the castle, the masters of the Orders and the other knights and lords quickly had the walls repaired and set in good order, for they were well aware that the next day the Moors would make every possible effort to take the city. Throughout that night there was dancing and celebration across the city and everyone was in high spirits, for they trusted in God's mercy that they would serve the city well enough to prevent the enemies of the Faith from causing them any harm.

The king of Granada and all the Moors believed that situated in this city of Córdoba was their supreme church, which had been the heart of their whole religion: it is the most beautiful of churches – in its time it had been a mosque – and they always held it to be a holy place. In addition, King Pedro was deeply hostile to this city as many of those who had been involved in the struggle against him were there within its walls. He also bore a grievance against the knights of Córdoba for having deserted him; and in every respect it was his desire that the Moors should capture and destroy the city. In spite of this, it was God's wish to come to the assistance of those who had placed their faith in Him.

On the next day the Moors reached the city, along with the king's forces, but they found it in better order than on the first day and, unable to inflict any damage on it, they withdrew.

1368: CHAPTER V

How the king of Granada captured and destroyed the city of Jaén, how King Pedro and the king of Granada returned to launch another attack on Córdoba, and how the king of Granada destroyed Úbeda.

After this King Pedro and the king of Granada remained for some days in their encampments near Córdoba, and from there the king of Granada returned to his own lands and King Pedro went back

otra vez torno el rrey de Granada con muy grand poder e fue para Iahen. E desque llegaron a la çibdat de Iahen, los que estauan dentro salieron a pelear en las barreras con los moros e ouieronsse de rretraer a la çibdat e los moros entraron en las barreras e cobraron toda la çibdat en su poder. E los christianos, los que pudieron, acogeronsse al alcaçar de la dicha çibdat, e los otros fueron muertos e catiuos. E avn despues los moros çercaron el alcaçar e los christianos non tenian viandas ningunas para tantos omnes commo ally se acogeron e desque vieron en tal afincamiento que eran perdidos del todo, fizieron su pleytesia de dar al rrey de Granada çierta quantia de doblas e que los desçercasse, e desto dieron en arrehenes personas çiertas. E los moros pegaron fuego a toda la çibdat e a las iglesias e derribaron las puertas mayores de la çibdat e grand parte de los muros, donde fue estragada e rresçibio muy grand daño e grand desonrra la çibdad de Iahen, que es vna de las mejores de aquella tierra, do sienpre ouo muy buenos guerreros.

E otra vez entro el rrey don Pedro e el rrey de Granada con el, con grandes conpañas, e llegaron a la çibdat de Cordoua; pero fallaronlos en tal guisa muy aperçebidos los que ý eran que non prouaron de llegar a ellos. E partio el rrey de Granada e fue por el obispado de Iahen e tomo la çibdat de Ubeda, que non era muy bien çercada, e entrola e rrobola e fizola quemar. E los christianos rrecogeronsse a vna fortaleza que es en la dicha çibdat, que dizen el castillo, e alli escaparon. E conbatieron a Andujar e non la pudo tomar. E despues por estas dos çibdades que anssi fueron destruydas, el rrey don Enrrique fizo muy bien rreparar de muros la çibdat de Iahen e la çibdat de Vbeda e preuilligolas en guisa que se poblaron.

E eso mesmo en estos tienpos, en ayuda del rrey don Pedro, el rrey de Granada entro las villas de Marchena e Vtrera e leuo quantos ý fallo catiuos a Granada, e perdiose mucha gente. E fue çierto que del lugar de Vtrera solo, que es de Seuilla, leuaron los moros honze mill personas omnes e mujeres pequeños e grandes. Otrossy los castillos que el rrey don Pedro ganara del rregno de Granada quando ayudaua

to Seville. The king of Granada then made his way back again with a vast army and headed for Jaén. When they reached the city, the defenders came out to fight against the Moors at the outworks but were forced to withdraw into the city. The Moors then made their way across the outworks and took possession of the whole city. Those of the Christians who were able to do so took refuge in the city's *alcázar* and the remainder were either killed or taken captive. Subsequently the Moors besieged the *alcázar* and, lacking provisions for such a large number of people taking refuge there and seeing that under such pressure they had no hope of escape, the Christians negotiated terms with the king of Granada: they were to pay him a certain sum in *doblas* and he was to halt the siege, and a number of people were handed over to him hostages. The Moors set fire to the whole city and to the churches, and they demolished the main gateways and a large part of the walls. The city of Jaén – one of the finest in those lands where there have always been oustanding warriors – was devastated and suffered great damage and humiliation.

    King Pedro, accompanied by the king of Granada and a large army, again moved onto the offensive and drew close to the city of Córdoba. However, they found its defenders so well prepared that they did not attempt to make an attack on them. The king of Granada then left Córdoba and moved through the diocese of Jaén: he seized Úbeda, whose walls were not strong, entering and looting the city and ordering it to be burned. The Christians took refuge in a fortified part of the city, known as 'the castle', and there they found safety. The Moors then attacked Andújar but were unable to capture it. Subsequently, in order to assist the two cities of Jaén and Úbeda which had suffered such destruction, King Enrique had their walls fully repaired and awarded them privileges to encourage their repopulation.

    Likewise during this period, seeking to give assistance to King Pedro, the king of Granada forced his way into the towns of Marchena and Utrera and carried off to Granada as captives all the people that he found there. Many people were lost. It was known for certain that just from the town of Utrera, which belongs to Seville, the Moors took 11,000 people, men and women, young and old. In addition, the castles which King Pedro had won from the kingdom of Granada when he assisted King

al rrey Mahomad contra el rrey Bermejo, todos los cobraron los moros e mas otros algunos; ca cobraron los moros en esta guerra nueua mente Belmez e los castillos de Canbil e Alhamar, los quales ganara el infante don Pedro, fijo del rrey don Sancho, en tienpo de las tutorias del rrey don Alfonso. Otrossy los castillos que el rrey don Pedro ganara commo dicho es, que eran Turon, Hardales, el Burgo, Cañete, Las Cueuas, cobraron los moros en esta guerra e fizieron mucho daño en tierra de christianos por la diuision que auia entre ellos.

E esto fecho el rrey don Pedro torno a Seuilla e sienpre fazia basteçer la villa de Carmona, que es a seys leguas dende, ca sienpre se rresçelaua que se auia de veer en algund peligro.

E el rrey don Enrrique estaua en el rreal que pusiera sobre la çibdat de Toledo e auia cobrado vna bastida que los de la çibdat auian fecho en vna iglesia sobre la puente de Alcantara que llaman Sant Seruande. E tenia el rrey don Enrrique de cada parte çercada la çibdat de Toledo, e de la otra parte de la puente de Sand Martin tenia fecha otra bastida e el tenia su rreal en la vega.

Capitulo VI°. Commo algunos de la çibdat de Toledo quisieron dar vna torre al rrey don Enrrique.

Assy acaesçio que algunos omnes que estauan dentro en la dicha çibdat de Toledo que amauan seruiçio del rrey don Enrrique, vn dia a medio dia tomaron vna torre de la çibdat que llaman la torre de los abades, que es muy alta e muy fuerte, e pusieronsse en ella, e llamauan 'Castilla por el rrey don Enrrique!'. E los del rreal fueronles luego acorrer e pusieron escalas a la torre e subieron quarenta omnes del rrey suso e pusieron ý çinco vanderas.

E los de la çibdat desque se vieron en tal guisa, llegaron todos e

Muhammed against the Red King were all captured by the Moors along with a number of others: during the present campaign the Moors retook Bélmez and the castles of Cambil and Alhabar, which had been seized by Prince Pedro, son of King Sancho, during the time of the minority of King Alfonso. Moreover, in the course of this conflict, the Moors also took the castles captured by King Pedro – as we have already explained –, which were Turón, Ardales, el Burgo, Cañete and Las Cuevas, and they caused great destruction in the Christian territories as a result of the divisions which existed there.

After all of this had taken place, King Pedro returned to Seville and devoted himself unceasingly to the preparation of the town of Carmona, six leagues away, for a siege: at all times he was afraid that he would find himself in danger.

King Enrique remained in the encampment that he had established outside the city of Toledo. He had seized a fortification which the people of the city had built on the site of a church called San Servando, looking down over the Bridge of Alcántara.[4] King Enrique now had the city of Toledo completely encircled and he had had another tower constructed on the far side of the Bridge of San Martín. His encampment stood on the flood plain.

1368: CHAPTER VI

How some citizens of Toledo attempted to hand over a tower to King Enrique.

It happened that, one day at mid-day, a number of men in the city of Toledo who were loyal to King Enrique seized the so-called Abbots' Tower, which is both of great height and very strongly fortified.[5] They occupied it with cries of 'Castile for King Enrique!' and at once the men from the king's encampment rushed to their aid. They put ladders up against the tower and 40 of King Enrique's men went up, raising five banners.

When the people of the city saw themselves in this predicament,

pusieron fuego de partes de la çibdat a vna puerta baxa de la torre e ardio luego, e alli pusieron mucha leña e mucha madera en guisa que el fuego fue muy grande, e el fuego subia a la torre. E los que auian subido suso e estauan por el rrey don Enrrique, que auian tomado su boz e se alçaran con la torre non pudian desçender yuso a la çibdat por el fuego nin estar en la torre, e ouieron a dexar la torre e desçender por las escalas que pusieron, e non pudieron al fazer.

Capitulo VII°. Commo algunos de la çibdat de Toledo fueron muertos por que querian dar entrada al rrey don Enrrique e commo cuydo cobrar el rrey don Enrrique la puente de Sant Martin e commo fizieron los de la çibdat.

Otrossy en aquel tienpo que el rrey don Enrrique touo la çibdat de Toledo çercada, algunos otros de la çibdat de Toledo por algunas vezes querian dar entrada a los del rreal; pero toda via se descubria e fueron muertos algunos en la çibdat por esta rrazon.

Otrosi el rrey don Enrrique fizo poner engeños a la puente de Sand Martin, ca los de la çibdat querian derribar la puente e los engeños de fuera tirauan a los onbres que labrauan en la torre de la puente. E el rrey don Enrrique fizo fazer alli vna bastida en guisa que cauauan la torre grande que tenian a la puerta de la puente.

E vn dia, teniendo los maestros que ya la torre estaua puesta en cuentos para le poder dar fuego e que caeria, dixeron al rrey que mandasse venir las gentes de omes de armas, ca fazian cuenta que sy aquella torre cayesse, que la çibdat era entrada, ca non auia dentro en la çibdat otra torre de que se pudiesse defender la puente. E commo

they flocked to the tower and set fire to a door at its foot, on the city side. It was quickly ablaze and they piled up a considerable amount of firewood and timber so as to produce a large fire which rose up into the tower. Those who had gone up, supporters of King Enrique who had declared their allegiance to him and had seized the tower, were unable to make their way down into the city because of the blaze, and likewise they could not remain on the tower. They had to abandon the tower and descend by means of the ladders that had been set up, for there was nothing else that they could do.

1368: CHAPTER VII

How some citizens of Toledo were killed because they wanted to allow King Enrique to enter the city; how King Enrique sought to seize the Bridge of San Martín; and how the people of the city reacted.

There were further occasions during the time that King Enrique was besieging Toledo when some others of its citizens tried to enable the troops from the king's encampment to enter the city. Their plans were always discovered, however, and this led to some people in the city being killed.

King Enrique also had siege engines put in place to fire on the Bridge of San Martín, for the city's defenders wanted to demolish the bridge and the attackers' siege engines were bombarding the men working on its tower. King Enrique had a siege tower erected there to enable them to mine the large tower that the defenders held at the gateway to the bridge.

One day when the engineers judged that the tower was ready to collapse, as it was now supported only on props ready to be set on fire, they informed the king that he should summon his men-at-arms: they reckoned that, if that tower was brought down, the way into Toledo was clear, given that there was no other tower in the city from which it was possible to defend the bridge. Although the people of Toledo

quier que los de la çibdat fazian vn muro de tapias muy grande en cabo de la puente, dentro en la çibdat, para la defender, pero avn estaua baxo, e el rrey don Enrrique, por conssejo de los maestros que pusieron los cuentos a la torre, mandoles poner fuego; pero non cayo la torre, que avn non fuera toda puesta en cuentos e perdiosse la obra e todo el trabajo que auia tomado en fazer aquellas cauas e poner aquellos cuentos a la torre.

E los de la çibdat quando vieron aquello, pensando que el rrey don Enrrique mandara cauar e poner otra vez los cuentos a la torre, lo qual assi se fazia, començaron de fazer derribar la puente de Sand Martin por medio el arco, a tirar las llaues de las piedras por que cayesse. E el rrey don Enrrique fizo poner dos engeños que tirauan a la puente e a los que labrauan en ella para la derribar; pero los de la çibdat acabaron primero su obra e derribaron la puente e cayo el arco. E commo quier que fue grand daño para la çibdat por se perder tal puente commo aquella, que era fermosa, enpero tenian ya que estauan seguros por aquella partida.

E assi paso lo que finco deste año que el rrey don Pedro estaua en Seuilla enbiando por todas la mas conpañas que pudia auer de los que tenian su partida e tratando con el rrey de Granada que le diesse ayuda para venir a acorrer a Toledo. Otrosy el rrey don Enrrique estaua en el rreal de Toledo enbiando por los que eran de su parte, que veniessen todos juntarse con el por quanto sabia nueuas que el rrey don Pedro auia de venir a desçercar la çibdat de Toledo e pelear con el.

Capitulo VIIIº. Commo las villas de Logroño e Bitoria e otras enbiaron rrequerir al rrey don Pedro commo farian.

Las villas de Logroño e de Bitoria e Salua tierra de Alaua e Santa Cruz de Canpesço tenian la partida del rrey don Pedro, e quando esta guerra se fazia, ellos estauan muy aquexados de caualleros e gentes

were constructing a very large defensive wall of rammed earth standing within the city at the end of the bridge, this had still not reached sufficient height, and so King Enrique, following the advice of the engineers who had put the props in place under the tower, ordered these to be set on fire. However the tower did not collapse as not all of it was as yet resting on props. The undertaking came to nothing and all the trouble taken over the mining and the placing of props under the tower was wasted.

When they saw this, assuming that King Enrique had ordered his men to dig more tunnels and once again put props in place – which indeed was being done – the people of the city began to work to bring down the Bridge of San Martín in the middle of the arch by removing the keystones so that it would collapse. King Enrique had two siege engines set up, bombarding the bridge and those who were working to demolish it. However the people of the city were the first to finish their task: they brought down the arch and the bridge collapsed. Although it was greatly to the detriment of Toledo to lose so beautiful a bridge, nevertheless the people now felt safe on that side of the city.

So it was that for the remainder of the year King Pedro stayed in Seville, summoning as many troops as he could from among his supporters and negotiating with the king of Granada for the provision of assistance in the relief of Toledo. Likewise, King Enrique remained in his encampment outside Toledo, summoning all his supporters to join him, for he had received reports that King Pedro was going to come to break the siege of Toledo and do battle with him.

1368: CHAPTER VIII

How Logroño, Vitoria and some other towns sent King Pedro a request for instructions with regard to the course that they should take.

The towns of Logroño, Vitoria, Salvatierra de Álava and Santa Cruz de Campezo had declared their support for King Pedro and during the course of this conflict they had suffered severe harassment from

que les fazian guerra por el rrey don Enrrique, e enbiaron al rrey don Pedro sus mensageros a Seuilla encubierta mente por los peligros de las comarcas que estauan por el rrey don Enrrique, por los quales le enbiauan dezir que ellos estauan en muy grand priesa e que se non podian defender e veyan bien que el non los pudia acorrer e que si su merçed era, que el rrey de Nauarra era su amigo e estaua junto con el su rregno, que les paresçia que era bien que se diessen a el e que se defenderian.

E el rrey don Pedro desque vio estas cartas que estas villas le enbiaron sobre esta rrazon que auedes oydo, enbioles su rrespuesta que les mandaua e rrogaua que en todas las maneras del mundo estudiessen firmes por el, que el fiaua por Dios que muy ayna los entendia acorrer a ellos e a los que tenian su partida e de les gualardonar los seruiçios que le auian fecho; pero en caso que el non los pudiesse tan ayna acorrer, que les mandaua que antes se diessen e entregassen al conde don Enrrique que al rrey de Nauarra e que nunca partiessen de la corona de Castilla. Otrosi que el fallara en el rrey de Nauarra pocas ayudas e que non era su voluntad que el cobrasse tales villas non auiendo rrazon por que.

Enpero asy acaesçio que los de las villas sobre dichas, lo vno por que lo tenian assy tratado con el rrey de Nauarra, otrossi por quanto don Tello, hermano del rrey don Enrrique, señor de Vizcaya, se auia visto con el rrey de Nauarra e tenia sus pleytesias con el contra el rrey don Enrrique su hermano, que non lo amaua nin lo queria bien nin quisiera venir a ayudarlo en esta guerra e estaua en Vizcaya en su tierra, e los dichos lugares de Bitoria e Logroño e Salua tierra e Santa Cruz dieronsse al rrey de Nauarra e vino a ellos a tomar la possession e vino con el rrey de Nauarra, don Tello a gelas fazer entregar. E estudieron por el rrey de Nauarra las dichas villas fasta otro tiempo

knights and soldiers who were waging war on them on behalf of King Enrique. They sent envoys to King Pedro in Seville, and they did so in secrecy on account of the threat posed by the areas which were in support of King Enrique. Through these envoys they communicated to the king that they were hard pressed and unable to defend themselves; it was clear to them that he could not come to their assistance and so they suggested that, if such was his will – since the king of Navarre was his ally and their towns were situated very close to his kingdom – they felt that it was right to accept the Navarrese monarch's lordship and thus be in a position to defend themselves.

Once he had seen the letters from these towns containing the proposal about which you have just heard, King Pedro sent them his reply: he commanded and entreated them that at all costs they were to remain unwavering in their support for him. He told them that, as he trusted in God, it was his intention to come very soon to assist them and those who had taken his side and to reward them for their loyalty to him. However, in case he proved unable to bring them aid with such speed, his command was that they should hand the towns over and surrender themselves to King Enrique rather than doing so to the king of Navarre, and that they should never separate from the Crown of Castile. He also said that he had received little support from the king of Navarre and that he had no desire for him to gain possession of towns such as these without due cause.

Nevertheless, it turned out that the people of those towns lost no time in handing them over to the king of Navarre. This was done on the one hand because they had already agreed with him that they would do so and on the other hand since King Enrique's brother Don Tello, lord of Vizcaya, had met with the king of Navarre and had negotiated a pact with him against his brother King Enrique: Don Tello was no friend or ally of his and had not been willing to come to his aid in the present campaign but rather had remained in his own territory in Vizcaya. The towns of Vitoria, Logroño, Salvatierra and Santa Cruz were handed over to the king of Navarre, who came to take possession of them accompanied by Don Tello, present in order to oversee their transfer. The towns remained subject to the king of Navarre until a later time, as we shall relate, and he installed garrisons

do contaremos commo paso. E puso el rrey de Nauarra en las dichas villas e logares conpañas de armas e daua ý sueldo e fazia guerra a Castilla.

Capitulo IXº. De lo que en este año acaesçio en el rregno de Aragon.

En este año que dicho auemos enbio el rrey don Pedro de Aragon a Çerdeña a don Pedro de Luna que era vn grand rrico omne de Aragon e con el mucha buena gente. E desque don Pedro de Luna llego en la ysla de Cerdeña, andudo luego por la tierra e fue poner su rreal delante la çibdat de Çerdeña do estaua el jurge de Arbolea, la qual çibdat dezian Orestan. E puso su rreal çerca la çibdat e non pusieron buena guarda en el, ca dexaua yr por viandas a los que querian yr.

E el jurge de Arbolea desque vio la poca hordenança de los de Aragon, allego su gente que estauan con el en la çibdat de Orestan e sin sospecha sallio al rreal e fueron luego desbaratados don Pedro e los suyos. E morio ý don Pedro de Luna e muchos buenos cauallleros e escuderos con el.

E quien el rreal quiere poner çerca de çibdat o villa do esta grand gente non lo deue poner muy çerca luego, ca es muy grand peligro segund aqui auedes entendido; otrossi deue guardar sienpre que las gentes non se partan por la tierra.

in the towns and villages, hired salaried troops and launched raids against Castile.[6]

1368: CHAPTER IX

Concerning what happened during this year in the kingdom of Aragon.

During the year about which we have spoken, King Pere of Aragon sent Don Pedro de Luna, an Aragonese magnate, to Sardinia, together with a large force of highly accomplished troops. Once Don Pedro arrived on the island of Sardinia he rapidly began to roam over its territory and established his encampment outside Oristano, the Sardinian city which was the seat of the Judge of Arborea.[7] His encampment was located close to the city. However, there was no close vigilance and those wishing to go off in search of provisions were allowed to do so.

On seeing the lack of organization on the part of the Aragonese, the Judge of Arborea assembled the troops that he had with him in the city of Oristano and made a surprise attack on the encampment. Don Pedro and his troops suffered a serious defeat, and Don Pedro de Luna met his death there along with many accomplished knights and squires.

Anyone who wishes to establish his encampment near to a city or town where there are a significant number of troops should not place it very close by, as this involves considerable risk, as you have seen in this case. In addition, he must always keep the troops from spreading out around the surrounding territory.

AÑO QUARTO

del rrey don Enrrique, que fue en el año del Señor de mill e trezientos e sesenta e nueue, e de la era de Çesar mill e quatroçientos e siete, e era AÑO VEYNTE que el rrey don Pedro rregnara.

Capitulo primero. Commo llegaron al rrey don Enrrique mensageros del rrey de Françia a confirmar sus ligas con el.

En el año quarto que el sobre dicho rrey don Enrrique rregno e era año de veynte que el rrey don Pedro rregnara, que fue año del Señor de mill e trezientos e sesenta e nueue quando andaua la era de Çesar en mill e quatroçientos e siete, e del Criamiento del mundo, segund la cuenta de los ebreos, en çinco mill e çiento e veynte e nueue años, e de los alarabes en sieteçientos e setenta e un años, estando el rrey don Enrrique sobre la çibdat de Toledo que tenia çercada, llegaron ý a el mensageros e enbaxadores del rrey don Carlos de Françia, por los quales le fiziera sauer que era guerra abierta entre el e el rrey de Ingla terra e que su voluntad era de lo auer por su amigo e por su aliado si a el pluguiesse.

E al rrey don Enrrique plogo mucho desto e commo quier que en el lugar de Aguas Muertas en el rregno de Françia, segund auemos dicho suso, fueron fechas amistades entre el rrey de Françia e el rrey don Enrrique estando ý el duc de Angeu e el cardenal de Boloña, enpero agora de nueuo fizieron sus amistades e sus rrecabdos de ligas e confederaçiones, las mas firmes que seer pudieron, en esta manera: primera mente, que el rrey don Carlos de Françia e el rrey don Enrrique de Castilla fuesen amigos de amigos e enemigos de enemigos e se ayudassen contra cualquier omne del mundo, e que esta mesma amistad durasse e fuesse firme entre ellos e sus fijos primeros herederos nasçidos e por nasçer, e que ninguno dellos non

YEAR FOUR (1369)

of the reign of King Enrique, which was the year of the Lord 1369 and, counting from the era of Caesar, 1407; and THE TWENTIETH YEAR of the reign of King Pedro.

1369: CHAPTER I

How King Enrique received emissaries sent by the king of France to confirm their alliance.

These events occurred in the fourth year of the reign of King Enrique – the twentieth year of the reign of King Pedro – which was the year of the Lord 1369; in 1407, counting from the era of Caesar; 5,129 years from the creation of the world by the reckoning of the Hebrews; and, according to that of the Arabs, it was in the year 771. While King Enrique was camped outside the city of Toledo, which he had placed under siege, he received emissaries and ambassadors sent by King Charles of France to inform him that war had been declared between himself and the king of England. He also told King Enrique that his wish was to have him as his friend and ally if he was willing.

King Enrique was delighted at this. As we related above, in the village of Aigues-Mortes in the kingdom of France, in the presence of the count of Anjou and the cardinal of Boulogne, an alliance had already been established between the king of France and King Enrique. However, they now confirmed their friendship and drew up their treaties and alliances, expressed in the strongest terms possible, as follows: firstly King Charles of France and King Enrique of Castile were to be allies of allies and enemies of enemies and to support each other against any man in the world; this same bond of friendship was to endure and to remain constant both between them and between their first-born heirs, those already born and those who would be born

pudiesse fazer pleytesia ninguna con enemigo alguno syn voluntad e consentimiento del otro, e otros articulos que fizieron sobre armadas de mar quando las ouiessen de fazer. E de todas estas cosas fizieron cartas, las mas firmes e mejores que seer pudieron.

Otrossy dixeron los dichos mensageros al rrey don Enrrique commo el rrey de Françia le enbiaua luego en su ayuda a mossen Beltran de Claquin con quinientas lanças. E acordadas e fechas estas ligas partieronse los enbaxadores del rrey de Françia, del rrey don Enrrique e tornaronsse para Françia.

Capitulo IIº. Commo el rrey don Pedro puso sus fijos en Carmona e ayuntaua sus gentes para venir a acorrer a Toledo, e commo fizo matar a don Diego Garçia de Padilla.

En este año sobre dicho el rrey don Pedro, antes que partiesse de Seuilla, leuo sus fijos e su thesoro todo e muchas armas a la villa de Carmona, e dexo con ellos omnes de quien se fiaua. E despues que esto ouo fecho partio de Seuilla e vino para Alcantara, e alli rrecogio conpañas suyas por que auia enbiado; ca estonçe vino alli a el Ferrand Alfonso de Çamora, que tenia la çibdat de Çamora, e los que estauan en Mayorga e otros muchos que tenian su parte en Castilla, e ayuntaronsse con el. E su entençion era de venir a acorrer a los de Toledo que estauan çercados e le auian enbiado dezir por muchas de vezes que non tenian viandas señalada mente pan, e que non se pudian tener luengo tienpo. Otrossy en estos dias antes que el partiesse de Seuilla, dixieronle commo Diego Garçia de Padilla, maestre que fuera de Calatraua e estonçe era señor de Val de Corneja e estaua con el, que trataua con algunos de la parte del rrey don Enrrique. E el rrey don Pedro fizolo tomar preso e poner en el algiue del castillo de Alcala de Guadeyra.

in the future; and neither of them was to enter into negotiation with any enemy without the agreement and consent of the other; and other articles were included concerning when naval expeditions were to be undertaken. On all these matters documentation was drawn up, as binding and comprehensive as possible.

The emissaries also told King Enrique that the king of France was sending Monsieur Bertrand du Guesclin to support him along with 500 lances. Then, once this alliance had been agreed and drawn up, the ambassadors of the king of France took their leave of King Enrique and returned to France.

1369: CHAPTER II

How King Pedro installed his children in Carmona and assembled his forces in order to go and relieve Toledo; and how he had Don Diego García de Padilla put to death.

In the course of this year, before departing from Seville King Pedro took his children, all his treasure and a large store of arms to the town of Carmona and left with them men in whom he trusted. Once he had done this he set out from Seville and headed for Alcántara where he assembled the forces that he had summoned. He was then joined in Alcántara by Fernán Alfonso de Zamora, who held the city of Zamora, by the men who had been in Mayorga and many others of his supporters in Castile. His intention was to go to the assistance of the people of Toledo, who were being besieged and who had written to him repeatedly to say that they had run out of provisions and in particular bread and that they could not hold out for much longer. During the period before he left Seville he was also told how Diego García de Padilla, previously master of Calatrava and currently lord of Valdecorneja, and who was one of his allies, was in discussion with supporters of King Enrique. King Pedro had him arrested and held in the dungeon of the castle of Alcalá de Guadaíra.

Capitulo III°. De otra carta que un moro de Granada sabidor, que dizian Benahatin, enbio al rrey don Pedro quando sopo que yua a la batalla de Montiel.

Estando el rrey don Pedro en Seuilla aparejandose para partir dende por yr a acorrer a Toledo, que estaua çercada, vn moro que dizian Benahatin, e era grand sabidor e filosopho e priuado del rrey de Granada, del qual diximos suso que le auie enbiado otra carta quando el rrey don Pedro torno de Vayona e vençio la batalla de Najara, e assi agora este mesmo moro desque sopo que partio el rrey don Pedro de Seuilla para acorrer a Toledo, penso que auia de pelear e enbiole otra carta, de la qual el tenor es este:

'Ensalçado rrey e señor que Dios honrre e guarde, amen. El tu sieruo Benahatin, pequeño philosopho e del consejo del rrey de Granada tu amigo, con todo rrecomendamiento e con el humildança, poderoso e nonbrado rrey entre los rreyes:

Non niego yo que el mi seruiçio non sea sienpre aparejado a onrra e ensalçamiento del tu estado e señorio rreal en quanto el mi saber alcançe e el mi poder sofrirlo pueda; las cosas que lo adebdan quales e quantas son, pues tu ya eres sabidor, non es menester rrepetir [de nueuo]. Pediste me que por industria del mi saber, con grand diligençia e acuçia de grand estudio, otrossy por manera de grand seso que en mi fallauas, en tus negoçios, que te fiziesse saber en qual manera podras palpar por verdadero saber vn dicho de profeçia, el qual dizes que fue fallado entre los libros e propheçias que dizes que fizo Merlyn, del qual las sus palabras, por los terminos que lo yo rresçibi son estas que se siguen: *En las partidas de Oçidente, entre los montes e la mar, nasçera vn aue negra comedora e rrobadora, e todos los panares del*

1369: CHAPTER III

Concerning another letter which a Moorish sage from Granada, by the name of Benahatin, sent to King Pedro when he learned that he was on his way to take part in the battle of Montiel.

While King Pedro was in Seville making ready to set off in order to go and relieve Toledo – which was under siege – he received a second letter from the Moor called Benahatin. This man was a great scholar and philosopher and an adviser of the king of Granada, and we have already told of how he had sent King Pedro a previous letter after his return from Bayonne and his victory in the battle of Nájera. So now this same Moor, having learned that King Pedro had left Seville to go to the assistance of the city of Toledo and considering that he was going to do battle, sent him another letter, the content of which is as follows:

'Glorious king and lord, may God honour and protect you, amen. It is in supplication and humility that your lowly servant Benahatin, a philosopher of minor importance and counsellor of your friend the king of Granada, addresses you, powerful and renowned king among kings.

I do not deny that, with regard to the sufficiency of my learning and the adequacy of my ability, the service that can I offer you is not always in keeping with the honour and praise which are appropriate to your standing and position of royal authority. As you are already aware of what lies behind this, there is no need for me to repeat it. You asked me through the application of my learning, most diligently and with great scholarly rigour, and through the intelligence that you have found in me with regard to your affairs, to tell you how you may fathom for its true meaning a prophetic text, which you assert to have been found among the books and prophecies that you say were produced by Merlin.[1] The words of this text, just as I received it, are the following: *In the western regions, between the mountains and the sea, will be born a black bird, voracious and thieving, hungry to take*

mundo querria acoger en si, e todo el oro del mundo ençerrara en su estomago e despues gormarlo ha e tornara atras e non peresçera luego por esta dolençia; ca dize caersele han antes las alas e secarsele han las plumas al sol e andara de puerta en puerta e non le querra ninguno acoger, ençerrarse ha en selua e morra ý dos vezes, vna al mundo e otra ante Dios, e desta guisa acabara.

Rey alto, rroguesteme, ca todo es en tu poder, rrogar e mandar, que yo pensaria quand graue era o podria ser, segund el menester en que estas, el deseo grande que as por seer çertificado en el entendimiento desta propheçia en que manera podras ende seer sabidor e que por la amistança e debdo de seruidunbre que en la tu merçed yo he, traspasasse yo en mi toda la mayor carga que yo pudiesse tomar deste tu cuydado; por que por el plazer de la mi esplanaçion, que en las mis palabras atiendes, ouiesses buena fiuza de sofrir lo aduenidero, e toda via que la verdat non te fuesse negada por amorio que contigo ouiesse, maguer que en algunas cosas o en todo pudiesses tomar mayor pessar de lo que tienes.

Rey alto e poderoso, sabe que yo, commo obediente al tu mandamiento, con cuydoso estudio seyendo partido de quales quier otros negoçios mundanales que a ello me agrauiassen, esforçe la materia sobre ello, escudriñe por todas partes el mi saber por cunplir lo que me enbiastes mandar e lo que por este estudio e mi entendimiento pude alcançar e acuerdo en que fuy ayuntado con otros grandes sabios syn vanderia e syn sospecha, e fablaron en esta materia commo quier non por manera de adeuinança, en que algunos rrahezes se ponen, la qual es rrepoyada en todo buen saber, e saluo sienpre antes e despues en cada lugar el solo e mejor [saber] de Dios e el su non semejante poderio, al qual toda cosa es ligera. E fue esta profeçia interpretada por la forma contenida, la qual es en cada seso della e cree que ha de seer trayda a esecuçion en la tu persona rreal, de lo qual Dios solo

for itself all the honeycombs in the world and which will devour and take into its stomach all the world's gold and then vomit it back up: it will recover and will not at first perish as a result of this malady. For the text says that first it will lose its wings and its plumage will burn dry in the sun; it will wander from door to door but no one will give it shelter; it will be confined in the forest where it will die twice: once to the world and once more before God; and in this way it will meet its end.

Illustrious king, you asked me – for all is in your power, both to ask and to command – to consider just how earnest was, or might be, according to the need in which you find yourself, your great desire for clarification in your understanding of this prophecy, and how you can be given knowledge of it. You asked me, by virtue of friendship and of the debt of service that I owe to your Grace, to take upon myself as much as possible of the burden of this concern of yours, in order that through the satisfaction provided by the explanation that you expect me to give, you may be confident of enduring the things which are to come. Moreover, you requested that the truth should not be kept from you on account of my close friendship with you, even though some things – or, indeed, everything – that I say may cause you to have greater cause for sorrow than is at present the case.

Illustrious and mighty king, I want you to know that, obedient to your command, through careful study and having removed myself from any worldly affairs that might have weighed upon me, I studied the related material meticulously, hunting through every part of my knowledge in order to carry out the task which you had written to entrust to me. What I managed to grasp by means of such study and through my own understanding was considered in collaboration with other men of great wisdom, without partisanship and without any lack of trust existing among us. They discussed this subject but not as though it were a riddle embodying some trivial matters – for this is condemned in all true scholarship – saving always, both first and last and in all places, the sole and superior wisdom of God and His power without peer, in comparison with which all things carry little weight. The prophecy was interpreted in terms of the meaning contained in each one of its elements. You may conclude that it is to apply to your

te guarde, e en que manera ella es e ha de ser puedes saberlo por las esplanaçiones que se siguen.

Rey alto ensalçado, sabe que esta profeçia enderezar a el hito de España contra el rrey que en ella era, que en fin del libro que me enbiaste dezir que seria rrey della, en la qual tierra agora non es visto seer rrey dende otro alguno sy non tu, que por derecho e antigüedad lo tienes, quanto mas pues que es manifiesto que tu eres el rrey en que la profeçia dize que nasçera entre los montes e la mar, ca el tu nasçimiento fue en la çibdat de Burgos, segund entendi, que bien puede seer dicho que es en tal comarca, e assy entiendo que el primero seso de los articulos de la propheçia que fabla del primer nasçimiento, que se prueua quanto cunple.

Siguesse adelante que dize que esta aue assy nasçida, que sera *comedora e rrobadora*. Rey, sabe que los rreyes que comen de los aueres e algos e rrentas que a el non son deuidos son llamados estos tales, comedores e rrobadores; pues si tu comes e gastas de las tus rrentas propias al tu señorio conuenientes, tu solo lo sabes; mas la tu fama es contraria, ca diz que tomas los algos e bienes de tus naturales e non naturales donde quier que los puedes auer, e fazes tomar e rrobar, e que esto, que non fazes por el puro derecho, e assy explana que el tu comer e rrobar sea tal commo lo que tiene la segunda explanaçion del segundo seso de la propheçia.

Otrossi dize que *todos los panares del mundo querra coger en sy*. Rey, sabe que pensando sola mente en esta explanaçion, por traer a buena concordança creedera, que falle quando el rrey don Alfonso tu padre era bivo e avn despues de su finamiento e despues aca que rregnaste algund tienpo, que todos los del tu señorio biuian a grand plazer de la vida por las buenas costunbres de que husaua tu padre, e este plazer les finco assy pendiente despues del su finamiento, en tienpo del tu señorio, el qual plazer auian por tan deleytoso que bien pudian dezir que dulçor de panares de miel nin de otro sabor alguno

own royal person; and from this may God, and God alone, preserve you! The manner of this – and the manner in which it is to be – you can learn from the explanations which follow.

Illustrious and exalted king, I want you to be aware that this prophecy is directed towards Spain, against the king reigning over her. At the end of the book that you sent me it said that this person would be her ruler; and in this land there is now no man who can be viewed as king other than yourself, for you hold this position by right and by seniority. It is all the more apparent, then, that you are the king that the prophecy states will be born between the mountains and the sea, for – as I have understood it – you were born in the city of Burgos, which can indeed be said to lie in just such a region. And thus I understand that the first element of the text of the prophecy, which at the beginning talks about the birth, is proven to be entirely true.

Next it is stated that this bird, born under such circumstances, will be *voracious and thieving*. My king, I want you to be aware that rulers who devour wealth, possessions and income which are not due to them are described in this way: voracious and thieving. For if you devour and consume your own income which belongs to the territory of which you are lord, you alone will know of it. However, your reputation goes against you, saying that you take the wealth and possessions both of your subjects and of others, wherever you have an opportunity to seize them, and that you have others take and steal, and that you do not do this by what is truly your right. And this demonstrates how your voracious and thieving nature coincides with the explanation of the second element of the prophecy.

The prophecy also states that the bird will be *hungry to take for itself all the honeycombs in the world*. I want you to be aware, my king, that, as I devoted my thoughts solely to the explanation of this prophecy in order to give an interpretation of it worthy of belief, I found that, when your father King Alfonso was alive, and even after his death and after you had reigned for some time, all those who lived under your lordship did so in great pleasure as a result of the noble ways of your father. This pleasure, moreover, continued to be felt after his death and during the time when the people lived under your lordship: so great for them were its delights that they might well have

non podria seer a ello comparado, de los quales plazeres son tirados tienpo ha todos los tus subditos por que tu eres el açidente dello por muchas amarguras e quebrantos e desafueros en que los as puesto, e pones de cada dia, faziendo en ellos muchas cruezas de sangre e de finamientos e otros muchos agrauios, los quales lengua non podria pronunçiar. Assy tengo que se explana este terçero seso desta profeçia de los panares, pues por el tu açidente fue el rrobador dellos.

Otrossi dize que *todo el oro del mundo metera en sy e en su estomago*. Rey, sabe lo qual creo que eres bien sabidor, maguer paresçe que non curas dello, que tan manifiesta es la tu cubdiçia desordenada de que vsas que todos los que han el tu conosçimiento por vso e por vista, e avn eso mesmo por oydas, o por otra qual quier conversaçion, tienen que eres el mas señalado rrey cubdiçioso desordenado que en tienpos passados ouo aqui en Castilla nin en otros rregnos e tierras e senoríos; por que tan descubierta e tan manifiesta es e tan grande la tu cobdiçia que muestras en acresçentar tesoros desordenados que non tan sola mente abonda lo hordenado mas avn siguiendo mal a mal, que tomas e rrobas algos e bienes de las iglesias e casas de oraçiones; assi acresçientas estos thesoros, que te non vençe conçiençia nin vergüença, e tan grande es el acuçia que en la cubdiçia pones que fazes nueuas obras e fuertes, assi de castillos commo de otra fortalezas e lauores, do puedas asossegar estos tales thesoros por que non puedes caber con ellos en todo el mundo, andando fuyendo de vn lugar en otro toda via con ellos, que el partir dellos te es graue de lo prouar; por lo qual todos afirmando el testo de la propheçia en este caso, e bien creo que si en el tu estomago los pudieses meter, por te non partir dellos e traer lo contigo, que te ofreçerias a ello. E assaz se muestra assi seer verdat por que bien sabes quanto tienpo ha en commo el tu henemigo, que se titulo en el tu nonbre de rrey, es con otros tus enemigos, la segunda vez entrado por las tierras e señorios dende, e

said that neither the sweetness of honeycombs nor that of any other taste could be compared to it. However, for some time your subjects have been deprived of these pleasures, and you have been the cause of this through the many bitter experiences, deep sorrows and acts of injustice to which you have subjected them and to which you continue to subject them each day, perpetrating on them many bloody atrocities, deaths and numerous other wrongs, such that no tongue could tell of them. And, since you were the cause of those pleasures being stolen from your people, this is how I consider that the third element of the prophecy, dealing with the honeycombs, is to be explained.

The text also states that the bird *will devour and take into its stomach all the world's gold*. My king, I want you to be aware that your inordinate greed is apparent. I believe that you already know this well, although it seems that you care little about it. Your greed is so manifest that those who know of you – from experience or from what they have seen or likewise through hearing about you or as a result of any dealings that they have had – all consider you to be the most conspicuous example of a king driven by inordinate greed that there has ever been here in Castile or in other kingdoms, lands and lordships. For so blatant, obvious and immense is the greed that you display in accumulating disproportionate amounts of treasure that not only are you not satisfied with what is seemly but, with evil following upon evil, you also take and steal wealth and possessions from churches and places of prayer.[2] You amass your treasure unrestrained by conscience or shame and so intense is your greed that you undertake the construction of new buildings and strongholds, both castles and other fortifications and structures, in which you can store such treasures securely; for there is not enough space in the whole world to hold you and those treasures as you constantly flee with them from one place to another, since parting from them is hard to endure. All of this confirms what the present section of prophecy's text says.[3] I can well believe that, if you could fit your treasures into your stomach and carry them with you so as not to part with them, you would be prepared to do so. There is sufficiently clear evidence of the truth of this: you are well aware how long has passed since your enemy, who has taken for himself your title of king – together with others who are opposed to you – invaded for a second time the lands and lordships of

donde tu te llamas rrey, afirmando el titulo que ha tomado rreal, e por non te partir desta cubdiçia faze te oluidar vergüença e bondad e estas te asentado en las postrimeras del tu señorio en esta frontera, açerca contigo de tus thesoros, pues de ti non los entiendes partir nin otrossi leuar contigo metidos en tu estomago, do los querrias poner si cosa fuesse e pudiesse seer; e dende oluidas la honrra e el estado que avies, el qual te va menguando cada dia: e assy tengo que se explana este quarto seso desta profeçia.

Otrossy lo al que desto se sigue, do dize que *lo gormara*. Rey, çierto es que el mucho cobdiçioso cubdiçia, e con escaseza desordenada que es su hermana, allega thesoros en esta manera. Puede le contesçer ende bien, commo contesçio al omne gloton que pone en su estomago mas vianda de aquella que la natura pide que puede sofrir, assi por el poner la demasia [es] que el estomago non puede sofrir de gormar lo hordenado e lo desordenado, por lo qual non se puede escusar que non rrecresca por ello el açidente, el qual trae desmayo e flaqueza en todos los miembros, e pues tu por esta manera llegas thesoros con cubdiçia desordenada, tengo que te aura contesçer por esta mesma forma: que perderas lo hordenado por lo desordenado e comunal mente todo en vno que lo gormaras por superfluydad, que es su ocasion, e rrecresçer te ha por ello el açidente, el qual verna en ti aquella dolençia que diz que pone en este quinto seso desta profeçia Merlin, e non seria fallado rremedio de sanidad e assi tengo que es esplanado el quinto seso desta materia.

Dize otrossy que *se le secaran las peñolas e se caera la pluma*. Rey, sabe que los philosofos naturales entre los otros negoçios que dellos manaron, que trataron muy biva mente en tales materias e semejantes seyendo puesto el caso e disputada la quistion entre ellos, e la absoluçion es esta: que las peñolas con que los rreyes ennoblesçen a si mesmos e anparan e defienden sus tierras e sus estados, que son los omnes grandes en sangre e en linaje, que son sus naturales, por

which you call yourself ruler, reinforcing his claim to the royal title. And your unwillingness to renounce your greed makes you forget all sense of shame and all integrity, and you find yourself rooted to the spot on this frontier at the very edge of your kingdom, close to your treasures; for neither is it your intention to part with them nor can you carry them with you, held within your stomach, where you would like to keep them if such a thing were possible. As a result of this you are forgetting all about the honour and the prestige which you used to possess, and your standing is sinking lower day by day. And that is how I consider that this fourth element of the prophecy is to be explained.

Let us also consider the following section, in which it is said that the bird will *vomit it back up*. My king, it is true that the man who is full of greed longs to acquire possessions and, together with the extreme miserliness which is the sister of covetousness, this leads him to amass treasure. In consequence the same thing can easily happen to him as happens to the glutton who fills his stomach with more food than nature requires or more than it can cope with: for in this way, as a result of being over-filled, the stomach cannot help vomiting up both what was sufficient and what was in excess, making the onset of illness inevitable, and this brings feebleness and loss of strength in all parts of the body. Since you in the same way amass treasures with inordinate greed, it is my belief that something similar is to happen to you: you will lose what was sufficient because of overindulgence and you will vomit it all up together out of excess, and you will be struck by sickness as a result, producing in you that illness which Merlin is said to mention in this fifth element of the prophecy; and no cure would be found. And this is how I consider that this fifth element of the prophecy is to be explained.

The text also says that the bird *will lose its wings and its plumage will burn dry in the sun*. My king, I want you to be aware that the natural philosophers, among the other subjects on which scholarship flowed from them, dealt keenly with such and similar matters, with the arguments being set out and the question debated among them. Their conclusion is as follows: the plumage by means of which kings lend themselves nobility and protect and defend their lands and their estates consists of the men, distinguished in bloodline and in lineage,

que estos son conparados e llamados 'alas' con que los rreyes buelan a vnas tierras e a otras, con quien fazen sus conssejos. E con las peñolas que destas tales alas se crian en los cuerpos de los rreyes, que ennoblesçen mucho sus personas e sus figuras, e que se fazen mucho apuestos por ello, e cresçen en su horgullo e apremian mucho en ello sus contrarios, e con estas alas pueden fazer muy ligeros buelos los rreyes quando los sus naturales son pagados dellos, en lo qual deuen mucho afirmar los rreyes por que entre ellos e los rreyes e los nobles en sangre non aya desmano a culpa del rrey; pero toda via guardando el conosçimiento rreal del rrey e la su alteza, lo qual en ninguna guisa non deue seer quebrado. E quando entre ellos assi se guarda ý es Dios terçero por guarda e por entre medianero e es el rrey çierto de sus alas en el tienpo de los menesteres, de lo qual desplaze mucho a sus enemigos, e desto todo, por tu ventura, muestrase contra ti lo contrario, por lo qual temo que la propheçia quiere çerrar en ti de grado en grado, siguiendosse a essecuçion, que en ti non ay ya alas de buelo nin peñolas con que afermoses tu persona rreal, assy que non paresçe seer en ti esfuerço alguno por fazer boladura syn lision de tu cuerpo o sin grand daño de tu estado, ca tus mal querientes pujan en la tu osadia, e puesto que alguna muestra quieras fazer so color de buelo diziendo que tienes plumas, sabe que muy fuerte cosa e muy graue es de encobrir lo que manifiesto es, ca esas tus plumas, con quien esa tu color piensas fazer, non son tales con que puedas fazer buelo ninguno por pequeño que sea syn te estar aparejada la lision ante dicha, mayor mente para el grand menester en que estas, ca lo manifiesto de ti es que las plumas enteras en los [codillos] que solias auer en tus alas con que bolar solias, que son caydas pues los tus naturales todos, los mas nobles e mas poderosos que a esto eran conparados, que fasta aqui tenias por peñolas de tu buelo, han puesto en oluido el amorio que te solian auer, e el señorio tuyo que fasta aqui obedesçian trataronlo

who are their vassals; for these are compared with and described as "wings" with which kings fly from one territory to another and it is with them that they take their counsel. Through the plumage of these wings growing on the bodies of kings, their person and their appearance acquire great nobility. It gives them an air of great elegance and they grow in pride and it is a powerful means by which to subdue their enemies. With these wings kings can fly with great ease when their vassals are contented with them: and on this kings must place great importance so that between them and those of noble blood no wrong occurs through fault of the king, although at all times it is necessary to recognize his exalted position, which in no way must be infringed. Moreover, when this relationship is preserved between them and God is present as an arbiter and intermediary and when the king is certain of his wings in times of need, his enemies suffer great discomfort. Your fate, however, is proving to be quite the contrary of all of this: as a result of which I fear that the prophecy is about to close in on you, step by step, steadily moving on towards its fulfilment, for you no longer have feathers for flight or plumage to enhance your royal person, so that you appear now to lack the strength which would enable you to fly without suffering serious injury to your body or grave harm to your standing. The audacity shown towards you by your adversaries is increasing and, even if you seek to give some appearance of flight, claiming that you do possess feathers, you should be aware that it is a serious matter and one of great consequence to disguise what is apparent: for those feathers of yours with which you seek to create that appearance are not such as to enable you to undertake any flight, however limited, without the prospect of suffering the injury of which I have spoken. This is especially true in view of the situation of dire need in which you find yourself: for what is apparent about your position is that whole feathers and the joints of your wings which previously enabled you to fly have all fallen away, since all your vassals, the most noble and the most powerful to whom this comparison applied – those that until now you had considered to be the plumage with which to support your flight – have forgotten all about the affection in which they used to hold you. They have negotiated with your opponent the same bonds of allegiance which used to keep them in obedience to

con el tu contrario. E la ocasion e el açidente por quien vino, fuera de Dios, tu eres el sabidor dello, e assy tengo que en esto se despone este sesto seso de la dicha profeçia.

Otrossi avn dize mas, que *andara este rrey de puerta en puerta e que ninguno non lo querra acoger*. Rey, sabed que todos lo sabemos que tan manifiesto es solamente esto contra ti: que synple saber de qual quier omne puede fazer su esplanaçion por que, mal pecado, tengo que los del tu señorio non quieren acogerte, yrado nin pagado, en quanto ellos pudiessen, por que sienpre quesiste que de los tuyos fuesses mas temido que loado e amado, e commo quier que en esa çibdat do estas agora asentado te ouiesses apoderar, pero Dios te libre del poderio del diablo por que del non sean tentados los que ý son para que fagan algund mouimiento contra la tu persona; ca oy dezir que dizen de ti e he temor que se querran mouer contra ty e assi tengo que se desplana la rrazon deste seteno seso.

Dize otrossy que *se ençerrara en la selua e que morra ý dos vezes*. Rey, sabe que lo que ami fue mas graue e el mayor afan que en esto tome, sy fue por apurar el seso deste vocablo que dize "en la selua", e para esto acarrea su entrepetraçion en esta guisa. Yo rrequeri los libros de las conquistas que pasaron fasta aqui entre las casas de Castilla e de Granada e de Benamarin, e por los libros de los fechos mas antigos que ý pasaron, falle escrito que quando la tierra que llaman de Alcaraz en el tu señorio, era poblada de los nuestros moros e fue perdida, e fue cobrada de los christianos, que auia çerca della vn castillo, que a ese tienpo era llamado por nonbre "Selua", el qual falle por estos mesmos libros que a essa sazon perdio luego este nonbre que auia de "Selua" e fue llamado por otro nonbre "Montiel" e que agora que asi es llamado, e assy tu eres aquel rrey que la profeçia dize que ha de seer ý ençerrado: luego esta es la selua o el lugar del ençerramiento segund por esta propheçia se pone, e en el auran de contesçer estas muertes e lo al que la profeçia dize. Dios solo es dello sabidor, al

you. Of the cause and the instrument which brought this about, apart from God, you are well aware. And so I consider that this is how the sixth element of the prophecy is to be interpreted.

The text also adds that the bird *will wander from door to door but no one will give it shelter.* My king, you should be aware that we all know this to be so clearly directed at you that it can be interpreted by the simple learning possessed by any man. For, to your great misfortune, it is my belief that – as far as it is within their power – those who live under your lordship are not willing to accept you whether your mood is one of anger or of contentment, because you have always desired to be feared rather than praised and loved by your people. Moreover, even if in that city where you are now established you were to be firmly in control, may God preserve you from the power of the Devil lest the people there be tempted by him to take part in some movement against your person. For I have heard what they are saying about you and I fear that they will try to move against you; and this is how I believe that the meaning of this seventh element is to be interpreted.

The prophecy also says that the bird *will be confined in the forest where it will die twice.* My king, I wish to tell you that the part of this task which caused me the greatest difficulty and over which I toiled the most was the elucidation of the phrase "in the forest", whose interpretation involved the following steps: firstly I sought out the books on the wars of conquest which have taken place up to the present day between the houses of Castile, Granada and Banū Marīn, and in those dealing with the events of greatest antiquity I discovered an account dealing with the time when the territory under your lordship which was known as Alcaraz was inhabited by our Moors and subsequently was lost and conquered by the Christians.[4] Nearby there was a castle, at that time known as *Selva*, which means "forest". As I discovered in those same books, shortly afterwards the castle lost this name of *Selva* and was given the different one of *Montiel*, and that is what it is currently called. Thus, you are that king who, according to the prophecy, is to be confined there and this, therefore, is the forest or place of confinement to which this prophecy refers. It is there that these deaths are to take place together with the other events mentioned in the prophecy. Only God has knowledge of this,

qual solo pertenesçe los tales secretos. E por que en este lugar canso el mi saber en este caso segund que era menester e non puedo mas alcançar, ca lo puse a mayor otro lugar e non ouo por industria, saluo por quanto se dexo vençer de alguna opinion que la mi ymaginaçion non parte despues aqui de sy, que tienen que bien assy commo en cada vno de los otros mienbros esta propheçia faze contra ti en cada materia, segund se sigue por las prouanças, que bien assy yra faziendo su curso por conclusion del vno al otro, de grado en grado, contra esta aue negra, que assi dize que nasçera, en la qual todas estas cosas han de seer conplidas.

E por que el postrimero seso en que faze conclusion del ençerramiento e de la muerte seria antes adeuinança que non alcançamiento de saber, lo qual en todo buen saber deue ser rrepoyado, dexa su explanaçion a aquel en quien es el poderio, que lo tal rreserua en sus secretos, e tu ventura que la quiera Dios guiar e desuiar, por que las cosas ante dichas non ayan lugar de fazer en ti la esecuçion que trae tan espantosa, en lo qual yo seria muy agradable, maguer en mis juizios fincasse contrario e non verdadero, lo qual seria muy ligero e agradable de lo sofrir, por que mayor buena andança seria a mi en la tu merçed del bien e vida segura que ouiesses, que non del contrario que temo.

E en lo que cunpliere mandame commo a tuyo e en esto me faras grand plazer, mas non me escriuas este vocablo "rrogar", por que en el tu rruego me fazes pesar e enojo, pues non me cae en rrazon, e sy algo fuy atreuido, non culpes la mi osadia por que de la parte del tu cuydoso seso me atreui e mandaste por tu carta que la verdat desto non te fuesse negada en aquello que el mi saber alcançasse. E yo fablo contigo segund lo entendi sobre ello, mas non por otra çertidunbre que pudiesse yo afirmar; pero sy en la tu corte hay omnes justos e sabidores de quien las tales cosas non se encubren, sometome a la mejor correbçion del su saber. Escrita en Granada.'

since such secrets belong to Him alone; for at this point my mind grew tired with this part of the task, as was inevitable, and it is not possible for me to make out any more. I set my intellect in another, loftier place and it remained at rest except insofar as it allowed itself to be overcome by a belief which since then has remained in my mind. This is that, just as in each of the other elements, this prophecy applies to you in every respect, as follows from the arguments, which will thus progress from conclusion to conclusion, step by step, applied to this black bird whose birth is described in the prophecy, and through which all these things are to become reality.

Since the final element, which contains the conclusion alluding to confinement and death, would amount to solving a riddle rather than the application of learning, and this in all true scholarship must be rejected, its explanation is left to the One in whom power resides and who retains such matters among His secrets. May God guide your fortune and prevent the events which have been described from bringing upon you so awful a conclusion. I would take great pleasure if this were to happen, even though as a result I would prove to be mistaken and wide of the truth in my judgements: it would be easy and pleasant to bear, for I would gain greater satisfaction from your enjoyment of prosperity and security than from its opposite, which is what I fear.

In whatever you require, command me as your servant and by doing so you will give me great pleasure, but do not write to me using this word "request", because with this word "request" you cause me unhappiness and annoyance, as it does not strike me as right. If I have been somewhat audacious, do not criticize my boldness, for it was on behalf of your troubled mind that I dared to speak freely; and your command in your letter was that the truth should not be kept from you inasfar as my learning could fathom it. I am speaking to you according to what I have understood of this matter, but not with any other certainty of which I could give firm knowledge. However, if in your court there are other just and scholarly men from whose understanding the meaning of such matters is not concealed, I submit myself to correction by their superior wisdom. Written in Granada.'

Capitulo IIII°. Commo el rrey don Enrrique sopo commo el rrey don Pedro queria partir de la çibdat de Seuilla para venir a acorrer a la çibdat de Toledo, que la tenia çercada el dicho rrey don Enrrique segund dicho es.

El rrey don Enrrique estando en el rreal que tenia sobre la çibdat de Toledo sopo que el rrey don Pedro queria partir de la çibdat de Seuilla e queria en todas guisas venir a acorrer la çibdat de Toledo. E enbio luego sus cartas al maestre de Santiago don Gonçalo Mexia e al maestre de Calatraua don Pero Moñiz e a los otros caualleros que estauan en Cordoua, que luego que sopiessen que el rrey don Pedro partia de Seuilla, que ellos partiesen de Cordoua e veniessen sienpre en par del, poniendo sus guardas commo cunpliessen e que supiessen que su voluntad era de pelear con el dicho rrey don Pedro, e que esse mesmo mandamiento auia fecho a todos los caualleros e gentes de armas suyos que estauan en Castilla e en Leon, que luego se veniessen para el al rreal do estaua.

E los maestres de Santiago e de Calatraua e los otros señores e caualleros que estauan en Cordoua desque vieron las cartas que el rrey don Enrrique enbiara commo dicho es, luego se aperçibieron e dexaron hordenados aquellos que en la dicha çibdat de Cordoua auian de fincar por guarda de la çibdat, e todos los otros luego que supieron que el rrey don Pedro partia de Seuilla, partieron de Cordoua e touieron sienpre su camino allegandose a Toledo segund que el rrey don Pedro fazia.

E quando el rrey don Pedro llego a la Puebla de Alcoçer, que es en la comarca e tierra de Toledo, ellos llegaron a Villa Real, que estaua por el rrey don Enrrique, que esta a diez e ocho leguas de Toledo. E eran los maestres e los otros señores e caualleros que partieron de Cordoua, entre los castellanos e ginetes, mill e quinientos omnes de armas.

E el rrey don Enrrique que estaua en el rreal que tenia sobre la çibdat de Toledo que tenia çercada, sopo por çierto commo el rrey

1369: CHAPTER IV

How King Enrique learned that King Pedro was intending to leave the city of Seville in order to come to the assistance of the city of Toledo, which – as has already been explained – was being besieged by King Enrique's forces.

While King Enrique was in his encampment outside the city of Toledo, he received reports that King Pedro was intending to set out from Seville and that he wished at all costs to come to the aid of the city of Toledo. He lost no time in writing to Don Gonzalo Mejía, master of Santiago, to Don Pero Muñiz, master of Calatrava, and to the other knights who were in Córdoba, instructing them that as soon as they knew that King Pedro was leaving Seville they should set out from Córdoba and shadow his progress closely, leaving a garrison in the city as was necessary; they should be aware that King Enrique intended to do battle with King Pedro and that he had sent a similar command to all his knights and men-at-arms in Castile and in León, instructing them all to report to him in his encampment without delay.

Once the masters of Santiago and Calatrava and the other lords and knights in Córdoba saw the letters which – as we already have said – King Enrique had sent, they at once made ready, leaving in place the men who were to remain behind to guard the city of Córdoba. The rest of them, as soon as they heard that King Pedro was leaving Seville, set out from Córdoba, always following his path and, just like him, heading for Toledo.

As King Pedro reached Puebla de Alcocer, which is in the area and the territory of Toledo, the men shadowing him arrived in Villa Real, which had given its support to King Enrique and is situated 18 leagues from Toledo. The troops accompanying the masters and the other lords and knights who set out from Córdoba, including Castilian horsemen and light cavalry, numbered 1,500 men-at-arms.

King Enrique, who was in his encampment outside the besieged city of Toledo, received confirmed reports that King Pedro had

don Pedro llegara a Alcantara e auia alli cogido las conpañas que le venian de Castilla e que eran ya en la Puebla de Alocoçer. Otrosi sopo commo los maestres de Santiago e de Calatraua e los otros señores que estauan por el e caualleros que eran de su partida que estauan en la çibdat de Cordoua eran partidos de la dicha çibdat e estauan en Villa Real. E desque todo esto esto fue çierto, ordeno de dexar çercada la çibdat de Toledo segunt estaua, por quanto en la çibdat non estauan si non pocas conpañas, que ya auia diez meses e medio que la tenian çercada e eran muchos de los que estauan dentro en ella, sallidos e venidos a la su merçed; otrossi muchos muertos e gastados e non tenian ya cauallos, de la grand fanbre que en la çibdat auia, ca la fanega de trigo en pan cozido valia mill e dozientos marauedis, e assi segund esto valian todas las otras viandas muy caras, e avn assy non las auian e comian los caullos e las mulas, e eran ya menguadas muchas de las gentes de guisa que estauan en la çibdat muy pocas; pero la çibdat es tan fuerte que pocos omnes la defendieran. E por esta rrazon dexo ý gentes de las suyas que guardasen la dicha çerca segund diremos.

Capitulo V°. Commo el rrey don Enrrique acordo de yr a pelear con el rrey don Pedro.

El rrey don Enrrique ouo su consejo que nin sabia çierto sy el rrey don Pedro venia por le dar batalla o por le fazer leuantar de la çerca por alguna manera, e pues la batalla estaua en dubda, que le cunplia dexar la çibdat çercada por que si la batalla non se fiziesse, non perdiesse el rrey don Enrrique el tienpo e trabajo que pusiera en la tener çercada, ca se rresçelaua que el rrey don Pedro fiziesse senblante que queria dar batalla, e en tanto que viesse la çibdat desçercada e al rrey don Enrrique leuantado del rreal, que faria commo pusiessen viandas en Toledo. E por esto ouo el rrey don Enrrique su consejo de dexar gentes

reached Alcántara, where he had met up with the troops coming to join him from Castile, who were now in Puebla de Alcocer. He also heard that the masters of Santiago de Calatrava, the other lords who supported him and the knights in Córdoba who were his allies had left that city and were now in Villa Real. Once all of this was known for certain, he gave instructions that the city of Toledo was to be kept under siege: there were only a few troops in the city, for they had been besieging it for ten and a half months, many of the people who had been inside had come out to place themselves at his mercy and many were dead or exhausted. They no longer had any horses, as a result of the serious shortage of food in the city, for a *fanega* of wheat in the form of baked bread cost 1,200 *maravedís*.[5] Likewise all other provisions were extremely expensive: even so they were impossible to obtain and people ate horses and mules. The number of defenders had diminished to the point that very few remained in the city, but it is so well fortified that it could have been defended by just a small force. So for this reason King Enrique left some of his troops there to maintain the siege, as we shall relate.

1369: CHAPTER V

How King Enrique resolved to go and do battle with King Pedro.

King Enrique consulted his advisers. He did not know for certain whether King Pedro was coming to do battle with him or in order to oblige him in some way to raise the siege. He determined that, since the battle was in doubt, it was best for him to continue with the siege of the city. This was so that, in the case of the battle not taking place, King Enrique would not have wasted the time and effort that he had put into besieging the city: there was a suspicion that King Pedro was making a show of intending to give battle and that, as soon as he saw that the siege had been raised and that King Enrique had left his encampment, he would have provisions taken into Toledo. For this reason King Enrique resolved to leave some of his troops in the encampment outside the city

de las suyas en el rreal sobre la çibdat de Toledo por que fincasse çercada e en este acuerdo fueron todos los que con el eran. E dexo el rrey don Enrrique sobre la çibdat de Toledo en el rreal, al arçobispo de Toledo don Gomez Manrrique, que era vn muy grand perlado e de grand linaje e tenia conssigo muy buena conpaña de omnes de armas. E dexo ý a Pero Gonçalez de Mendoça, mayordomo mayor del infante don Iohan su fijo, e a don Ferrand Perez de Ayala e a don Diego Garçia de Toledo e a Diego Gomez de Toledo e otros caualleros e escuderos con ellos, que eran seysçientos omnes de armas e pieça de ballesteros e peones con ellos.

E el rrey don Enrrique partio del rreal de Toledo e fuesse para vna villa que dizen Orgaz, que es a çinco leguas de Toledo, e alli venieron a el los maestres de Santiago e de Calatraua e don Iohan Alfonso de Guzman, que fue despues conde de Niebla, e don Alfonso Ferrandez de Monte Mayor, adelantado mayor de la frontera, e don Gonçalo Ferrandez de Cordoua, e Diego Ferrandez su hermano, alguazil mayor de Cordoua e muchos otros caualleros e escuderos que estauan en Cordoua. Otrossy alli llego a el mossen Beltran de Claquin, que venia de Françia, e eran con el e con otros estrangeros que el rrey tenia primero consigo, fasta seysçientas lanças. E assi ayunto el rrey don Enrrique alli todas sus conpañas para pelear, que pudian seer todas fasta tres mill lanças, e de ginetes e omnes de pie non curo de ayuntar saluo aquellos omnes que yuan con los señores e caualleros, e segund cada dia solian andar.

E alli fizo el rrey don Enrrique toda su hordenança de la batalla con acuerdo e consejo de los que ý eran con el, e mando que la auanguarda ouiesse mossen Beltran de Claquin e el maestre de Santiago don Gonçalo Mexia e don Pero Moñiz maestre de Calatraua e don Iohan Alfonso de Guzman e los otros caualleros de Cordoua que alli eran, e toda la otra gente que fuesse con el en otra batalla. E non fizo otras alas nin mas batallas.

E partio el rrey don Enrrique de Orgaz e luego sopo commo el rrey don Pedro pasara por el campo de Calatraua e que era çerca de vn lugar e castillo de la horden de Santiago que dizen Montiel e que la conpaña que ally venia con el era esta: don Ferrando de Castro e el

of Toledo in order to maintain the state of siege; and all those present were in agreement. In the encampment outside the city of Toledo King Enrique left Archbishop Gómez Manrique of Toledo, a prelate of very high standing and distinguished lineage who had a fine company of men-at-arms at his service. He also left there Pero González de Mendoza, chief steward to his son Prince Juan, Don Fernán Pérez de Ayala, Don Diego García de Toledo and Diego Gómez de Toledo, and with them some other knights and squires: a force amounting to 600 men-at-arms together with a good number of crossbowmen and footsoldiers.

King Enrique set out from the encampment at Toledo and headed for a town called Orgaz, situated five leagues from Toledo, and there he was joined by the masters of Santiago and Calatrava and by Don Juan Alfonso de Guzmán, who was later to become count of Niebla, Don Alfonso Fernández de Montemayor, governor general of the Frontier region, Don Gonzalo Fernández de Córdoba and his brother Diego Fernández, head constable of Córdoba, and many other knights and squires who had been in Córdoba. Another arrival was Monsieur Bertrand du Guesclin, who had come from France, together with a number of other foreigners – as many as 600 lances – who had accompanied the king in the past. And so at Orgaz King Enrique drew up all his forces ready to fight: probably altogether as many as 3,000 lances. He did not trouble to assemble a force of light cavalry or men on foot, with the exception of those who habitually accompanied the lords and knights.

There and then King Enrique drew up his battle formation with the agreement and advice of the men accompanying him. He instructed that the vanguard was to be composed of Monsieur Bertrand du Guesclin, the master of Santiago Don Gonzalo Mejía, the master of Calatrava Don Pero Muñiz, Don Juan Alfonso de Guzmán and the other knights from Córdoba who were present, while all the other troops were to be with him in the other batallion. He drew up no other flanks and no other batallions.

King Enrique set off from Orgaz and quickly learned how King Pedro had crossed the Territory of Calatrava and was close to a town and castle belonging to the Order of Santiago and bearing the name of Montiel.[6] King Pedro had with him Don Fernando de Castro, the

conçejo de Seuilla e de Carmona e Xerez e Eçija, e Ferrand Alfonso de Çamora e los que con el estauan; otrossi cauallos e escuderos e otros que estauan por su partida en Mayorga, que pudian seer todos castellanos e ginetes tres mill lanças, e cauallos de moros que el rrey de Granada le enbiara en su ayuda, con vn cauallo de Granada que venia con ellos por mayor, eran mill e quinientos de cauallo. E sopo el rrey don Enrrique que el rrey don Pedro era en Montiel: pero dizianle que queria desuiar el camino que primero truxiera e que queria yr camino de Alcaraz, que estaua por el, pero non lo sabia çierto.

Capitulo VI°. Commo fue la pelea de Montiel.

El rrey don Enrrique ouo su consejo de acuçiar su camino quanto pudiesse e catar manera commo peleasse con el rrey don Pedro, ca sabia que si la guerra se alongasse que el rrey don Pedro auria de cada dia muchas aventajas. E por esto ouo su consejo e acordo de acuçiar la batalla e fizolo assy. E andudo quanto pudo en guisa que llego çerca del dicho castillo de Montiel do estaua el rrey don Pedro. E algunos de los que yuan con el ponian fuego por la tierra por veer el camino, ca la noche era muy escura.

E el rrey don Pedro non sabia nueuas çiertas del rrey don Enrrique nin que era partido del rreal que tenia sobre la çibdat de Toledo, e tenia sus conpañas derramadas por las aldeas enderredor de Montiel, ca dellos posauan dos leguas dende e otros a vna legua de Montiel donde el estaua, e assy estauan todos. E aquella noche el alcayde del castillo de Montiel, que era vn cauallo de la horden de Santiago e comendador de Montiel que dizian Garçi Moran, que era asturiano, e el e los suyos vieron grandes fuegos a dos leguas del lugar de Montiel, e fizieronlo saber al rrey don Pedro commo paresçian grandes fuegos a dos leguas del castillo donde el estaua, e que catassen si eran de sus enemigos. E el rrey don Pedro dixo que pensaua que serian don

militias of Seville, Carmona, Jerez and Écija, and Fernán Alfonso de Zamora and those in his company; and also in his army were knights, squires and others of his supporters from Mayorga, amounting to some 3,000 lances, including Castilian horsemen and light cavalry. In addition there were Moorish knights – 1,500 horsemen – sent to aid him by the king of Granada, with a knight from Granada as their commander. King Enrique learned that King Pedro was in Montiel. He was told that his adversary intended to make a detour from his original route and head for Alcaraz, which had given him its support, but he did not know this for certain.

1369: CHAPTER VI

How the battle of Montiel was fought.

King Enrique determined to hasten his pace as much as possible and seek a way of engaging King Pedro in battle, for he was aware that if the war became drawn out King Pedro would gain considerable advantage with every day that passed. For this reason he consulted his advisers and decided to try to precipitate the battle. He acted accordingly, advancing as quickly as he could in order to reach the castle of Montiel where King Pedro had installed himself. Some of those accompanying King Enrique lit fires along the ground so as to make out their way, for it was a very dark night.

King Pedro knew nothing for certain of King Enrique, not even that he had left his camp outside the city of Toledo. He had his forces spread out through the villages around Montiel: all scattered, some of them billeted two leagues away, others one league from where he was in Montiel. That night the governor of Montiel castle – a knight of the Order of Santiago, an Asturian by the name of Garci Morán –, together with his men, saw large fires burning two leagues away from Montiel. They informed King Pedro that these fires could be seen two leagues from where he was in the castle and they advised him that they should investigate whether they had been lit by his enemies. King

Gonçalo Mexia e don Pero Moñiz e los que partieran de Cordoua, e que se yuan juntar con los que estauan sobre el rreal de Toledo. E esto era por que non sabia ningunas nueuas. Pero el rrey don Pedro enbio luego sus cartas a todos los suyos que posauan en las aldeas que al alua del dia fuessen luego con el en el lugar de Montiel donde el estaua.

E quando fue grand mañana, otro dia, llego el rrey don Enrrique e los suyos, que de la media noche auian andado a vista del lugar de Montiel. E las gentes del rrey don Pedro que el enbiara al camino do paresçian los fuegos tornaronsse diziendo al rrey don Pedro commo el rrey don Enrrique e los suyos venian muy çerca. E el rrey don Pedro e los suyos armaronsse e pusieron su batalla çerca del dicho logar de Montiel e los que posauan en las aldeas, de los suyos, non eran llegados todos.

E el rrey don Enrrique aderesço sus gentes para la batalla, e mossen Beltran de Claquin e los maestres de Santiago e de Calatraua e los otros señores e caualleros e los de Cordoua, que eran en la auanguarda, quando mouieron por yr a la batalla para juntar con los del rrey don Pedro, toparon en vn valle que non pudieron pasar. E el rrey don Enrrique e los que con el yuan, que era la segunda batalla, pasaron por la otra parte e aderesçaron para los pendones del rrey don Pedro e luego que llegaron a ellos fueron desbaratados, que el rrey don Pedro nin los que con el eran nin los moros non se touieron punto nin mas, antes començaron de se yr. E los del rrey don Enrrique, los vnos siguieron los moros e alcançaron e mataron dellos e los otros se detouieron peleando con los del rrey don Pedro fasta que el rrey don Pedro se ençerro en el castillo de Montiel, que estaua y luego e algunos de los suyos con el, e algunos morieron e otros fuyeron. E fue esta batalla miercoles catorze dias de março deste dicho año a ora de prima.

E en esta batalla non morieron de los del rrey don Pedro omnes de cuenta, saluo vn cauallero de Cordoua que dizian Iohan Ximenez, e la rrazon por que pocos morieron fue por que los vnos posauan en las aldeas, que non eran llegados a la batalla, e los otros que y eran rrecogieron se con el rrey al castillo de Montiel.

Pedro said he thought that it would be Don Gonzalo Mejía and Don Pero Muñiz and the men who had set out from Córdoba, who were on their way to join up with those in the encampment outside Toledo. All this was because he had received no reports. However, King Pedro promptly wrote summoning all those of his men who were billeted in the villages, instructing them to join him in Montiel at dawn.

Then, when the next day dawned, King Enrique and his troops arrived, having marched through the night in view of Montiel castle. The men that King Pedro had sent out onto the road where the fires could be seen returned to him with reports of how King Enrique and his forces were drawing very close. King Pedro and his troops armed ready for combat and drew up their battle lines near to the town of Montiel, although those who had been billeted in the surrounding villages had not yet all arrived.

King Enrique headed his troops straight towards the field of battle. Monsieur Bertrand du Guesclin, the masters of Santiago and Calatrava, the other lords and knights and the men from Córdoba, all of whom were in the vanguard, when they moved forward towards the place where they were to join battle with King Pedro's troops, found themselves in a valley along which they could not advance. However, King Enrique and those with him in the second section of the army, passed along the other side of the valley and made straight for his adversary's standards. As soon as they reached them, King Pedro's forces gave way: neither he nor the troops in his company nor the Moors held firm for any length of time but instead they began to retreat. Of King Enrique's troops, some pursued the Moors, catching them up and killing a number of them, and the others remained behind, continuing to fight with King Pedro's army until he took refuge, together with some of his men, in the nearby castle of Montiel. Some of his supporters were killed and others fled. The battle had taken place at the hour of Prime on Wednesday the 14th of March of the year in question.[7]

No men of distinction among King Pedro's troops died in this battle, with the exception of a knight from Córdoba by the name of Juan Jiménez. The reason why few men died was that some of the troops had been billeted in the surrounding villages and had not arrived in time for the battle, whilst others who had taken part withdrew with the king into the castle of Montiel.

Capitulo VIIº. Commo Martin Lopez de Cordoua, que se llamaua maestre de Calatraua sopo commo el rrey don Pedro era vençido e tornosse para Carmona.

Luego que la batalla de Montiel fue desbaratada segund dicho es, algunos de los del rrey don Pedro que partieron de ally fallaron a Martin Lopez de Cordoua, que el rrey fiziera maestre de Calatraua, en Baeça, que venia con conpañas al rrey don Pedro para seer con el en la batalla, e contaron le commo el rrey don Pedro e los que con el eran fueron desbaratados.

E el maestre don Martin Lopez desque estas nueuas sopo tornosse para Carmona do estauan los fijos del rrey don Pedro, los cuales eran estos. El rrey don Pedro despues que morio doña Maria de Padilla, ouo fijos de vna dueña que estaua en su casa e criara al infante don Alfonso su fijo e ouo dos fijos della, vno que dizian don Sancho e otro que dizian don Diego, e queria los el rrey don Pedro muy grand bien a la madre e a ellos, e dexara los en Carmona. Otrossi estauan en Carmona otros fijos que el rrey don Pedro ouiera de otras dueñas.

E el maestre don Martin Lopez luego que en Carmona llego, apoderosse de todo lo que ý era assi de thesoro commo de los alcaçares de la villa, que son tres, e auia los fechos e enfortalesçidos mucho e basteçidos de muchas viandas e de muchas armas el rrey don Pedro.

Recogieronsse con el dicho Martin Lopez en la dicha villa de Carmona fasta ochoçientos omnes de cauallo castellanos e ginetes e muchos ballesteros.

1369: CHAPTER VII

How Martín López de Córdoba, who termed himself master of Calatrava, learned that King Pedro had been defeated, and how he returned to Carmona.

Shortly after they had been put to flight in the battle of Montiel, as we have described, in Baeza some of King Pedro's supporters who had left the battlefield came across Martín López de Córdoba, whom the king had created master of Calatrava. He was coming with companies of troops to fight on King Pedro's side in the battle and they told him how King Pedro and his army had been defeated.

On hearing this news, Don Martín López, the master, returned to Carmona to join the sons and daughters of King Pedro. Among them were two sons that, after the death of Doña María de Padilla, he had fathered by a lady of his household who had brought up his son Don Alfonso; one was called Don Sancho and the other Don Diego, and King Pedro, who was very fond both of them and of their mother, had left them in Carmona.[8] Also in Carmona there were some more children that King Pedro had fathered by other ladies.

As soon as Don Martín López, the master, arrived in Carmona, he took charge of everything there, both the treasure and the town's *alcázares* – of which there are three –, which King Pedro had built up, fortified heavily and equipped with a large supply of provisions and arms.

Together with Martín López, some 800 Castilian horsemen and light cavalry and also a large number of crossbowmen withdrew into the town of Carmona.

Capitulo VIII°. Commo el rrey don Pedro sallio de Montiel e morio.

El rrey don Enrrique desque ouo desbaratado la dicha pelea de Montiel e vio al rrey don Pedro acogido al castillo que ý era, puso muy grand acuçia en fazer çercar de piedra seca [faziendo] una pared al lugar de Montiel [enderredor] por rreçelo que el rrey don Pedro non se fuesse de ally. E asy fizo e puso muy grandes guardas de dia e de noche enderredor del lugar de Montiel por rreçelo que el rrey don Pedro non se fuesse de alli.

Asi fue que estaua con el rrey don Pedro en el castillo de Montiel vn cauallero de Gallizia que dizian Men Rodriguez de Senabria, que auia seydo preso en la villa de Briuiesca quando el rrey don Enrrique la tomo quando entrara en el rregno nueua mente, segund auemos contado. E mossen Beltran de Claquin por que aquel cauallero le dixo estonçe quando fuera preso que era natural de la tierra de Trastamara, que el rrey don Enrrique diera estonçe por condado al dicho Beltran de Claquin, pago su rrendiçion por el, que eran çient mill florines, a vn cauallero que le tenia preso que dizian mossen Bernal de la Sala, por lo qual el dicho Men Rodriguez estudo con mossen Beltran vn tienpo e despues partiosse del e fuesse para el rrey don Pedro.

E por que conosçia el Men Rodriguez a mossen Beltran, fablo con el del castillo de Montiel, donde se acogera quando el rrey don Pedro fuera desbaratado e dixole que si a el pluguiesse que el queria fablar con el secreta mente. E mossen Beltran dixole que le plazia e seguro le que viniesse a el e el Men Rodriguez sallio de noche al mossen Beltran, por quanto mossen Beltran tenia la guarda de aquella partida donde el e los suyos posauan, e Men Rodriguez le dixo assi: 'Señor mossen Beltran, el rrey don Pedro mi señor me mando que fablasse con vos e vos dize assi que vos sodes vn muy noble cauallero e que sienpre vos preçiastes de fazer fazañas de buenos fechos e que vos veedes el estado en que es el e que, si a vos pluguiesse de lo librar de aqui e poner en saluo e seguro e seer vos con el e de la su partida, que

1369: CHAPTER VIII

How King Pedro left Montiel and met his death.

Once King Enrique had won the battle of Montiel and had seen King Pedro find protection in the nearby castle, he urgently set about having the castle and town of Montiel surrounded by a dry stone wall, in his concern that King Pedro should not get away. He took this measure and, lest the king escape, he had Montiel heavily guarded day and night.

It happened that with King Pedro in the castle of Montiel there was a Galician knight called Men Rodríguez de Sanabria. This man had been taken prisoner in the town of Briviesca when King Enrique had seized it after entering the kingdom for the second time, as we have related. Since at the time of his capture Men Rodríguez had told Monsieur Bertrand du Guesclin that he was a native of the lands of Trastámara, of which King Enrique had recently created Monsieur Bertrand count, the Breton knight had paid Men Rodríguez's ransom – of 100,000 florins – to Monsieur Bernardon de la Salle, the knight who was holding him prisoner. As a result of this Men Rodríguez remained with Monsieur Bertrand for some time before taking his leave of him and going to join King Pedro.

As Men Rodríguez knew Monsieur Bertrand, he spoke to him from the castle of Montiel, where he had taken refuge following King Pedro's defeat, and told him that, if he was willing, he wished to talk with him in private. Monsieur Bertrand agreed to this and gave him a guarantee of safe conduct so that he could come to him. Men Rodríguez left the castle by night to meet Monsieur Bertrand, who was responsible for the guarding of the area where he and his men had their quarters. 'Monsieur Bertrand,' Men Rodríguez said to him, 'my lord King Pedro has commanded me to speak with you: he says to you that you are a knight of outstanding nobility, that you have always prided yourself on committing deeds of great integrity and that you can see the position in which he finds himself. I am to tell you that, if you are willing to allow him to leave this place, escort him to safety,

el vos dara las sus villas de Soria e Almaçan e Atiença e Monte Agudo e Deça e Moron por juro de heredad para vos e los que de vos vinieren. Otrossy que vos dara dozientas mill doblas de oro castellanas e yo pido vos por merçed que lo fagades assi, ca grand honrra auredes en acorrer vn rrey tan grande commo este, e que todo el mundo sepa que por vuestra mano cobra su vida e su rregno.' E mossen Beltran dixo a Men Rodriguez: 'Amigo, vos sabedes bien que yo so vn cauallero vasallo del rrey de Françia, mi señor e su natural, e por su mandado so venido aqui en esta tierra a seruir al rrey don Enrrique. Por quanto el rrey don Pedro tiene la parte de los ingleses e el es aliado con ellos, espeçial mente contra el rrey de Françia mi señor, e yo siruo al rrey don Enrrique e esto a sus gajes e a su sueldo, e non me cunple fazer cosa que contra su seruiçio e su honrra fuesse nin vos me lo deuriades consejar sy algund bien e cortesia de mi rreçibistes, e rruego vos que non me lo digades mas.' E Men Rodriguez le dixo: 'Señor mossen Beltran, yo entiendo que vos digo cosa que vos sea sin verguença e pido vos por merçed que ayades vuestro conssejo sobre ello.' E mossen Beltran desque oyo todas las rrazones que el dicho Men Rodriguez le dixo, rrespondiole que pues tales rrazones le dizia que queria auisarsse e saber que le cunplia fazer en tal caso.

E Men Rodriguez se torno al castillo de Montiel al rrey don Pedro. E algunos dixieron despues que Men Rodriguez dixera esto al mossen Beltran con arte e que fuera en conssejo por que el rrey don Pedro fuesse escarnesçido commo despues fue. E avn dizian que maguer que Men Rodriguez fue despues preso con el rrey don Pedro, quando el fue preso, que todo fue arte e sabiduria del dicho Men Rodriguez por quanto despues dio el rrey don Enrrique al dicho Men Rodriguez en Gallizia dos lugares, que son Alariz e Milmanda en tenençia e a Oynbra por juro de heredad; pero esto non paresçio despues asy, que Men Rodriguez era buen cauallero e non era de creer que el fiziesse tal cosa contra su señor, ca despues desto touo el sienpre la parte del rrey don Pedro e morio teniendo su partida del rrey don Pedro.

E despues que esto asi paso entre el dicho mossen Beltran e el

make yourself his ally and take his side in the conflict, he will grant you some of his towns – Soria, Almazán, Atienza, Monteagudo, Deza and Morón – for you and your descendants to enjoy as your own. He will also give you 200,000 gold Castilian *doblas*. I implore you to be willing to do this, for you will win great honour by assisting a king as great as this one and through everybody knowing that it is by your hand that he is regaining his life and his kingdom.' 'My friend,' Monsieur Bertrand replied to Men Rodríguez, 'you are well aware that I am a knight, vassal and subject of the king of France and it is at his command that I have come to this land to serve King Enrique. Since King Pedro has given his support to the English and is their ally, specifically against my lord the king of France, and I am in the service of King Enrique, in his employ and receiving his pay, it is not fitting that I should do anything which is disloyal to him or which brings him dishonour; nor, if you have received any benefit or courtesy from me, should you advise me to do it. So I ask you to say no more to me of this matter.' 'My lord Monsieur Bertrand,' said Men Rodríguez, 'it is my intention to put to you a proposal which brings you no shame and I beg you to seek counsel on it.' Having heard all the arguments that Men Rodríguez put forward, Monsieur Bertrand replied that, in the light of such suggestions being made to him, he wished to seek advice and determine what it was right for him to do in such a case.

Men Rodríguez returned to King Pedro in the castle of Montiel. Later it was claimed by some people that Men Rodríguez had said these things to Monsieur Bertrand with a different intention and that he had been part of a plan to trick King Pedro, as subsequently happened. It was also claimed that, although Men Rodríguez was later taken prisoner at the same time as King Pedro was captured, this was all trickery and cunning on the knight's part, in view of the fact that King Enrique later gave Men Rodríguez tenure of the two villages of Alariz and Milmanda in Galicia as well as Oimbra as a permanent inheritance. However afterwards this did not appear to be true: Men Rodríguez was a fine knight and it was not to be believed that he would have acted in this way against his lord, since subsequently he always took the side of King Pedro and he died supporting his cause.

After this encounter had taken place between Monsieur Bertrand

dicho Men Rodriguez, otro dia mossen Beltran conto esta rrazon a caualleros e escuderos parientes e amigos suyos que alli eran con el, espeçial mente a vn su primo que dizian mossen Oliuer de Mauni e dixoles todas las rrazones que el Men Rodriguez le dixera, e que les demandaua consejo que faria. Enpero luego les fazia saber que en ninguna manera del mundo el non faria tal cosa seyendo el rrey don Pedro enemigo del rrey de França su señor, e eso mesmo del rrey don Enrrique, a cuyos gajes el estaua en su seruiçio, mas que les preguntaua que si esta rrazon que Men Rodriguez lo acometiera sy la diria al rrey don Enrrique o sy faria mas sobre ello ya que lo acometiera que el fiziesse cosa que fuesse contra seruiçio del rrey de França e el rrey don Enrrique a cuyas gajes el estaua, que era caso de trayçion.

E los caualleros sus parientes con quien mossen Beltran tomo este conssejo le dixieron a mossen Beltran que ellos en esse mesmo conssejo eran, que el non fiziesse cosa que fuesse contra seruiçio del rrey de França, otrossi contra seruiçio del rrey don Enrrique a cuyas gajes el estaua e que bien sabia que el rrey don Pedro era enemigo del rrey de França por la amistad que tenia con el rrey de Ingla terra e con el prinçipe de Gales su fijo contra la casa de França. E dixeronle que les paresçia que esta rrazon la fiziesse luego saber al rrey don Enrrique, e el fizolo assi e dixole todas las rrazones que le dixera el dicho Men Rodriguez de Senabria.

E el rrey don Enrrique ge lo agradesçio mucho e dixole que loado fuesse Dios, que mejor guisado tenia el de le dar aquellas villas e doblas que le prometiera el rrey don Pedro que non el. E dixole luego el rrey don Enrrique al dicho mossen Beltran que el ge las daria las villas que el rrey don Pedro le prometiera otrossy las doblas; pero que le rrogaua que el dixiesse a Men Rodriguez de Senabria quel rrey don Pedro viniesse a su posada del dicho mossen Beltran e le fiziesse seguro que le pornia en saluo, e desque ý fuesse que gelo fiziesse

and Men Rodríguez, on the following day Monsieur Bertrand told some knights and squires, members of his family and friends of his who were present there with him – and in particular one of his cousins called Monsieur Olivier de Mauny – about what had been discussed. He informed them about all the proposals that Men Rodríguez had put to him and said that he was asking them for advice with regard to what he should do. However, he immediately made them aware that in no way in the world would he do such a thing, as King Pedro was an enemy of his lord the king of France and likewise of King Enrique, in whose pay and service he was. Moreover, he also asked them whether he should tell King Enrique about the proposal which Men Rodríguez had put to him, and whether he should take further action in this respect given that he had been urged to do something which was disloyal to the king of France and to King Enrique – in whose pay he was –, for it was a treasonable act.

The knights, relatives of his, whom Monsieur Bertrand consulted on this matter, told him that they agreed with him that he should not commit any act of disloyalty to the king of France or likewise to King Enrique, in whose pay he was; and they pointed out that, as he was well aware, King Pedro was an enemy of the king of France through his alliance with the king of England and his son the prince of Wales against the House of France. They told him that in their opinion he should report this matter at once to King Enrique. He followed their advice and repeated to the king everything that Men Rodríguez de Sanabria had said to him.

King Enrique thanked him warmly and told him that – thanks be to God! – he was in a better position than King Pedro to hand over to him the towns and the sum in *doblas* that he had been promised. Immediately afterwards King Enrique informed Monsieur Bertrand that he would give him the towns promised to him by King Pedro and also the *doblas*. However, he asked Monsieur Bertrand to inform Men Rodríguez de Sanabria that King Pedro was to go to his quarters and he told him to give him an assurance that he would take the king to safety; and, as soon as King Pedro was there, Monsieur Bertrand was to let King Enrique know. Although Monsieur Bertrand was hesitant about doing this, on the urging of some of his relatives he agreed to

saber. E commo quier que el mossen Beltran dubdo de fazer esto; pero por acuçia de algunos parientes suyos fizo lo asi. E non touieron los que esta rrazon sopieron que era bien fecho e dizen algunos que quando el torno la rrespuesta a Men Rodriguez, que el le assegurara que pornia al rrey don Pedro en saluo, e que algunos de sus parientes de mossen Beltran que fueran en el consejo e avn pasaran juramentos muy grandes entre ellos en manera que el rrey don Pedro se touo por assegurado dende.

E en tal manera se fizo, que finalmente el rrey don Pedro estaua ý tan afincado en el castillo de Montiel que non lo podia sofrir, que algunos suyos se venian para el rrey don Enrrique, otrossi por que non tenian agua si non poca, e con esto e con esfuerço de las juras que le auian fechas aquellos con quien Men Rodriguez de Senabria tratara sus fechos, auenturosse vna noche el rrey don Pedro e vinosse para la posada de mossen Beltran e pusosse en su poder armado de vnas fojas e en vn caualo. E assi commo alli llego, descaualgo de un cauallo ginete en que venia, en la posada de mossen Beltran, e dixo le a mossen Beltran: 'Caualgad que ya tienpo es que vayamos.' E non le rrespondio ninguno por que ya lo auian fecho saber al rrey don Enrrique commo el rrey don Pedro estaua en la posada de mossen Beltran. Quando esto vio el rrey don Pedro, dubdo e penso que el fecho yua a mal e quiso caualgar en el su cauallo ginete en que venia, e vno de los que estauan con mossen Beltran trauo del e dixole: 'Esperad vn poco.' E touolo e non lo dexo partir. E vino con el rrey don Pedro esa noche don Ferrando de Castro e Diego Gonçalez, fijo del maestre de Alcantara e Men Rodriguez de Senabria e otros.

E luego que alli llego el rrey don Pedro, e tardaua en la posada de mossen Beltran commo dicho auemos, sopolo el rrey don Enrrique, que estaua ya aperçebido e armado de todas sus armas, e el baçinete en la cabeça, esperando este fecho, e vino alli armado e entro en la posada de mossen Beltran. E assi commo llego el rrey don Enrrique trauo del rrey don Pedro, e non lo conosçio, ca auia grand tienpo que non lo auia visto. E dizen que le dixo vn cauallero de los de mossen Beltran: 'Catad que este es vuestro enemigo.' E el rrey don Enrrique avn dubdaua si era el. E dizen que dixo el rrey don Pedro: '¡Yo so! ¡Yo so!' E estonçe el rrey don Enrrique conosçiole e feriolo con vna daga

do so. Those who knew about what had been said did not consider that it was the right thing to do. There are those who claim that, in giving his reply to Men Rodríguez, the Breton knight had assured him that he would take King Pedro to safety and moreover that some of Monsieur Bertrand's relatives had been involved in the discussions and even in the swearing of weighty oaths, in such a way that King Pedro was made to feel secure.

The situation developed in such a way that in the end King Pedro found himself so completely trapped there in the castle of Montiel that he could no longer endure it. Some of his men were going over to King Enrique, and in addition they had hardly any water left. As a result of this, and encouraged by the oaths sworn by the men with whom Men Rodríguez had been negotiating, one night King Pedro ventured out from the castle and made his way to Monsieur Bertrand's quarters. Mounted and armed with swords, he placed himself in his hands. As soon as King Pedro arrived he dismounted from his jennet, and there in Monsieur Bertrand's quarters he said to the knight, 'Mount your horse, it's time for us to be on our way.' No-one answered him, for they had already notified King Enrique that King Pedro was in Monsieur Bertrand's quarters. On seeing this, King Pedro hesitated and, grasping that something was wrong, he tried to mount the jennet on which he had come. One of the men who were with Monsieur Bertrand caught hold of him, saying, 'Wait a moment.' He hung on to him and did not allow him to leave. That night King Pedro was being accompanied by Don Fernando de Castro, Diego González, son of the master of Alcántara, Men Rodríguez de Sanabria and a number of other men.

As soon as King Pedro had arrived and found himself detained in Monsieur Bertrand's quarters, the news reached King Enrique. He was already prepared, fully armed and wearing his bascinet, waiting for this to happen.[9] He made his way there in his armour and entered Monsieur Bertrand's quarters. As soon as he went in, King Enrique caught hold of King Pedro but did not recognize him: it had been a long time since he had last seen him. It is claimed that one of Monsieur Bertrand's knights said to him, 'Look, this is your enemy!' King Enrique was still in doubt as to whether it was indeed him, but men say that King Pedro then exclaimed, 'It is me! It is me!' At that point King Enrique

por la cara. E dizen que amos a dos, el rrey don Pedro e el rrey don Enrrique, cayeron en tierra. E el rrey don Enrrique lo firio estando en tierra de otras feridas. E alli morio el rrey don Pedro a veynte e tres dias de março deste dicho año. E fue luego fecho grand rruydo por el rreal: vna vez diziendo que era ydo el rrey don Pedro del castillo de Montiel e luego otra vez, en commo era muerto.

E morio el rrey don Pedro en hedad de treynta e çinco años e siete meses; ca el rrey don Pedro nasçio año del Señor de mill e trezientos e treynta e tres años e rreyno año del Señor de mill e trezientos e çincuenta años, e de la era de Çesar mil e trezientos e ochenta e ocho años, e fino en este año que es el año del Nasçimiento del Señor de mill e trezientos e sesenta e nueue e de la era de Çesar mill e quatroçientos e siete años. E asi biuio el rrey don Pedro treynta e çinco años e siete meses, segund que dicho auemos, ca se cunplieron sus treynta e çinco años en agosto e el fino mediado março adelante en el otro año. E fue el rrey don Pedro assaz grande de cuerpo e blanco e rruuio, e çeçeaua vn poco en la fabla, e era muy caçador de aues e fue muy sofridor de trauajos. E era muy tenprado e bien acostunbrado en el comer e beuer, e dormia poco e amo mucho mugeres, e fue muy trabajador en guerra e fue cubdiçioso de llegar tesoros e joyas. E valieron las joyas de su camara treynta cuentos en piedras preçiosas e en aljofar e baxillas de oro e de plata e en paños de oro e otros apostamientos. E auia en moneda de oro e de plata en Seuilla en la Torre del Oro e en el castillo de Almodouar, setenta cuentos, e en el rregno e en sus rrecabdadores en moneda de nouenes e cornados treynta cuentos. E en debdas de sus arrendadores, otros treynta cuentos, assi que ouo en todo, çiento e sessenta cuentos, segunt despues fue fallado por sus contadores de camara e de las cuentas. E mato muchos en su rregno, por lo qual le vino todo el daño que auedes oydo. E por ende diremos aqui lo que dixo el propheta Dauid: 'Agora los rreyes aprendet, e seed castigados todos los que judgades el mundo, ca grand juyzio e marauilloso fue este e muy espantable.'

E rregno el rrey don Pedro en paz syn otro le tomar su titulo, diez e seys años conplidos, del dia que el rrey don Alfonso su padre fino, que fino en el mes de março en el rreal de Gibraltar, segund dicho auemos, año del Señor mill e trezientos e çinquenta años e de la era de Çesar

recognized him and struck him with a dagger across the face. It is said that the two of them, King Enrique and King Pedro, fell to the ground, and as they struggled there King Enrique struck his adversary more blows. And it was there that King Pedro died on the 23rd of March of the year in question. At once a great commotion spread throughout the encampment, as there circulated first the news that King Pedro had left the castle of Montiel and, shortly afterwards, that he had been killed.

King Pedro died at the age of 35 years and seven months. He was born in the year of the Lord 1333 and came to the throne in the year of the Lord 1350, in 1388 counting from the era of Caesar; and he died in this year, which was, from the year of the Lord's birth, 1369, in 1407 counting from the era of Caesar. Thus – as we have already said – King Pedro lived for 35 years and seven months, as he reached the age of 35 in August and died in mid-March in the following year. King Pedro was quite strongly built, pale-skinned and fair-haired, and he spoke with a slight lisp. He was a great hunter of birds and he had considerable powers of endurance. He was very temperate, had good habits with regard to eating and drinking, slept little and had a marked fondness for women. He was very active in times of war and he felt a great desire to acquire treasures and jewels. The jewels of his chamber were worth 30 million in precious stones, pearls, gold and silver plate, gold cloth and other fine items. In gold and silver coin he had 70 million in the Tower of Gold in Seville and the castle at Almodóvar; throughout the kingdom and in the hands of his tax-collectors there were 30 million in *novenes* and *cornados*, and in debts owed by his tenants a further 30 million.[10] So in all he possessed 160 million according to the reckoning made subsequently by those responsible for the accounts of his chamber and those of the kingdom. He killed a large number of people in his realm, as a result of which he suffered all the ills of which you have heard tell. Therefore, at this point we shall use the words of the prophet David: 'Now, O kings, act wisely. Take warning you judges of the earth.'[11] For this was a great, wondrous and terrible judgement.

King Pedro reigned in peace, with no other man taking his title, for 16 full years, from the day of the death of his father King Alfonso – which occurred, as we have said, in the month of March in the encampment outside Gibraltar, in the year of the Lord 1350, in 1388

mill e trezientos e ochenta e ocho fasta quel rrey don Enrrique entro en el rregno e se llamo rrey en Calahorra en el mes de março, año del Señor mill e trezientos e sesenta e seys, e de Çesar mill e quatroçientos e quatro. E rregno tres años en contienda con el rrey don Enrrique.

counting from the era of Caesar – until King Enrique entered the kingdom and took the title of King in Calahorra in the month of March of the year of the Lord 1366, 1404 counting from the era of Caesar. For three years he reigned in conflict with King Enrique.[12]

NOTES

YEAR 14 (1363)

1. Since the late nineteenth century, **Murviedro** has been known as Sagunto (or Sagunt).
2. The Orduna text appears to imply that the king of Aragon and prince Ferran, as well as King Pedro's half-brothers, had been in France. There is no evidence to suggest that this is the case and the translation follows the text of other editors (see, for example, Llaguno Amirola, 1779, 369).
3. **the spring of Almenara:** King Pere's chronicle also describes this episode, but states that the Aragonese army waited on 'the plains of Nules, near the spring of La Losa' (Mary Hillgarth, 1980, ii, 538).
4. **Don Sancho:** in fact King Pedro was to make Sancho lord of Villena and endow him with a number of other properties. **Isabel** later bore the king a second son, who was named Diego (Estow, 1995, 213).
5. **Castellón de Burriana:** In the fourteenth century this was the name given to what is now Castellón (or Castelló) de la Plana, also known just as Castellón (or Castelló), the principal city of the present-day province of the same name. The town of Burriana (or Borriana) is situated some 13 kilometres to the south.
6. The castle of **la Muela** is situated above the town of Monroyo (or Mont-roig) in the present-day province of Teruel.
7. **Launac** is situated about 25 kilometres north-west of Toulouse. For the context of this battle and its consequences, see Vernier, 2008, 57–59 and Fowler, 2001, 61–69.
8. For the role of the mercenaries of the 'free companies' in the battle of Launac and more generally during this period, see Vernier, 2008, 57–58, Fowler, 2001, 66–68, and also 1362, VIII, note 8.

YEAR 15 (1364)

1. **Don Felipe de Castro:** Don Felipe IV de Castro Alemany became a firm friend of Count Enrique and after his marriage to Juana in 1366 he joined him in his campaigns (see 1367, III). He was taken prisoner at Nájera but was eventually freed by his brother-in-law, now king, in 1369. Richly endowed with lands in Castile, he did not return to Aragon, but a year later he was killed by his own vassals in Paredes de Navas (Fantoni y Benedí, 2000, 68).
2. **a river known as the Cullera:** this is now known as the River Júcar (or Xúquer).

3. **'solano'**: this is literally a wind that comes from the direction in which the sun rises. It is the name given to a strong and destructive hot east wind.
4. Other editors include this chapter at the beginning of the following year, as the episode in question occurred early in 1365 (see, for example, Llaguno Amirola, 1779, 390).
5. **the first ruler to bear that name**: this king is known today as Jean II. Jean I, the posthumous son who was the successor to Louis X, had lived for just five days in 1316.

YEAR 16 (1365)

1. This was the battle of Montpensier, fought on the 3rd of June, 1362: Count Enrique's Castilian troops, numbering about 400, defeated a much larger force, killing some 600 men and taking 200 prisoners (Fowler, 2001, 54–55).

YEAR 17 (1366)

1. **Sir Eustace**: this is Eustache (Eustache) d'Auberchicourt, a Frenchman who had spent some time under the command of the Black Prince but had also fought as a mercenary in the service of a number of different causes including that of the king of Navarre.
2. **the emperor of Germany**: Karel (Karl or Charles) IV reigned as Holy Roman Emperor from 1355 until his death in 1378, and also as king of Bohemia from 1346.
3. **Muhammad el Cabezani**: this figure has been identified with Faraj ibn Ridwān, who had previously been sent by Muhammad V to support King Pedro against the king of Aragon (Abbady, 1964, 11; see also 1363, III).
4. **King Enrique**: the Orduna text follows manuscript tradition in calling Enrique 'King' at this point, whilst other editors opt for the title 'Count', which Orduna (1997, 128) suggests was used in this passage of the original text of the *versión vulgar*.
5. **had himself crowned**: the meaning of the Spanish text ('se corono') could be that King Enrique was crowned by another person, presumably a bishop or an archbishop. It could also, however, mean that he actually crowned himself. There was a long tradition of self-coronation on the part of the Castilian monarchs and one of the most famous examples was that of Alfonso XI, Enrique's father, which also took place at **las Huelgas**. The convent of Santa María la Real de las Huelgas had been founded in 1187 by King Alfonso VIII and his wife Leonor (or Eleanor). It was without doubt significant that Enrique chose for the ceremony to be performed at the place where his father had crowned himself in 1331. Ironically, it was also the birthplace of King Pedro.

346   *Crónica del rey don Pedro*

6. **Count of Trastámara:** for the origin and importance of this title, see 1350, III, note 7 and Introduction, note 1.
7. The so-called **Five Towns** were Salvatierra de Tormes, Montemayor del Río and Miranda del Castañar (all situated in the present-day province of Salamanca) and Granadilla and Galisteo (Cáceres). See Llaguno Amirola, 1779, 409.
8. **Martín Yáñez:** the Orduna text gives the name Martín López here, but it is made clear elsewhere that the man responsible for the store of gold and silver was Martín Yáñez, the king's chief treasurer.
9. An **estoc** was a long, sharply-pointed sword, generally for two-handed use, of a kind first introduced in the fourteenth century. From Guarda, King Pedro was accompanied by his escorts for a further 130 kilometres, heading northwest towards **Lamego.** From there they had to travel a further 100 kilometres northwards to Chaves, which is situated close to the frontier with Galicia.
10. This is the same **Juan Diente** who first appeared as one of King Pedro's guards, involved, for example, in the deaths of the master of Santiago Don Fadrique (1358, III) and Prince Joan (1358, VI).
11. The **Feast Day of Saint John** (St John the Baptist) falls on the 24th of June. The day on which the murder took place, the Feast of Saints Peter and Paul, was five days later.
12. **to be given to:** the Orduna text reads 'entrar' (to enter), but the translation follows other editions in taking this as 'entregar' (to hand over).
13. One *quintal* was equivalent to 112 lbs (Estow, 1995, 230) or approximately 51 kilograms.
14. **Count Alfonso** was an illegitimate son of King Enrique. At this point he was just 11 years old.
15. It is not entirely clear here who is offering allegiance to whom: according to some versions of the text (see, for example, Llaguno Amirola, 1779, 425), it is Juan Rodríguez de Biedma who is offering his allegiance to Don Álvar Pérez de Castro. Don Álvar was Don Fernando de Castro's half-brother but, whilst Don Fernando remained unfailingly loyal to King Pedro, Don Álvar – having accompanied King Pedro through Portugal (see chapter X, above) – he then switched his allegiance to King Enrique (see chapter XII).
16. **February of the year in question:** given that King Pedro arrived in Bayonne at the beginning of August 1366 (Estow, 1995, 231), this must in fact have been February 1367.
17. *dinero*: one *dinero* was, indeed, worth one tenth of a *maravedí* (see, for example, Lincoln, 2017, 577).
18. **the Bayonne canal:** Bayonne stands at the confluence of the River Adour and its tributary the River Nive. Until its course was changed in the sixteenth century, the River Adour flowed parallel to the coast for some 15 kilometres before reaching the sea at Capbreton and, after flooding which occurred in the mid-fourteenth century, further north at Vieux-Boucau.

19. **his wife the princess:** in 1361 the prince had married his cousin, Countess Joan of Kent.
20. John of Gaunt, **duke of Lancaster**, was ten years younger than his brother the prince of Wales. He accompanied him to Spain and fought in the battle of Nájera. In 1371 he married King Pedro's daughter Constanza and in 1386 he was to lay claim – unsuccessfully – to the throne of Castile.

YEAR 18 (1367)

1. Pierre, **Le Bègue de Villaines** was a prominent member of the free companies, fighting alongside Bertrand du Guesclin. He was to play a significant role in King Enrique's victory at Montiel and in the capture of King Pedro, for which he was generously rewarded. The nickname *Bègue* means literally 'the stammerer'.
2. **Pero López de Ayala:** this is the first occasion on which the chronicler records his presence among King Pedro's opponents. We last heard of him as figuring among the few remaining supporters of the king who accompanied him back from Burgos to Seville in March 1366 (see 1366, IV).
3. **knights in full armour:** both here and in the description of the right flank, the translation follows the Orduna text, but other editions give *caballos* (horses) rather than *caualleros* (knights). This reading is backed up by other sources, including the account given by Jean Froissart, and it would indicate that Enrique's army was making use of the kind of heavily armoured cavalry commonly employed north of the Pyrenees (Villalon and Kagay, 2017, 229).
4. **the king of Naples:** Jaume III of Majorca had refused to swear allegiance to the king of Aragon and as a result had been driven out of his kingdom. His son Jaume, after being imprisoned in Barcelona for some years, eventually escaped and found refuge with Queen Giovanna (Joanna) of Naples. They married in 1363, although in fact Jaume never ruled as king.
5. **on the day of the battle:** this appears to imply that the present chapter describes the organization of the army on the day of the battle of Nájera itself. The chronology is potentially confusing here. In chapter IV King Enrique was reviewing his forces at Bañares and organizing them ready for the forthcoming battle. In chapter V the prince of Wales and King Pedro are shown to be going through the same process, but the content of the subsequent chapters makes it clear that their army is still at the point of preparing to enter Castile and, presumably, some way short of readiness for battle. For details of the ensuing campaign, see Villalon and Kagay, 2017, 199–218.
6. **bearing a letter:** what follows is the most detailed account included in any of the chronicles of this correspondence between the prince of Wales and King Enrique. Different sources, however, vary in what they tell us of the number, order, tone and content of the letters that were exchanged. For a review of

these, see Villalon and Kagay, 2017, 218–21. A third letter appears to have been written by King Enrique from Santo Domingo de la Calzada at an earlier point in the campaign and there may have been four letters altogether. Delachenal (1909–31, 3:398) examines the copies of the actual letters which survive and concludes that Pero López de Ayala 'purely and simply fabricated' the text of his versions.

7. **our dear and beloved relative:** in the course of his letter the prince of Wales repeatedly mentions his bond of kinship with King Pedro. In 1170 Eleanor Plantagenet, daughter of Henry II of England, married King Alfonso VIII of Castile. Through her daughter Berenguela she was directly related to the line of kings of Castile from Fernando III to King Pedro. In addition, Eleanor of Castile, wife of Edward I and grandmother of Edward III, was the daughter of Fernando III, king of Castile and León. See Introduction, p.11.

8. **Saint James:** According to legend the body of Saint James the Greater (Santiago) had been transported to Galicia and subsequently transferred to Santiago de Compostela, where his tomb became the object of veneration by pilgrims over the centuries. Tradition credited Saint James with intervention in battle on behalf of Castilian forces against Muslim enemies.

9. **Santisteban del Puerto** is a town situated in the present-day province of Jaén.

10. **Lazarus Sunday** is the fifth Sunday in Lent. The battle took place on Saturday the 3rd of April (see chapter XIX). The date is confirmed by Froissart and in King Pedro's own correspondence (Orduna, 1997, 197 and Díaz Martín, 1975, 431).

11. **Pope Benedict:** Pedro Martínez de Luna became a cardinal in 1375 and was elected pope, as Benedict XIII, in Avignon in 1394. With the kingdom of France withdrawing its support from the Avignon 'antipopes', he was eventually to lose the support of his cardinals and ultimately find himself excommunicated, receiving recognition only in Aragon. In Spanish he is known as Papa Luna.

12. **the pass of Jaca:** this is probably the pass of Somport (also known as the pass of Aspe or Canfranc).

13. The Vizcayan port of **Castro Urdiales** was of considerable commercial importance, but it was also of critical significance as a naval base and as the location of Castile's main royal shipyards.

14. **the French were beginning to wage war:** for an account of the growing unrest in Guyenne and of the strategy of the French monarchy in provoking discontent among the Gascon lords, see, for example, Barber, 1978, 207–10.

15. *reales*: the *real* was a silver coin introduced by King Pedro. It was initially worth three *maravedís*. For the *dobla*, see 1355, XV, note 8.

16. **Benahatin:** in the translation this name has been left in the distorted form in which the chronicler uses it, but there is convincing evidence (Garcia, 1999, 20) to identify both the name and the figure described by the chronicler with

Muhammad ibn al-Khatīb, who was an adviser to King Pedro's ally Muhammad V and a polymath best known for his work as an historian and as a poet. It is possible to view Benahatin's two letters as apocryphal and it could be argued that López de Ayala attributed them to Ibn al-Khatīb under this name but invented or extensively elaborated their content. The points which they make are highly appropriate to, and reinforce very effectively, the arguments that he has been developing over the course of the *Crónica*. On the other hand, critical opinion is now inclined to view them as genuine (see particularly Garcia, 1999). Garcia (1999, 21) cites a passage in which Ibn al-Khatīb states that he wrote to King Pedro to give him advice and suggests that a more extensive correspondence took place. Other versions of the letters apparently sent by the Moor to the king have survived independently and it is possible (Moure, 1993) that the letters which appear in the *Crónica* are derived from a translation from Arabic into romance carried out by a Jewish scholar. The two letters probably circulated independently as propaganda before their inclusion in the *Crónica* (Moure, 1993, 79), but it is also highly likely (Garcia, 1999, 37) that López de Ayala adapted them for his own, very specific purposes.

17. **who ... bears the title of ruler:** that is, King Enrique.
18. **of which he might himself be accused:** here the translation follows the reading of Llaguno Amirola and others rather than the version ('excused' instead of 'accused') which appears in the Orduna text.
19. **will I say what I have said ... in whose court I have lived:** the translation of this sentence follows the reading in the Llaguno Amirola text rather than Orduna's rather more problematic version.
20. **Pero Girón ... master of Alcántara:** there is no evidence that Pero Girón held this position. Pedro Alfonso de Sotomayor had recently been appointed master of Alcántara, replacing Martín López de Córdoba who was now master of Calatrava (Novoa Portela, 2002, 333).
21. **put to death with great cruelty:** Doña Urraca was burnt alive, a notorious event which was the origin of a vivid popular legend concerning the loyalty of one of Doña Urraca's ladies who threw herself into the flames to die with her (see, for example, de Mena, 2017, 140–42).
22. **Asturias de Santillana** was an administrative district which took in the centre and west of present-day Cantabria together with the extreme eastern part of what is now the Principality of Asturias. The district of **Trasmiera** corresponded to the part of Cantabria which lies to the east of the River Miera.
23. **the tower of the bridge of Avignon:** this was the Tour Philippe-le-Bel, which stood at the western end of the bridge and had been constructed at the beginning of the fourteenth century and extended some fifty years later. The bridge spanned the River Rhône, linking the territory of the king of France to the west with the enclave under the authority of the Pope to the east.

24. **three towns:** today these are Thézan-lès-Béziers, Servian and Cessenon-sur-Orb.
25. **the Bastard of Béarn:** this was Bernard de Foix, the illegitimate half-brother of Gaston Fébus, count of Foix (see 1357, IV, note 3). He later married a member of the de la Cerda family, thus inheriting considerable wealth and property, and remained in Castile under King Enrique.
26. **the Valley of Andorra:** Andorra was originally known as 'les valls d'Andorra'.
27. It is not possible to identify the exact name of the squire here called **Dolet**. Froissart calls him Talebot and in printed texts of the *Crónica* he appears as Tobete (Llaguno Amirola, 1779, 514).
28. **much against their will:** it was under pressure from the French cardinals that in 1370 Pope Urban V was to return to Avignon. Shortly afterwards he fell ill and died.
29. **Cardinal Gil** de Albornoz had in the first instance been a soldier. Between 1353 and 1357, on behalf of Pope Innocent VI, with the aid of a mercenary army he reduced to submission the feudal lords who had achieved virtual control of the Papal States. He returned to Italy for two further campaigns between 1358 and 1363. For the cardinal's role in helping to arrange the marriage between King Pedro and Blanche of Bourbon, see Estow, 1995, 141–42.

YEAR 19 (1368)

1. **the *seisén* ... worth six *dineros*:** that is, six tenths of a *maravedí*.
2. **other kinds of coin:** these were *reales* and *cruzados*: in Orduna's text the account of the minting of these coins (including an explanation of the reasons behind it and the consequences) is to be found in 1369, XI (Orduna, 1997, 297). In other editions it is in chapter III of the first year of the *Chronicle of Enrique II*.
3. For the role of the Marinid prince 'Abd al-Rahmān ibn 'Alī ibn **Abū Yaflūsin**, known to the chronicler as Abenfaluz, see Abbady, 1964, 33.
4. The strategically important site of the castle of **San Servando** was occupied from the late eleventh century by a Benedictine monastery from which the castle took its name. The monastery was destroyed after only 22 years, but almost a century later the ruined complex was granted to the Knights Templar, under whom it was converted into a fortress. This in turn lost its importance in the early fourteenth century after the dissolution of the Templars and fell into neglect, but the text appears to suggest that a new defensive structure had recently been constructed on the site by King Pedro's supporters.
5. **Abbots' Tower:** the 'Torre de los Abades' is a large rectangular structure of Islamic origin, jutting out from the city walls, which served to protect the access to a gateway.
6. **until a later time, as we shall relate:** the recovery of Vitoria and Logroño by King Enrique is recounted in 1373, VIII–IX (Orduna, 1997, 348–50).

7. For the role of the Judges of **Arborea**, see 1352, VIII, note 5.

YEAR 20 (1369)

1. **Merlin:** the tradition of prophecies attributed to the sage Merlin has its origin in the works of Geoffrey of Monmouth, composed in the first half of the twelfth century. However, it was the Venetian known as Richard d'Irlande who in the 1270s composed *Les Prophésies de Merlin*, a work which spawned a variety of imitations, particularly in France, Italy and Spain, usually of an apocalyptic nature and possessing a strong political content. Pero López de Ayala was not the first Castilian writer to cite Merlin as the source of a prophecy: the *Poema de Alfonso XI*, composed by Rodrigo Yáñez in 1348, also does so on two occasions. There is a further allusion to Merlin's prophesies in the *Visión de Alfonso X*, a politically motivated work probably composed during the final years of the reign of Enrique II. For a detailed study of this tradition and its significance, see Alvar, 2015, 333–44. In addition, Garcia (1999, 30–36) has identified close links between López de Ayala's account and French texts, notably the *Chanson de Duguesclin*, contemporary with the *Crónica*.
2. **not only are you not satisfied with:** for the sake of clarity, the translation of this sentence follows Llaguno Amirola's reading (1779, 540: 'non solo non te abasta ...') rather than that of the Orduna text.
3. The translation here follows Llaguno Amirola (1779, 540: 'Por lo qual todo, es afirmado ...').
4. The mountains of **Alcaraz** are situated in the present-day province of Albacete. The town of Alcaraz itself and its fortress occupied a strategically important position on the lower slopes and they were captured by Alfonso VIII from the Muslims in 1213 in the wake of his victory at Las Navas de Tolosa. The town of Montiel and its castle are situated some 30 kilometres from Alcaraz: the Castillo de la Estrella at Montiel had been handed over by Alfonso VIII to the Order of Santiago, to which it belonged until it was placed in the hands of King Pedro (see 1354, XIV).
5. The precise size of a *fanega*, a unit of dry capacity, varied between localities, but as a general rule it is defined as being approximately equivalent to 55.5 litres. Here it is probably equivalent to just over 40 kilograms.
6. **the Territory of Calatrava:** this area of natural beauty, situated around the town of Almagro in the present-day province of Ciudad Real, continues to be known as the 'Campo de Calatrava'. It was the most important of the territorial estates of the Order from which it takes its name.
7. **Prime** is the first of the canonical hours of prayer and corresponds to the first hour of daylight.
8. The **lady of his household** is Doña Isabel, mentioned in 1363, V.

9. **bascinet:** this was a kind of helmet which had various forms, but the one worn by King Enrique would probably have extended down at the back and the sides as far as the base of the neck, leaving part or all of the face exposed.
10. ***novenes*** and ***cornados*** were both coins made of *vellón* (billon, an alloy of silver with a larger amount of copper or another base metal). *Cornados* (or *coronados*) were so called because they bore the image of crowned head of the king.
11. **Now, O kings ...:** this is taken from Psalms 2:10. The quotation from the psalm does not include the sentence which follows, although the punctuation of the Spanish text suggests that it does.
12. In Orduna's edition the narrative for year 4 of King Enrique's reign continues as chapter IX, but in other editions of the text this material is included as the opening section of a separate chronicle. The account for the remainder of the year 1369 deals principally with: the surrender of the castle of Montiel and the capture of most of King Pedro's key supporters; the submission of most cities, including Toledo; continuing resistance in a number of areas, notably that by Don Martín López in Carmona; how King Enrique sent for his daughter Leonor from France; the declaration of support for the king of Aragon by the castle of Requena (situated on the frontier between Castile and the kingdom of Valencia) and the struggle which ensued; the minting of a new coin, the *cruzado*, and a new form of the *real*, which were used to pay King Enrique's armies and the foreign mercenaries (thus fuelling inflation); the claim laid by King Fernando I of Portugal to the throne of Castile and the outbreak of hostilities; King Fernando's short-lived invasion of Galicia and King Enrique's retaliation; the unsuccessful siege of Guimarães and the capture of Bragança; how Don Fernando de Castro took refuge in Guimarães; the loss of Algeciras to the Moors of Granada; and the time spent by King Enrique in Toro, where he made arrangements for the payment of the foreign mercenaries and for the dispatch of troops to the various remaining centres of conflict in Castile and on its frontiers.